Civic Engagement in Food Systems Governance

The local food movement is one of the most active of current civil engagement social movements. This work presents primary evidence from over 900 documents, interviews, and participant observations, and provides the first descriptive history of local food movement national policy achievements in the US, from 1976 to 2012, and in the UK, from 1991 to 2012, together with reviews of both the American and British local food movements. It provides a US–UK comparative context, significantly updating earlier comparisons of American, British, and European farm and rural policies.

The comparative perspective shows that, over time, more effective strategies for national policy change required social-movement building strategies, such as collaborative policy coalitions, capacity building for smaller organizations, and policy entrepreneurship for joining together separate rural, farming, food, and health interests. In contrast, narrowly defined single-issue campaigns often undermined long-term policy change, even if short-term wins emerged. By profiling interviews of American and English movement leaders, policymakers, and funders, the book demonstrates that democratic participation in food policy is best supported when funders incentivize groups to work together and overcome their differences.

Alan R. Hunt has served as Senior Policy Analyst at the Northeast Midwest Institute, Washington D.C., and as Director of Policy and Research at Wholesome Wave, Bridgeport, Connecticut. He was a Fulbright Scholar at the Centre for Rural Economy at Newcastle University, Newcastle, UK from where he received a Ph.D. in Rural Development. He currently lives and works from his family's farm in Hampton, New Jersey.

"This book fills a long-standing gap in academic research on the formation and growth of local food movements. The comparative approach is well-researched, providing evidence-based insights into processes of political and social change. It is a must-read for anyone studying food systems in the US or UK."

—*Becca Jablonski, Special Assistant Professor of Food Systems and Regional Economics, Colorado State University, USA*

"This is an authoritative study of local food movements in Britain and America, drawing on the author's extensive research and policy experience. It is full of insights for policy analysts, food farming and environmental campaigners, and students of politics."

—*Philip Lowe, OBE, Duke of Northumberland Professor of Rural Economy, Newcastle University, UK*

"Hunt's research benefits from his experience building bridges between groups holding very different views of farm and food policy matters, amplified by personal insights from his family's agricultural background. The result is policy analysis centered on people."

—*Gary R. Matteson, Vice President of Young, Beginning, and Small Farmer Programs, The Farm Credit Council, USA*

Civic Engagement in Food Systems Governance

A comparative perspective on American and British local food movements

Alan R. Hunt

LONDON AND NEW YORK

First published 2015
by Routledge
2 Park Square, Milton Park, Abingdon, Oxon OX14 4RN

and by Routledge
711 Third Avenue, New York, NY 10017

First issued in paperback 2017

*Routledge is an imprint of the Taylor & Francis Group,
an informa business*

© 2015 Alan R. Hunt

The right of Alan R. Hunt to be identified as author of this work
has been asserted by him in accordance with sections 77 and 78 of
the Copyright, Designs and Patents Act 1988.

All rights reserved. No part of this book may be reprinted or
reproduced or utilised in any form or by any electronic, mechanical,
or other means, now known or hereafter invented, including
photocopying and recording, or in any information storage or
retrieval system, without permission in writing from the publishers.

Trademark notice: Product or corporate names may be trademarks or
registered trademarks, and are used only for identification and
explanation without intent to infringe.

British Library Cataloguing-in-Publication Data
A catalogue record for this book is available from the British Library

Library of Congress Cataloging in Publication Data
Hunt, Alan R. (Alan Robert)
    Civic engagement in food systems governance: a comparative
    perspective on American and British local food movements/
    Alan R. Hunt.
    pages cm. – (Routledge studies in food, society and environment)
    Includes bibliographical references and index.
    ISBN 978-1-138-88843-2 (hbk) – ISBN 978-1-315-71343-4 (ebk)
    Local foods – Government policy – United States. 2. Local foods –
    Government policy – Great Britain. 3. Nutrition policy – United
    States – Citizen participation. 4. Nutrition policy – Great Britain –
    Citizen participation. I. Title.
    TX360.U6H87 2016
    363.8′5610973–dc23
    2015016578

ISBN 13: 978–1–138–49700–9 (pbk)
ISBN 13: 978–1–138–88843–2 (hbk)

Typeset in Bembo
by Florence Production Ltd, Stoodleigh, Devon

Contents

List of illustrations	vii
List of agencies, organizations, and abbreviations	ix
Author notes	xii
Preface	xiii

1 Local food policies as a lens on American and British food movements   **1**

Introduction 1
Toward a theory of food systems practice 3
Quantifying key terms and concepts 5
Defining local food and its projects 8
Developing the British–American comparison 12
Conclusion 21

2 Local food in national American policy, 1976–2012: Increasing inclusion, increasing policy success   **22**

From producer market development to food system development, 1976–2008 29
From low-income access to local food to community empowerment, 1989 onward 37
Fresh, healthy, and local food in schools: From pilot projects to national program, 1994 onward 43
Conclusion: Increasing inclusion, increasing policy success 55

3 Local food in national English policy, 1991–2012: Policy decline with increased contention   **59**

Pre-crisis era: Nutrition and rural development 65
Post-farm crisis era: Reconnecting farmers and consumers, 2001–2007 76
World food price crisis era: Mobilizing awareness of Britain's connection to global food issues, 2007–2012 90

vi *Contents*

Conclusion: The available policy windows did not align with advocacy group interests 100

4 English case study: The co-option of local food policy by environmental interest groups 105

Uncovering overlooked policy narratives of local food 105
Food miles narrative origins and intersection with local food narratives 109
Contention, counter-mobilization, and discrediting 115
The environmental shift: Co-option of the local food narrative 119
Conclusion: A culture of non-participatory decision-making enabled the co-option of local food 140

5 American case study: Overcoming barriers to policy change due to civil society coordination failure 142

Competing narratives: Political "win" and policy "failure" 142
The "insider" strategy: Working the legislative process 148
Contrasting "insider" and "outsider" advocacy strategies with policy outcomes 161
Conclusion: Empowerment as an alternative to rivalry 164

6 Making space for collaboration in the food system: Three practices for overcoming exclusion 169

Advocacy repertoire: Political communication as a cultural script 171
Contrasting American and British advocacy repertoires 171
Sustaining change: Empowerment, policy entrepreneurship, and capacity building 190
Conclusion 201

7 Toward a theory of food systems practice 203

Civic participation in food systems governance: A theory of food systems practice 204
The shift toward movement building 214
Conclusion 216

Appendix 1 Organizations interviewed	218
Appendix 2 Proposed interview topics list	220
Appendix 3 Participation observation events	222
References	225
Index	269

Illustrations

Figures

1.1 Semiotic square of four narratives of local food and the entities enabled by each narrative	12
2.1 Diagram of the farm-to-school program's reauthorization, 2009–2010	54
3.1 Simplified diagram of British and European institutions	71
3.2 England's proposed development spending by scheme, 1999–2007	72
3.3 Actual Rural Enterprise Scheme spending by activity in 2001	73
3.4 Diagram of SSFF implementation by economic, environmental, and social sustainability	84
3.5 Masthead of IIED's "Fair Miles" opinion article	97
4.1 Overlapping elements of Sustain's local food policy narrative and food miles policy narrative	113
4.2 Logo of the *Farmers Weekly* food miles campaign	115
4.3 Organizations with which RDPE Network participants have an existing partnership	122
4.4 Partner organizations of Food Issues Census respondents	123
4.5 Wordle from the Food Issues Census depicting factors that help and hinder food issues	136
5.1 Proposed structure of the Farm and Food Policy Project	150
5.2 "Evolved Structure" of the FFPP	151
5.3 Food desert newsletter from Representative Bobby Rush	160

Tables

1.1 Methods and sources of information for observing the policy process	17
1.2 Comparison of prevailing structural characteristics of food movements in the US and England	20
2.1 Summary of American programs supporting local food activities, including spending levels	24
2.2 Funding history of the Value-Added Producer Grant Program fiscal years 2001–2012	36

viii *List of figures and tables*

3.1	Summary of major English government policy reports	61
3.2	Timeline of local food policy milestones in England	64
3.3	LEADER implementation in England, including funding levels	69
3.4	Proposed expenditures of selected RDPE Measures relevant to local food activities, 2007–2013	86
3.5	Proposed expenditures of Rural Economy Grant Schemes relevant for local food	99
4.1	Timeline of selected national media report titles on food miles and the world food price crisis	118
5.1	Comparison of funding levels of selected conservation programs between the House Farm Bill floor vote and the Farm Bill as engrossed and placed on the Senate calendar	143
5.2	Timeline of WKKF's policy grant-making and the Farm and Food Policy Project	147
5.3	Excerpts of relevant policy goals and recommendations on local food systems in *Seeking Balance*	154
5.4	A comparison of the "outsider" and "insider" strategies used in the 2008 Farm Bill	162
6.1	Typology of stakeholder participation	184
6.2	Comparison of the level of stakeholder engagement by organization/network for national-level local food policies in the US and England	186
6.3	Funding characteristics of local projects in the US and England	199
7.1	A comparison of marketism, interest group, and food system narratives and practices	206

Agencies, organizations, and abbreviations

American units of government

AMS, Agricultural Marketing Service
CCC, Commodity Credit Corporation
CRS, Congressional Research Service
DOD, Department of Defense
FNS, Food and Nutrition Service
GAO, Government Accountability Office
MSD, Marketing Services Division
NRCS, Natural Resource Conservation Service
OMB, Office of Management and Budget
RBCS, Rural Business Cooperative Service
USDA, United States Department of Agriculture

American programs

B&I, Rural Business & Industries Loan and Loan Guarantee Program
CFP, Community Food Projects
EBT, Electronic Benefit Transfer
FFVSP, Fresh Fruit and Vegetable Snack Program
FMNP, Farmers Market Nutrition Program
FMPP, Farmers Market Promotion Program
HFED, Healthy Food Enterprise Development Center
HUFED, Healthy Urban Food Enterprise Development Center
SFMNP, Senior Farmers Market Nutrition Program
SNAP, Supplemental Nutrition Assistance Program (formerly Food Stamps)
VAPG, Value-Added Producer Grant Program
WIC, Special Supplemental Nutrition Program for Women, Infants, and Children

British units of government

DEFRA, Department for Environment, Food, and Rural Affairs, 2001–
DFID, Department for International Development

x *Agencies, organizations, and abbreviations*

MAFF, Ministry of Agriculture, Fisheries, and Food, 1952–2001
NAO, National Accountability Office
NHS, National Health Service
RDA, Regional Development Agency

British reports, programs, and EU-related programs

CAP, Common Agricultural Policy
ERDP, English Rural Development Programme
LEADER, Liaison between rural development actions (translated from French: Liaison Entre Actions de Développement de l'Économie Rurale)
LIPT, Low-Income Project Team
PMG, Processing and Marketing Grant
PSFPI, Public Sector Food Procurement Initiative
RDPE, Rural Development Programme for England
REG, Rural Economy Grant
RES, Rural Economy Scheme
SFFS, Sustainable Farming and Food Strategy (used interchangeably with SSFF)
SSFF, Strategy for Sustainable Farming and Food (used interchangeably with SFFS)

European units of government

EC, European Commission (also, European Community)
EC DGA, European Commission Directorate-General for Agriculture
EU, European Union

American organizations

AFT, American Farmland Trust
CFSC, Community Food Security Coalition
CNF, Child Nutrition Forum
EDF, Environmental Defense Fund (also abbreviated to ED)
FFPP, Farm and Food Policy Project
FMC, Farmers Market Coalition
FRAC, Food Research & Action Center
HFCWG, Healthy Food and Communities Work Group (part of FFPP)
NAMWG, New Agricultural Markets Work Group (part of FFPP)
NANA, National Alliance for Nutrition and Activity
NEMWI, Northeast Midwest Institute
NFFC, National Family Farm Coalition
NFSN, National Farm to School Network
NFU, National Farmers Union
NSAC, National Sustainable Agriculture Coalition

SAC, Sustainable Agriculture Coalition
WKKF, W. K. Kellogg Foundation

British organizations

CLA, Country Land and Businessowners' Association
CPRE, Campaign (formerly "Council") for the Protection of Rural England
EFF, Esmée Fairbairn Foundation
FARMA, National Association of Farmers' Retail & Markets Association
FCFCG, Federation of City Farms & Community Gardens
FOE UK, Friends of the Earth UK
IIED, International Institute for Environment and Development
LEAF, Linking Environment and Farming
MLFW, Making Local Food Work
NEF, New Economics Foundation
NFA, National Food Alliance
NFU, National Farmers Union
SA, Soil Association
SAFE Alliance, Sustainable Agriculture Food and Environment Alliance
Sustain, Sustain: the alliance for better food and farming
WWF UK, World Wildlife Fund UK

Other abbreviations

ITO, Indian Tribal Organization (US)
NGO, Non-Governmental Organization
QUANGO, Quasi-Autonomous Non-Governmental Organization
SMO, Social Movement Organization

Author notes

Style accommodations were made for differences in American, British, and European formats. A hybridized reference format was needed: American and British citation styles utilize each country's legal citation system as a basis for formatting foreign legal references. This meant that significant contextual information could be lost, such as the origin country, legislative chamber that introduced a bill, action undertaken by the legislature, and full legal citation. The American Psychological Association's 6th Edition citation style served as base style, with modifications for government documents, statues, and bills based upon the Harvard Blue Book Uniform System of Citation 19th Edition. The citation style for reports was modified to include both the organizational author (including governmental sub-agency) and individual author.

Financial support

The first year of research was supported by a US–UK Fulbright Scholar award. Newcastle University awarded an International Postgraduate Scholarship and the School of Agriculture, Food, and Rural Development graciously reduced tuition fees and provided travel funding. Also, I was a short-term consultant to the Swedish University of Agricultural Sciences (SLU) and World Wildlife Fund UK.

Acknowledgements

This research would not have been possible without the participation of British and American policy practitioners, funders, and policymakers. Thank you.

Academic research and book writing inevitably become a family project. My wife and daughter made several accommodations for me pursue this research and write this book. My wife's aunt also provided helpful editorial guidance. Thank you Elizabeth, Madison, and Jessie.

Preface

National policies have a direct impact on the decisions made by landowners, which in turn affects farm management, wildlife, and families, potentially for generations. On my family's farm, the U.S. Department of Agriculture (USDA) paid for the installation of a pond as a secondary water supply for my grandfather's greenhouses. It brings countless bird and amphibian species to our backyard and cultivated my curiosity of the outdoors. Other policies were less beneficial. The USDA paid him to plant autumn olive (*Elaeagnus umbellata*), a woody shrub native to Asia that yields red berries attractive to birds. In his lifespan, attitudes about using invasive plants to provide wildlife habit changed. What one generation decides is the "right way" to do things has a lasting impact, incurring costs for later generations. This taught me that enshrining a popular idea into policy is not just a thought exercise. It can instill real burdens for people on the ground. Often, it is the perspective of stakeholders who are best able to directly communicate that valuable on-the-ground perspective. A guiding question for framing the research for this book is: *How have stakeholders been included in the policy process, and has the policy process responded to their interests and concerns?*

Balancing long-term outcomes, on the landscape and families, with short-term outcomes, like passing a Bill, is fundamentally difficult. In the New York region, the farmland preservation movement sought policies to protect farmland from its rapid conversion to other uses in the 1980s and 1990s. Located 50 miles west of New York City and six miles from an interstate highway, the backdrop of my childhood was fields turning to bare orange earth and then to subdivisions and strip malls. Observing this trend, it seemed ironic that the individual pursuit of a rural life resulted in the loss of that rural quality of life *en masse*. The worst dreams I have are of my family's farm being turned into a commercial development, the neighboring farms being developed, and needing to move to find again that sense of rural place.

I watched the land preservation movement develop a very successful message to "save farms." This resulted in state-wide public referendums with voters allocating more than \$2.5 billion for preserving farms and "open space" in New Jersey. However, many of the farmers wishing to "sell out" were near retirement age. The message to "save farms" did not cultivate support for farm

xiv *Preface*

viability measures such as business planning, farm transition planning, and beginning farmer development. In 2005, my family sought to preserve our farm. The state proposed to preserve our farm as "open space" through a direct purchase and letting it transition into forest. We declined. Presently, there is no public support for business planning to make an existing farm more viable.

I have seen the beneficial impact of narrowly defined advocacy group messages and their downsides. Narrowly framed campaigns preserved the *land* but did not preserve *farming*. The initial framing of an issue can endure for decades within public discourse and governmental institutions. Thus, I question: *How do advocacy group messages align with the interests of the affected stakeholders, and align with political feasibility?*

Agriculture and policy were not initial interests for me despite their presence in my upbringing. In line with the outdoor recreation I pursued with my family and Boy Scouts, I focused my college education on environmental studies. Through college, I explored different landscapes: rural Maine, a term in Oslo, Norway, a term in Norwich, England, and a short term in Russia. In the spring of 2002, I encountered my first farmers' market in Norwich, England.

In this 700-year-old farmers' market, many vendors advertised products as "local," "farm fresh," or "hand dug." This context sparked my curiosity about local food as an economic development strategy for my community and farm. I explored this market in greater depth for a course on Consumer Cultures and interviewed vendors about why they marketed products as "local." My interest in the United Kingdom as a research site was born from this project, from the tantalizing similarities with American culture and insightful differences.

I then studied local food in the United States. I surveyed a Maine beef producer and shoppers at the Portland Public Market about the potential for marketing beef locally (Hunt, 2003). For my Master's research, I returned to Maine, surveying both producers and consumers to understand how their interactions impact the surrounding landscape (Hunt, 2005, 2007a). Through this research, I drew on examples in Britain where agencies had created marketing promotions linking consumer's food purchase to maintaining the surrounding countryside (Countryside Agency, 2002, 2004; Peak District National Park Authority, 2005). When I shared the results with the Maine Department of Agriculture, I met Gus Schumacher, a former undersecretary at the USDA, and was hired at the Northeast Midwest Institute in Washington, DC. as an agricultural policy specialist in 2005.

The Northeast Midwest Institute is a small "think and do tank" that provides policy research and analysis for the House and Senate Northeast–Midwest Coalitions. My time there gave me an inside perspective on how advocacy groups interact with Congress and Executive Branch agencies. I worked with the Farm and Food Policy Project (FFPP), a three-year cross-sector alliance seeking change in farm, food, and rural policies through the 2008 Farm Bill. Its prominence and connection to over 450 organizations exposed me to a variety of policy strategies, communications strategies, organization types, and

Preface xv

funder priorities. I became curious about their different ways of defining problems, proposing solutions, framing messages, and communicating to the public and policymakers.

Having more questions than answers, I wanted to return to academia to study these themes through a doctoral degree. I wanted an outsider's perspective and visited a number of British universities to research their programs. I chose Newcastle University's Centre for Rural Economy, a social science unit located in the School of Agriculture, Food, and Rural Development, because of its interdisciplinary setting, international perspective, and focus on industrialized countries. I began a Ph.D. in Rural Development in September, 2010 which was completed in July, 2013.

I thought research would explain several professional frustrations. One frustration was that the decentralization of the local food movement made policy work difficult. There are several well-organized advocacy coalitions yet many more unaffiliated local organizations. In one national group, the National Sustainable Agriculture Coalition, their members voted on and carried out mutually developed policy agendas. Through my time in the UK, I saw that decentralization was more than "normal," it was a central part of a *local* food movement. I learned that well-organized, stakeholder-led coalitions were an exception, in both the UK *and the US*, because the most visible policy advocacy often was carried out by media-savvy environmental interest groups.

Early in the research process I conducted background interviews, hoping to find a cross-sector policy alliance similar to the FFPP in the UK. A national, cross-sector alliance promoting local food did not and had not existed in England. Through one advising session, I realized that my "no data" situation was, in fact, my data: a cross-sector coalition had not formed. Rather than two similar, "like" cases, the two case studies resulted in a divergent or "extreme" case. This realization drove me to ask about how organizations do and don't work together in interviews.

This type of iterative refinement of tentative ideas and re-checking those ideas with further empirical evidence is central to the development of a theory in the grounded theory approach (Charmaz, 2006, pp. 102–104). The following questions helped focus, refine, and frame my research.

- Is it a uniquely American tradition of civic participation for individuals to work together and more of a British phenomenon for great individuals to work singly? *Is culture the main driver for coalition formation?*
- Are advocacy coalitions uniquely well suited to the American federal system and centralized interest groups uniquely well suited to the British, and principally English, central government? *Are political structures a defining feature, creating incentives and disincentives for coalition formation?*
- Do coalitions emerge after a period of high conflict? *Is there an evolutionary cycle to how organizations respond to conflict over time?*
- Was "local food" a more significant issue to mobilize public and policymaker support at a national level in the US and less significant in

xvi *Preface*

the UK? *Did both countries have relevant, national policies, which stakeholders used or could use to further local food projects?*

This last question was especially clarifying.

In both the US and the UK, individuals, farmers, businesses, schools, government leaders, and others were forming local food projects. Both American and British policymakers were interested in local food and national advocacy groups promoted local food to policymakers. The initial difference was in *how* local food policy was promoted. Many British interest groups favored media communications and American coalitions favored direct communication to policymakers (Hunt, 2011b).

A by-product of the comparative research is that we often default to focus on what is "better" or "worse." For the issue of local food, forming the local food project is a central goal: it is about ordinary people in a variety of roles engaging in tangible work around the issues of food. Engaging as a stakeholder is a principal outcome. I refined my initial research question by focusing on stakeholder engagement.

- In these two countries, what has been the political impact of national-level advocacy on local food?
- How do advocacy group messages align with the interests of the affected stakeholders, balancing their interests and stakeholder interests with political feasibility?
- How have stakeholders been included in the policy process, and importantly, has the policy process (including NGOs and policymakers) responded to their interests and concerns?

While the second question reflects my observations about the farmland preservation movement, and the third reflects observations of working within a cross-sector alliance, these are not the questions I began my research. They emerged from the research. Through my American experience, I thought stakeholder-led groups were comparatively "normal." It was through the interviews of British organizations, where professional-led interest groups and stakeholder-led groups were both active on local food issues, that I began to focus on a linkage between stakeholder participation and policy outcome.

And yet, questions about stakeholder participation are biased *in principle*. Concerns about participation, of who is included and excluded, in a political process are defining concerns of democratic governance. A policy outcome can be measured simply. Did a bill become law? Were resources increased or harms reduced? Answering questions about how participation affects the translation of stakeholder needs into policy ideas and outcomes is more difficult. I hope that I have provided the solid description and insight needed to fairly compare the advocacy group and policy processes of two democratic countries.

1 Local food policies as a lens on American and British food movements

Introduction

Popular interest in local and regional foods has increased through the 2000s and 2010s. Prior to this popular recognition of local food, leaders of the American and British food movements pioneered local food production, processing, distribution, and marketing as the economic and social components of sustainable agriculture, or, more commonly in Europe, as *alternative food networks*. A record of the discourses, ideas, purposes, and needs for local food system development is observable in national-level policy documents in each country.

A retrospective analysis of the national policy development is possible, owing to the quality and availability of government documents, in both countries. This includes bills, laws, regulations, reports, government data, debates in the Congress and Parliament, and the views of proponents of local food (as captured in testimony and report quotations). The policies provide a record of decisions made about how to define the goals and anticipated outcomes of local food policy.

In the US, it is possible to trace national advocacy to 1975, the year prior to the enactment of the Farmer to Consumer Direct Marketing Act of 1976. In the UK, specifically England (which is the focus of this research), the first national policy that encouraged local food activities came with the introduction of LEADER in 1991, an EU rural development program. The aim of this book is to describe the establishment of national policies, analyzing the interactions between national advocacy groups, local-level or grassroots organizations, and national policymakers.

Government records and advocacy group documents are not complete pictures of what constitutes "local food." Not all the local food advocacy could be pursued through national policy. Within the topical focus on local food and within the context of national policy, broader issues of social movement formation are discussed.

The degree of social inclusion and exclusion within local food projects is a relatively recent concern expressed by academics, such as P. Allen (2004, 2010), DeLind (2011), Hinrichs and Allen (2008), Hinrichs and Kremer (2002), and

2 American and British local food policies

Winter (2003). However, policy records provide evidence that policy leaders in the US and UK pursued policies to address inequalities *from the outset.*

Hinrichs and Charles (2012) consider that the level of social inclusion of local food projects varies in the US and assert that "before the most recent Farm Bill in 2008, few Farm Bills offered provisions directly supporting the development of local food systems" (Hinrichs & Charles, 2012, p. 171). In the following section several national policies are listed that were authorized earlier through the Farm Bill, Child Nutrition Act, and other related acts, including a Women Infants and Children's Farmers Market Nutrition Program, the Community Food Project program, the Value-Added Producer Grant, and a Senior Farmers Market Nutrition Program.

Given the nature of the American policy process, where constituents and advocates typically bring their policy ideas to Members of Congress for introduction as a Bill, local food proponents were well aware of the potential of social exclusion, and actively sought to address it through national policies for the past several decades. This type of oversight by academic observers, both in the US and UK, is not uncommon and indicates the need for a dedicated analysis of both countries' policy texts concerning local food.

Research on the food movement and local food systems in the US has proceeded with little analysis after nearly four decades of national policy activity, much of which has privileged social inclusion. Recent British scholarship on an English funding program, using empirical evidence on local food projects, has repositioned local food projects as socially inclusive (Kirwan et al., 2013). While this research is in dialogue with and presents arguments that respond to the concerns identified by other scholars, such as defensive localism and social exclusion, it has not been framed by those concerns.

This book emphasizes reporting information gathered from primary documents—policy documents, advocacy group documents, interviews, and participant observation—over academic publications. They represent a virtually untapped well of information to understand American and British food movements, and are accessible to the public. More than 1,100 primary documents were reviewed.

This research began with observations, using a grounded theory approach (Charmaz, 2006). The evidence is gathered before hypotheses are formed, and theorization occurs in the final stages of research. The grounded theory approach integrated easily into the context-building required for international comparative research (Hantrais, 2009) and case study development (Eisenhardt, 1989; Snow & Trom, 2002; Yin, 1993, 2003).

In discussing local food, one would expect the local context to be critically important, yet cultural and political differences are often overlooked. DuPuis and Goodman (2005) grouped scholarship on American, European, and British local food movements together without examining the differences in the movements. Yet, American, British, and continental European perspectives on local food reflect differences in political and cultural contexts (see Barnes, 2008).

Cultural understandings of the same terms differ between countries. Blake, Mellor, and Crane (2010) applied the American notion of middle class (which is based on average income) to justify their selection of a sample of local food consumers from the British middle class (which is based upon profession and university education and typically includes individuals of above-average income). In another example, the emphasis of who has power in society is different in American and British conceptions of *food democracy*. American scholars Hassanem (2003, 2008) and Hamilton (2004, 2005, 2011) emphasize the empowerment of ordinary citizens and British scholars Barling, Caraher, and Lang (2009) focus more on institutional approaches, such as governments reducing food poverty, decreasing corporate influence, and interest groups engaging in media campaigns or protests.

The normal or default ways in which people organize for political action often differ between countries. Starr (2010) considered whether the American local food movement was a social movement by using European literature on new social movements, when European social movements had developed from labor movements and American movements had developed from a pluralistic tradition (della Porta, 2002, p. 295).

The Introduction introduces key differences and similarities between the US and UK, and shared meanings of local food. The second chapter begins with the development of national-level local food policies in the US, exploring policies specific to local food and those policies used to support local food. The development of English local food policies, including the interaction of the British government with the European Union, is in Chapter 3, and introduces the issue of limited advocacy group collaboration. Chapter 4 examines those issues through a case study on "food miles" advocacy in England. Chapter 5 utilizes a case study from the 2008 US "Farm Bill" and illustrates how poor advocacy group collaboration was increased through a new policy alliance, called the Farm and Food Policy Project. Chapter 6 makes a direct comparison between both countries based primarily on public speeches and interviews of American and British policy leaders. Chapter 7 concludes with a *theory of food systems practice*, the aim of which is to formalize the assumed "playbook" used in many local-level food projects, and suggests that its application by national-level advocacy groups may improve policy outcomes over time.

Toward a theory of food systems practice

The experience of food is very rich, crossing all human senses. It influences our physiology. Its cultivation and harvesting has transformed our planet. It can be produced as nearby as our homes. It can crisscross the earth before it reaches our plates. Its distribution and availability is not universal, and is subject to weather, climate, insects, pathogens, genetic extinction, trade restrictions, and poverty. There is no one way to perceive, understand, or interact with food. Food escapes universalisms.

4 American and British local food policies

Food is critical to existence, and its availability is critical to social stability. Hunger, high food prices, and inattention to agricultural producers have sparked many successful revolts and changes of government (Lang, Barling, & Caraher, 2009, pp. 285–286; Tarrow, 1998). Most countries have a range of policies designed to support their agricultural sectors and have policies designed to influence consumer food prices. Because the challenges faced in agricultural production and food distribution are varied in their cause, policy responses differ. While there is a history of cross-discipline policy responses in food and agriculture, the advent of modern agriculture brought greater specialization and reliance on sciences to enhance production and reduce losses.

The local food movement challenges specialization through reintroducing the social dimension of agriculture, often changing people's relationship through food. Linkages between food production, distribution, processing, marketing, and consumption are often changed locally and regionally because it is a level at which individuals are able to come together and form relationships with tangible, physical, and visible outcomes. This involves linkages that are often:

- *multi-sector*, involving perspectives from production, harvesting, processing, distribution, retailing, citizens and consumers, governmental institutions, laborers, and restaurant workers;
- *multi-level*, including local, county, national, and international perspectives;
- *interdisciplinary*, and informed by multiple disciplinary perspectives, data, and tools including those from agricultural sciences, anthropology, development studies, economics, environmental sciences, nutrition, and sociology;
- *participatory*, including citizens and stakeholders in decision-making;
- *inclusive orientation*, as more rather that fewer perspectives are engaged in decision-making; and
- *multi-objective*, as a result of a diversity of perspectives involved in decision-making, decisions typically prioritize and carry out multiple goals simultaneously.

Utilizing the term "food system" elevates interconnection as the defining feature. This follows from Rountree, that "The 'whole' is of higher organizational status than the 'parts' and has its own identity" (Rountree, 1977, p. 249). Its use in the field is meant to shift thinking and action toward the simultaneous pursuit of sustainability and social justice (Clancy, 1994, p. 77). It differs slightly from the use of local food network or links used more commonly in the UK (Hinrichs & Charles, 2012), which signify interconnection but with less emphasis on the whole. Even though terms differ, equity within the food system is a shared concern in the US and UK.

Quantifying key terms and concepts

What is a social movement?

The definition of a new social movement used by Gerlach and Hine (1970) is applicable for the geographic dispersion of a local food movement. A new social movement is decentralized, segmented, and reticulated (as cited in Tarrow, 1998, p. 129). It has no single leader (decentralized authority), is composed of heterogeneous and largely autonomous local groups (segmentation), and is connected through network-based relationships (reticulated) (Tarrow, 1998, p. 129).[1] Only part of a social movement is organized. Its widespread influence comes from unorganized individuals sharing in its beliefs and carrying out supportive actions autonomously from movement organizations.

A social movement is more than its structure. A social movement's aim to influence society is fundamentally political. Its political changes are achieved through collective action. For Tarrow, a social movement is a group of individuals engaged in "collective challenges based upon common purposes and social solidarities, in sustained interaction with elites, opponents, and authorities" (Tarrow, 1998, p. 4). Tarrow identified that solidarity originates from consensus (Tarrow, 1998, p. 6). Consensus can be formed through deliberation among heterogeneous social groups who recognize the interdependence of their interests or from socially homogenous groups who possess a set of shared beliefs, achieving consensus. For the study of food movements, an emphasis can be placed on consensus achieved through deliberation.

A food movement is a diverse collection of organizations and unorganized stakeholders that engage substantially on food issues. The organizations range from farm and rural development groups to urban agriculture and environmental groups and public health groups. A subset of the food movement is active in local projects relating to the local and regional production, distribution, and consumption of food. This is a local food movement.

The American and British local food movements are textbook examples of a social movement:

- there is no single organization that represents local food;
- each country has hundreds of organizations pursuing local food projects for diverse goals; and
- they are interconnected by a mix of formal and informal networks.

US Examples:

- The U.S. Department of Agriculture (USDA) Farmers Market Directory lists over 8,000 markets (USDA, 2013b).
- The USDA National Farm to School Census lists over 40,000 schools involved in local food purchasing projects (USDA, 2014b).

6 *American and British local food policies*

- A 10-year review of Community Food Projects lists nearly 200 projects (Tuckermanty et al., 2007).
- The website Local Harvest lists over 20,000 members engaged in direct marketing (Local Harvest, 2012).

UK Examples:

- The Making Local Food Work (MLFW) project supported 1,600 community food enterprises that involved over 7,000 producers (MLFW, 2012).
- There are over 550 farmers markets and over 4,000 farm shops (DEFRA, 2012a; UK: Rise in number of farm shops, 2011).
- There are about 260 recognized community food projects (Sustain, 2003).

In both countries, local food projects have involved low-income residents (Briggs et al., 2010; Cohen, 2002; Fisher, 1999; FOE UK, 2001; Garnett, 1996; Kantor, 2001; Sustain, 1999a, 2001, 2003; Tuckermanty et al., 2007). Also, local projects are typically connected to regional or national networks and associations.

Social movement organizations, interest groups, and advocacy groups

American and British scholars describe citizen participation and collective action on food policy change as "food democracy" (Hamilton, 2004, 2005, 2011; Hassanein, 2003, 2008; Lang et al., 2009). Decentralized action should not be misconstrued as disorganized. Organizations seeking to mobilize a constituency to form a consensus for political goals are considered social movement organizations (SMOs). This is in contrast to interest groups, which primarily rely on media-oriented campaigns (Kriesi, 1996, pp. 152–153). The term *advocacy group* is used to include SMOs, interest groups, and other NGOs (e.g. trade associations) in policy advocacy.

SMOs include the direct participation of citizens and/or stakeholders in the organization. The main American advocacy groups that have promoted local food policies are: the National Sustainable Agriculture Coalition (NSAC), the Community Food Security Coalition (CFSC), and the National Farm to School Network (NFSN). These are all social movement organizations that utilize a grassroots organizing model (Kriesi, 1996; Rucht, 1996). These organizations, as well as some in the UK, including FARMA and the Federation of City Farms & Community Gardens (FCFCG), operate as a special type of SMO called an *advocacy coalition* (Sabatier, 1993; Sabatier & Jenkins-Smith, 1993). In an organized advocacy coalition, stakeholders from different organizations or perspectives participate directly in the coalition's decision-making through participating on a board or voting during general membership meetings.

By contrast, an interest group has "sufficient resources – in particular, institutionalized access, authority, and expertise – which means that they normally do not have the recourse to the mobilization of their constituents" (Kriesi, 1996, p. 153). They rely on media messages to mobilize supporters to create "a movement without incurring the costs of building and maintaining mass organizations" (Tarrow, 1998, p. 131). Media mobilization techniques have fewer opportunities for empowerment and learning how to overcome social divisions (Evans & Boyte, 1986; Tarrow, 1998, pp. 129, 132–133). National advocacy groups in England that promoted local food without participation of stakeholders in policy decisions include the Campaign for the Protection of Rural England (CPRE), the Soil Association (SA), and Sustain. Their political authority derives not from stakeholders that they serve as members, but by the visibility of their position, access, and influence. Because of their national prominence, they are considered by their peers as part of the local food movement (FEC, 2011) even though they do not directly represent local food stakeholders.

Who is a stakeholder?

Stakeholder theory developed from the business sector to identify individuals and groups not directly involved in business transactions but who could be affected by the business' activities. In public policy, the term *stakeholder* describes the groups of entities and individuals who bear the benefits, costs, and risks of policy success, failure, and policymaker inaction (Freeman, 1984; Mitchell, Agle, & Wood, 1997).

Local food stakeholders are heterogeneous. They include individuals who are economically and socially dependent on the success of local food projects. This includes small farm operators and individuals dependent on the social relationships formed through local food projects, such as community gardens. Dependency exposes them to risks of failure of a local food project. Thus, an advocacy group's ability (or inability) to influence the policy process can have a direct impact on local food stakeholders even if they are not directly engaged in public policy advocacy.

Not all stakeholders are able to fully participate. Society is embedded with preexisting constraints to participation (e.g. resources, time, knowledge, historical discrimination, etc.). These factors affect who participates in a local food project. A local food project is neither fundamentally inclusive nor exclusive; inequality can be increased, maintained, or reduced.

A local project can reproduce preexisting social inequalities, such as middle-class outsiders undertaking a "greening" project in a predominantly lower-income neighborhood without resident support (Hexham Community Partnership, 2012). Much academic concern has been placed on local food projects being a place where preexisting social exclusion are reproduced (Allen, 2004, 2010; DeLind, 2011; Hinrichs & Kremer, 2002).

A local project can seek to overcome preexisting social inequalities. It can reduce divisions between: producers and consumers (e.g. community-supported agriculture, CSA), urban consumers and rural producers (e.g. farmers markets);

8 *American and British local food policies*

and people with lower incomes and higher incomes (e.g. community gardens; public benefits used at farmers' markets, farm-to-school projects). It can improve access to healthy, affordable, and fresh foods for different races and ethnicities. When social divisions are reduced, the skills and capacity of individuals to work across differences is increased (Gaventa & Barrett, 2010; Putnam, 2000, pp. 19–21).

Local food projects in the US and UK have created situations where social inequalities can be addressed (for some examples see: Community Council of Devon (2010); Community food and health (Scotland) (2014); Fisher (1999); Morgan and Sonnino (2006); Sustain and MLFW (2009); Tuckermanty et al. (2007). Systematic studies of the degree of social inclusion or exclusion of potential participants in local food projects are extremely limited, of which Kirwan et al. (2013) may be the first. Because local food projects bridge divisions (e.g. cross-sector, spatial, producer/consumer, etc.), they are *oriented* towards inclusion.

Defining local food and its projects

The local-level activities that constitute local food projects are varied. The term "local food project" is used to describe formalized activities at the local level, and can include regional-level activities. Local food projects aim to increase the availability of local and regional food through production, processing, distributing, marketing, and consumption within that locality or region. They may include, but differ from, *locality* foods. (Locality foods are intended for consumption beyond their production region but are labeled with that place's identity, usually as a quality mark; e.g. Parmesan cheese, Champagne sparkling wine, etc.) The projects may be a not-for profit or for-profit activity. Some may include a small portion of non-local products in their projects. Despite their different forms and goals, their commonality is reorienting social relationships through food in a defined, proximate location.

Most local food projects are collaborative, and the success or failure of a project (e.g. new food hub, a small abattoir, or a farmers' market) affects individuals beyond those directly engaged in the project's management. The level of collaboration needed for a local food project is variable and extends along a continuum of interdependence (e.g. as with an abattoir) through to joint project implementation and partnerships (e.g. common with a farm-to-school project). Some local food activities are not collaborative, such as sales made directly between a producer and a consumer from the farm or via the Internet. These activities are local food projects in the sense that the individual producer assumes traditionally separate roles of production, distribution, and marketing.

Within this meaning of local food project, an emphasis is placed on relationships between producers and purchasers. In some places there has been a push to define local or regional food by distance. In England, a radius of 30 miles is frequently cited by advocacy groups as a way to define "local."

American and British local food policies 9

However, advocacy group documents show that local is considerably more flexible in meaning, especially for large urban areas and rural counties (CPRE, 2011b, c, d, e, f, g, 2012a, b, c, d, e, f, g; FARMA, 2010). Distance-based measures also vary in the US. The variability in characterization of local food illustrates that the attributes of local food are socially constructed. The definitions of "local" food originate from the individuals that initiate the project and may be shared between other similar projects. Locally and regionally produced and consumed foods are "sub-national."

Some trade associations portray local as national in order to maintain cohesion among its diverse membership (NFU Food Chain Staff, 2012). Equating local with national is instrumental to maintaining cohesion in the National Farmers Union (NFU) and other national trade associations. This is a function of a highly specialized and regionalized agriculture in a country with a small land area. An example offered by the NFU was with pork breeds, where a region's common breeds are still linked with their breeding origin. The promotion of a locally distinctive breed from one region (e.g. Hampshire) might harm the market of pork producers from another region (e.g. Berkshire), thus increasing dissention among association members. As with other definitions of local food, this definition is socially constructed.

The "value" of local food originates from the relationships between producers and consumers, reflecting Granovetter's (1985) concept of social embeddedness. Previous research demonstrates that social relationships have a causal influence on local food sales and are correlated with producers changing their production methods to utilize fewer chemicals (Hunt, 2007a), and can influence on-farm biodiversity (Goland & Bauer, 2004). The European Commission (EC) envisioned the LEADER program's support of local agriculture through the reformation of social relationships (Sylvander, 1993 (revised 1995)). Values of local food are attributed through social processes: economic transactions, beliefs, sensations (e.g. taste, smell), and management practices.

The goals of local food projects are defined by its participants. Projects may be formed or shaped by external factors, such as criteria from public funding sources (EC, 1991; Gale, 1997). External influences can displace, distort, blend, and enable locally defined goals. Four policy narratives of local food are apparent in both American and British policy texts: transformation, instrumentalism, marketism, and individualism.

Transformation

Local food is taken into account on its own, with distinctive attributes, processes, and outcomes, and a transformation occurs. A change of status of its participants occurs through their participation in a local food activity. Producers may gain income, community development may be maintained or increased, employment may be generated, and consumer access to fresh foods may increase. This narrative has a revelatory aspect where "knowing where one's food comes from" is a gateway to further food system awareness. Values of inclusion; grassroots and

10 American and British local food policies

participatory democracy; overcoming traditional social, economic, cultural, and disciplinary boundaries; and an equality of power across all food system participants are prevalent. Ideologies that polarize local food to corporately controlled global food systems exist, as exemplified within the food sovereignty and alternative agriculture movements. Transformation is based on actions, not words. Aspiration is undergirded with pragmatism. Outcomes range from minimal levels of local food awareness as a consumer to projects that reorganize social, economic, and environmental relationships, such as with CSAs. Activities towards food localization can occur simultaneously in rich and developing countries and practices can be exchanged through international networks: local food is not isolationist. Actions through individuals and groups of individuals are relatively privileged over action from public policy. Public policy can play an important corrective role with social, economic, and environmental inequities. Transformation is least prevalent in English policy documents and most prevalent in American policy documents.

Instrumentalism

Local food is used to support or achieve other, predefined policy objectives. Local food policies were developed in a well-defined policy environment, with preexisting narratives of agricultural support, rural development, and food poverty. Preexisting policy priorities are used to enable local food activities. Local food is often subordinated within preexisting narratives, but not necessarily marginalized. When subordinated to other narratives, local food may be in conflict with the main narrative's assumptions. This is especially true when local food is integrated with government narratives that use consumer choice and "productivist" frames in agricultural policy. Advocates of local food may intentionally subordinate their narratives to gain allies or to access resources from pre-established funding sources. Instrumental narratives may be an authentic narrative of the local food movement, be imposed by an external entity (government), or be a hybrid narrative formed through negotiation or deliberation. The instrumentalism narrative appears frequently in early US policies on local food and is the main narrative in English policy documents.

Marketism

Local food, and the actions of individuals related to local food, is subsumed within existing economic and political relationships. Local food is often considered as "just another product" to be offered through existing production, processing, distribution, and marketing activities. For example, local food may be considered another "consumer choice" label alongside natural and organic. Outcomes are oriented towards private gains to retailers, distributors, and producers. Retailers compete by price. Non-economic outcomes are considered a beneficial by-product of economic transactions. The impacts of individuals are often only viewed in the aggregate, as a product of consumer demand.

American and British local food policies 11

Individuals are considered as passive consumers, though businesses may acknowledge the need for educating individuals about food, diet, and health. Actions by the private sector are privileged over the actions of government and individuals. The primary goal of public policy for local food is economic development. Critiques of preexisting social and economic arrangements are not prevalent. Marketism positions local food as an innovation and an implicit critique of a staid status quo. This narrative appears frequently in English policy documents and rarely in American policy documents.

Individualism

Local food conveys individual benefits to the producer and consumer. It is a product available to those who can purchase it. This narrative often appears as the consumer-oriented "twin" to the corporation-oriented marketism narrative. The main difference is that actions by individuals, as consumers and small business owners, are advantaged over governmental and corporate institutions. An idealized form of economic competition is communicated, where multiple independent and small businesses compete in a competitive marketplace. Market power is kept in check by regulatory authorities. Adequate access to information allows individuals to make informed choices. This includes choices for individual benefit, such as selecting healthy food; for the benefit of others, such as through purchases of Fairtrade products; and the benefit of non-humans, such as conserving physical and wildlife resources through organic or Rainforest Alliance Certified products. Retailers compete by offering products with social and environmental claims. Consumption choices may challenge the status quo and while also conveying an elevated social status or "warm glow" of impure altruism. Public policy is viewed as a way to help satisfy individual needs and to provide an active counterweight to the influence of businesses. This includes efforts to limit food advertising to children, provide calorie counts in restaurants, promote nutrition standards, government regulation that protects "independent" businesses, and resources for small business development. The individualism narrative appears frequently in news media, food magazines, and advertising. It rarely appears in American and English policy documents.

Relationships between the four narratives can be illustrated through a semiotic square (Fieldman, 1995). The semiotic square in Figure 1.1 is composed of two axes, one of which represents the shared or individual nature of goods while the other represents the degree to which that good's availability is influenced by individuals or institutions. Within these relationships certain groups of individuals and entities are empowered to provide locally produced goods (shown in the circles in Figure 1.1).

Government policies specific to local food are generally designed to support or enable its activities, rather than regulate, restrict, or control. Often, governmental policies seek to enable a wide range of market-oriented or community-based actions. Only at the extreme of government provision does

12 *American and British local food policies*

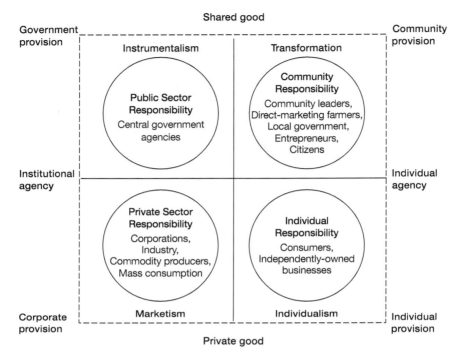

Figure 1.1 Semiotic square of four narratives of local food and the entities enabled by each narrative.

a government directly control the marketing and distribution of food, as does the USDA with the provision of surplus foods to individuals on low incomes (*Agricultural Adjustment Act*. Section 32 (as amended)). Other extreme outcomes are illustrated in the corners of the square.

All four narratives appear in each country. The instrumental narrative was promoted most by English interest groups: local food could reduce negative effects from climate change. The transformation narrative was promoted most by American SMOs: local food could improve the economic viability of small farm operators and lead to the self-empowerment of low-income communities to meet their food needs.

Developing the British–American comparison

There is a long history of comparisons between American and British cultures and political institutions. Nearly two hundred years ago, de Tocqueville observed that American and English political activity had (and still has) two different default styles of political action.

The English often perform great things singly, whereas the Americans form associations for the smallest undertakings. It is evident that the former people consider association as a powerful means of action, but the latter seem to regard it as the only means they have of acting.

(de Tocqueville, 1835/40 [1997], para. 5)

Social movement scholars describe these different, default cultural patterns of action as *advocacy styles* or *repertoires* (Swidler, 1986; Tarrow, 1998; Tilly, 1993; Zald, 1996). Because these ways of organizing or protesting are familiar and well known, they can be powerful tools to mobilize supporters. However, they can limit opportunities for learning and "constrain the choices available for collective action" (Tilly, 1993, p. 264). An international comparison of social movements requires grounding in each country's advocacy style in relation to its political institutions, governance style, and history (della Porta, 2002; Hantrais, 2009; Howlett, 2002).

Differences in political processes impact how national policies developed and were communicated to national policymakers. Although both are democratic, America's federal system developed differently from Britain's parliamentary system. The American political system was partly a reaction to the British governing style in the colonial era.

In *The Federalist Papers*, James Madison considered that the British Constitution could allow one branch of government to exert control—perhaps tyrannical control—over other branches because "the legislative, executive, and judiciary departments are by no means totally separate and distinct from each other" (Madison, 1788, para. 2). As a result, he promoted separate legislative (law-making and spending decisions), executive (implementation, administration, and enforcement), and judicial branches (independent judgments rendered by individuals removable by neither branch of government). These principles are enshrined in the American Constitution, and rely on the will of the Congress to reach consensus on law, funding the government, and granting (or restricting) the powers of the executive branch to carry out the law. With such decentralized authority, there are multiple points within the overall governmental framework at which NGOs can influence and change national policy. Also, because political majorities are needed in both the House and the Senate of the Congress, numerically small coalitions of Members of Congress often provide critical votes—and critical avenues—for policy change. American advocacy coalitions, like those in the food movement, utilize a decentralized membership structure, allowing members to cultivate direct relationships with Members of Congress *as constituents*.

In Britain, the English government has comingled legislative and executive authorities whereby the Parliament selects the chief executive (the Prime Minister) and the Cabinet departments' leaders are generally staffed by sitting Members of Parliament (MPs). The comingling of legislative and executive powers incentivizes English policymakers to form most policy through agency reports. *Why go through the labor of passing a law, when once "in" government, you*

14 *American and British local food policies*

can both direct funding and policy to your priorities? Favoring agency actions over more time-consuming laws can result in quick policy formation. It can also result in political instability (Pike et al., 2011), low motivation to conduct oversight (Schlesinger, 1992), limited transparency of government documents (observed and discussed in Chapter 3), and uncertain accountability to stakeholders (Verney, 1992). Policies frequently change when the majority or coalition changes in Parliament. With a preference for reports and policy actions from the executive agencies, versus laws, incoming governments can easily change policy. Laws are more difficult to change and more costly to introduce. In general, this has resulted in major rural policy shifts when parties change and minor shifts when government leadership changes within the existing majority or coalition (Pike et al., 2011).

British oversight is also limited. English Parliament leaders are also leaders of the executive agencies. There is little incentive for members of the same party or coalition to conduct critical oversight on their colleagues, *or themselves*. By contrast, the American Congress can call members of the executive branch to testify to Congress. If responses are unsatisfactory, funding may be withheld.

The main checks on parliamentary authority come externally. This is often through media attention, the government's appointment of "independent" inquiry panels, and the formation of semi-permanent, quasi-autonomous NGOs (QUANGOs) that provide oversight or guidance on government policymaking (Greve, Flinders, & Thiel, 1999). For example the Sustainable Development Commission advised the government on sustainable food policies (Lang, Dibb, & Reddy, 2011). Neither process is truly independent of Parliament; both are created from parliamentary action. As a result, NGOs are often in the role of providing independent oversight through mobilizing public opinion via media campaigns.

Differences in American and British institutions had an impact on this research, notably access to reliable expenditure data. It was relatively easy to identify a program's funding level in the US. Each branch of government needed consistent, transparent, and detailed budgets to coordinate spending activities. This resulted in many documents citing the same spending numbers. However, British spending figures were less reliable and difficult to find. Detailed annual budgets were not published for specific programs. When budgets were available, current and prior year funding levels in annual reports were inconsistent across reports. For most British programs it was impossible to identify funding changes over time *if expenditures were stated at all*.

Stakeholder participation also varied. A commitment to stakeholder consultation has been an increasing focus of British government leaders. Yet, consultation processes are ad hoc and not universally applied to all major policy decisions. While consultation results in greater information availability, the consultation process rarely holds policymakers accountable to stakeholder's input. A common refrain among food policy advocates was that the reports from a consultation process would grow dusty on a shelf. While the English policy process is open to stakeholder views, through the Parliament and the executive agencies, uncertain policy processes and accountability procedures diminish stakeholder participation and can reduce trust in government.

The US' Administrative Procedures Act (APA) of 1946 requires that stakeholders be consulted for significant policy changes (Appel, 2000; Bingham, Nabatchi, & O'Leary, 2005). Even an unsuccessful lawsuit can increase agency diligence and responsiveness to public comments (Appel, 2000). Stakeholders can sue the government if it fails in its consultation responsibilities. These are significant oversight authorities. Black and Hispanic farmers brought legal action against USDA over deficiencies in its implementation of the APA resulting in class action settlements in excess of $2 billion (Cowan & Feder, 2012; Feder & Cowan, 2010). The APA offers significant guidance to federal agencies when implementing the law and developing programs. The threat of taking the government to court is often an effective threat; social movements often lacking sufficient financial resources and legal expertise to sue.

Both governments are relatively open to stakeholder views when policy is formulated and revised. In both countries, national legislators showed interest in local food. In the US, between 1976 and 2012, 18 national policies were developed by Congress which could support local food (Ferd Hoefner [NSAC Policy Director], 2011). In Britain, MPs debated issues concerning local food in connection with major national policy proposals (House of Commons, 2002), bills were introduced which would support local food (*Food Justice Strategy Bill*, 2003, 2004), and MPs asked local food stakeholders to present their policy proposals (Sue Miller [Liberal Democrat, Chilthorne Domer], 2011). Further, debates in Parliament demonstrate a highly nuanced understanding of local food. Winter reported on local food debates involving protectionist or "defensive localism" (House of Commons, 2002; Winter, 2003). However, national policy records from the same period show a two-track policy dialogue. One discussed the needs of large-volume producers vulnerable to international competition (which included protectionist proposals). A separate, coincidental dialogue focused on the needs of smaller-volume producers who marketed products directly to consumers (which favored marketing and quality improvements, increased supermarket access, cooperative formation, and promoting a food culture). Knowledge of the needs of local food stakeholders is observable in national policy debates in both countries. What differs is the political action process.

Stakeholders were mobilized differently in each country. In both the US and England, stakeholder-led organizations provided an authentic voice on local food issues. American proponents of local food were more likely to interact directly with policymakers. In England, environmental-oriented interest groups defined the local food policy narrative through media campaigns. As a result, policy narratives from English stakeholder-led groups were overshadowed by the media campaigns.

Policies in the US and UK covered similar policy issues: agriculture, rural development, and on-farm conservation. Both the US and the UK (as a member of the European Union) regularly renew agriculture-related policies

16 *American and British local food policies*

on a 5- or 6-year basis. An EU agricultural attaché observed that the EU's Common Agricultural Policy (CAP) is the EU's "Farm Bill," the informal name applied to American farm, food, rural, and conservation legislation (Trarieux, 2005). Because of their frequent renewals, both provide opportunities for regular incremental policy changes and are multi-sector policies.

In the US, the "Farm Bill" includes policies for agricultural loans, subsidies, and crop insurance; on-farm conservation projects; rural development; and one of the US' main social welfare programs, the Supplemental Nutrition Assistance Program (SNAP). Similarly, the EU CAP contains policies for agricultural subsidies; rural development; and on-farm conservation projects. It has no specific social welfare program for nutrition. Both policy vehicles have shifted from higher levels of agricultural subsidization to lower levels. This is due to obligations agreed to in the General Agreement on Trade and Tariffs through the World Trade Organization and an increasingly urban population demanding more "public goods" in exchange for continuing farm programs (Berry, 1982; Brasier, 2002; Cox, Lowe, & Winter, 1986; Doering, 1999; Lehrer, 2008; Lowe & Wilkinson, 2009; Malone, 1986; Morgan, 2010; Moyer & Josling, 1990; Potter, 1998). National demographic trends and international trade obligations have put the US and UK on "common trajectories of change" (Braiser et al., 2012, p. 214).

However, the UK has devolved most authority on CAP implementation to the countries in its union. Authority for implementing most CAP policies devolved to Scotland in 1998 (Scottish Parliament), Wales in 2006 (National Assembly for Wales, 2014), and Northern Ireland in 1998 (Department of Agriculture and Rural Development. Northern Ireland, 2013; HM Government, 2013). However, before official devolution, greater authority was often granted for rural development programs (Bryden & Warner, 2012).

England remains governed through the UK Parliament. The same agencies and individuals who implement agricultural and rural policies in England through the Department for Food, Environment and Rural Affairs (DEFRA) also negotiate with the EU on the CAP and represent Britain's agricultural and food interests internationally. In general, when referring to "Britain" or the "UK," it refers to activities that encompass all four nations. When referring to England, it is to the country of England and organizations that primarily work in England. Typically, advocacy groups in England communicate issues related to England, or Great Britain, in its role as an EU member state. The CAP emerged in the 1980s with British sustainability advocates focusing policy activities on its agri-environmental programs but not its rural economic development policies.

Multi-level observations of the policy process were needed to compare policymaking in both countries. Observations were made of three different units of the policy process: national policies, advocacy groups and their policy environment, and the agency of individuals involved in policy formulation. As shown in Table 1.1, each of the three parts of the policy process was analyzed

Table 1.1 Methods and sources of information for observing the policy process

Unit of observation	Main methods	Main sources	Perspectives
National policies	Narrative analysis	• Government documents	• Government agencies • Legislature • Some quotes or republished advocacy group statements in government documents
	Policy outcomes	• Government documents • Advocacy group documents	• Multiple governments • Multiple organizations from different advocacy sectors
Advocacy group processes & their policy environment	Two-case comparative study	• US—Documents from government and advocacy groups	• Government • Funders • Multiple organizations from different advocacy sectors
		• England—Interviews	• Multiple organizations from different advocacy sectors
	Use of an extreme case Participant observation	• Researcher-selected • Stakeholder conferences • Small group meetings • Policy communication events • Consultancy	• American and English • Firsthand experience • Firsthand experience • Some quotes from notes or audio recording • Firsthand experience
Individual agency	Individual perspectives	• Interviews, especially funders	• Multiple American and English organizations from different advocacy sectors
		• Public speeches from movement leaders	• Varied by context

18 *American and British local food policies*

from different types of information sources, with multiple perspectives observed and reported within those sources.

Interviews were used to explore the motivations of individuals and gain insights that are not otherwise written or recorded. Active interviewing techniques were utilized, which are highly interactive (Gubrium & Holstein, 2003; Holstein & Gubrium, 1995; Hugh-Jones, 2010; Mason, 2002; Roulston, 2010). Twenty-three individuals were interviewed in the UK, including representatives from environmental and agricultural NGOs, policymakers, and funders (listed in Appendix 1). Fewer individuals were interviewed in the US because access to documentary information detailing individual and organization perspectives was available. During the initial British interviews, topics became more targeted, focusing on understanding the English policy environment, policy targets, collaboration, and the role of funders.

- How groups engage in policy (what they consider policymaking) and in what venues (e.g. Parliament, DEFRA, EU, media).
- Indications of how and when groups collaborate (i.e. acting jointly in some manner) across interests; barriers and inducements to collaborate.
- Understanding group decision-making processes and whether farmers, low-income individuals, or local/grassroots groups were included in decision-making or agenda-setting of group activities.
- How organization members get information needed to inform their strategic decisions.
- The role of funders in "setting the rules of the game."
- A potential British case study on local food policy at the national level.

(from Hunt, 2011a, p. 1)

The full set of initial interview questions are included in Appendix 2.

Participant observation was utilized to understand what was "normal" in a setting, and thus may escape reporting in an interview (Lichterman, 2002; Whyte, 1984). A list of participant observation activities is included in Appendix 3, these ranging from attending farmers' markets in both countries, attending practitioner conferences in both countries, farm site visits, and working as a food policy consultant in both countries.

To balance the use of *elicited* information—information that the researcher generates or co-develops through the research process—are *extant* sources (Lichterman, 2002, p. 141). Extant texts are any form of information that exists outside of the research process, independent of the researcher's observations (Charmaz, 2006). In this research, extant texts, such as government and advocacy group documents, are used to "provide an independent source of data from the researcher's collected firsthand materials" and experiences (Clemens & Hughes, 2002, p. 38). Most documents exist in the public domain. Two sets of primary documents, not in the public domain, provided critical insights into each country's policy process. First, permission was given to take and use printed and electronic files from my employment at the Northeast

Midwest Institute, to develop the American case study in Chapter 5. Second, permission was given to use materials gathered by Professor Philip Lowe and Neil Ward in a communal archive at the Centre for Rural Economy at Newcastle University. Both sets of internal documents were crucial for reconstructing collaborative advocacy efforts for locally produced food.

Documents were not assessed for the validity of their claims. Following from Janow (1996) texts were used as 1) as signifiers of beliefs (e.g. meanings of local food, desirable citizen actions, expected roles of government and NGOs, etc.), and 2) indicators of actions (e.g. decision-making, funding, communication to/from government, etc.). Assessing the symbolic qualities of texts was important to understand normal patterns of policy advocacy, such as:

- who was and was not represented in advocacy communications;
- the intended purpose of the texts, and what was *unsaid*;
- the relative priority of local food to other priorities; and
- the conditions through which advocacy narratives were manipulated or ignored.

Documents were analyzed for their narrative, policy outcomes, and relationship of intended outcomes to actual outcomes (Charmaz, 2006; van Eeten, 2007; Yin, 2003).

As discussed in the Preface, this research began with an assumption that national-level advocacy on local food policy would be collaborative in both countries. However, in both countries, contention rather than collaboration appeared to be normal in national policy advocacy. In the US, collaboration across sectors and issues areas was well-supported, and policy collaboration on local food appeared "normal." Significant resources and capacity had been developed in response to earlier coordination failures, principally between environmental and sustainable agriculture groups. Advocacy groups promoting local food in the US had adopted stakeholder-led advocacy coalitions at their time of formation. In England, high contention between national advocacy groups *and* high segmentation by sector, issue, and organization was the norm. As a result, national policy perspectives on local food were highly fragmented. However, local food activities in the US and UK were relatively similar at the local level, typically reflecting cross-sector collaboration and increased capacity of participants (see also Hinrichs & Charles, 2012). Thus, the national policy activities were the main point of divergence.

The emergence of an extreme case led to theoretical refinement on the conditions under which collaboration occurred or was inhibited (Charmaz, 2006, p. 102; Lichterman, 2002; Snow & Trom, 2002). Focusing on the divergences of advocacy group activities enabled theorization about factors which contribute to collaborative policy action and the formation of holistic local food narratives and competitive policy actions and single-sector narratives of local food (Charmaz, 2006; Hantrais, 2009; Mathison, 1988; Yin, 2003). A critical difference between the countries was the degree to which funders of

Table 1.2 Comparison of prevailing structural characteristics of food movements in the US and England

Site of political activity	US	England
National policy institutions		
Institutions	Representative democracy Separation of executive & legislative powers	Representative democracy Comingled executive & legislative powers
Processes	Strong legal protection for stakeholder consultation	Ad hoc stakeholder consultation
Advocacy group processes & their environment		
National policy content	Typically cross-sector Multi-objective Holistic "food systems" narrative	Typically single-sector Single objective Environmental-centric "food miles" narrative
Inter-organization relationships	Cooperative Formation of cross-sector policy coalitions	Competitive Interest groups dominate stakeholder-led groups
Advocacy organization structure	Social movement organizations Advocacy coalitions Cross-sector Multi-issue Stakeholder leadership	Interest groups Single sector Single issue Staff leadership
Connective structures	National coalitions National networks (e.g. National Farm to School Network, National Good Food Network) Cross-sector regional conferences	One national network (e.g. Sustain) Short-lived networks (e.g. Making Local Food Work, Tasting the Future, Food Poverty Network) Single-organization conferences
Local food projects		
Collaboration	Citizens, farmers, businesses, NGOs, govt., schools	Citizens, farmers, businesses, NGOs, govt., schools
Inclusion	Urban–rural partnerships Often includes low-income issues	Some urban–rural partnerships Sometimes includes low-income issues

NGOs encouraged national advocacy groups to work collaboratively and the degree to which funders scrutinized how those organizations included stakeholders in their internal decision-making. However, several observations were similar between the two countries, supporting the validity of the American–British comparison (Table 1.2).

Conclusion

American and British contexts differ but there are similarities in local food activities, policy needs, and the openness of the policy process to stakeholder input. A long-term policy analysis allows for the observation of how beliefs are transmitted to policymakers and how those beliefs change with time (Clemens & Hughes, 2002; Sabatier, 1993; Sabatier & Jenkins-Smith, 1993). Each country's period of observation begins with its first national-level local food policy. Through the evidence gathered with this research, it can be observed that increasing the inclusion of a social movement over time brings new allies, which in turn provides new opportunities to cultivate and add political champions to a social movement. The theory of food systems practice introduced here, and revisited in Chapter 7, seems to have been effective in forming local food projects in both countries and was utilized to great affect in the US. It may be useful in other policy settings.

In the US, the local *food system* perspective served as a *collective action frame* to mobilize diverse stakeholders. In England, local food appeared as another single issue seemingly appropriate for advancement by specialist interest groups. *Does breadth contribute to alliance formation and learning new advocacy tactics, or does its accompanying coordination tie up advocacy resources? Does specialization and reliance on a few, well-honed tactics deliver reliable policy outcomes?* The following chapters explore these questions.

Finally, a democratic society is not just focused on outcomes. The equity of its process matters, with its principles based upon broadening inclusion and direct participation. The evidence in this book illustrates these are not just idle concepts, but vital strategies for achieving political success.

Notes

1 After this point, decentralization refers to dispersion of both authority and geography. Segmentation is used to describe separation or division between organizations.

2 Local food in national American policy, 1976–2012

Increasing inclusion, increasing policy success

This chapter focuses on a *narrative analysis* of national-level local food policies in the US, from the first national policy's introduction in 1975 to the end of 2012. Narrative policy analysis is a qualitative approach to examining policy change (Roe, 1994; van Eeten, 2007). Analysis follows three tracks. First, w*here did the local food narrative originate and how did it evolve through the policy process over time?* Second, *what is the content of the narrative?* What does the language in the policy tell us about the goals of the local food movement, its needs, and preferred and politically acceptable means to achieve those goals? Third, *what is the trajectory of policy outcomes over time?* Are policymakers increasing or decreasing their support for local food; is funding increasing or decreasing; are policies increasing in number or breadth, or declining or being narrowed? Narrative analysis focuses on program impacts to a lesser degree than formal program evaluation.

The chapter has two aims. The primary aim is not to establish an "authoritative" history, but *a* history that re-links policy events and activities suitable for narrative policy analysis. A historical review on national local food policies was not available as "few movement groups have lots of time to spend on outside researchers" (Lichterman, 2002, p. 125). Conducting a historical review was necessary to understand long-term trends, a process that requires researchers to "discover evidence originally collected by others and make evidence speak to core theoretical questions" (Clemens & Hughes, 2002, p. 201). This reconstruction of movement history is often only possible because movement groups "produced official documents archived by government institutions" (Clemens & Hughes, 2002, p. 201). Example documents include reports, public comments, and testimony entered into official record, records of policy debates in a legislature, and formal policy records (e.g. legislation, regulations, grant awards, program evaluations). The second aim is to develop theoretical insights related to food systems practice introduced in Chapter 1.

From 1975 through 2012, 18 policies were identified regarding local food (Table 2.1). Four policies are presented in Chapter 5. Eleven are reported here and grouped by three themes:

Local food in national American policy 23

- producer market development, beginning in 1975;
- low-income access and community development, beginning in 1989; and
- local food in schools, beginning in 1994.

Focusing only on the outcomes of final legislation minimizes the preceding stages of social movement activities. These include mobilizing supporters, forming and articulating cogent policy proposals, and experiencing resistance (which is often difficult to observe through official policy documents). One decision faced by a movement's policy leaders is deciding whether the movement's issues will develop better through engaging with existing governmental institutions and established policy communities or opposing them.

A social movement's influence and public support often originate from being *unlike* existing organizations and institutions. Engaging with existing institutions and policy communities can undermine public support of the movement's message and identity, if its goals appear manipulated or co-opted. Facing this risk, some social movement leaders and social movement organizations decide not to engage with policymakers, waiting for better future conditions. Occasionally movement leaders adopt messages and tactics designed to prevent integration with existing institutions to establish a "pure" moral authority (Taylor, 1995). Yet, working at the political margin can over time result in a cycle of increasing radicalization that further marginalizes the social movement, which Laclau (1996) characterized as "ghettoization" (p. 51).

A movement may split over the tension to oppose or engage, resulting in a radical wing and a more moderate wing (Tarrow, 1998, pp. 146–147). A moderate wing may propose and practice transformative ideas, but utilizes socially accepted tactics. It engages directly with policymakers, lobbies, and reaches out to the media. Engaging with policy is an uncertain process, yet "what is certain is that there is no major historical change in which identity of *all* intervening forces is not transformed. . . . The increasing awareness of this fact explains the centrality of the concept of 'hybridization' in contemporary debates" (Laclau, 1996, p. 52). This concept of narrative *hybridization* is a good measure of narrative policy change in a relatively stable policy environment.

Outsiders are often accommodated in American agricultural policy. Maintaining public support of agricultural programs has required ally cultivation from urban-associated political interests (Berry, 1982). Local food was a newcomer to the well-developed agricultural, nutrition, and conservation policy communities and institutions, some of which are 150 years old (Sheingate, 2001). Power and influence shifts within existing institutions. Over time, newcomers become incumbents or important allies. This is a fact illustrated with the rising political influence of nutrition and anti-hunger groups from the late 1960s (Berry, 1982) and conservation groups since the 1980s (D. W. Johnson, 1991–1992; Malone, 1986). Outsiders can become insiders. But they face newcomer challenges. They possess less knowledge, skill, policymaker access, and familiarity with the policy process relative to incumbent interests.

Table 2.1 Summary of American programs supporting local food activities, including spending levels[1]

Program/ policy	Date enacted	Main policy problem	Intended outcomes	Location of focus	Beneficiaries	Key metaphors	Spending at start★	Spending in FY 10
Farmer-to-Consumer Direct Marketing Act	1976	Develop and expand direct marketing opportunities	Mutual benefit of consumers and farmers	State level and lower	State governments Market managers Farmers Consumer organizations	Mutualism Consumer access linked with producer income	$1,500,000 (FY 77)	Not published
Women, Infants, and Children Farmers Market Nutrition Program	1988	Nutritional inadequacy Limited awareness of farmers markets	Change in fresh produce consumption Access to farmers markets	States Indian Tribal Organizations	Low-income mothers and children Farmers	"Fresh nutritious unprepared foods"	$3,000,000 (FY 88)	$19,900,000
Department of Defense (DOD) Fresh	1994★	Improve food quality and "provide new markets for small farmers"	Improve variety	Schools "Small-resource farmers"	Schoolchildren; smaller-volume producers	Fresh produce Quality	$3,200,00 (FY 96)	$66,000,000
Community Food Projects	1996	Lack of low-income community self-determination Poverty Dependency	Increase self-reliance Develop linkages between 2 or more sectors	Communities	Low-income individuals Non-profits with community work experience Small and medium-sized farms	Self-reliance Comprehensiveness Innovation Entrepreneurship Mutual benefit of "agricultural producers and low-income consumers"	$1,000,000 (FY 96)	$5,000,000

Value-added Producer Market Development Grant Program	2000	Lack of marketing opportunity for non-contract producers	Increase producer revenue	Individuals and groups of individuals	Independent farmers and ranchers Producer cooperatives	Independence Producer ownership and control	$15,000,000 (FY 01)	$20,400,000
Senior Farmers Market Nutrition Program	2001★	Provide resources to low-income seniors	Increase domestic consumption of agricultural commodities Develop new direct markets	States Indian tribal organizations	Low-income seniors Direct-marketing farmers	"Fresh, nutritious, unprepared, locally grown fruits, vegetables, honey, and herbs"	$15,000,000 (FY 01)	$20,600,000
Farmers Market Promotion Program	2002	Direct market development	Expansion of direct markets Access for food assistance beneficiaries	States Communities	Groups of producers Communities Food assistance beneficiaries	Increase domestic consumption Promotion	$1,000,000 (FY 06)	$5,000,000
Fresh Fruit and Vegetable Snack Program	2002	Improve child nutrition Produce industry market development	Increase produce consumption Increase produce industry sales	Schools, including Indian tribal organizations	Low-income children	Fresh fruits and vegetables	$3,000,000	$65,000,000
Purchases of Locally Produced Foods (in school food)	2002	Legal ambiguity	Encourage purchases of locally produced food	Schools	None mentioned in acts	Locally produced, unprocessed products	Regulation – Not applicable	Regulation – Not applicable

Table 2.1 continued

Program / policy	Date enacted	Main policy problem	Intended outcomes	Location of focus	Beneficiaries	Key metaphors	Spending at start*	Spending in fy 10
Access to Local Foods and School Gardens (farm-to-school)	2004	Diet-related disease Lack of markets for smaller farms Urban-rural disconnect	Healthy food access Support for smaller farms Nutrition and agriculture education Community involvement	Schools	Schools with high portions of low-income students Small and mid-sized farms	Fresh, healthy food Sustained community commitment Linkages	$5,000,000 (FY 13 – proposed)	0
Healthy Food Education and Replicability – Pilot Program for High-Poverty Schools	2008	Lack of support for experiential learning on food and farm issues	Nutrition education and vegetable gardening experience	Schools in high-poverty communities	Schoolchildren from families with low incomes	"Hands-on" experience People's Garden	$1,000,000 (FY 10)	$1,000,000
Healthy Urban Food Enterprise Development Center[1]	2008	Lack of start-up funds Lack of technical assistance Lack of information on replicable models	Improve access to healthy and local food in underserved communities	Urban, rural, and tribal communities with limited healthy food access, high diet-related disease, or persistent poverty	Non-profit and for-profit businesses Producers Residents in underserved communities	Fresh, healthy food Consumer food access Producer market access Underserved communities	$1,000,000 (FY 09)	$1,000,000

Policy	Year	Problem	Purpose	Geography	Stakeholders	Definitions	Authorization	Appropriation
Locally or Regionally Produced Products priority in the Rural Business and Industries Loan and Loan Guarantee Program[1]	2008	Lack of finance for economically viable local and regional food projects	Ensures USDA reserves 5% of an existing fund for local and regional food projects	Urban, rural, and Indian tribal organizations with limited healthy food access, high diet-related disease, or persistent poverty	Non-profit and for-profit businesses, including producers engaged in local and regional food production or marketing	Defines locally or regionally produced agricultural food products Underserved communities	$49,700,000 (FY 08)	$49,700,000
Study and report on food deserts[1]	2008	Limited awareness of scope of food deserts Lack of intra-agency coordination	Information on location and causes of food deserts Improved agency coordination	Areas with limited access to affordable and nutritious food	Policy analysts Community planning agencies and activists	Defines "food desert"	Not published	Not published
Study on the Impacts of Local Food Systems and Commerce[1]	2008	Lack of information on economic, nutritional, & environmental impacts	Information on local food impacts and barriers to expansion	National	Policy analysts Community activists	Local food systems	Not published	Not published
Food Safety Modernization Act: Suspension of registration for direct sales[2]	2010	Compliance burden for small businesses and farmers	Exempts farm shops, farmers' markets, and CSAs from registration	National	Small-volume or small-sales farms with direct sales	None	Regulation – Not applicable	Regulation – Not applicable

Table 2.1 continued

Program/policy	Date enacted	Main policy problem	Intended outcomes	Location of focus	Beneficiaries	Key metaphors	Spending at start★	Spending in FY 10
People's Garden Grant Program	2011★	Lack of financial resources in some impoverished communities	"Facilitate the creation of produce, recreation, and/or wildlife gardens" Informal education	Urban and rural areas	Communities	Community collaboration People's Garden	$750,000 (FY11 – proposed)	Not applicable
Farm To School Census [2,3]	2012	Lack of information on local food purchases by schools	Baseline on current practices Identify future priorities	National, including Indian tribal organizations	Policy analysts Community activists	None	$5,000,000 (FY12 – proposed)	Not applicable

★Some programs are not funded when enacted but are funded at a later date. Programs only start when funding is provided
★★Began as a USDA pilot program
FY = Fiscal Year
1 Included in Chapter 5
2 Self-explanatory, not elaborated further
3 The Healthy, Hunger Free Kids Act of 2010 authorized USDA to collect information on farm-to-school programs, formalized into a Farm to School Census in 2012

In the 2000s the agricultural policy community tolerated the expansion of local food programs. For example, a new program like the Farmers Market Promotion Program helped retain the agricultural share of the USDA budget. In the 2010s, the nutrition and anti-hunger groups learned that including programs, like Farm to School, could add support to their overall policy priorities. These outcomes came *over the long term* with periods of resistance and tenuous policy outcomes.

A few summarizations can be made with a long-term view.

- Attention to the affordability of food has been a concern of local food advocates since at least 1975 and was a central concern in subsequent national local food policies.
- Social movement organizations proposed policy narratives that embodied a transformative intent and integrated with preexisting policy narratives.
- Direct engagement with policymakers was favored and resulted in long-term supporters in Congress and with executive branch civil servants.
- Resistance primarily originated from anti-hunger and nutrition policy communities, or the food industry, not the agricultural policy community.
- Preexisting agricultural funding streams, laws, and agencies provided a "beachhead" for new policy development.
- Policies supporting local food increased in number, scope, and funding over time, principally due to the cultivation of Congressional supporters by advocacy coalitions.

This chapter details the work of balancing social movement priorities with political feasibility, which led to increasing support for local food.

From producer market development to food system development, 1976–2008

Farmer-to-Consumer Direct Marketing Act of 1976

Introduced in Congress in 1975 and passed in 1976, the Farmer-to-Consumer Direct Marketing Act authorized the USDA to promote "development and expansion of direct marketing of agricultural commodities from farmers to consumers" through funding, technical assistance, coordination with the states, facilitation, and research (*Farmer-to-Consumer Direct Marketing Act*, 1976a). At the time, public interest and use of farmers' markets experienced resurgence (Allison, 2001; Pyle, 1971; Shakow, 1981), in part from an economic recession. This Act further defined and reinvigorated activities that were broadly authorized in the 1946 Agricultural Marketing Act, which provided USDA services for wholesale and terminal markets (Wann et al., 1948).

Mutuality is a central outcome of direct to consumer marketing. The USDA was charged to implement a program "for the mutual benefit of consumers and farmers" (*Farmer-to-Consumer Direct Marketing Act*, 1976b). The Act defined

30   *Local food in national American policy*

direct marketing activity as individual farmers and groups of farmers selling directly to "individual consumers, or organizations representing consumers, in a manner calculated to lower the cost and increase the quality of food to such consumers while providing increased financial returns to the farmers" (*Farmer-to-Consumer Direct Marketing Act*, 1976b). Historically, the goals are linked to city ordinances on farmers' markets and public markets (Allison, 2001; Pyle, 1971; Shakow, 1981).

The USDA promoted states' direct-to-consumer marketing efforts including conference sponsorship, technical assistance to formalize marketing laws and regulations, and sharing information among market managers (Eileen Stommes, 1998; *Farmer-to-Consumer Direct Marketing Act*, 1976a; USDA, 2001a). The USDA carried out a survey of farmers' markets and has maintained a national directory of farmers' market locations in the US since 1994 (Payne, 2002; USDA, 1998). Funding was provided at $1.5 million in 1977 and 1978 and henceforth included in the core USDA Agricultural Marketing Service budget.

Several characteristics of American local food legislation can be observed in this Act. Through the narrative of "mutualism," it targets two sectors of the food system producers and consumers. It proposes multiple objectives: increasing producer income while simultaneously lowering the costs and increasing the quality of food for consumers. The Act's language is market-oriented in wording but transformative in outcome. USDA resources are directed to direct marketing, a counter-trend to commodity market development and increasingly distant relationships between producers and consumers (Lyson, 2004). Legislative incrementalism is evidenced as a preferred form of policy change. Earlier statutes are used as a beachhead from which to expand future legislation: the Farmer-to-Consumer Direct Marketing Act further defined USDA's market development role within the 1946 Agricultural Marketing Act. Likewise, the Farmer-to-Consumer Direct Marketing Act would be modified to include the Senior Farmers Market Nutrition Program and Farmers Market Promotion Program in 2002.

Farmers Market Promotion Program

The Farmers Market Promotion Program (FMPP) was added to the Farmer-to-Consumer Direct Marketing Act of 1976 in 2002 through the Farm Bill (*Farm Security and Rural Investment Act*, 2002d). The program sought to support activities for the mutual benefit of producers and consumers. It was first funded at $1 million in 2006 by the Bush Administration from preexisting USDA funding sources. In 2008, the FMPP was revised, given a mandatory funding stream, and a 10 percent set aside for projects increasing the use of Electronic Benefit Transfers (EBT) for Food Stamp beneficiaries. The program's focus and its politics benefitted a wide range of interests.

FMPP political support crossed traditional geographic divisions and party lines. The 2008 revisions were supported by a coalition of urban, rural, and suburban Members of Congress, with leadership in the House originating from a group of newly elected "Blue Dogs" (fiscally conservative Democrats) on the Agriculture Committee (*Amendment to H.R. 2419 Offered by Mr. Kagen of Wisconsin*, 2007; The Blue Dogs of the Democratic Party, 2006). Senate support came from states with diversified agricultural sectors and supporters of fruit and vegetable production. Political support from senior party leaders for policies proposed by newly elected Representatives and Senators enabled the FMPP to be funded at a level higher than originally proposed by advocates (*Amendment to H.R. 2419 Offered by Mr. Kagen of Wisconsin*, 2007; *Local Food and Farm Support Act*, 2007).

The FMPP includes all forms of direct-to-consumer marketing conducted by farmers. The narrative is market-oriented and aims to encourage promotion and development activities to increase the consumption of domestically produced foods:

The purposes of the Program are:

(A) to increase domestic consumption of agricultural commodities by improving and expanding, or assisting in the improvement and expansion of, domestic farmers markets, roadside stands, community-supported agriculture programs, agri-tourism activities, and other direct producer-to-consumer market opportunities; and

(B) to develop, or aid in the development of, new farmers markets, roadside stands, community-supported agriculture programs, agri-tourism activities, and other direct producer-to-consumer marketing opportunities.

(Farmers Market Promotion Program, 2008a)

Farmers markets, roadside stands[2], CSAs, and agri-tourism are forms of direct *and local* marketing because they are primarily face-to-face interactions bounded by producers' and/or consumers' limited willingness to travel. There is no restriction that direct sales also be local sales. Internet or mail-based sales, made directly between farmer and consumer, could be funded through the FMPP.

Congress did not define "farmers market" or any other direct marketing activities. The USDA Market Services Division (MSD) required that projects benefit "two or more agricultural farmers/vendors that produce and sell their own products through a common distribution channel" (USDA, 2006, p. 13334). In 2010, definitions for CSA, farmers markets, roadside stands, and direct-to-consumer marketing were introduced (USDA, 2011c). Entities eligible for direct marketing support included: "agricultural cooperatives; producer networks, or producer associations; local governments; nonprofit corporations; public benefit corporations; economic development corporations; regional farmers' market authorities; and Tribal governments" (Farmers Market Promotion Program, 2008b; 2011c, pp. 3046–3047).

The 2008 FMPP revisions encountered resistance from two policy communities. A competing legislative draft promoted by the Environmental Defense Fund, a mainstream environmental interest group, wanted "projects

32 Local food in national American policy

that will support, encourage, or promote the transition to organic and other environmentally beneficial forms of agricultural production" (*Healthy Farms, Foods, and Fuels Act of 2007*, 2007b, d). The focus on organic and environmental forms of production was not supported by the Sustainable Agriculture Coalition (which included organic farming organizations), the Farmers Market Coalition, and other organizations in the Farm and Food Policy Project (*Food Outreach and Opportunity Development for a Healthy America Act of 2007*, 2007; *Local Food and Farm Support Act*, 2007; NEMWI, 2008b).

Second, political resistance was encountered with expansion at farmers markets of the use of EBT terminals (e.g. debit card readers) for Food Stamps, now called the Supplemental Nutrition Assistance Program (SNAP). Community food security advocates and farmers market managers sought a permanent legislative fix to the Food Stamp program to ensure that wireless EBT terminals could be used.

The FNS experimented with EBT technology in 1984, and in 1995 EBT technology was trialed at farmers markets (USDA, 2011g). A 1998 USDA study on EBT feasibility concluded that EBT implementation was feasible but costs and implementation could be a barrier to widespread use (USDA, 2010b; Wright et al., 1998). Concerns about the shift from paper to electronic benefit were communicated to the USDA prior to the EBT transition through a government-funded study, pilot project results, and communications from farmers market managers, small farm operators, and food security advocates (Fisher, 1999; Harold L. Volkmer et al., 1998). By 1999, some advocates found there was "little political will among USDA and the states to develop a farmer friendly EBT system" (Fisher, 1999, p. 44).

When EBT systems were fully implemented in 2004, Food Stamp sales at farmers markets dropped to less than $1.6 million per year (Briggs et al., 2010, p. 2). Earlier redemption levels vary by source. The Agricultural Marketing Service (AMS) indicated that Food Stamp sales at farmers markets were estimated at $75–100 million annually (USDA, 1998), the level also reported by Fisher (1999). The Administrator of the USDA FNS indicated in 1990 that Food Stamp redemptions at farmers markets were about $82 million (Betty Jo Nelson [USDA FNS Administrator], 1991, p. 5). The ERS observed that Food Stamp redemptions declined from $134 million to $58 million for all direct-to-consumer markets, perhaps due to cutbacks in the Food Stamp program (Kantor, 2001, p. 22). More recent USDA FNS data show sales at farmers markets just above $9 million in 1993 (Briggs et al., 2010, p. 1). Regardless of source, Food Stamp redemptions dropped with the adoption of EBT at farmers markets 100 to 10 times below their paper redemption levels.

As a result, farmers market and community food security leaders focused on disseminating a "work around" system at farmers' markets. This included the use of one, central EBT terminal operated by market staff. Food Stamp recipients could swipe their benefit card to receive market-only currency (wooden tokens, or paper script) to make their food purchases (for an example see Megill, 2005).

Local food in national American policy   33

Resistance to increasing social inclusion at farmers markets did not originate from the local food movement. Political resistance against the "grassroots efforts to mobilize existing modest resources" of farmers markets and managers were a negative influence on access to local foods by persons of low income (Markowitz, 2010, p. 77; Young et al., 2011).

Local food groups sought to reverse the exclusion imposed by a federal policy change, and mobilized their modest community-based resources to increase access. With USDA inaction, and a lack of political support from nutrition policy gatekeepers, the FMPP became an *alternative venue* to support the financial costs, capacity building, and promotion needed for successful EBT implementation. While the shift to EBT was administered by the FNS, the AMS, a farm program agency, provided assistance for EBT.

The development of the FMPP follows the multi-sector, multi-objective goals evidenced in the Farmer to Consumer Direct Marketing Act. The development of work-around systems for EBT and the inclusion of EBT projects in the FMPP show that advocates of local food sought to increase market access for people with low incomes. These policies were developed in a participatory manner, with stakeholders (farmers market managers, food security and sustainable agriculture advocates, community-based groups, state agencies, and federal agencies) engaged in a multi-level dialogue.

Value-Added Producer Grants: A program for independent producers

The Value-Added Producer Market Development Grant Program (VAPG) originated in the final version of the 2000 Agricultural Risk Protection Act during a farm crisis of poor weather, low export demand, and low prices in both commodity and livestock agriculture (*Agricultural Risk Protection Act of 1999; Agricultural Risk Protection Act of 2000–Conference Report; A bill (H.R. 2559) to amend the Federal Crop Insurance Act*, 2000; Committee on Agriculture, 2001; *The Farm Financial Crisis*, 1999; Womach & Becker, 2001). The policy tools provided in the 1996 "Freedom to Farm" legislation, written when prices were high, were considered inadequate to address the natural and economic crisis (*The Farm Financial Crisis*, 1999; Lehrer, 2008). Simultaneously, consolidation of large-volume processors and distributors in the livestock and grain sectors and a declining number of small-volume processors and distributors took place (MacDonald et al., 2000; Ollinger et al., 2005).

The VAPG was framed as a response to industry trends of consolidation. It aimed to provide grant funds for producers to independently or cooperatively build their own, producer-controlled processing, distribution, and marketing systems. Some proponents of value-adding framed it as a necessary response to the negative outcomes of agri-business consolidation. In a 1999 Agriculture Committee Hearing, Representative Thune [R-SD] framed his support for value added agriculture as a way to stem rural decline from industry consolidation:

34 *Local food in national American policy*

I do think it is clearly an issue which, if, in fact, the smaller, independent producers start going by the wayside, a lot of those small towns are, too, and that, in my judgment, is something that is not in the long-term best interest of our country. And that is why I think this whole issue of consolidation is so important, not only just again to the smaller producers, but to the entire way of life and the entire economic well-being of rural parts of the country. . .

(Agribusiness Consolidation, 1999)

Because this frame provided a negative critique of an agri-business practice, VAPG had a tenuous development. Hearings on value-adding were held in in the House Small Business Committee rather than the House Agriculture Committee (*Helping Agricultural Producers "Re-grow" America: Providing the Tools*, 2000; *Helping Agricultural Producers Regrow Rural America*, 1999). VAPG's inclusion came late in the Agricultural Risk Protection Act of 2000 even though it was proposed three years earlier (Library of Congress, 2000; *Value-added Agricultural Products Market Access Act of 1997*, 1997; *Value-Added Development Act for American Agriculture*, 2000a, b). Senator Grassley, Iowa Republican, indicated its authorization and funding was resisted by the American Meat Institute (Chuck Grassley [R-IA], 2000). State-based, but not national farm organizations, endorsed the program. The legislation had bipartisan support, from President Clinton, and endorsements from the Missouri Farm Bureau Federation, Missouri Soybean Association, the former chair of South Dakota's Farm Bureau, the South Dakota Beef Industry Council's board, and the Minnesota Corn Growers (*Helping Agricultural Producers "Re-grow" America: Providing the Tools*, 2000; *Helping Agricultural Producers Regrow Rural America*, 1999).

Members of Congress wanted to be identified as supporters of farmers and ranchers in their districts; yet, they also wanted to avoid confrontation with industrial interests in their states. Some Congressional "supporters" communicated their support for the VAPG *only after* Congress had sent the final bill to the White House for the President's signature (John Ashcroft [R-MO], 2000; Library of Congress, 2000; *Value-Added Development Act for American Agriculture*, 2000b). The program focused on independent, non-contract producers and cooperative development. Its narratives were market-oriented, featuring the use of common business development tools (business planning, value-adding, and capital access) as strategies to benefit independent producers. Opposition focused on VAPG's surrounding *frame*, not its content.

Industry opposition appeared symbolic and aimed at market control. The $35 million in the original proposals and $15 million provided in the final legislation were unlikely to alter the structure of the American meat industry (*Agricultural Risk Protection Act of 2000*, 2000; Chuck Grassley [R-IA]). Further, the impact of the VAPG was intentionally limited to not have sectorial impacts: "It is not the intention of the Managers that grants made under this section will interfere with existing markets" (Managers on the part of the House and

Local food in national American policy   35

the Senate at the Conference for H.R. 2559, 2000). There were no overt references to agribusiness consolidation in the program's final legislation (*Agriculture Risk Protection Act* of 2000, 2000).

Successive revisions demonstrated Congress did intend for the VAPG to transform marketing opportunities for small-volume producers and cooperatives. The 2002 Farm Security and Investment Act (2002 Farm Bill) directed support to majority producer-owned businesses and provided a definition of value-added agriculture.

One part of the definition for "value-adding" was that "a greater portion of the revenue [be] derived from the marketing, processing, or physical segregation of the agricultural commodity or product is available to the producer" (*Farm Security and Rural Investment Act*, 2002c). The 2002 revisions aimed to change the marketing opportunities available for producers, enhance revenue relative to prevailing marketing options, and expand customer base (*Farm Security and Rural Investment Act*, 2002c).

Through the 2008 Farm Bill, the transformation-oriented narrative in VAPG expanded to a wide range of marginalized producer groups: socially disadvantaged farmers,[3] small and mid-sized farms,[4] family farms,[5] and beginning farmers.[6] The Act emphasized the connection to consumers through the development of "mid-tier supply chains"[7] and the aggregation and marketing of "locally-produced agricultural food products" (*Food, Conservation, and Energy Act of 2008*, 2008k). Ten percent of the VAPG funds were reserved for mid-tier value chains, which were defined as:

> local and regional supply networks that link independent producers with businesses and cooperatives that market value-added agricultural products in a manner that—
>
> (A) targets and strengthens the profitability and competitiveness of small and medium-sized farms and ranches that are structured as a family farm; and
>
> (B) obtains agreement from an eligible agricultural producer group, farmer or rancher cooperative, or majority-controlled producer-based business venture that is engaged in the value chain on a marketing strategy.
>
> (*Food, Conservation, and Energy Act* of 2008, 2008g)

Revisions focused on transforming a producer's relationship from a passive "price taker" role to a more active "price maker" role through development of producer-controlled supply chains. Once enacted, the emphasis on "non-interference" with existing markets diminished.

While the language of the VAPG is market-oriented, the goals are transformative, aiming to 1) increase producer market power, 2) provide equity in the supply chain, 3) support marginalized groups, and 4) include diverse forms of agricultural production. The VAPG goals were cross-sector, involving

36 Local food in national American policy

producers in processing and marketing roles and including a greater emphasis on consumer marketing in the 2008 revisions. The program focused on producer income and market access. Proponents like Representative Thune linked the viability of independent producers to the social sustainability of rural communities. This extended to increasing program access for socially disadvantaged and beginning producers.

Despite the program's increasing orientation to advocates' concerns, the VAPG's unstable funding stream weakened its effectiveness (Table 2.2). The Agriculture Committees provided mandatory or automatic annual funding for VAPG. However, funds were frequently reappropriated to programs requiring discretionary or ad hoc annual funding, such as the Special Supplemental Nutrition Program for Women, Infants, and Children (WIC; Keith, 2010).

Several nutrition programs rely on discretionary annual funding. A commonly cited reason for this is that anti-hunger and nutrition policy communities favor discretionary funding to mobilize their supporters on an annual basis. Pragmatically, anti-hunger and nutrition advocates had successfully outcompeted other funding priorities in the annual appropriations process (Oliveira & Frazao, 2009, p. 39; Richardson, 2010). In other words, when the overall USDA budget decreases, Congress prioritizes discretionary funding for nutrition programs over discretionary items in the rural development agency budget, like VAPG, and

Table 2.2 Funding history of the Value-Added Producer Grant Program fiscal years 2001–2012[8]

Fiscal year	Congressional funding authorization		Congressional funding appropriation		USDA solicitation	USDA reported expenditure	
	Millions of dollars						
	M	D	M	D	Total	M	D
2001	15		15		20	25*	
2002	0	0	0	0	33	0	0
2003	40			No limit	27.7	51	
2004	40			15.0	13.2	30	1
2005	40		15.5		14.3	0	14
2006	40		*20.3*		19.475	2	34
2007	40		*20.3*		19.3	1	23
2008	40		*18.9*		18.4		20
2009	15	40	15	3.9	18	1	0
2010	0	40		20.4	0**	15	7
2011	0	40		18.9	37	N/A	N/A
2012	0	40		14	N/A	N/A	N/A

M = Mandatory funding; D = Discretionary funding
* USDA does not identify as mandatory or discretionary; ** Funding of two fiscal years combined due to guideline delay in 2010
N/A = not available
Italics = cannot be confirmed by a second source

Local food in national American policy 37

environmental programs. While this arrangement works well for the influential anti-hunger and nutrition policy communities, it can displace the priorities of other marginalized groups (e.g. socially disadvantaged producers) and reduce funding available for water quality protection and improvement.

In addition to a tenuous funding history, VAPG also suffered from implementation delays in 2002–2004. Also, improperly written regulations resulted in revisions of program guidelines, compromising funding availability in 2009–2011 (USDA, 2009c, 2010c, 2011i). VAPG has not been a priority for funding or implementation and its advocates were unable to affect external factors that impact the VAPG.

From low-income access to local food to community empowerment, 1989 onward

Linking low-income access to fresh and healthy foods to local producers: WIC and Senior Farmers Market Nutrition Programs

The WIC Farmers Market Nutrition Program (WIC FMNP) and Senior Farmers Market Nutrition Program (SFMNP) provide vouchers for produce purchases made directly from farmers by social groups with low fresh produce consumption. The political development of the FMNP illustrates classic features of American policy development: policy entrepreneurship, the use of state policy as a model for federal policy, and national-level experimentation through pilot and demonstration projects.

The programs were based on the 1986 Farmers' Market Coupon program created in Massachusetts (Commonwealth of Massachusetts, 2011). The concept originated in 1982, in conversation between Gus Schumacher and Hugh Joseph, a Tufts University nutrition student, who had organized the Lowell Massachusetts farmers' market in 1980. Later, Tufts University hosted a meeting that led to the pilot concept implemented by Schumacher (Joseph, 2014).

In 1988, Schumacher worked with Senator John Kerry [D-MA], to enact a national-level WIC FMNP pilot program that provided federal funding to Massachusetts and several other states (*Farmer to Family Nutrition Enhancement Act*). Their proposal passed into law as a three-year, ten-state pilot program through the Hunger Prevention Act of 1988 (*Hunger Prevention Act of 1988;* Oliveira et al., 2002). In 1992, Congress made the WIC FMNP permanent and eligible to more states (*Farmers' Market Nutrition Act of 1991;* Oliveira et al., 2002; *WIC Farmers' Market Nutrition Act of 1992*, 1992a, b; *WIC Supplemental Benefits Act of 1991*).

The WIC FMNP expanded on the public health goals of WIC, emphasizing access to unprocessed, fresh foods. Its purpose is to:

(1) provide resources to women, infants, and children who are nutritionally at risk in the form of fresh nutritious unprepared foods (such as fruits and vegetables), from farmers markets; and

38   *Local food in national American policy*

(2) expand the awareness and use of farmers markets and increase sales at such markets (*WIC Farmers' Market Nutrition Act of 1992*, 1992a).

By linking these two goals, the WIC FMNP encourages low-income families to access fresh, locally produced[9] foods purchased directly from farmers, benefiting both groups.

The 1994 Child Nutrition Act enhanced these goals, allowing states with the WIC FMNP to use funds for promoting the

> development of farmers markets in socially or economically disadvantaged areas, or remote rural areas, where individuals eligible for participation in the program have limited access to locally grown fruits and vegetables.
> (*Healthy Meals for Healthy Americans Act* of 1994, 1994a)

With modest funding ($15–20 million per year), small benefits of $10–30 per year are provided to a quarter to a third of all WIC recipients (USDA, 2012g). Benefits to producers are also dispersed, reaching 18,487 farmers, 4,079 farmers' markets (three-fifths of farmers' markets in 2012), and 3,184 roadside farm stands (USDA, 2012g, p. 2). Funding constraints limited the transformative potential of the WIC FMNP, resulting in Congress capping benefits at low levels to maintain broad program access (G. S. Becker, 2006).

To create the SFMNP, Schumacher repeated a pattern of cross-sector policy entrepreneurship and policy skill. In 2000, Schumacher proposed the SFMNP at a time when attention on agency actions was elsewhere: national elections occurred three days after his proposal was issued (USDA, 2000a). Similarly, the request for applications on December 1 and announcement of awardees in January, 2001 took place when attention was on the incoming Bush Administration and the new Congress (USDA, 2000a).

While the WIC FMNP was added to a preexisting program, the SFMNP required a new funding stream. Schumacher proposed funding the SFMNP pilot at $10 million, through preexisting authorities in the Commodity Credit Corporation (CCC) Charter Act, a depression-era farm program. However, $15 million in pilot program awards were announced 16 days before the end of the Clinton Administration on January 4, 2001 (Committee on Agriculture, Nutrition, and Forestry, 2001).

A year later, Congress followed Schumacher's lead and codified the SFMNP's funding from the CCC. Like Schumacher, Congress drew from the CCC's preexisting policy goals to "increase the domestic consumption of agricultural commodities by expanding or aiding in the expansion of domestic markets or by developing new and additional markets, marketing facilities, and uses" (Specific powers of Corporation; USDA, 2000a). The SFMNP aimed to:

(1) provide resources in the form of fresh, nutritious, unprepared, locally grown fruits, vegetables, honey, and herbs from farmers markets, roadside stands, and community supported agriculture programs to low-income seniors;

Local food in national American policy 39

(2) increase the domestic consumption of agricultural commodities by expanding or aiding in the expansion of domestic farmers markets, roadside stands, and community-supported agriculture programs; and
(3) develop or aid in the development of new and additional farmers' markets, roadside stands, and community-supported agriculture programs

(USDA, 2000a).

Building on past legal precedent, the SFMNP was added to the Farmer-to-Consumer Direct Marketing Act of 1976 through the 2002 Farm Bill. Congress authorized the SFMNP for $15 million annually in 2002, with an increase to $20.6 million in 2008 (*Farm Security and Rural Investment Act*, 2002a; Managers on the part of the House and the Senate for H.R. 2419, 2008c).

Through two different political positions, Schumacher demonstrated the innovation, follow-through, willingness to collaborate, and risk-taking characteristics of policy entrepreneurs (Roberts & King, 1991) and political skill at joining separate agricultural and nutrition policy streams (Kingdon, 1984).

The difference in funding sources and legal justifications affected how the WIC and Senior FMNPs were implemented. Relatively small funding allocations and restrictions on administrative costs limited WIC FMNP expansion in some states (Dollahite et al., 2005; *Healthy Meals for Healthy Americans Act of 1994;* Johnson, Cowan, & Aussenberg, 2012; USDA, 2000a). One factor was opposition from mainstream anti-hunger organizations for fear that new programs would "take money away" from larger, preexisting nutrition programs (Winne, 2008, p. 151). Both programs are administered by the Food and Nutrition Service and USDA rarely requests increases for program funding.

However, by virtue of SFMNP being funded from an agricultural program and authorized to be added to an act promoting direct-to-consumer marketing, it enjoyed less regulation, less bureaucratization, and more innovation. For example, the SFMNP has only six legal subparagraphs, three of which are the purposes described earlier. The codified version of the WIC FMNP has 31 legal subparagraphs, most of which are dedicated to the details of program administration. Even though both programs are managed by FNS, the legal authorities at FNS have often been subjected to lawsuits (Berry, 1982). The additional legal flexibility in the SFMNP allowed Maine to provide benefits through a CSA subscription model and helped Alabama expand its farmers markets (NSAC, ca. 2009).

Like WIC FMNP, funding constraints limited the SFMNP. The SMFNP serves a smaller group of individuals, 863,097 seniors. Yet in fiscal year 2011 it was widely available from "19,069 farmers at 4,598 farmers' markets as well 3,445 roadside stands and 141 CSAs" (USDA, 2012f, p. 2). Because of benefit dispersion, a Congressional Research Service report indicated:

> some policymakers and anti-hunger advocates have questioned whether the administrative costs of operating farmers' market nutrition programs

40 *Local food in national American policy*

are justified by the relatively low level of benefits low-income persons receive through these programs; they have suggested that the money might be better spent by improving traditional food assistance program benefits under food stamps and WIC.

(Becker, 2006, p. 6)

There is a circular logic in play here. Anti-hunger advocates have critiqued the FMNPs for delivering a low level of benefits yet have not sought to expand the FMNPs' funding to provide a more substantial benefit. Instead, they suggested reallocating funds to other priorities. Despite lobbying from the farmers market and sustainable agriculture community, expanded funding for the FMNPs was sidelined by larger and more influential interest groups (Feeding America, 2009; FMC, 2009; FRAC, 2009; Tropp & Barnham, 2008). As with resistance on expanding EBT access, resistance in expanding the FMNPs was seen as a negative influence on access to local food in low-income communities (Young et al., 2011).

The FMNPs are multi-objective, linking nutrition and food affordability goals with supporting producer market development. They are funded by the federal government, administered by the states (which can experiment in implementation), and implemented by farmers and market managers. They are multi-level and form and sustain relationships across sectors (e.g. producers, consumers, market managers). Increasing the participation of people with low incomes at farmers markets are stated goals. The FMNPs' principles of equity and inclusion demonstrate that advocates were able to hybridize their transformative goals into existing institutions.

Self-determination and self-reliance in low-income community food systems:
Community Food Projects

The Community Food Project (CFP) program[10] articulates community change based on the self-empowerment of low-income communities and the self-mobilization of local resources to meet locally defined food, farm, and nutrition issues. The CFP program prioritized projects that linked "2 or more sectors of the food system" (*Federal Agriculture Improvement and Reform Act*, 1996). The 1996 Farm Bill introduced the CFP program and defined a CFP as

a community-based project that requires a 1-time infusion of Federal assistance to become self-sustaining and that is designed to—

(1) meet the food needs of low-income people;
(2) increase the self-reliance of communities in providing for their own food needs; and
(3) promote comprehensive responses to local food, farm, and nutrition issues.

(*Federal Agriculture Improvement and Reform Act*, 1996)

These goals were to be carried out by non-profit organizations that have experience in:

(A) community work, particularly concerning small and medium-sized farms, including the provision of food to people in low-income communities and the development of new markets in low-income communities for agricultural producers; or
(B) job training and business development activities for food-related activities in low-income communities.
(*Federal Agriculture Improvement and Reform Act*, 1996)

The program focused on promoting "entrepreneurial projects," "innovative linkages between the for-profit and nonprofit food sectors," and encouraging "long-term planning activities and multi-system, interagency approaches" (*Federal Agriculture Improvement and Reform Act*, 1996). It encouraged information sharing and collaboration at all levels.

The program had a modest start with $1 million in 1996 and $2.5 million in subsequent years. Yet, its narrative is rooted in transformative change by empowering communities through a participatory approach rather than responding to externally defined priorities of federal anti-hunger and farm programs (Winne, Joseph, & Fisher, 1997). The CFP program's enactment in the 1996 Farm Bill legitimatized the community food security approach and was a watershed for food justice movements (Coglianese, 2001; Kathy Ozer [NFFC Executive Director], 2011).

Collaboration, holistic approaches to the food system, mutualistic market interactions, and a bottom-up problem-solving approach were enhanced and embedded into the CFP's renewal in the 2002 Farm Bill (*Farm Security and Rural Investment Act*, 2002b). A second clause was added to the CFP definition which could also allow projects to

meet specific State, local, or neighborhood food and agricultural needs, including needs for—

(A) *infrastructure improvement and development*;
(B) planning for long-term solutions; or
(C) the creation of innovative marketing activities *that mutually benefit agricultural producers and low-income consumers.*
(additions to the 1996 Farm Bill language shown in italics,
Farm Security and Rural Investment Act, 2002b)

Collaboration, coordination, and planning elements of CFPs were strengthened to:

encourage long-term planning activities, and multisystem, interagency approaches *with multi-stakeholder collaborations, that build the long-term capacity*

42   *Local food in national American policy*

of communities to address the food and agricultural problems of the communities,
such as food policy councils and food planning associations.

(additions to the 1996 Farm Bill language shown in italics,
Farm Security and Rural Investment Act, 2002b)

Documentation developed by the USDA in the lead-up to the CFP program's renewal indicated a wide variety of projects were supported by the CFP program. This included outreach for the Food Stamp program, community gardens, farmers markets, farm-to-school initiatives, and CSAs (Cohen, 2002; Kantor, 2001).

A community of food practitioners had formed, leading the USDA to develop the Community Food Assessment Toolkit to formalize assessment methods and disseminate project examples (Cohen, 2002). This Toolkit furthered wider dissemination of practices for including residents from low-income communities as integrated team members; and mapping food availability and developing policy responses at the neighborhood level (Cohen, 2002, pp. 11, 15, 136).

To increase diffusion of community food practice and identify replicable projects, Congress authorized a Community Food Security Learning Center as part of the CFP (*Farm Security and Rural Investment Act*, 2002b). Information sharing would address "common community problems" including the "loss of farms and ranches; rural poverty; welfare dependency; hunger; the need for job training; and the need for self-sufficiency by individuals and communities" (*Farm Security and Rural Investment Act*, 2002b). The CFP program forged a new, more comprehensive policy narrative and engaged local-level stakeholders in boundary-breaking activities (Kobayashi, Tyson, & Abi-Nader, 2010; Tuckermanty et al., 2007), but the CFP program's development remained limited due to competition for nutrition program funding.

The 2002 Farm Bill provided the CFP program with $5 million annually for five years even though the Farm Bill budget runs ten years. A level of $10 million per year was included in the Senate's draft of the 2008 Farm Bill, but the House provided no annual funding (*Food and Energy Security Act of 2007*, 2007a, b). Thus, advocates for CFPs needed to mobilize their supporters to maintain the $5 million baseline level. This shifted their activities away from expanding the program to $10 million per year to defending its $5 million funding level (HFCWG, 2006b). Through grassroots mobilization, CFP advocates were able to maintain the CFP program (Artur Davis [D-IL] & Bobby Rush [D-IL], 2007a, b).

Community Food Projects were not a priority of the anti-hunger and nutrition policy community. In the 2008 Farm Bill there was a $3.2 billion *net* increase for nutrition programs, which increased benefits and reduced barriers to Food Stamps (Johnson, 2008). When the 2008 Farm Bill was finalized it "extend[ed] all significant expired authorities in the (renamed) Food Stamp Act and other laws covered by the nutrition title indefinitely, *with the exception of funding for community food projects* (extended through FY2012)" (emphasis added, Johnson, 2008, pp. 100–101).

The transformative narrative and bottom-up approach of CFPs faced competition from a similar program, the Hunger-free Communities Infrastructure Grants promoted by some anti-hunger and nutrition advocacy groups. It funded similar activities to the CFP, but excluded requirements for community participation and cross-sector linkages. Instead, it favored capital investments in physical infrastructure such as food bank facilities. The bottom-up approach of community food projects conflicted with the top-down approach of nutrition programs that provided individual income assistance.

Fresh, healthy, and local food in schools: From pilot projects to national program, 1994 onward

Only some of the US' nutrition and food programs are authorized through the Farm Bill. The Child Nutrition Act, and related acts, are renewed on a 4–6-year cycle and include provisions for the WIC, school meals, and nutrition standards. Both WIC and school meal programs are means-tested and are available to families on low incomes. Locally produced food procurement has increased in political popularity as a school food purchasing practice. Resistance to its development through public policy occurred through lack of funding and the Bush Administration's concerns about potential policy conflicts with the World Trade Organization (WTO).

American policies on local food in school meals are grouped into three categories: agency learning activities, enabling policies, and start-up support. Preceding the authorization of a farm-to-school program in 2010, USDA staff engaged in *policy learning* activities, which familiarized USDA staff with the farm-to-school concept. This included "learning through doing": agency staff worked alongside project implementers to learn how farm-to-school projects developed, gave financial and technical support for pilot projects, and hosted practitioners and staff workshops. School food *enabling policies* emphasized the use of fresh fruits and vegetables and provided flexibility for food service directors to purchase local food. Some programs aimed to provide *start-up* support, to form local food projects. These three types of policy support are introduced and explained here.

Agency learning activities and pilot projects, 1994–2000s

Farm-to-school policy began with technical assistance, facilitation, and modest support of community-developed projects from local, regional, and national headquarters by USDA staff. Pilot projects began in 1994 and aimed to support procurement of fresh products from limited-resource farmers located near schools (USDA, 1994). In 1997 technical assistance and resources were provided to an African-American rural farmer cooperative in Florida (Ritchie & Chen, 2011; Schofer et al., 2000; Tauber & Fisher, 2001). This was a formative

44   *Local food in national American policy*

collaborative learning experience for USDA staff from AMS, FNS, the Rural Business and Cooperative Service (RBCS), the Natural Resources Conservation Service (NRCS), and local extension offices.

The partnership's collaborative, multi-agency approach was recommended for replication by the USDA National Commission on Small Farms to "foster local and regional food systems for the benefit of small farms, rural community citizens, and low-income people in rural and urban areas" (Schofer et al., 2000, pp. 6–7). A collaborative, multi-level style of convening local and national agency staff, school food service authorities, and producers was reproduced in other regions of the country during the late 1990s and early 2000s.

The USDA launched town hall-style meetings and workshops with farmers, USDA staff, and occasionally Congressional representatives. A 1998 North Carolina meeting brought out 175 African-American and limited-resource farmers (USDA, 2000b). A similar meeting with the National Association of Black Farmers was held in Virginia (USDA, 2000b). In 2000, the USDA conducted the Small Farms/School Meals Workshop Regional Forum, in Kentucky (Tropp & Olowolayemo, 2000). The workshop report listed several states' attendees and indicated farm-to-school projects were underway in Kentucky, Ohio, North Carolina, and California. Many were using the Department of Defense (DOD) Fresh program (Tropp & Olowolayemo, 2000).

Sustainable agriculture advocates were part of these learning activities. A 2002 Iowa event cited the participation of the Practical Farmers of Iowa, which was a member of the Midwest Sustainable Agriculture Working Group and the Sustainable Agriculture Coalition (It's win-win: From farm-to-school, 2001). Both organizations had relationships with Senator Harkin [D-IA], Senate Agriculture Committee Chairman, who would introduce an amendment in the 2002 Farm Bill supporting farm-to-school projects. The Practical Farmers of Iowa had also received a Community Food Project grant (Tuckermanty et al., 2007). Learning activities on farm-to-school crossed USDA agencies, local institutions (e.g. extension, university agriculture programs), and stakeholder interests (e.g. African-American producers, rural interests, sustainable agriculture advocates, and schools).

Enabling policies: Tools for local food procurement

Department of Defense FRESH program, 1994 onward

The Department of Defense (DOD) Fresh program began in 1994 when the USDA formed a partnership with the DOD for utilizing its procurement network to provide cost-effective fresh fruits and vegetables to school food buyers (USDA, 2011b). The initiative aimed to increase the number of small farm operators, limited resource farmers, and farmers markets listed as approved vendors in the DOD system (USDA, 1994). While not limited to local produce, the USDA expected DOD Fresh would "improve the quality of the foods used by those schools that are close to particular growing areas as well as providing important new markets for small farmers" (USDA, 1994).

The pilot program was authorized by Congress soon after the USDA-DOD partnership began. It was framed as a pragmatic innovation that "piggybacked" on existing, efficient purchasing and delivery systems (*Healthy Meals for Healthy Americans Act of 1994;* Tropp & Olowolayemo, 2000; USDA, 1994). The House Agriculture Chairman and Chair of the Congressional Hispanic Caucus described it as an innovative way to "provide a wide variety of produce purchased at low cost" through existing purchasing systems (Eligio "Kika" de la Garza [D-TX], 1994). The simple program purpose, use of an existing distribution system, and funding availability from an existing source eased program development: nothing new needed defining or creating.

The 1996 funding was $3.2 million and reached eight states, many of which were not dominant fruit and vegetable producers: South Dakota, Wyoming, Colorado, New Hampshire, Texas, Maryland, and South Carolina (Tropp & Olowolayemo, 2000). By 2005, the program had a $50 million budget and 12 out of 45 states used the DOD Fresh program to procure at least some locally sourced produce (USDA, 2005c). In 2010, it expanded to $66 million (USDA, 2011b). The DOD Fresh program's funding originated from Section 32 of the 1935 Agricultural Adjustment Act, an indication of how long-standing policies can be repurposed for new uses (*An Act to Amend the Agricultural Adjustment Act and other purposes,* 1935; *Farm Security and Rural Investment Act,* 2002g; Managers on the part of the House and the Senate H.R. 2646, 2002b). Funding for DOD Fresh did not directly compete for funding with other nutrition programs.

However, reliance on DOD's purchasing system made the program vulnerable to administrative changes beyond USDA's control. During 2006–2007, the DOD shifted to a "prime vendor" system (Scott, 2006; USDA, 2011b). While fruit and vegetable purchases were still decentralized and implemented through 14 regional offices and 45 contracts (38 of which were held by small vendors), it concentrated purchases into larger-volume, long-term contracts (Scott, 2006; USDA, 2011b). A 2006 DOD letter indicated that its suppliers are "full-line produce provider[s]," an unlikely claim for many smaller-volume farmers (Scott, 2006). Relying on a preexisting system outside of USDA control was an early program development advantage, but the lack of control reduced the ability of the USDA to meet its goal of support for small farm operator purchases.

Fresh Fruit and Vegetable Snack Program, 2002 onward

The Fresh Fruit and Vegetable Snack Program (FFVSP), a competitively awarded grant program, provides free snacks to public schoolchildren regardless of income. A four-year pilot project began through the 2002 Farm Bill (*Farm Security and Rural Investment Act,* 2002e). The program expanded through

46 *Local food in national American policy*

funding increases in the 2004 Child Nutrition Act and the 2008 Farm Bill. Like DOD Fresh, it relied on funding from Section 32 funds (*Agricultural Adjustment Act. Section 32 (as amended)*; Becker, 2009; *Food, Conservation, and Energy Act of 2008*, 2008i). The program provided flexibility and additional funding to purchase fresh fruits and vegetables from vendors (many of which were local) chosen by the school district (Buzby, Guthrie, & Kantor, 2003).

Early program emphasis was on nutrition and support for schools with low-income children. Congress directed the USDA to "carry out a pilot program to make available to students . . . free fresh and dried fruits and fresh vegetables throughout the school day" (*Farm Security and Rural Investment Act*, 2002e). Additional guidance about outcomes was included in the Manager's Amendment. Evaluation goals included: feasibility (measured in students' interest), methods for providing the snacks, lessons learned, and changes in student and teacher attitudes during the pilot's duration (Managers on the part of the House and the Senate H.R. 2646, 2002c).

The pilot program's legislation originated in the Senate and was championed by Agriculture Committee Chairman Harkin (Buzby et al., 2003; Lorelei DiSogra [United Fresh Produce Vice President], 2012). Chairman Harkin was able to maintain his bill's funding level at $6 million and a $200,000 evaluation study even though the House did not include the program (*Farm Security and Rural Investment Act*, 2002e; Managers on the part of the House and the Senate H.R. 2646, 2002c). The connection to children's nutrition was an important motivation for many Congressional supporters. Four states—Indiana, Iowa, Michigan, and Ohio—and an unspecified Indian Tribal Organization (ITO, government-recognized Indian tribal group) were to be funded (Managers on the part of the House and the Senate H.R. 2646, 2002c). The USDA provided funding to 25 schools in each state, and seven in the Zuni Pueblo (Buzby et al., 2003).

Operational feasibility, geographic diversity, and socio-economic character-istics were the primary criteria used in the evaluation. The pilot program evaluation, conducted by the USDA's Economic Research Service (ERS), indicated that "most participating schools consider the pilot program to be very successful and feel strongly that the pilot should continue" (Buzby et al., 2003, iii). Changes in nutritional outcomes were not part of the assessment. Fourteen schools made purchases directly from producers or farmers' markets. The ERS study concluded that "an expanded program could create new markets for domestic fruits and vegetables" (Buzby et al., 2003, p. 15).

Two months after the ERS communicated its findings, *both* the House and Senate introduced bills to expand the program through the 2004 Child Nutrition Act reauthorization. The Senate bill targeted schools that had a majority of students receiving free and reduced lunches, a provision retained in the final legislation (*To amend the Richard B. Russell National School Lunch Act to reauthorize and expand the fruit and vegetable pilot program*, 2003). The House bill favored expanding the program nationally by funding 25 schools in each state and schools on ten Indian reservations (*To promote improved nutrition for*

Local food in national American policy   47

students by expanding the Fruit and Vegetable Pilot Program under the Richard B. Russell National School Lunch Act, 2003). Both the House and Senate proposals contained findings and purposes sections linking the consumption of fresh fruits and vegetables to public health goals (reduction of diet-related disease), but no new purposes were added to the program. While both the House and Senate proposed substantial funding increases, respectively $75 million and $78 million,[11] the final 2004 Child Nutrition Act provided $9 million in annual mandatory funding from Section 32 funds (*Child Nutrition and WIC Reauthorization Act of 2004*, 2004b; *To amend the Richard B. Russell National School Lunch Act to reauthorize and expand the fruit and vegetable pilot program*, 2003; *To promote improved nutrition for students by expanding the Fruit and Vegetable Pilot Program under the Richard B. Russell National School Lunch Act*, 2003).

The final legislation continued to allow purchases of dried fruit (*Child Nutrition and WIC Reauthorization Act of 2004*, 2004b). The new legislation and mandatory funding made the program permanent, retained the preexisting schools, and expanded to three additional states (25 schools each) and two more Indian reservations. Throughout the mid-2000s, new states were added, primarily those of Members of the subcommittees for agricultural appropriations in order to secure the political support for the program's overall funding (Lorelei DiSogra [United Fresh Produce Vice President], 2012).

Like the VAPG, the FFVSP faced competition from other nutrition programs in the annual appropriations process. The FFVSP was not a priority of the anti-hunger and nutrition interest groups. During the 2004 and 2010 Child Nutrition Act reauthorizations, it was not supported by the National Alliance for Nutrition and Activity (NANA), composed of nutrition groups, school trade associations, and public health groups (CS Mott Group for Sustainable Food Systems, 2009; NANA, 2004, 2008a). The School Nutrition Association did not advocate for the FFSVP (Bulls Eye Resources, 2008; CS Mott Group for Sustainable Food Systems, 2009; School Nutrition Association, 2008a, b), nor did the Child Nutrition Forum, composed of anti-hunger and some nutrition groups (Child Nutrition Forum, 2008; CS Mott Group for Sustainable Food Systems, 2009). Expansion of the FFVSP's funding in the 2008 Farm Bill came as part of a broader expansion of fruit and vegetable (specialty crop) programs (Lehrer, 2008).

The 2008 Farm Bill expanded the program to all states, territories, and all ITOs, though a minimum number of tribal organizations was not specified. It removed dried fruit from the existing statute, required that the states inform low-income school districts of the program's availability (including the ITO schools), and provided mandatory funding from Section 32 at $1.2 billion over 10 years (*Food, Conservation, and Energy Act of 2008*, 2008c). Any lingering ambiguities about the use of program funds for products other than fresh fruit and vegetables were firmly addressed in the Manager's Statement:

> As the name of the program makes clear, it is the intent of the program to provide children with free fresh fruits and vegetables. It is not the intent

48 *Local food in national American policy*

of the Managers to allow this program to provide other products, such as nuts, either on their own or comingled with other foods, such as in a trail mix. The Managers support the inclusion of all fruits and vegetables in the federal nutrition programs where supported by science . . .

> (Managers on the part of the House and the
> Senate for H.R. 2419, 2008a, p. 106)

The 2008 reauthorization represented the first inclusion of public health narratives in the FFVSP, overcoming their exclusion in earlier bills.

The expanded and better-funded FFVSP articulated a model of behavior change: to have a positive health impact for low-income children through the substitution of fresh produce in place of less healthy food. One new criterion for assessing applications was "a plan for implementation of the program, including efforts to integrate activities carried out under this section with other efforts to promote sound health and nutrition, reduce overweight and obesity, or promote physical activity" (*Food, Conservation, and Energy Act of 2008*, 2008c). A new evaluation was required, and emphasized public health outcomes, including "increased consumption of fruits and vegetables" and "decreased consumption of less nutritious foods" (*Food, Conservation, and Energy Act of 2008*, 2008c). A $3 million USDA-funded study by Abt Associates indicated that FFVSP increased produce consumption, that the produce consumed did not increase caloric intake, and that produce was substituted for other food consumption (Olsho, Klerman, & Bartlett, 2011).

The FFVSP faced resistance from anti-hunger and nutrition interest groups in the annual funding process and was often excluded from their priorities for major reauthorizations. Even after mandatory funding was secured in 2008, the School Nutrition Association proposed redirecting FFVSP funds to increase school meal reimbursements (Bulls Eye Resources, 2008; Lorelei DiSogra [United Fresh Produce Vice President], 2012; School Nutrition Association, 2008a, 2008b). The external tensions on the FFVSP centered on spending priorities: increasing school meal access or providing higher-quality food to existing low-income students. It faced internal tensions over which products should be considered "healthy food" because the "specialty crop" industry backed the Fresh Fruit and Vegetable Snack Program and included producers of dried fruit, nuts, and white potatoes.

Geographic preference in school meal procurement

While the USDA was learning how schools could increase their purchases of fresh and locally produced foods, government policies were ambiguous about whether schools could prefer food service contractors that supplied local products. Farm-to-school advocates worked to introduce a floor amendment in the 2002 Farm Bill permitting local food purchases (*Senate Amendment 2585*, 2001). Although the House Bill did not have a similar provision, the Farm Bill conference committee retained the amendment (Managers on the part of the House and the Senate H.R. 2646, 2002a). The modification required the Secretary of Agriculture to:

> encourage institutions participating in the school lunch program under this Act and the school breakfast program . . . to purchase, in addition to other food purchases, locally produced foods for school meal programs, to the maximum extent practicable and appropriate.
>
> (*Farm Security and Rural Investment Act*, 2002f)

Three days after the 2002 Farm Bill was passed, the USDA issued a memorandum asking State agencies responsible for implementing the school meal programs to encourage the purchase of locally produced foods (USDA, 2005c). The memorandum indicated school food authorities still had an "obligation to adhere to all applicable procurement requirements" and were "reminded that all purchases must be made competitively, consistent with Federal and State procurement laws and regulations" (USDA, 2005c, p. 35). To farm-to-school advocates, it seemed they had achieved a major legislative victory.

The USDA was less supportive of local food procurement as the Bush Administration took an active role in an international trade agenda. *Locally applied* preferences for local foods could be misunderstood as a national *mandate* for local food purchasing. The USDA reversed its earlier 2002 position and issued ambiguous guidances about the legality of local food procurement. A 2003 "Q&A" published by the USDA cited a federal regulation predating the 2002 Farm Bill as "prohibit[ing] the use of in-State and local geographic preferences in the award of contracts" (Garnett, 2007, p. 3). In 2005, the USDA FNS issued a guide on how to purchase locally produced foods, which included the memorandum issued three days after the 2002 Farm Bill *and not* the more recently issued documents (USDA, 2005c). Ambiguous guidance led advocates of geographic preference to enlist outside legal expertise.

The Community Food Security Coalition (CFSC), a proponent of geographic preference, sought additional support. The Harrison Institute of Public Law, at Georgetown University in Washington, DC published a memorandum challenging Administration policy (Caplan, 2006). The Institute's memorandum was based on normal legal precedence: the language of an Act cannot be superseded by a regulation or the Committee's report on the Act. In response, the USDA FNS issued a new memorandum, which stated "that [their] interpretation is incorrect and FNS disagrees with it as a result" (S. C. Garnett, 2007, p. 1).

To overcome agency resistance, advocates enlisted the support of their Congressional champions. In May, 2007, a bipartisan group of 17 Senators sent a letter to the Secretary indicating that the USDA's interpretations were against the intent of the law (Herb Kohl [D-WI] et al., 2007). This, too, proved ineffective at changing FNS' position.

50   *Local food in national American policy*

As a consequence, CFSC, supported by the Harrison Institute's legal expertise, re-mobilized their Congressional supporters to introduce new local food procurement legislation (Larsen & Forster, 2008). The 2008 Farm Bill included new geographic preference language that made minor modifications to the original 2002 language (*Food, Conservation, and Energy Act of 2008*, 2008h). The Administration vetoed the 2008 Farm Bill because it was "inconsistent with our objectives in international trade negotiations" (Bush, 2008, para. 2). Congress overruled the veto, passing the legislation into law. Two months after the Farm Bill passed, the USDA issued a new memorandum allowing schools to apply a geographic preference within a competitive bidding process (Long, 2008).

The 2008 Farm Bill's Conference Committee introduced a new clause that locally produced foods should only be "unprocessed agricultural products" (*Food, Conservation, and Energy Act of 2008*, 2008h). The addition of "unprocessed" in the 2008 Farm Bill was unexpected by farm-to-school advocates but not unwelcome (Larsen & Forster, 2008), with the regulation clarifying an assumption that local foods were generally considered minimally processed.

Public comments received on USDA's proposed regulation on the new procurement provisions also revealed an assumption about the meaning of local food. Most of the 77 commentators considered locally produced foods as "whole" foods (USDA, 2011d). USDA issued its final regulation stating, "unprocessed locally grown or locally raised agricultural products means only those agricultural products that retain their inherent character" and excluded highly processed products produced by food manufactures rather than farmers (USDA, 2011d, p. 22607).

Conflicts over geographic preference were not related to the geographic preference narrative or partisanship. The Bush Administration's initial support, shift to opposition during 2003–2007, and renewal of support for geographic preference in 2008 were due to the rise and fall of its international trade agenda (Lehrer, 2008; Morgan, 2010; Morgan & Sonnino, 2008). Limiting Congress' 2002 geographic preference legislation was a way for the Administration to control political risk during WTO negotiations. Through sustained interaction with government and ten years of advocacy, farm-to-school advocates transformed government procurement regulations, allowing local school districts the opportunity to include locally produced products in their procurement bid specifications (Long, 2011; NFSN, 2011).

Start-up support: A national farm-to-school program, 2003 onward

The development of a national farm to school program occurred in three stages:

- initial authorization without funding in the 2004 Child Nutrition Act;
- the addition of a school garden program for high-poverty schools in the 2008 Farm Bill and funding for gardens in 2010; and
- reauthorization with mandatory funding in the 2010 Child Nutrition Act.

Local food in national American policy 51

Transformative narratives of farm-to-school projects were present from proposal through implementation. Funding support for the farm-to-school program was initially resisted by the anti-hunger and nutrition policy communities.

The Farm-to-Cafeteria Acts of 2003 provided resources to address common barriers faced by food service directors in making local linkages. These included establishing relationships with producers and processers, coordinating purchases with producers or aggregators, retraining kitchen staff to use raw products, developing new menus (requiring nutritional analysis), using seasonal products, and cultivating a taste among children for different foods (*Farm-To-Cafeteria Projects Act of 2003*, 2003a, b; Tropp & Olowolayemo, 2000; USDA, 2005c). Grant funds were aimed at start-up costs and not intended for subsidizing purchase of local foods.

While the legislative proposals were unfunded, the 2004 Child Nutrition Act authorized a farm-to-school program, Access to Local Foods and School Gardens (*Child Nutrition and WIC Reauthorization Act of 2004*, 2004a). Its purposes were:

(A) to improve access to local foods in schools and institutions participating in programs under the Richard B. Russell National School Lunch Act (42 U.S.C. 1751 et seq.) and Section 4 of this Act through farm-to-cafeteria activities that may include the acquisition of food and appropriate equipment and the provision of training and education;
(B) at a minimum, be designed to procure local foods from small- and medium-sized farms for school meals;
(C) to support nutrition education activities or curriculum planning that incorporates the participation of schoolchildren in farm and agriculture education activities; and
(D) to develop a sustained commitment to farm-to-cafeteria projects in the community by linking schools, agricultural producers, parents, and other community stakeholders.

(*Child Nutrition Improvement and Integrity Act*, 2004)

The farm-to-school concept is based upon economic and social embeddedness; the economic role of farmers providing food is overlaid with and intertwined with their role in community (Granovetter, 1985; Hinrichs, 2000). Senator Leahy observed that

> when these connections are made, children receive healthful, fresh food choices at school and positive hands-on educational experiences about the foods that are produced in their region. At the same time, farmers not only strengthen their local markets, but become more involved with the schools in their community.

(Patrick Leahy [D-VT] et al., 2006)

52 *Local food in national American policy*

Securing funding for the newly authorized program was the priority for its advocates.

During the 2008 Farm Bill, Senator Sanders introduced an amendment for "high-poverty" schools to the Access to Local Foods and School Gardens program (Bernie Sanders [I-VT], 2007; *Food, Conservation, and Energy Act of 2008*, 2008d; Tom Harkin [D-IA] et al., 2007). "High poverty" was defined as schools where 50 percent of the eligible children received free or reduced-price school lunches. In 2010, Sanders secured $120,000 for Vermont schools as well as an additional $1 million for school gardens. This funding was provided through the People's Garden Initiative, an effort linked to First Lady Michelle Obama's "Let's Move" campaign (Bernie Sanders [I-VT], 2009, 2010; *Conference Report to Accompany H.R. 2997*, 2009; USDA, 2011h).

As the 2009 Child Nutrition Act reauthorization drew near, CFSC and the National Farm to School Network (NFSN) sought support from the Child Nutrition Forum (CNF), an alliance of anti-hunger and nutrition groups, but it offered only tacit support for the farm-to-school program:

> Improved nutritional health for our children can be achieved by increasing meal reimbursements to help schools, sponsors and providers improve meals and snacks and increasing children's access to fruits and vegetables in all forms (including those sourced from regional farms), whole grains and low-fat milk and reduced-fat dairy products.
>
> (Child Nutrition Forum, 2008, p. 3)

NANA also decided not to support farm-to-school programs in 2008 (Hunt & Kalb, 2008; NANA, 2008b, 2009). This set back farm-to-school advocates who had anticipated being included in both policy forums. By March, CNF's Congressional supporters introduced bills supporting their priorities (CFSC, 2010; *Child Nutrition Promotion and School Lunch Protection Act of 2009*, 2009a, b; *National and State Organization Sign-On Letter Urging Support for Prioritizing Low-Income Children's Access to Healthy Meals*, 2009). Farm-to-school was not included in bills promoted by the CNF, nor did NANA support farm-to-school.

The exclusion of farm-to-school from legislative proposals drove farm-to-school advocates to form a separate policy initiative for its reauthorization and funding. Advocates began legislative outreach in February of 2009 and had drafted farm-to-school legislation by April, 2009 (Elsener, 2009). Additional funding to support policy outreach efforts was not secured until late spring.

Engaging in child nutrition was new for sustainable agriculture advocates, like the National Sustainable Agriculture Coalition (NSAC), and there was a learning curve (Hunt, 2009). By the summer, NSAC had become one of five convening organizations of the Farm to School Collaborative, a "cross-sector alliance of school, nutrition, rural, and sustainable agriculture groups and farmers that support Congressional enactment of $50 million in mandatory funding for farm-to-school programs in the 2009 Child Nutrition Reauthorization" (NFSN et al., 2009).[12]

Farm to school was an Obama campaign priority. It was part of its rural policy platform, though not part of its nutrition platform (Obama for America, 2008a, b), illustrating the divisions between the nutrition policy community and advocates of farm-to-school. Farm-to-school became one of the White House's eight priorities for the Child Nutrition Act reauthorization (Kohan, 2010).

After introducing legislation to stem the depth of a recession, the Obama Administration signaled to Congress its next legislative priority was healthcare policy. The resulting legislative delay on the Child Nutrition Act provided time for farm-to-school advocates to overcome the setbacks of the CNF and NANA. Farm-to-school advocates identified a sponsor for their legislation in the House and cultivated supporters from the House minority caucuses. This replicated a successful urban–rural strategy used in the 2008 Farm Bill. However, the House sponsor, Representative McCollum [D-MN], was uneasy about introducing a bill recommending mandatory funding, delaying the bill's introduction.

In November 2009, three critical events happened, changing the Farm to School Collaborative's strategy. First, advocates sought out additional potential House champions for the farm-to-school legislation (Lott, 2009a, b). Second, Representative McCollum no longer supported mandatory funding for a farm-to-school program (Lott, 2009c; *The National Farm to School Act*, 2009). Third, the Collaborative sought other bills to include their legislation (Lott, 2009b; United Fresh Produce, 2010). Consequently, Representative Farr's [D-CA] Children's Fruit and Vegetable Act of 2009, supported by United Fresh Produce, was the first bill proposing mandatory funding for a farm-to-school program. This bill was followed by Representative Holt's [D-NJ] Farm to School Improvements Act of 2010 (H.R. 4710) .

Representative Holt became the new House champion. His bill (H.R. 4710) had 31 co-sponsors from 23 states, including Members of the three minority caucuses in the House, and Chair of the House Education and Labor Committee (which oversaw child nutrition policy). It was included as part of the Committee Chair's Improving Nutrition for America's Children Act (*Improving Nutrition for America's Children Act*, 2010). Four weeks later, a companion piece of legislation was introduced by Senator Leahy (S. 3123) and was cosponsored by 17 Senators from 14 states (*Growing Farm to School Programs Act of 2010*, 2010). Thus, six bills supported farm-to-school programs (see Figure 2.1). In 2010 the House and Senate passed versions of the Child Nutrition Act (H.R. 5504 and S. 3307), both of which included mandatory funding for a farm-to-school program (*Healthy, Hunger-Free Kids Act of 2010*, 2010b; *Improving Nutrition for America's Children Act*, 2010).

The Child Nutrition Act's renewal rested upon new budget estimates for the House and Senate bills (Congressional Budget Office, 2010a, b). Congress was increasingly reluctant to propose new federal spending during the recession. The Senate bill (S. 3307) responded to this political pressure by cutting farm conservation programs to pay for child nutrition increases. Conservation

54 *Local food in national American policy*

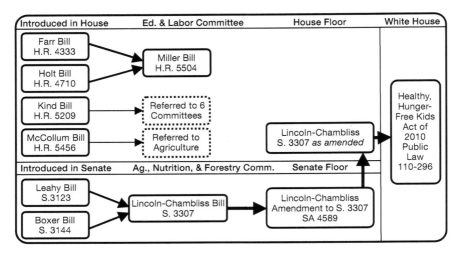

Figure 2.1 Diagram of the farm-to-school program's reauthorization, 2009–2010.

advocates mobilized their supporters and instead the Chair of the Senate Agriculture Committee introduced an amendment (SA 4589) to direct the last six months of stimulus-related SNAP benefits to pay for the new child nutrition funding (*An amendment to the bill S. 3307, to reauthorize child nutrition programs, and for other purposes*, 2010; Democratic Policy Committee, 2010). The Healthy, Hunger-Free Kids Act of 2010 was passed in a "lame duck session," authorizing $40 million in mandatory funding for a new farm-to-school program (*Healthy, Hunger-Free Kids Act of 2010*, 2010a).

The final language is nearly identical to advocate proposals. Compared with the 2004 authorization, the new program was twice as long with a new set of eligible entities, evaluation criteria, provisions for technical assistance, and a revised list of eligible activities (*Child Nutrition and WIC Reauthorization Act of 2004*, 2004a; *Healthy, Hunger-Free Kids Act of 2010*, 2010a). It directed the USDA to

> carry out a program to assist eligible schools, State and local agencies, Indian tribal organizations, agricultural producers or groups of agricultural producers, and nonprofit entities through grants and technical assistance to implement farm-to-school programs that improve access to local foods in eligible schools.
>
> (*Healthy, Hunger-Free Kids Act* of 2010, 2010a)

With limited grant funds, the Secretary was directed to "achieve regional balance, consider geographical diversity and equitable treatment of urban, rural, and tribal communities" (*Healthy, Hunger-Free Kids Act of 2010*, 2010a).

Local food in national American policy   55

Geographic diversity was paired with criteria favoring proposals serving a high proportion of low-income children in the Criteria for Grant Selection section:

(A) Make local food products available on the menu of the eligible school.
(B) Serve a high proportion of children who are eligible for free or reduced-price lunches.
(C) Incorporate experiential nutrition education activities in curriculum planning that encourage the participation of schoolchildren in farm- and garden-based agricultural education activities.
(D) Demonstrate collaboration between eligible schools, non-governmental and community-based organizations, agricultural producer groups, and other community partners.
(E) Include adequate and participatory evaluation plans.
(F) Demonstrate the potential for long-term program sustainability.
(G) Meet any other criteria that the Secretary determines appropriate.
(Healthy, Hunger-Free Kids Act of 2010, 2010a)

The transformative narrative of farm-to-school was matched with agency actions to promote socio-economic and geographic equity in the selection of grantees (USDA, 2012d).

The legislative development of farm-to-school was frustrated by anti-hunger and nutrition interest groups. Farm-to-school was not directly opposed by CNF and NANA. However, these gatekeepers did not engage in its development or offer support to farm-to-school advocates. Farm-to-school advocates had to cultivate their own champions and allies; demonstrating newcomers must *display* their political support through public backing and *mobilize* their own resources to gain access to the policy process.

Congressional supporters of farm-to-school policy provided crucial political support for the Child Nutrition Act's reauthorization. As a result, "food advocacy organizations now also regard farm-to-school programs as a fundamental part of their agenda to improve nutrition" (Robert Wood Johnson Foundation, 2011, p. 6). Farm-to-school advocates were not accepted as an essential part of child nutrition policy until they enlisted Congressional champions, and supporters who were *politically significant* for the Act's passage.

Conclusion: Increasing inclusion, increasing policy success

Through these 11 policies, proponents of local food undertook actions that succeeded in sustained narrative hybridization over four decades. Advocates successfully linked their transformative narratives with preexisting, market-oriented agricultural policy narratives. Local food proponents sought to support self-determination of low-income communities (e.g. CFP), expand markets for smaller-volume producers (e.g. FMPP, VAPG, FMNPs), and link people with low incomes to local food (e.g. FMNPs, farm-to-school, geographic

56 *Local food in national American policy*

preference, FFVSP, DOD Fresh). Policies increased in number, scope, and funding; none were repealed or defunded between 1976 and 2012.

In an overall strategy of direct engagement with policymakers, several advocacy tactics were used:

- grassroots mobilization linked with direct lobbying;
- policy collaboration;
- formation of political coalitions in the legislature;
- cultivation of allies;
- engaging agency officials in policy-oriented learning (e.g. pilot projects, workshops); and
- policy entrepreneurship (e.g. joining of policy streams for small farms and sustainable agriculture with food assistance for low-income groups).

These tactics were used consistently across time, and avoided direct confrontation with established interests.

Preexisting policy narratives served as beachheads to hybridize older policies with newer local food policies. The Commodity Credit Corporation, established in 1933, funded the SFMNP. The FFVSP and DOD Fresh were funded through Section 32 of the 1935 Agricultural Adjustment Act. The FMPP and SFMNP were added to the policy framework established by the 1946 Agricultural Marketing Act. The transformative intent of policies proposed by local food advocates did not conflict with, nor aim to displace, preexisting policies and statutes.

Resistance was observed when a narrative, used to justify the policy critiqued agribusiness practices (VAPG), conflicted with an Administration's priority (international trade and local procurement), and had limited support by advocacy group gatekeepers (EBT, FMNP expansion, farm-to-school funding). When advocates encountered resistance with dominant interests, policy development was shifted to alternative policy venues as with VAPG and EBT. Opposition to local food *policies* was nonpartisan.

Local food policies had both Republican and Democrat proponents. President Bush's second-term administration provided discretionary funding for the FMPP in 2006 and 2007 before the Democrat-controlled Congress provided mandatory funding through the 2008 Farm Bill. The Bush Administration both supported and opposed geographic preference, because international trade negotiations were a high-profile part of its political agenda. When partisanship on local food occurred, it was directed at President Obama by conservative Republicans opposed to the Administration's message of *"Know Your Farmer, Know Your Food,"* not the existence of local food policies in the *"Know Your Food"* message Congress had enacted and funded (John McCain [R-AZ], Saxby Chambliss [R-GA], & Pat Roberts [R-KS], 2010). While partisan political views have affected local food, these influences were not *because of* local food. For local food, significant points of resistance originated from other advocacy groups in overlapping policy communities.

Local food in national American policy   57

Policymakers were reluctant to take on the policy proposals of local food advocates without the support of gatekeeper organizations, as observed with the introduction of EBT and the lack of funding when farm-to-school was first authorized. The decision to maintain the WIC program through discretionary, annual funding had negative consequences for other policies. This pressure included policies that increased access for fresh healthy foods for people with low incomes, including the FFVSP and WIC FMNP. But the expansion of these policies to a larger number of people was frustrated by limited support from anti-hunger and nutrition advocacy groups and the Food and Nutrition Service.

By observing national policies, one can conclude that the local food movement's political agenda was centered on increased inclusion for people with low incomes. While attention to issues of food affordability, nutrition, and access are preexisting concerns of the USDA, local food advocates actively mobilized their own resources to develop nutrition programs (FMNPs, farm-to-school) while devoting fewer resources to programs that could only benefit farmers (e.g. the VAPG). Throughout its development, the local food movement has been aware of the potential for social inequity and acted on those concerns through national policy.

Notes

1 Fiscal year 2010 expenditures were the most recent year in which all program expenditures were available at the time research was completed (*Agriculture Risk Protection Act of 2000*, 2000; *Farm Security and Rural Investment Act*, 2002a; *Farmer-to-Consumer Direct Marketing Act*, 1976b; *FDA Food Safety Modernization Act*, 2010; *Federal Agriculture Improvement and Reform Act*, 1996; *Food, Conservation, and Energy Act of 2008*, 2008a; *Hunger Prevention Act of 1988*, 1988; Managers on the part of the House and the Senate for H.R. 2419, 2008b; NSAC, 2010; OMB, 2011; USDA, 2011b, 2013a, 2012d, 2006, 2001b, 2012e, 2011e, 2011f, 2000a, 2011h).
2 Equivalent to the British term "farm shop," although some farm stands are self-service.
3 For the VAPG, a socially disadvantaged farmer or rancher is a member of a socially disadvantaged group "whose members have been subjected to racial, ethnic, or *gender* prejudice because of their identity as members of a group without regard to their individual qualities" (emphasis added, USDA, 2012b). Another definition of socially disadvantaged farmer, used for making farm loans, excludes gender (USDA, 2012c).
4 Congress does not define a small or mid-sized farm. The USDA considers a small farm as one with less than $250,000 in annual sales and a mid-sized farm as less than $1 million in annual sales (USDA, 2011i).
5 Congress does not define "family farm." The USDA Farm Services Agency uses a definition that includes a farm where both "physical labor and management" are provided by family members by "blood or marriage, or are a relative," which "use full-time hired labor in amounts only to supplement family labor" (USDA, 2012a). This includes nearly all farms in the US (about 98 percent) and excludes farms owned by non-family corporations (Newton & MacDonald, 2009).
6 The definition of beginning farmer and rancher used by USDA is based upon a Congressional definition of beginning producer used for eligibility in public and private farm credit programs. The most frequently cited components of the lengthy

58 *Local food in national American policy*

definition are that a beginning farmer and rancher: 1) "has not operated a farm or ranch, or who has operated a farm or ranch for not more than 10 years," (7 U.S.C. § 1991(11)(b)); 2) "materially and substantially participates in the operation of the farm or ranch,"(7 U.S.C. § 1991(11)(d)(i)(I)(aa)); and 3) "provides substantial day-to-day labor and management of the farm or ranch" (7 U.S.C. § 1991(11) (d)(i)(I)(bb)).

7 The term originates from the "Agriculture of the Middle" research initiative (Agriculture of the Middle, 2012). Several researchers from this initiative participated in the Farm and Food Policy Project's "Family Farm Revitalization Work Group" to develop the mid-tier value chain concept in this legislation (NEMWI, 2006a).

8 Note: Different types of documents were used to create the table: statutes, the White House's annual budgets (OMB, 2002, 2003, 2004, 2005, 2006, 2007, 2008, 2009, 2010, 2011), funding announcements in the *Federal Register* (USDA, 2005a, 2007, 2008, 2009b, 2011a, 2004, 2005b, 2009c, 2001b, 2002, 2003), and budget summaries from the National Sustainable Agriculture Coalition, which were the most reliable of the four document types (NSAC, 2010, 2011; SAC, 2005b).

9 USDA developed regulations ensuring that only locally grown foods were eligible in the program (1994b).

10 I served on the review panel for CFP grants for one fiscal year.

11 The Senate bill did not provide a total cost, though a total cost can be estimated from the bill. The bill proposed to add 920,000 students from 46 states, 20,000 students in ITO schools, and 40,000 students to the four original states while maintaining the preexisting 64,377 students (*To amend the Richard B. Russell National School Lunch Act to reauthorize and expand the fruit and vegetable pilot program*, 2003). At $75 per student per year, the program would provide about $78 million per year.

12 I participated in the collaborative as a representative for the Wallace Center.

3 Local food in national English policy, 1991–2012

Policy decline with increased contention

Episodic policy change shaped English policy narratives of local food, in contrast to incremental development observed in American policy. Major policy shifts occurred due to: a change of majority party or coalition in Parliament (and consequently, government administration); government leadership change without a party or coalition change; regular policy cycles associated with the EU CAP or other EU policies; and events portrayed as national or international "crises" in mainstream media. Pike et al. (2011) observed that major rural policy shifts occurred with governmental party changes and minor shifts occurred when government leadership changed within a party's tenure in the government. Advocacy groups were able to influence EU policies and their implementation in the UK, and were able to frame and reframe media coverage of crisis events.

The relevant policy events span more than a decade and are segmented by researcher-defined episodes (Sabatier, 1993; Sabatier & Jenkins-Smith, 1993). Each episode is defined by the opening of a window of political opportunity and closes with a significant shift reframing or closing of that opportunity (Kingdon, 1984). The opening and closing of policy windows associated with two crisis events are used to divide this chapter into three sections (della Porta, 2002).

Each section reviews government and advocacy group narratives and actions relating to local food. Also, each section highlights a characteristic feature of English policymaking that affected local food policy. The three sections are:

- *Pre-crisis era.* From 1991 through 2000, before the Foot and Mouth Disease (FMD) outbreak in 2001, local food policy proceeded on two separate tracks related to food poverty and health and rural development. This section focuses on the use of government-created stakeholder workshops in policy formulation. The four national-level policies that enabled local food projects were established in this era. This window closed with the reframing of farm, food, and rural policies in response to the FMD outbreak (see Ward, Donaldson, and Lowe, 2004).
- *Post farm crisis era.* From 2002 through 2007, policies were shaped by the "farm crisis" caused by the FMD outbreak. This crisis drove the renaming

of the Ministry of Agriculture, Fisheries and Food (MAFF) to the Department for Environment, Food and Rural Affairs (DEFRA). Policymakers promoted a narrative of "reconnection" to promote a renewed trust in the farm and food industry. Local food was central to the reconnection narrative. This reframing also supported the EU-wide shift from farm production subsidies to agri-conservation (or green) payments and non-farm rural development. Once the immediate crises passed, government policy aligned with narratives promoted by environmental and farm advocacy groups. New local food policies were not established and by the era's end, some policies were discontinued.

- *World food price crisis era.* From 2008 onward, international concerns, increasing global food prices, and climate change framed both government and advocacy group narratives. The section focuses on scientific knowledge and expertise in policy formation. Several national reports raised the profile of food issues, including local food: Food Matters (2008), a new national food strategy called Food 2030 (2010), and a Foresight report on food (2011). Two governments, scientists, and industry challenged local food claims by environmental groups. As a result, contention increased and policymaker interest in local food decreased.

The main narrative policy reports of each era, selected for their significance and representative characterization of issues in that era, are summarized in Table 3.1.

This chapter focuses on part of what British researchers consider "policies," a combination of statutory, regulatory, and programmatic decisions made by Parliament and Cabinet agencies. The Parliament, British government, and devolved authorities also implemented and negotiated on EU policies. Other agencies and informal institutions had a role in the governance of food issues.

In England it was common for ad hoc "programs" to be established by the government, government-funded QUANGOs, and non-governmental organizations. Typically, these programs had a combination, but not all, of these features:

- Institutions were created by government actions but operated independently of Cabinet agency oversight.
- Lack of a formal policy process once created (e.g. regulation formation).
- Lack of formal or transparent decision-making processes.
- Selection of which groups to fund or support without a formal selection process (e.g. no open competition).
- Programs were short-lived.

Several short-lived entities are introduced to indicate their role with the local food sector and are not discussed further.

The Countryside Agency was formed through a statutory process, but was short-lived and typically provided resources to local food on an ad hoc basis.

Table 3.1 Summary of major English government policy reports

Report	Main policy problem	Intended outcomes	Geographic focus	Audience	Key metaphors
Low-income, Food, Nutrition, and Health: Strategies for Improvement (1996)	Food access for people with low incomes	Improve physical access & affordability for healthy food Local Food Partnerships	Communities in Great Britain	Health professionals Planners Government Retailers	Community Community food projects
Independent Inquiry into Inequalities in Health Report (1998)	Declining rate of health improvement due to persistent inequalities	Identify policy priorities	Great Britain	Department of Health Health policy community	Inequality
National Strategy for Urban Renewal: Local Shops Access (2000)★	Food retailers moving to urban fringe Poverty Crime	Proactive planning Community engagement & leadership	Urban areas in Great Britain	Planners Government Agencies Retailers	Access
Rural White Paper (2000)★	Rural decline Underinvestment in services	Modernization Investment in services Countryside preservation	English rural towns The countryside	Rural people Farmers	Rural-proofing
Farming & Food: a sustainable future (2002)	Farm crisis Lack of public trust	Food safety reform Shift to "green payments"	England & Great Britain	Farm community Public EU	Reconnection
Sustainable Farming and Food Strategy (2002)★	Economic, environ., & social sustainability of agriculture Public health	Farm subsidy reduction EU compliance	Primarily England	Farm community Civil society EU	Reconnection Competiveness
Food Matters (2008)★	Global food prices Lack of National Food Strategy	Identify priorities for a National Food Strategy	Primarily England	Informed Public	Cultural change
Food 2030 (2010)★	Lack of National Food Strategy	National Food Strategy	Primarily England Global trade partners	Primarily global trade partners	Food security
Future of Food and Farming (2011)	How a global population of 9 billion by 2050 can be fed healthily and sustainably	Marshaling support for global food systems	Primarily global trade partners	Coalition supporters Business community Scientists	Sustainable intensification

★ Denotes national strategy document

62 Local food in national English policy

It promoted local food from its 1999 inception, launched an "Eat the View" local food campaign, and was merged into another agency, Natural England, by statute in 2006 (Countryside Agency, 1999, 2002, 2004; Enteleca, 2001; *Natural Environment and Rural Communities Act 2006*, 2006).

A QUANGO, Food from Britain, was created by statute in 1983 to promote British food products domestically and internationally and supported the formation of Regional Food and Drink Groups (Elliott J. et al., 2005). These Groups promoted foods from the English regions (e.g. promotional brochures, festivals, development of EU protected status for British foods). However, their leadership typically did not include community-based organizations (e.g. farmers market associations) and their funding processes were not transparent. They ended in 2009 and were abolished in 2014 by statute (DEFRA, 2014a).

Another QUANGO, but with a non-governmental revenue stream, the BIG Lottery Fund, established a competitive grant program for local food. Through its "Changing Spaces" environmental grant-making program, the Royal Society of Wildlife Trusts established The Local Food Program with just under £60 million in 2007. Separately, the BIG Lottery funded the establishment by the Plunket Foundation of the Making Local Food Work (MLFW) program (Kirwan et al., 2014; MLFW, 2008). Both are considered "programs," and were multi-year competitive grant programs. However, neither was established through public policy.

There were relatively few public policies that supported the local food sector. All were associated with the EU and most were grant programs. By the end of the pre-crisis era, England had deployed four policies that enabled local food activities. These policies were:

- the LEADER program, established in 1991;
- the Regional Development Agencies (RDAs) legislative act in 1998;
- the Rural Enterprise Scheme (RES) in 2000; and
- the Processing and Marketing Grant (PMG) in 2000.

All of these policies had the potential to support local agricultural and food activities (Curry et al., 2002, pp. 43, 46; EC, 1991).

A few summarizations can be made about local food policy narratives in comparison to the narratives presented from the US (Chapter 2):

- Policy documents primarily consider local food as *instrument* to reach other goals, such as rural development or public health and a *transformation* narrative is also present.
- Local food is often associated with *sustainable food*, but narrowly framed as an environmental issue. A narrow framing is espoused by governmental institutions and environmental activists.
- The term *food chain* is used to describe the business linkages from farm to retail store. It does not consider individuals as both consumers and citizens and generally excludes the environment, unlike the *food systems* narrative.

Local food in national English policy 63

- Local food is not considered a "niche" market, as organic food was considered in the UK (Tomlinson, 2007).
- Local food was understood as separate from *locality* food, which is typically exported for consumption away from the area of production or harvesting (Curry et al., 2002, p. 10).

Narratives of local food were hybridized in British and English government policy reports. Compared with the US, the narratives of the British government were more critical of local food and exposed advocacy group narratives to manipulation, one of the risks of *narrative hybridization* (Laclau, 1996). Governmental responses to advocacy groups' narratives need to be taken in context: British interest groups frequently sought to attack and undermine the credibility of policymakers (discussed in chapters 4 and 6). Also in comparison with the US, British government procedures had a lower level of government accountability to stakeholders. The recommendations of stakeholder workgroups were ignored, the government did not consistently follow through on its own recommendations, and scientific evidence was manipulated. Yet, when the British government was accountable to the EU for program implementation, the policy process was more regular and transparent.

The EU CAP provided a predictable vehicle for policy change. It was typically renewed on six-year cycles with a mid-term review of its progress and one to two years of negotiations preceding the each policy's finalization (Table 3.2). These recurring policy windows were not considered a significant target for most English advocacy groups that supported local food, though British environmental groups were active in shifting farm subsidies to conservation payments (Falconer & Ward, 2000; Lowe & Wilkinson, 2009). Rather, for local food, many British advocacy groups sought policy windows opened by crises portrayed in the national media. Demonstrating that EU policy windows were *de-linked* from the media-oriented policy eras was a significant research finding.

Using media campaigns, English sustainable agriculture and food interest groups mobilized supporters to create "a movement without incurring the costs of building and maintaining mass organizations" (Tarrow, 1998, p. 131). The resulting disconnection decreased opportunities for stakeholders to learn advocacy skills and concentrated policy knowledge and expertise in relatively few organizations and individuals (Tarrow, 1998, pp. 129, 132–133). Without a direct link between English local food stakeholders and national interest groups, it is necessary to question whether the prominent *national* policy narratives of local food were authentic narratives used by *local* stakeholders.

The connective structures (Diani, 1995, 2002) between English advocacy groups and local food stakeholders are discussed in Chapter 4. What follows is a detailed representation of policies related to local food from 1991 through to 2013. A lengthier characterization of British policies can be found in Hunt (2013).

Table 3.2 Timeline of local food policy milestones in England[1]

Year	Policy	Milestone	Relevance to local food in England
1991	EU Community Initiative	LEADER Program began (1991–1993)	Utilizes several streams of EU funds Support for "local agriculture" Local Action Groups required cross-sector stakeholder participation
1992	"MacSharry reform" of CAP	Begins shift of farm payments from production support to income support	Processing and Marketing Grant (1991–1993; 1994–1996)
1994	EU Community Initiative	LEADER II (1994–1999)	Expands LEADER in geographic scope and funding
1998	Regional Development Act	England forms Regional Development Agencies	New agency administers all EU funds, including CAP & LEADER Agencies encourage regional food & drink promotion
2000	"Agenda 2000" CAP reforms	New English Rural Development Program (ERDP) (2000–2006)	Processing and Marketing Grant (PMG) Rural Enterprise Scheme (RES)
	EU Community Initiative	LEADER+	Expands LEADER in geographic scope and funding
2003	"CAP reform"	De-links farm payments from production support Payments shift to agri-environmental programs	Mid-term review of the ERDP with policy recommendations for the PMG and RES
2007	CAP "Health check"	New Rural Development Program for England (RDPE) (2007–2009) LEADER Approach	Shifts to "measures" for adding value, cooperative development, farm diversification, non-farm microenterprises, and tourism LEADER becomes part of the CAP Expansion of LEADER in geographic scope and funding (5% of CAP funds)
2010	(Coalition government formed)	RDPE replaced by Rural Economy Grant (2010–2013) RDAs abolished	Shifts to "themes" for rural development, agri-food projects, dairy assistance, and targeted assistance for 5 sub-regions Rural development recentralized LEADER administration shifted to Local Action Groups

Pre-crisis era: Nutrition and rural development

This era is characterized by exploratory approaches into wider food system issues, collaboration across professional disciplines, and greater engagement of stakeholders and NGOs in policy formation. From 1991 to 2000, policymakers investigated the nutritional and health links to food quality and food access for people with low incomes. Both Conservative and Labour governments linked local food with preexisting policy narratives of social exclusion, community deprivation, rural development, and public health. Despite the near convergence of rural and urban-oriented policy streams about the access to food shops, they remained separate issues.

Nutrition, health, and food shop access

Low Income Project Team, 1993–1996

The Department of Health's 1992 *Health of the Nation* report set in motion a series of policy activities and reports on the linkage between diet and severe disease, such as stroke and cancer (Nelson, 1997). A Nutrition Task Force was established in 1993. The Task Force formed a cross-sector Low Income Project Team (LIPT) to examine how food and diet affected people on low incomes. The work of the LIPT represents the most detailed governmental account of the interests and needs of community-based local food projects across all policy eras.

Three years later, the LIPT published *Low Income, Food, Nutrition and Health: Strategies for Improvement.* It recommended the formation of local food partnerships to enable "local authorities, food retailers, and low-income communities themselves to make joint decisions about the provision of a healthy and affordable food supply" (1996; Nelson, 1997, p. 91). Nelson, a participant in the LIPT, indicated that these partnerships "include the right of citizens to have access to a safe, health-enhancing and affordable food supply (different from the consumer's right to buy what they can afford in a market over which they have *no* control)" (emphasis in original, Nelson, 1997, p. 92).[2]

Self-mobilization of lower-income communities and the empowerment of individuals living on lower incomes were a policy priority for the LIPT. Yet, the LIPT also acknowledged barriers to the replication of local food partnerships, especially establishing best practices. As a result, the LIPT proposed the development of a national network of local food projects "to stimulate and facilitate the development of projects and to encourage evaluation of their effectiveness" (Nelson, 1997, p. 92).

After the LIPT ended, some participants, including "representatives of national and local government departments, local community projects, food retailers, funding agencies (including Research Councils), and academics," met to develop a "a coordinated national strategy" (Nelson, 1997, p. 93). This resulted in an ad hoc *Forum on Diet and Health in Low-income Families* held at

66 *Local food in national English policy*

the Royal Society for Medicine. Seventy participants developed a list of barriers to address domestic food poverty (Nelson, 1997, p. 96). Local food projects were considered a primary vehicle to reduce barriers to healthy food. Project examples included "food co-ops, cookery courses, healthy-recipe leaflet development, community cafes selling cheap healthy foods, food and nutrition education courses, meal provision for those with special needs, food coupons, etc." (Nelson, 1997, p. 100).

The Forum identified constraints on local food project formation, including: "Lack of a national support strategy for local activity; the physical and administrative distances between low-income communities and policymakers; . . . the need for funding to be given for projects before their impact has been proven; unwillingness to experiment with unproven methods; . . . recognition that the physical distance between out-of-town supermarkets and low-income communities creates serious problems of access; . . . recognition of the need for partnerships which cross public and private sector boundaries and embrace the diversity of problems which arise from the diversity of low-income communities" (Selected barriers from Nelson, 1997, p. 96).

In response to these constraints, Nelson indicated that local food projects want:

- to form networks at a local level but have access to a national forum;
- local communities to set their own agenda; to liaise and develop partnerships with retailers;
- help with research into community needs, the effectiveness of local projects, and dissemination of the findings; to work with pressure groups who can lobby for change at a national level.

(Nelson, 1997, p. 96)

Local project leaders, researchers, and pressure groups all wanted a "common forum" that would cut across disciplines and carry forward the work begun in the LIPT (Nelson, 1997, p. 97). New efforts were needed: preexisting non-governmental networks and governmental activities were considered insufficient to develop local food projects.

Independent Inquiry into Health Inequalities, 1998

The LIPT's 1997 report languished until after the May 1997 national elections. In July, the newly elected Labour government launched an *Independent Inquiry into Health Inequalities*, which picked up some of the LIPT's issues. The *Inquiry* identified food affordability, limited access to food shops in lower-income communities (called "food deserts"), and the EU CAP's impact on diet as future national policy directions for food policy (Acheson, 1998, section on Reducing food poverty and improving retail provision). The issue of health inequality became the focus of the Social Exclusion Unit, established within the Cabinet Office (December 1997).

Local food in national English policy   67

Within the Social Exclusion Unit, unequal access to food shops was a focus of the urban-oriented *National Strategy for Neighbourhood Renewal*. A parallel rural focus on local food shops appeared in the 2000 Rural White Paper, extending to local food supply chains, and the availability of farmers' markets, abattoirs, and livestock markets (Department of the Environment, 2000, pp. 7, 75, 77, 84, 89, 92–94, 166). Both reports responded to a trend of food retailers moving away from city centers into larger retail spaces at the urban fringe.

Urban redevelopment and food shop access: Bringing Britain Together

The Labour government favored stakeholder consultation and launched 18 working groups, called Policy Action Teams (PATs), to gather input on urban redevelopment as part of its *Bringing Britain Together* initiative. The remit of Team 13 included good retailing practices, the use of food cooperatives in housing estates, and strategies to promote healthy eating (Social Exclusion Unit, 2001). Their goal was "to develop a strategy to increase access to affordable shops for people in poor neighbourhoods" (Social Exclusion Unit, 2001, p. 248). Of its 48 participants, four identified themselves as community workers or small business owners (Policy Action Team 13, 2000, pp. 66–68). Organizations with rural or agricultural ties were not in attendance aside from MAFF staff.

The recommendations of PAT 13 communicated a distrust of consultation processes; that local governments would not follow through on concerns raised by stakeholders. The Team described these "hollow consultations" as instances when

> communities are consulted about the future pattern of shopping facilities in their neighbourhood but are not listened to, their views not acted upon; often it appears that consultation is not integrated with discussions with local retailers and a common understanding of the constraints and drivers for successful retailing is not developed.
>
> (Policy Action Team 13, 2000, p. 36)

To address these concerns, the team recommended a change in how local councils implemented the planning process. They wanted use of "*neighbourhood planning processes, such as 'planning for real', to help articulate the community's vision and devise a strategy for achieving improved access to shopping and services*" (emphasis in original, Policy Action Team 13, 2000, p. 37). Additionally, they recommend national government support for community-owned food shops to help communities respond to locally identified needs.

PAT 13 made two recommendations for financing community-owned food shops, both tied to preexisting programs. One recommendation was for the Regional Development Agencies to establish a revolving loan fund to invest in refurbishing retail stores (Policy Action Team 13, 2000, p. 40). The government disagreed with this financing model on the basis that existing, but

68   *Local food in national English policy*

unspecified, agencies already were doing this work (Social Exclusion Unit, 2001, p. 174).

A second recommendation was similar: a government-funded "Community-led, Community-owned Development Trust" to be located in the Department of Environment, Transport, and Regions (Policy Action Team 13, 2000, p. 40). The government placed the Development Trust model as a proposed topic for a future meeting for the Department of Environment, Transport, and Regions to discuss existing case studies on the model, rather than start a new initiative (Social Exclusion Unit, 2001, p. 175).

The Minister for Small Business and E-Commerce encouraged the community-owned retailing work to be continued by a university professor, Tim Lang, and a lone advocate, Toby Peters of Community Owned Retailing Limited (Companies House; Social Exclusion Unit, 2001, pp. 170–171).

Only one of Team 13's food retailing recommendations was accepted without qualification: large food retailers were to improve their "community involvement practices" (Social Exclusion Unit, 2001, p. 127). However, the government admitted this outcome was "non-quantifiable" (Social Exclusion Unit, 2001, p. 127).

The *National Strategy for Neighbourhood Renewal* process was intended to empower communities and increase stakeholder involvement (Robinson, Shaw, & Davidson, 2005). Instead, it confirmed the fears of stakeholder participants, resulting in a "hollow" consultation without stakeholder recommendations being accepted into government policy.

New approaches to regional and rural development

Links between the rural economy and development actions: LEADER I (1991–1994) and LEADER II (1995–1999)

LEADER was introduced by the European Commission in 1991 to empower local rural communities to determine their own development objectives rather than respond to development priorities set by a central government. The acronym derives from the French *Liaison Entre Actions de Développement de l'Économie Rurale* and means "Links between the rural economy and development actions." LEADER sought to change a top-down culture of rural policymaking to a bottom-up, community-led approach. Recently, the European Commission wrote:

> The bottom-up approach means that local actors participate in decision-making about the strategy and in the selection of the priorities to be pursued in their local area. . . . LEADER conceives the local people as the best experts on the development of their territory. It can be seen as a *participatory democracy* tool supplementing the electoral *parliamentary democracy*.
> (European Network for Rural Development, 2012,
> emphasis in original)

Local food in national English policy 69

The promotion of "local agriculture" was one of five initial priorities (EC, 1991). Later iterations of LEADER did not retain the phrase *local agriculture,* although local agricultural and food projects remained eligible through LEADER.

LEADER's influence on local food activities in England was twofold: it promoted locally initiated agricultural and food projects and established local-level governance to fund those projects. In 1992, small-scale pilot projects for impoverished rural communities were launched. England's first LEADER project supported a "Folk Arts and Cider Festival" and a "Festival of Food and Drink" to "promote off-season tourism" in the Southwest (EC DGA, 1994, Festivals, para. 4).

After LEADER I, successive iterations of LEADER expanded in geographic scope and funding, facilitating the formation of an increasing a number of local LEADER groups (Table 3.3). In LEADER II, EU evaluators identified English projects supporting the "organic food chain, regional marketing, niche products, quality improvement and market placement of local products" and "rare varieties and breeds, orchard meadows" (Austrian Institute for Regional Studies and Spatial Planning, 2003a, p. 203).

The activities supported by LEADER I and LEADER II were enabled, or *animated*, through *Local Action Groups* (LAGs), which required the participation and decision-making of a cross-sector group of local stakeholders (EC, 1991). The EC DGA considered rural and agricultural development as a socially mediated process reliant upon local human capital, local resources, and local relationships:

> Before trying to bring a development project into being, it is ne-cessary [sic] to identify the potential human capital in a community and the economic potential of a value-added approach. It is also necessary - and this is absolutely vital - to win the con-fidence [sic] of local players, to give them optimism and a positive vision of their future, so that they genuinely wish to be part of a development process.
>
> (Pujol, 1994 (revised 1995), Chapter 2, para. 2)

Promoting the self-confidence of local-level stakeholders was considered necessary to meet LEADER's capacity-building goals because "remote,

Table 3.3 LEADER implementation in England, including funding levels

Phase	Duration	Local action groups	Total funding
LEADER I	1991–1993	1	£1 million
LEADER II	1994–1999	21	£20 million
LEADER+	2000–2006	26	£112 million
LEADER Approach	2007–2013	65	Minimum 5% of RDPE

(ekosgen, 2010, pp. 5, 9, 20, 23.)[3]

70 *Local food in national English policy*

disadvantaged rural areas, [are] especially where the self-confidence of the local population has been undermined by centuries of cultural and political repression" (Ray, 1998, p. 86).

The EU evaluators of LEADER considered LEADER II in England a model for the rest of Europe because of the cultural change embodied in projects related to direct marketing, use of the cultural landscape in branding efforts, and agricultural tourism (Austrian Institute for Regional Studies and Spatial Planning, 2003a, p. 168). Despite its model European status, the English government wished the program prioritized economic development objectives.

LEADER was often subjected to central government interference (Austrian Institute for Regional Studies and Spatial Planning, 2003a, b, 2006; Carnegie UK Trust Rural Programme, 2010; ekosgen, 2010, 2011; Metis GmbH, AEIDL, & CEU, 2010; Ray, 1998, 2000, 2002; Shucksmith, 2000, 2012). The Treasury's matching funds for LEADER projects were withheld at times and government managers favored evaluating projects by short-term job creation statistics rather than long-term capacity-building measures (ekosgen, 2010; Office of the Deputy Prime Minister, 2006; Ray, 1998; Shucksmith, 2000; von Meyer et al., 1999). Also, delays in the start of each LEADER program resulted in significant gaps in the pay for local-level LEADER coordinators, resulting in a loss of program facilitation expertise as staff sought other jobs. LEADER was unable to change the larger social, historical, and political context of political authority operational in local English communities.

Yet, LEADER was resistant to overt manipulation and co-option: its implementation, and the involvement of local stakeholders, was a European Commission requirement. Its bottom-up focus on stakeholder participation did not fit into prevailing, top-down narratives of the British government's rural development policy. In the 176-page 2000 Rural White Paper, *Our Countryside*, LEADER was only listed three times: first, on page 81, in a small text box separate from the main report; second, passingly on page 156; and third, in a one-paragraph description in the Appendix.

LEADER was an "orphan" program. It was a requirement of the EU. The Treasury was exposed to political risk if the LAGs made poor spending decisions. And, perhaps most importantly, British policymakers could not credibly try to take credit for LEADER's positive outcomes: they would have to acknowledge the EU origins of LEADER and that local stakeholders were capable of making their own spending decisions.

English "devolution:" Regional Development Agencies, 1998–2011

The Parliament passed the Regional Development Authorities Act in 1998, which was intended to regionalize the administration of central government and EU-financed programs (*Regional Development Agencies Act 1998*, 1998; Ward, Lowe, & Bridges, 2003). English "devolution" was implemented from the top down and did not create an elected body of representatives for England. Devolution in Scotland and Wales included the formation of national assemblies

Local food in national English policy   71

with elected representatives. The English narrative of regionalism did not coincide with greater local autonomy and participation in decision-making (Hewitt & Thompson, 2012). Figure 3.1 is a simplified diagram illustrating the location of British governmental institutions and their relationship to EU institutions involved in the CAP.

The RDAs were to "co-ordinate regional economic development and regeneration, enable the English regions to improve their relative competitiveness and reduce the imbalances that exist within and between the regions" (Allen, 2002, p. 23). By 2000 the nine RDAs became the main governmental units responsible for implementing EU rural development programs. In addition to formal policies, the RDAs provided ad hoc support to the Regional Food and Drink Groups, sponsored food festivals, and provided financial assistance for local food business incubators (Elliott J. et al., 2005). It is their formal policy activities that are considered next.

Implementing the English Rural Development Program, 2000–2006

The English Rural Development Program (ERDP) represented a shift away from an agriculture-centric rural policy and to a geographic approach to rural community development that was more common in Europe (Falconer & Ward, 2000; Lowe & Ward, 1998; Marsden & Sonnino, 2008; Pike et al., 2011; Ward & Lowe, 2004). This shift resulted in significant opposition from Britain's agricultural lobby groups (EU Committee, 2008, pp. 15, 42–43,82; Falconer & Ward, 2000).

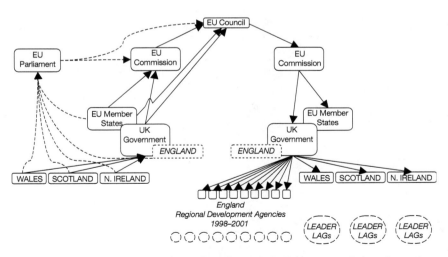

Figure 3.1 Simplified diagram of British and European institutions. Policy formation is depicted on the left and policy implementation on the right.[4] Entities with separate governing authorities bounded by solid lines.

Beginning in 2000, two ERDP initiatives, the Rural Enterprise Scheme (RES) and the Processing and Marketing Grant (PMG), could be used to support local and regional food activities (Curry et al., 2002; DEFRA, 2002d). Several activities related to local food production and marketing were identified as a "key national priority" by MAFF:

> Priorities for action at national level include: collaborative groupings of producers; initiatives linking parts of the food chain; marketing of organic products; consumer and quality assurance schemes (including traceability); specialty foods and initiatives involving protected name status.
> (MAFF, 2001, p. 39)

MAFF funds could be used for "establishing farmers markets," "developing and promoting the regional/local branding of products (including use of EU protected designations. . .)," and "establishing collaborative marketing groups to market products to an enhanced standard" (MAFF, 2001, p. 39).

While the EU-initiated programs presented a window of opportunity for England's rural development groups, rural development policy was at a disadvantage. Compared with agriculture it had less influence and funding, as illustrated in Figure 3.2 (Lowe & Ward, 1998; Ward & Lowe, 2004). Nine out of ten schemes in the ERDP were dedicated exclusively to producers (MAFF, 2001). Most rural development funding was devoted to agri-environmental payments for farmers. Unlike farm and conservation payments, rural development funds required a match from the Treasury. Only the Rural

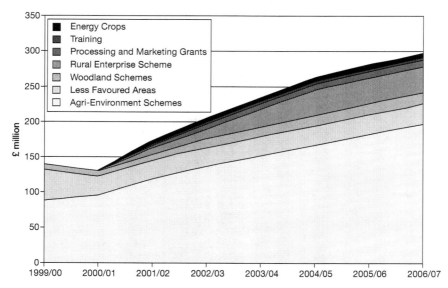

Figure 3.2 England's proposed development spending by scheme, 1999–2007; DEFRA (2002a, section 7.2.4).

Enterprise Scheme (RES) was available to non-farmers and it was still available to farmers.

The RES clustered several different EU policy objectives into ten types of eligible activity, each of which had different application criteria. The eligible activities were:

- setting up farm relief and farm management services;
- marketing quality agricultural products;
- basic services for the rural economy and population;
- diversification of agricultural activities;[5]
- agricultural water resources management;
- development and improvement of infrastructure;
- encouragement of tourist and craft activities;
- investment in agricultural holdings;
- renovation and development of villages; and
- protection of the environment in connection with agriculture (MAFF, 2001, pp. 11–12).

Several sources show that local food activities were funded through the RES (DEFRA, 2002c; Evans, 2003; Ilbery et al., 2010; Little et al., 2012; Watts et al., 2009). The degree to which the RES supported local food activities was not identified by DEFRA, NGOs, or academic researchers. Expenditure data in Figure 3.3 show that 73 percent of RES expenditures in 2001 were for agricultural activities related to agricultural diversification, farm relief, and management services.

While the RES encompassed a variety of uses, including non-farm support, the Processing and Marketing Grant was narrowly targeted to farmers wishing to undertake substantial projects costing £70,000 and higher (MAFF, 2001).

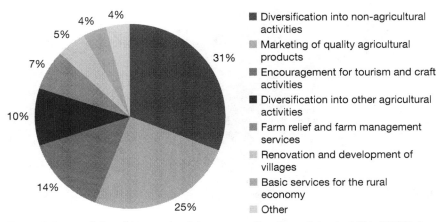

Figure 3.3 Actual Rural Enterprise Scheme spending by activity in 2001 (DEFRA, 2002b, p. 5).

74   *Local food in national English policy*

The PMG funded collaborative and cooperative marketing efforts (Plunkett Foundation, 2003). Few sources report the use of the PMG for local food projects (Ilbery et al., 2010; Little et al., 2012; Watts et al., 2009). Like the RES, the degree to which the PMG supported local food activities was not established by DEFRA, NGOs, or academic researchers.

Previous PMG schemes existed in 1991–1993 and 1994–1996, but had been discontinued. Throughout the ERDP, government-funded evaluators focused outcomes assessments on national, sector-wide impacts of the PMG and not individual farmer impacts (ADAS & University of Reading, 2003; Elliott, 2003). The small share of ERDP funds allocated to the PMG suggests that national, sector-level impacts were an inappropriate focus of program outcomes. The PMG did, however, result in individual producer benefits (Elliott, 2003, p. 6) and regional impacts (Watts et al., 2009).

Limited government intervention a by-product of advocacy group segmentation

Prior to the farm crisis, there was awareness of limited access to food shops in rural and urban areas; a connection to food quality, health, and income; and a desire to diversify the rural and agriculture economies. Local food was part of these policy dialogues. However, urban–rural linkages were not established in policy as they were in the US. This was due to a higher level of segmentation between urban, rural, and agricultural advocacy groups in Britain than in the US.

If national policymakers lacked a coherent direction on local food, so too did British advocacy groups. Framings of local food, its expected outcomes, and the actions needed to enable food localization differed across *and within* organizations. Many British farm, rural, and food advocacy groups remained focused on domestic issues even though EU-initiated programs were creating new *domestic* policy opportunities.

In 1994, the SAFE Alliance promoted changes to the CAP to "support organic and low input, more sustainable agriculture" and reduce surpluses on the world market (SAFE Alliance, 1994, p. 49). The report did not include recommendations on LEADER, even though the first LEADER pilot had just concluded and LEADER II was expanding to 21 English communities. Instead, SAFE focused on critiquing the food industry's use of long-distance food transport resulting in excessive food miles (SAFE Alliance, 1994). SAFE merged with the National Food Alliance (NFA) in 1998 to form Sustain.

In 1999, Sustain's food miles report, *Still on the Road to Ruin*, did not mention the CAP, rural development funding, or LEADER. It recommended government "assistance to be set aside for direct marketing schemes" including "cheap loans and grants" and support for mobile abattoirs (Sustain, 1999b, p. 16). Higher priorities for Sustain were labeling food products with their country of origin and a new carbon tax for food transport (Sustain, 1994, republished 2011, p. 55; 1999b, p. 16).

Local food in national English policy 75

By contrast, a 1996 *urban* agriculture report jointly authored by SAFE and NFA discussed *rural* issues more thoroughly than either food miles report. It proposed direct "local food links" between rural growers and urban consumers (T. Garnett, 1996). Sustain continued this food poverty work, which focused on urban agriculture projects and local food networks. Its network was urban-oriented and did not make explicit connections to rural food poverty (Sustain, 1999a, c).

Sustain's food poverty and urban agriculture work exemplified the lack of consensus on how to frame local food. There was also a lack of consensus with how to pursue policy change. Policy targets, strategies, and tactics differed across organizations. Through 2001, at least three national advocacy groups— Sustain, the Council for the Protection of Rural England (CPRE),[6] and Friends of the Earth UK (FOE–UK)—published reports that promoted local food (Bullock, 2000; CPRE, 1998 (reprinted 2002), 2001a, g, 2002; FOE UK, 2001; Garnett, 1996; SAFE Alliance, 1994; Sustain, 1999a, b, c, 2001).

Sustain favored criticisms of the food industry, in order to mobilize its supporters and gain media attention. CPRE favored local resistance, in order to mobilize its stakeholders against domestic food retailers, such as Tesco supermarkets, through its *Food Webs* report. Unlike Sustain and CPRE, FOE-UK favored direct interaction with the government and issued detailed policy recommendations. One recommendation was that RDAs direct the Agricultural Development Scheme and Rural Enterprise Scheme to support farmers markets; and another that Parliament develop new legislation to reduce barriers for farmers markets (Bullock, 2000, pp. 17, 19, 24–28). The lack of consensus in advocacy groups prevented the formation of a *collective action frame* and common policy goals needed for *consensus mobilization* (Tarrow, 1998, p. 113).

The lack of collective action frame and segmentation between advocacy groups affected national policymakers' response to local food. The most prominent example is the *Food Poverty Eradication Bill*, and later versions, called the *Food Justice Bill*, introduced in Parliament between 2001 and 2005. These bills supported the development of "local food poverty eradication strategies" (Deputy Speaker, 2002; Food Justice, 2005; *Food Justice Strategy Bill*, 2003, 2004; *Food Poverty (Eradication) Bill*, 2001; *Food Poverty Eradication Bill*, 2001). They adopted a community-initiated approach to address poverty, as suggested by the LIPT. Similar to the LEADER approach, local groups of stakeholder-led "local food authorities" would promote "local food economies" to address food poverty. While these bills did not exclude rural area activity, they did not make explicit links to rural development or preexisting rural policies like LEADER. The initial bill was endorsed by 12 organizations, including Sustain and FOE-UK, but lacked support from farmers, rural groups (including CPRE), and urban agriculture groups (Dalmeny, 2001). The final bill, in 2005, listed two farm organizations as supporters, one of which was the Soil Association (SA) (Food Justice, 2005). Likely, if one of the *Food Justice* bills had passed, it would have resulted in an overlap with LEADER and its LAGs.

76 *Local food in national English policy*

Fragmentation within and across policy communities resulted in a fragmented policy response. It is not surprising that national policymakers did not establish dedicated policies for local food and that local food projects had limited support through existing rural development programs.

Post-farm crisis era: Reconnecting farmers and consumers, 2001–2007

After 2001, the English government sought to address the underlying economic conditions believed to have contributed to practices enabling the FMD outbreak (Curry, Sir Donald et al., 2002). With televised culling of livestock herds (some programs showing the burning of carcasses) and closure of popular walking paths through the countryside, Prime Minister Blair personally managed the government's crisis response, events thoroughly detailed by Ward et al. (2004). The "farm crisis" created a significant window of opportunity to reframe Britain's farm, rural, and food policies (Ward et al., 2004; Wilkinson et al., 2010b).

Prior to the crisis, there was a need to nullify the British agricultural lobby's opposition to accepting EU CAP reforms on agri-environmental payments and compliance measures. The farm crisis provided the Blair government with a significant focusing event to increase public pressure on farm lobby groups.

An independent Policy Commission on the Future of Farming and Food was formed to conduct wide-ranging consultations to inform the Government policy response (The "Curry Commission"). The Commission solicited public and stakeholder input from a broad range of interests in September, 2001 and received comments from 303 individuals and 330 organizations (Policy Commission on the Future of Farming and Food, 2001). Additional input was sought through four meetings grouped by stakeholder interests: farmers, consumers, the food industry, and the "Green Groups" (Wildlife and Countryside Link, 2001b). Through these four sectorial groupings, the Curry Commission created *collaborative* policy windows.

An NGO facilitator managed each stakeholder grouping and organized a two-hour meeting with the Curry Commission (Wildlife and Countryside Link, 2001b). The Green Groups were coordinated by the Wildlife and Countryside Link and included at a minimum: the CPRE, the Council for British Archaeology, FOE-UK, the National Trust, the Royal Society for the Protection of Birds, WWF (UK), and the Youth Hostel Association (Wildlife and Countryside Link, 2001b, p. 3). They understood the Commission's meeting was a collective policy window: they wanted a "slick choreographed approach" to their proposals and prepared a "Hymnsheet" of talking points (Wildlife and Countryside Link, 2001b, pp. 2–3).

The Green Groups also recognized that the policy window available for their environmental priorities was dependent on their linkage with socio-economic goals:

Local food in national English policy   77

Policy Commission likely to make recommendations in two key areas:

Commercial prospects for farming. . .*[and]*

What would an efficient, market driven **public support** for farming look like (a blue-print for how public money should be spent, NOT just £bns more on agri-environmental schemes).
(emphasis in original, Wildlife and Countryside Link, 2001b, p. 1)

Through policy collaboration, the separate, pre-crisis era policy narratives of economic competiveness and sustainability were presented alongside each other (Wildlife and Countryside Link, 2001c).

Environmental and wildlife organizations linked their recommendations to rural development policy and preexisting concerns about access to food shops (CPRE, 2001b–f; FOE UK, 2001; La Trobe, 2002; Wildlife and Countryside Link, 2001a, c). CPRE indicated that the ERDP could be used to support local "access to affordable fresh foods in 'food deserts'" (CPRE, 2001f, p. 2). The facilitator of consumer groups, the National Consumer Council, communicated that food poverty and affordability was understood as an urban *and rural* issue:

Enterprises that keep wealth within local agricultural communities should also be encouraged to stop small farms dying off, and to help local people have cheap access to fresh produce at a fair price via not-for-profit enterprises.
(National Consumer Council, 2001, p. 10)

The shared policy window motivated advocacy groups to stitch their narratives together. Input to the Curry Commission portrayed local food as both a social and economic component to sustainability, and linked urban and rural concerns about access to food shops and food affordability.

Promoting "reconnection" and local food in the Sustainable Farming and Food Strategy, 2002

The Commission's *Farming and Food: A sustainable future* characterized local food as a way to enhance farm income, promote rural development, provide more food choices, reconnect consumers and farmers, and restore trust following the FMD epidemic (Curry, Sir Donald et al., 2002; DEFRA, 2002e). The Curry Commission is often credited with framing the government's policy response to local food (Kirwan & Maye, 2013). However, it did not propose new policies related to local food. The Curry Commission report was primarily symbolic, enhancing the visibility and establishing legitimacy of local food activities.

Local food was not portrayed as a niche and could be mainstreamed. Consumers were encouraged to make local food purchases through mainstream

78 *Local food in national English policy*

supermarkets, because local foods were not accessible from regular farmers' markets (Curry et al., 2002, pp. 45–46). Local food was not promoted as a way for communities to increase their agency in the farm and food system. Rather, the Commission emphasized *stability* by linking local food to preexisting policies, institutions (e.g. the RDAs and Food from Britain), and policy narratives.

Local food was a central component in the Commission's policy narrative reconnecting producers and consumers following the farm crisis. It aspired for policies that could "reconnect consumers with what they eat and how it is produced" (Curry et al., 2002, p. 30). The producer–consumer relationship was social, based upon "closeness" rather than a geographic measure (Curry et al., 2002, pp. 44–45).

Local food was framed in a marketism narrative: "The expanding market in local food — cutting out the middle man, and reducing transport costs — presents opportunity" (Curry et al., 2002, pp. 16–17). However, opportunity anticipated through more direct producer–consumer relationships in the marketism narrative struggled when addressing the scale of producers reaching supermarkets.

The direct-to-consumer approach of "cutting out the middle man" was perceived as a barrier for larger volume producers:

> A final barrier is access to customers. Local producers have found some innovative solutions to the problems this presents. Some producers are delivering through box schemes or opening farm shops, while farmers markets have been embraced with enthusiasm. Farmers markets are a successful way forward for some, and we strongly welcome the way this sector has grown. But their scale means that they cannot currently be a major distribution channel for any but the smallest producers.
>
> (Curry et al., 2002, p. 45)

The Commission recommended that the RES and PMG support local food activities and increase the volume of local food distribution (Curry et al., 2002, p. 44). No one model for increasing local food processing and distribution was favored (Curry et al., 2002, p. 43). The Commission recommended that the current grant levels on the PMG be increased *and decreased* to "allow smaller enterprises access to funds. This may be important in stimulating the small local producers who will supply local food markets" (Curry et al., 2002, p. 43).

The Commission carefully crafted a policy narrative focused on larger-volume producers—the report's main agricultural audience—while avoiding alienation of smaller-scale producers who had substantial public support. The Curry Commission's recommendations promoted *stability* through the continued reliance on preexisting private and public food system institutions. These included supermarkets, the RDAs, and QUANGOs, like Food from Britain and its associated Regional and Food and Drink groups (Curry et al., 2002, pp. 46, 119).

Despite a focus on mainstream markets, the Commission acknowledged the transformational potential of local food projects. The Commission observed that "consumers want more authentic food" and that the local food sector "has been created by small farming and food businesses that have gone against the recent trend of consolidation" (Curry et al., 2002, p. 16). Yet, the "reconnection" narrative was not a paradigm shift and was applied to reestablish trust in farmers, the government, and the food retail industry.

It was also politically pragmatic. Curry sought to sway a reluctant farm community to accept agri-environmental payments in lieu of production subsidies (Ward et al., 2004) and signal to the European farming community that Britain would push for a market-oriented farm policy in the 2003 CAP reform. Although the Commission's recommendations were non-binding, the government accepted most recommendations in its *Sustainable Farming and Food Strategy* (DEFRA, 2002d; HM Government, 2002). The reconnection narrative made the local food sector a legitimate part of agricultural policy, through elevating and not marginalizing its activities. It was a high water mark for the influence of local food proponents on a major governmental policy report.

The Strategy for Sustainable Farming and Food, 2002

Environmental sustainability became the narrative focus of the government's response to the Curry Commission's recommendations through a command paper called the *Strategy for Sustainable Farming and Food* (SSFF) (DEFRA, 2002d, 2006c; HM Government, 2002). The "farm crisis" resulted in a renaming of the Ministry of Agriculture, Fisheries and Food to the Department for Environment, Food, and Rural Affairs. Despite the renaming, post-crisis policy focused on the agricultural sector.

The environmental narrative was only a frame containing traditional agricultural and rural concerns: the report was not organized by the common triad of economic, social, and environmental sustainability. The first section of the report was structured topically, with sections on:

- promoting cooperation and reducing inefficiency in the food chain;
- promoting agri-environmental schemes;
- attracting new farmers;
- increasing food safety;
- addressing animal welfare issues; and
- how rural economic conditions differ from urban areas (DEFRA, 2002d, p. 4).

Adding value, through local food, was the first initiative proposed in the SSFF, to support "reconnecting with the market" (DEFRA, 2002d, p. 15).

Local food was linked to economic competiveness, a metaphor recurring throughout the SSFF:

80 Local food in national English policy

the Curry report stressed the importance of **adding value** to increase returns from the market and so improve competitiveness. One way is to respond to the demand for locally produced foods; both delivered direct to local consumers, through box schemes for example, and made available through farmers markets, multiples and other retailers. It makes excellent business sense and there are clear benefits to the environment if transport and packaging are reduced. And farmers markets not only benefit producers, but help bring life to town centres and connect consumers with the rural economy.

(emphasis in original, DEFRA, 2002d, p. 16)

DEFRA acknowledged the potential of local food to transform relationships between producers and consumers, revitalize rural towns, and improve the rural economy. Like the Curry Commission report, local food was not marginalized or considered a "niche." It was one of many strategies to promote value-added agriculture through the PMG and RES (DEFRA, 2002d, p. 16).

Partnerships were encouraged with the farming sector, food chain, and business community. The SSFF justified the need for collaboration by quoting FOE-UK: "Farmers need to be prepared to work in partnership with other farmers and with consumers, and in co-operatives to build local markets" (DEFRA, 2002d, p. 22).[7] NGOs (principally wildlife and animal welfare organizations) were specifically named to help coordinate with the Regional Development Agencies on SSFF implementation (DEFRA, 2002d, p. 47). However, "working together" on local food was limited to organizations favored by the government. Stakeholder organizations directly engaged in local and regional food were not invited to participate with the RDAs, including FARMA, FCFCG, CPRE, Sustain, and the SA.

Government support for collaboration within the supply chain was to be promoted through a new, privately operated but government-funded entity, the English Farming and Food Partnerships (DEFRA, 2002d, p. 22; 2005). The term "partnerships" is misleading—its membership was entirely composed of farmer-controlled businesses. Its main policy recommendation was for the government to establish a loan fund for small and medium agriculture-related businesses (English Farming and Food Partnerships, 2009).[8] While the *narrative* of the SSFF indicated the need for producers to collaborate with non-farmers, the *actions* taken by the government excluded non-farmer organizations as delivery partners in forming local food linkages.

The SSFF made two recommendations for local food, which were not related to agriculture. One focused on addressing health and food poverty, and was introduced through a quote from the National Consumer Council:

Our research among low-income consumers has shown that they would like greater access to locally produced food, which has not had a damaging effect on the environment and which meets high animal health and welfare standards.

(DEFRA, 2002d, p. 16)

Local food in national English policy 81

The proposal was the placement of "five a day co-ordinators" in regional Primary Care Trusts[9] to "help support new community initiatives funded by the New Opportunities Fund, many of which will link farmers directly to low-income consumers" (DEFRA, 2002d, p. 38). Other policies related to food poverty were not proposed.

The second non-agricultural policy was the Public Sector Food Procurement Initiative (PSFPI), to "encourage sustainable procurement of food, including organic food" (DEFRA, 2002d, p. 18). The emphasis on sustainable food rather than local food represented a shift from the Curry Commission's recommendations to favor locally produced food in government procurement (Curry et al., 2002, p. 104).[10] The PSFPI was to establish "how far, without breaching the EU procurement rules, public procurement can focus on sustainable products and ensure that English and indeed all UK producers are fairly considered" (DEFRA, 2002d, p. 20).

Local food purchasing was considered illegal by the British government in the early 2000s (Public Sector Food Procurement Initiative, 2006, p. 4). Great care was made to ensure that sustainable food purchasing was not equated to local food purchasing in England (Morgan & Sonnino, 2008, p. 176). The PSFPI developed guidance materials for small farm operators to make procurement bids (DEFRA, 2006b, 2007a, b; Public Sector Food Procurement Initiative, 2006). Emphasis later shifted to seasonal foods. Both government and advocacy group narratives of the PSFPI deemphasized use of "local" as a criterion in food procurement (Sustain, 2011c).

The SSFF used narratives of local food selectively and instrumentally. The transformative narrative of local food was bypassed and no new policies were implemented for local food. Greater inclusion of local food stakeholders in food policy institutions and greater citizen engagement, through community food projects, were not promoted in the SSFF. While the SSFF's narrative appealed to an environmental agenda, as did the Curry Commission's report, its policy content focused on agricultural policy.

Shifting narratives in the Strategy for Sustainable Farming and Food three years on

Following the Curry Commission report, DEFRA engaged in several research-oriented activities to learn more about the local food sector. In 2003, DEFRA formed a Working Group on Local Food and commissioned research on policy options for local food throughout the 2000s (DEFRA, 2003a, b, 2009a, b). One recommendation directed the government to use the term "regional quality foods" to encompass *locality* foods and local foods consumed near their point of production.

In addition, DEFRA favored promoting the ERDP schemes for local food in the year following the farm crisis. In a set of 55 case studies of ERDP projects, 85 percent were examples of local food production and marketing even though the majority of ERDP funds were spent on agri-environmental programs

82 *Local food in national English policy*

(DEFRA, 2002c). Also, midterm reviews of the RES and PMG provided well-substantiated and detailed recommendations for programmatic changes beneficial for the local food sector (ADAS & SQW Limited, 2003; ADAS & University of Reading, 2003; Elliott, 2003; Evans, 2003; Plunkett Foundation, 2003; Rural Partnerships Limited, 2003).

DEFRA's priorities began to shift. The Working Group on Local Food ended in 2003 after it had published a report on a multi-agency approach to supporting the local food sector (DEFRA, 2003b). The government did not include local food as a policy objective. Instead, it sought to use food miles as an outcomes indicator for the "reduced environmental cost of the food chain" (number 4.10 in Figure 3.4). Other government documents from 2005 and 2006 showed that the government had not made progress on applying the RES and the PMG to the local food sector's needs (Andrews & Dunn, 2005; DEFRA, 2006c).

In July 2006, DEFRA reviewed its progress on implementing the SSFF in a report entitled *Sustainable Farming and Food Strategy: Forward Look* (DEFRA, 2006c). The predominant narratives were consumer choice and environmental sustainability of local food. In the cover letter, the then Secretary of State for Environment, Food, and Rural Affairs, David Miliband, promoted DEFRA's efforts at making government procurement more sustainable. Of local food, he stated:

> as consumers we all have a role to play, in ensuring that our patterns of consumption respect environmental limits. For the farming and food sector this presents real opportunities both to meet the demand for high quality, seasonal or locally sourced produce delivered through strong local food chains and, importantly, to help deliver our future energy needs.
> (forward by David Milliband, Secretary of State for Environment, Food, and Rural Affairs in DEFRA, 2006c, p. 4)

Rather than utilize government policy to support the local food sector, *A Forward Look* promoted the non-profit sector engaging in consumer behavior change to meet objectives defined in the SSFF.

A Forward Look focused on the roles that civil society should take in promoting local food *without* government support. The government still directed civil society on how its actions could support government-defined policy objectives, such as "bring[ing] direct access and greater awareness of the health benefits of fresh fruit and vegetables to those on lower incomes" (DEFRA, 2006c, p. 47). As in earlier policy reports, the government wanted to be associated with local food. Yet, it made no new commitments to support the sector's development. Nor did *A Forward Look* measure progress on goals established for the local food sector in *Strategy for Sustainable Farming and Food*.

The shift to an environmental narrative emphasized a linkage of food miles to environmental sustainability, value-adding, and collaboration, and the

Local food in national English policy   83

exclusion of local food from social sustainability, as shown in DEFRA's 2005 strategic plan (Figure 3.4). Observing these changes, Sir Don Curry, who chaired the *Implementation Group for the Sustainable Farming and Food Strategy*, issued his own three-year look back on post-farm crisis policies. He asserted that "creating opportunities for locally produced food" was an important social policy outcome but was disappointed in the shift away from the Curry Commission's "reconnection" narrative (Curry, 2006, p. 2). *A Forward Look* represented a pullback from the government's role in promoting social outcomes through farm and food policy.

Post-crisis changes to the ERDP: Ending schemes linked with local food

With the ERDP ending in 2006 and a new program established for 2007–2013, the government had an option of continuing existing schemes into the new program. The government had received information to improve the RES and PMG in their 2003 midterm reviews (ADAS & SQW Limited, 2003; Elliott, 2003; Evans, 2003). It commissioned the Plunkett Foundation to issue recommendations to increase food supply chain collaboration through the PMG (Plunkett Foundation, 2003). However, the government seized upon negative criticisms to justify ending the RES and PMG in 2006. Of the four enabling policies established in the pre-crisis era, only the RDAs and LEADER remained by 2006.

The government closure of the RES and PMG was not part of a well-established plan, despite its claims that ending the two schemes was based upon *Rural Strategy 2004* (DEFRA, 2006a, para 2). It had recommended *increasing* RES funding and maintaining the PMG in the *Rural Strategy* (DEFRA, 2004b, p. 31). As late as 2006, DEFRA communicated to the House of Commons that the RES and PMG "have been very popular and successful across the country" (Gardiner, 2006). *Why would DEFRA close very popular programs?*

DEFRA was facing another public credibility crisis. It needed to consolidate political support from its traditional agriculture industry allies. One way to do so was to close farm diversification programs unpopular among the mainstream agricultural community (Cumulus Consultants Ltd, 2006; NAO, 2004, p. 46; Plunkett Foundation, 2003; Shucksmith & Herrmann, 2002).

In the wake of the farm crisis, DEFRA's public support was still weak, and it was losing support from its strongest stakeholder community (Hyder Consulting (UK) Limited, 2008, p. 115). At the time, DEFRA's competency to administer farm programs was in question. In 2006, a third inquiry by the National Audit Office (NAO) was underway for payment delays affecting the majority of English farmers (NAO, 2006). Delays and improper payments were so severe the EU imposed fines for non-compliance totaling nearly £500 million by 2011 (NAO, 2011, p. 4; 2009, p. 29).

A NAO report recommended closing some ERDP schemes, due to program overlap (NAO, 2004). The audit identified duplication between the RES and

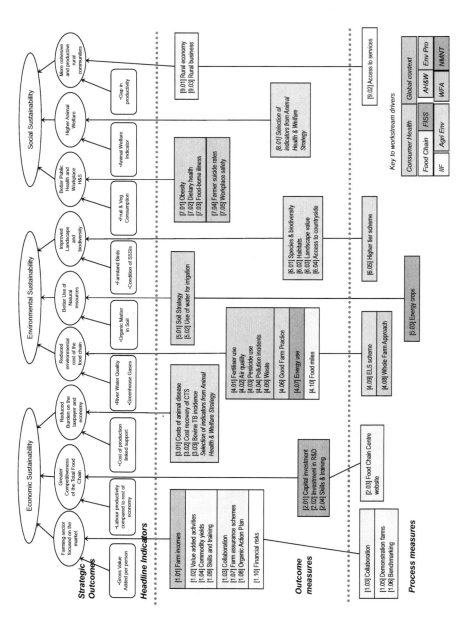

Figure 3.4 Diagram of SSFF implementation by economic, environmental, and social sustainability. (Andrews & Dunn, 2005, p. 5.)

Local food in national English policy   85

the Vocational Technical Scheme, not between the RES and PMG. Rather than cite the 2004 NAO report, and shift blame to the NAO, DEFRA accepted responsibility for scheme closure by claiming it was part of *Rural Strategy 2004*. Relatively few farmers were served by the PMG and RES and, unlike other programs, these programs lacked vocal supporters.

DEFRA's credibility crisis follows a pattern that Ruckelshaus identified as "battered agency syndrome" (Ruckelshaus, 1996; Weaver, 1986). It was safer to accept blame from a small number of users, gain credit from the mainstream farm community for ending "unneeded" programs, and avoid drawing further attention to the NAO. Reducing negative public criticism and re-solidifying support with its traditional agricultural allies trumped the concerns of a few program users.

The new Rural Development Program for England, 2007–2010

Like the ERDP, the new Rural Development Program for England (RDPE) supported a broad range of farm, agri-environment, forestry, and rural development activities. The RDPE replaced the ERDP's ten schemes with 28 "measures" (DEFRA, 2008a). This shift was primarily a change in nomenclature as supported activities were nearly identical to the ERDP (EC, 1999, 2005).

Local food activities previously eligible in the RES and PMG were now dispersed across five measures (listed in Table 3.4). Of the five, two were eligible for non-farmers (Measures 312 and 313). Yet, unlike the ERDP, government policy did not promote the measures for local food activities.

Of the five measures, only one connected with government policy reports: Measure 124, for cooperative development, was linked to the SSFF (DEFRA, 2008a, Section 5, pp. 30–31). This measure also supported activities formerly supported by the closed PMG. Only one of the 28 measures made an explicit link to local food: Measure 313 for rural tourism (DEFRA, 2008a, pp. 5–123, 124–125). With a dispersion of eligible activities across measures and inconsistent expenditure data from the RDPE, it is not possible to analyze the RDPE for parity with SSFF goals.

The RDPE gave the RDAs new flexibility to prioritize their deployment of the Measures (RDPE Network & Rural Services Network, 2009). As a result, regional plans varied in their priorities. Some regions did not offer all measures. Of the nine regions, only the Southeast prioritized local or regional food (RDPE Network, 2009). The Southeast ranked "quality food sales" as its third priority out of nine in total (RDPE Network, 2009, p. 3). The Southeast's plan allocated a high level of funds for agricultural value-adding, the second highest allocation of Measure 123 in England (Hyder Consulting (UK) Limited, 2010).

The government change in 2010 resulted in a 2–3-year duration of these Measures. Inconsistent implementation and frequent program changes continued through the RDPE.

86   *Local food in national English policy*

Table 3.4 Proposed expenditures of selected RDPE Measures relevant to local food activities, 2007–2013

RDPE measures	Proposed expenditures 2007–2013
Farmer-only Measures from Axes 1 and 3	
Adding value to agricultural and forestry products: Measure 123 (restricted to micro-enterprises)	£ 111,023,252
Cooperation for the development of new products: Measure 124	£ 64,114,395
Farm diversification into non-agricultural activities: Measure 311 (included retailing and processing)	£ 123,844,172
Measures eligible for non-farmers and farmers from Axis 3	
Support for the creation and development of micro-enterprises: Measure 312	£ 52,709,525
Encouragement for tourism activities: Measure 313 (includes "promotion of tourism activities linked to quality regional and local food culture and rural crafts")	£ 38,123,742

(DEFRA, 2008a, Section 5, p. 124; 2008b.)

LEADER+ (2000–2006) and the LEADER Approach (2007–2013)

Even though LEADER supported local food projects, it was not linked to the Curry Commission's "reconnection" narrative of local. Unlike the English rural development programs, LEADER continued on its own trajectory established through EU regulations. It was not affected by the World Food Price discussed in the following section.

The preexisting tensions between central government authority and local authority over program expenditures persisted and increased with LEADER+ (2000–2006) and the LEADER Approach (2007–2013). By 2013, the LEADER Approach had become the most significant source of public funds applicable to local food projects (see Tables 3.3 and 3.4).

Despite the apparent continuity of LEADER's development, its implementation was subject to delays, disruption, and interference. Due to the implementation gaps between LEADER II and LEADER+, and between LEADER+ and the LEADER Approach, program access, the meetings of the LAGs, and staffing for LAG facilitation were disrupted (Carnegie UK Trust, 2010; DEFRA, 2004a; Hyder Consulting (UK) Limited, 2008).

The English government criticized LEADER for its focus on capacity building instead of economic performance. The lack of economic indicators as performance measures were characterized as "peculiarities" reflecting a "lack of control over reported achievements by Program management" (Office of the Deputy Prime Minister, 2006, pp. 10, 112). Programmatic control and fiscal management, not the self-mobilization of local communities, was the

Local food in national English policy   87

focus of the English government's administration of the LEADER program (Carnegie UK Trust Rural Programme, 2010, pp. 30–31).

Tensions between central government and the LAGs increased when the RDAs became responsible for overseeing LEADER+:

> In some areas, LAG officers have highlighted that RDAs have retained decision-making powers (rather than just sign-off) which has been seen to actively disengage LAGs. Similarly, there have been reported tensions at times between (RDA) desire for outputs and LAG pursuit of innovative and bottom-up approaches.
>
> (ekosgen, 2011, p. 66)

These tensions resulted in the formation of two separate rural policy networks (Austrian Institute for Regional Studies and Spatial Planning, 2003a, p. 238). Agricultural producers favored the better-funded agriculture-centric ERDP and RDPE, which could support larger projects than LEADER. Many non-farm stakeholder groups favored LEADER over the ERDP and RDPE, partly due to its capacity-building approach. As a result, agriculture-related projects were not a spending priority of the LAGs in LEADER+ (ekosgen, 2010).

While specific information on local food activities is limited, LEADER+ continued to support local food activities (Carnegie UK Trust Rural Programme, 2010). The single English case study conducted by EU evaluators showed that Northumberland County had a priority for "adding value to local products" (Metis GmbH et al., 2010, p. 68). As with LEADER II, the EU evaluators of LEADER+ considered its capacity-building outcomes a prime example of LEADER's intended outcomes: "In England, LEADER+ is seen by some communities as the first time they have had involvement in designing a funding stream at strategy level" (Austrian Institute for Regional Studies and Spatial Planning, 2006, p. 68).

The LEADER Approach (2007–2013) represented a significant shift: It became part of the CAP and was no longer a separate European Community Initiative for rural development. With the mainstreaming of LEADER, the European Commission solidified the LEADER Approach as a *process* for rural development activities, composed of:

(a) area-based local development strategies intended for well-identified subregional rural territories;
(b) local public-private partnerships (hereinafter local action groups);
(c) bottom-up approach with a decision-making power for local action groups concerning the elaboration and implementation of local development strategies;
(d) multi-sectoral design and implementation of the strategy based on the interaction between actors and projects of different sectors of the local economy;
(e) implementation of innovative approaches;

88 *Local food in national English policy*

(f) implementation of cooperation projects;

(g) networking of local partnerships.

(EC, 2005, Article 61)

While the terminology differed from the LEADER I "support for 'local agriculture,'" the LEADER Approach remained a transformational, bottom-up strategy for rural development, including local food and agricultural products. In England, the LEADER Approach enabled several rural and market towns within commuting distance of major urban employment centers to maintain their own identity and autonomy (ekosgen, 2011, p. 65). The LEADER Approach funded farm shops and cafes, value-adding infrastructure (both on- and off-farm), farmers markets, micro-breweries, and food-related tourism (Carnegie UK Trust Rural Programme, 2010; Cumbria Fells and Dales RDPE Local Action Group, 2011; ekosgen, 2011; England's Regional Development Agencies, 2009; Southeast England Development Agency, 2009).

Central government could interfere with LEADER. However the EU requirements for a bottom-up approach through the LAGs, multi-sector participation, and "ring fenced" funding (*The Future of the Common Agricultural Policy. Volume I: Report*, 2008, p. 10) inoculated LEADER against "capture" by the national farm lobby and central government (Marsden & Sonnino, 2008; Shucksmith & Rønningen, 2011).

The features that inoculated LEADER against capture also limited advocacy group interest in LEADER. The multi-sector approach prevented a clear linkage of LEADER actions with any single advocacy group's goals. As a result, LEADER remained "orphaned" by both DEFRA and the advocacy community even though LEADER was a program well-suited for promoting bottom-up, local-level change in the food system.

Crisis-induced collaboration was not sustained among advocacy groups

The farm crisis opened a window of opportunity to engage with DEFRA on local food. Advocacy group policy collaboration influenced the Curry Commission's support of local food. Yet, collaboration was not sustained after the government issued policy positions in the SSFF. The last documented collaborative effort on local food was a 2003 discussion paper funded by three charitable trusts and with input from 27 organizations (Sustain & Food Links UK, 2003). Absent political necessity or external funding, the Green Groups did not collaborate on their own.

Amidst the opportunity to engage with DEFRA on local food, the attention of many wildlife, environmental, and countryside advocacy groups returned to their narrow interests with agri-environmental programs. FOE-UK, which developed detailed recommendations for the ERDP, did not issue further reports on local food policy. Wildlife and Countryside Link, which developed the narrative and policy links between rural development and agri-environmental policy, issued no further reports on local food policy. CPRE did not expand its lobbying on CAP to include rural development policies and focused only on agri-environmental payments (CPRE Policy Staff (b), 2011). Sustain did not target policy activities on existing programs, but on developing the food miles concept (Sustain & Food Links UK, 2003, p. 23).

The government would have observed diminishing advocacy group support for local food on the ERDP *before* making its policy decisions to close the RES and PMG in 2006. The government pullback from priorities established in the SSFF followed diminishing advocacy activity on local food and the ERDP.

Sustain's 2006 recommendations for the RDPE exemplify diminished advocacy group activity observable by the government. In its recommendations for a "more competitive and sustainable agriculture" in the new RDPE, Sustain did not refer to the RES or PMG, comment on how RDAs should implement the new RDPE, or recommend minimum or maximum grant funding levels for microbusinesses Sustain wished to promote (Sustain, 2006b, section 4). Their LEADER recommendations were equally vague: "we would call for a significant streamlining of administrative processes to support local decision-making" (Sustain, 2006b, section 6). Even though Sustain had rural and agricultural members, its one-paragraph recommendations for LEADER were so brief they provided no alternative perspective on information from government-funded evaluations.

In the resulting policy gap, the farm lobby reasserted its influence and "recaptured" England's rural development programming. A strategy of the farm lobby—waiting for environmental groups to shift their policy focus away from farm issues—was employed successfully in the 1980s (following from Wilkinson, Lowe, & Donaldson, 2010, pp. 339–340). In the 1980s, environmental groups narrowed their policy focus in the 1980s due to limited resource availability (Wilkinson et al., 2010). This was not the case in the 2000s. Sustain and the SA focused resources on a food miles campaign (Kenneth Hayes [Soil Association], 2007; Schleisman, 2003; Sustain & Food Links UK, 2003). Significant new resources were provided through two non-governmental grant programs, the first of which began as early as 2005 (Kirwan et al., 2014; MLFW Staff, 2011). Although the Curry Commission had raised awareness of the connection between English rural development programs and the local food sector, most national advocacy groups promoting local food did not focus on those policies.

A window for rural development groups identified in 1998 by Lowe and Ward and broadened by the Curry Commission, had passed by the end of the post-farm crisis era (Marsden & Sonnino, 2008; Shucksmith, 2009; Shucksmith & Rønningen, 2011). The result was an English Rural Development Program and Rural Development Program for England, which were primarily "rural in name only." Most funds went to agri-environmental payments and farmers remained eligible for nearly all rural programs. Community groups could access only a limited share of these funds.

90 *Local food in national English policy*

The post-farm crisis era can be characterized as one of missed opportunities for local food. While rural development programs were being regularly revised at the EU and national levels, the attention of England's main sustainable agriculture and food interests groups shifted towards climate change policy.

World food price crisis era: Mobilizing awareness of Britain's connection to global food issues, 2007–2012

A policy window on climate change opened in the late 2000s, culminating from an intense issue attention cycle, beginning in mid-2006 (Carter, 2008). During this time, climate change was elevated from low-profile to an issue of cross-party consensus (Carter, 2014). Britain undertook some domestic (e.g. the Climate Change Act) and foreign policy actions supporting climate change (with the EU Lisbon Treaty). However, by the end of 2010, significant counter-mobilization resulted in increased fragmentation on climate change policy (Carter, 2014). Local food was swept up in that counter-mobilization.

Attention to linkages between food transportation and climate change increased in the early 2000s (Schleisman, 2003; Sustain, 1999b; Sustain & Elm Farm Research Centre, 2001). By 2005, DEFRA began to explore scientific evidence that could quantify the environmental impacts of food transport through a lifecycle analysis approach (Smith et al., 2005). Potential reductions in energy used in food transportation were of interest to many domestic food industry groups (DEFRA, 2007c, d; This is Money, 2006). Public, media, policymaker, and advocacy group attention to issues of climate and food was high in 2007 and peaked in 2009 (Carter, 2014; Lockwood, 2013). Attention to climate change coincided with a period of international food shortages, due to poor weather conditions and higher fuel prices for food transport.

Three simultaneous events combined to form a "food crisis." The global average price of staple cereal crops doubled in 2007 (Wiggins, Keats, & Compton, 2010). Energy prices spiked, increasing the cost of food transportation (UN Food and Agriculture Organization, 2008). Third, the combination of these two trends resulted in an additional 173 million people becoming food insecure (The High Level Panel of Experts on Food Security and Nutrition, 2011). With a shift away from domestic self-sufficiency, a goal of the *Agriculture Act* of 1947, Britain had increased its reliance on food imports from less developed countries for fresh fruits and vegetables (DEFRA, 2010b; Food Chain Economics Unit, 2007). At the heart of the world food price crisis was a debate on social equity within a globalized food production and distribution system. Britain was maintaining its own food supply by importing some food from countries with food shortages.

English policymakers took a new interest in food policy. Three significant national policy reports were published and discussed, covering issues of global food security, Britain's reliance on food imports, and environmental sustainability. *Food Matters*, released in 2008, considered local food as part of a cultural shift in public attitudes toward food and a healthier diet (Cabinet

Office, 2008, pp. 9, 62, 64–66, 96). In 2010, a new, national food strategy *Food 2030* was issued (HM Government, 2010). It communicated that local, community food projects were beneficial, yet reducing food miles could introduce unintended harm to the environment and people in less developed countries (HM Government, 2010, pp. 15, 47). As local food was elevated, there was increased scrutiny from other government agencies, researchers, industry groups, foreign governments, and international development advocacy groups.

In 2011, the multi-year, research-intensive Foresight project on food sustainability issued its report, *The Future of Food and Farming: Challenges and choices for global sustainability* (Foresight, 2011d). The Foresight report was even more critical of local food and indicated that reducing food miles undermined economic development opportunities in less developed countries (Foresight, 2011d, p. 141).

This section begins with the introduction of two government reports, *Food Matters* and *Future of Food and Farming*, to illustrate how contention increased with local food due to its linkage to climate change. The second part describes development of the Coalition government's rural development policy in relation to its "localism" agenda.

Policymaker interest in local food, on both the environmental and rural policy fronts, declined in this period. Two national policies were linked to local food projects by 2012. With rural policies being the main means of public support for the local food sector since 1991, significant questions can be raised about policy target selection by advocacy group leaders. The organizations credited with promoting local food to policymakers were not pursuing the policy vehicles that offered the best chances of politically feasible public sector support for the local food sector.

Evaluating environmental claims of reduced food miles in government policy reports

Food Matters: Manipulation of government-funded research

Food Matters was issued by the Cabinet Office, and communicated high-level governmental interest in food issues across Cabinet departments. It acknowledged both the increasing popularity of local food and the multiple motivations that make up that public interest. This public interest was framed as an issue of consumer choice:

> (23) The increasing demand for 'local food' has multiple motivations, including wanting to support local food producers, a growing interest in provenance and its associations with quality, and in some instances a perception of lower environmental impact. The local food movement can play a part in reconnecting consumers with food producers, providing new market opportunities for farmers and small-scale food manufacturers,

92 *Local food in national English policy*

strengthening social capital within communities, and providing a focus for local economic development.

(Cabinet Office, 2008, p. 15)

The use of the marketism language of consumer choice and market opportunities allowed the government to position public interest in local food as one of many market-driven trends, and not a threat to mainstream markets (Cabinet Office, 2008, pp. 18, 19, 64).

Yet, within the marketism narrative, the transformative potential of local food was noted:

> These trends are seen by some as not just indicative of a renewed interest in the provenance and quality of food, but representative of an alternative food system that co-exists with 'conventional' systems of farming, food manufacture and retail.
>
> (Cabinet Office, 2008, p. 64)

The government used a "co-existence" metaphor to avoid critiques of the conventional retail system and avoided labeling local food as a niche market.

The Cabinet Office was aware that local food was increasingly contested. *Food Matters* avoided the use of the term "local food" and substituted specific forms of local food activities such as "farmers markets," "allotments," and "seasonal" food. While the government described the positive impacts of these activities, it proposed no new policy actions (Cabinet Office, 2008, pp. 62–64). Instead, it portrayed local food activities as part of a social marketing approach to policy change.

Most descriptions of local food activities were located in a section entitled "engaging people in the great food debate" (Cabinet Office, 2008, p. 62). The government was not a neutral arbitrator of competing scientific claims. The government's many positive examples of local food activities were bounded by a critique of local food's association with food miles:

Behind the warm glow of 'sustainable' and 'local' food propositions lies the reality of a complex world in which there are few simple answers or universal solutions.

(23) [shown earlier]

(24) But the environmental case for 'local' is less clear. **'Food miles' are a poor indicator of the environmental impact of food products** and small-scale production is not necessarily resource-efficient or low-impact.

(emphasis in original, Cabinet Office, 2008, p. 15)

The citation for the statement about the food miles indicator is a highly selective citation taken out of context from a 2005 DEFRA-commissioned report on *the Validity of Food Miles as an Indicator for Sustainable Development* (Smith et al., 2005).

The first sentence of the first finding of the 2005 report stated, "**A single indicator based on total food kilometres is an inadequate indicator of sustainability**" (emphasis in original, Smith et al., 2005, p. ii). This paragraph continued to argue that what was needed was "**a suite of indicators** which reflect the key adverse impacts of food transport" (emphasis in original, Smith et al., 2005, p. ii). Following this statement were three findings indicating that: data existed to track food transport, food transport had growing impacts on greenhouse gas emissions, and *total* social, economic, and environmental costs of food transport in the UK exceeded £9 billion per year.

The 2005 report had not proposed a single, miles-based measure. It accounted for the complexity of food transport by proposing a four-part metric that considered the differential environmental, economic, and social costs of food transport (Smith et al., 2005, p. iii). The combined use of the four indicators, three of which are distance-based, were found to be consistent and "strongly synergistic with the principles on which both the Sustainable Farming and Food Strategy and the draft Food Industry Sustainability Strategy are based" (Smith et al., 2005, p. 91).

In addition to the critique of environmental claims associated with food miles, *Food Matters* made an economic, equity-based argument against food miles. It cited information generated in a study funded by the Department for International Development (DfID): "there are social equity arguments for imports as well as more local food – UK demand for fresh produce grown in Africa supports over 700,000 workers and their dependents" (Cabinet Office, 2008, p. 15; Legge et al., 2006). The *Food Matters* report implied that a preference for local food would divert potential food purchases away from African growers. However, the DfID-commissioned study indicated that the decreasing British supermarket purchases of African produce were due to the growers' costs in complying with retailer food safety standards on pesticide usage (Legge et al., 2006, p. 46). The DfID-commissioned study confirmed the smallholder's "vulnerability from dependence on export sales," an issue identified by Sustain in its 1994 *Food Miles Report* (Legge et al., 2006, pp. iii, 24; Sustain, 1994, republished 2011, p. 8).

"Debate" in *Food Matters* seemed focused on the government injecting its views of food miles into the public debate, exacerbating rather than resolving competing environmental claims about local food.

Foresight: Ignoring peer-reviewed evidence in favor of opinion

Foresight is a government think tank devoted to analyzing future scenarios and identifying potential government policy responses. Its aim is to inform and influence British policymaking through issuing non-binding recommendations (Foresight, 2011a). The Foresight process is portrayed as a comprehensive effort to marshal scientific evidence to inform government policymaking (Foresight, 2011a, g). The development of a report by Foresight represents a significant political investment in a policy topic.

94   *Local food in national English policy*

The *Future of Food and Farming: Challenges and choices for global sustainability* focused on the sustainability of the international food trade, in terms of maintaining Britain's ability to import food despite potential supply chain disruptions from economic and environmental conditions. This framing of *food security* downplayed local food (Kirwan & Maye, 2013).

This Foresight report began during Brown's Labour government and was published in Cameron's Conservative–Liberal Democrat Coalition government. Its two-year development solicited input from 400 experts from 35 countries and commissioned 100 "peer-reviewed" publications (Foresight, 2011d). At least three types of documents were generated by Foresight:

- peer-reviewed journal articles;
- *Working Papers,* not peer-reviewed and occasionally written by a single author; and
- government-authored *Synthesis Reports* which interpreted a wide range of evidence, including Working Papers and commissioned, peer-reviewed research.

All three types of document are publically available on the Foresight website. However, Foresight is unclear about which publications it considered peer-reviewed: some publications were peer-reviewed journal articles and others were reviews of existing evidence on a topic.

The Foresight process was not free from government influence. All publications were government-funded and the Foresight process was also chaired by government Ministers (Foresight, 2011e). Its High Level Stakeholder Group was co-chaired by the Ministers for DEFRA and DfID (Foresight, 2011e).

Its expert panel had conflicts of interest, and its decision-making process was not transparent. The Lead Expert Group included the current Director of the International Institute for Environment and Development (IIED), whose organization was leading counter-mobilization efforts against the food miles narrative through blogs, reports, media, and government outreach (Buxton, 2011; Chi, MacGregor, & King, 2009; Foresight, 2011f; IIED, 2006, 2007; Legge et al., 2008; MacGregor & Vorley, 2006; Sarch, 2006; Sustain, 2006a). It also included Jules Pretty, the lead author of research indicating conditions under which local food production and distribution reduced greenhouse gas emissions (Foresight, 2011f; Pretty et al., 2005).

The decision-making process of Foresight was neither public or transparent. Foresight did not describe how it analyzed evidence or how it made decisions. With government Ministers chairing the process and the government funding its research and information gathering, the conclusions of Foresight cannot be considered independent policy positions. As a result, the Foresight process lacks many of the elements that give credibility to scientific evidence, such as independence from the political process, transparent methodology, and minimization of bias.

Local food in national English policy 95

Throughout the Foresight process on the *Future of Food and Farming*, evidence was either ignored or used selectively in order to substantiate a negative critique of food miles, and by association, local food. However, analyses of evidence generated in each document type communicated rationales for supporting local food activities. Recommendations on local food differed across documents, but none of the documents reviewed dismissed it outright— except the final report.

Peer-reviewed publications in academic journals offered the most thorough consideration of the pros and cons of local food and the food miles concept. A peer-reviewed review article on *Food Consumption Trends and Drivers* recommended a direction towards food localization in its penultimate sentence of its conclusion:

> As Feenstra (2002) aptly put it—we should endeavour towards 'A collaborative effort to build more locally-based, self-reliant food economies—one in which sustainable food production, processing, distribution, and consumption are integrated to enhance economic, environmental and social health'.
>
> (Kearney, 2010, p. 14)

Thus, the transformative narrative of local, bottom-up influences on the food system governance was present and available for consideration in the Foresight process. Another peer-reviewed article indicated reducing "food miles" in the post-farm gate supply chain could reduce carbon emissions. The remit of the researchers who made this observation was limited to analyzing energy usage *before* products left the farm (Woods et al., 2010, p. 1993). Their conclusion was based upon research by Pretty et al. (2005). Jules Pretty was on the Lead Expert Group (Foresight, 2011f). Thus, scientific evidence and expertise was available to debate the environmental outcomes of reduced food miles. Neither peer-reviewed article was cited in the final *Future of Food and Farming* report or related Working Papers and Synthesis Reports.

A Working Paper generated by the Foresight process, *Review of levers for changing consumers' food patterns*, considered the greater use of seasonal meats and field-grown crops in the UK as a medium priority, benefitting sustainability, but with some potential for unintended consequences (Stockley, 2011, p. 6). Stockley's paper referred to neither Kearney's nor Woods et al.'s peer-reviewed papers.

A Foresight Synthesis Report on *Changing Consumption Patterns* included Stockley's seasonal food recommendation verbatim (Foresight, 2011b, p. 5; Stockley, 2011, p. 6). *Changing Consumption Patterns* also referred to the work of the UK's Sustainable Development Commission, which had found positive environmental impacts for seasonal food and no evidence of related social inequities (Foresight, 2011b, p. 6). It noted that public policies often aimed to "maintain vibrant local food industries" and support the "competitiveness of local rural economies" (Foresight, 2011b, pp. 16, 17). This Synthesis Report

96   *Local food in national English policy*

made no recommendations on the promotion of seasonal food consumption, but directed readers to another Synthesis Report on *Meeting the Challenges of a Low Emissions World.*

Meeting the Challenges of a Low Emissions World drew on Stockley's Working Paper. It indicated that there is credible evidence that some food transportation is unnecessarily long, citing Pretty et al. (2005), and that as a result some food could be produced closer to where it is consumed (Foresight, 2011c, p. 16). It found that:

> Well-managed GHG [greenhouse gas] reduction strategies could also bring a range of collateral benefits, including. . . . A more diverse and localised production system that supports rural economies, increased adoption of sustainable practices [and] a reduction in food processing and transport.
>
> (Foresight, 2011c, pp. 10–11)

The Synthesis Report indicated that these changes would reduce greenhouse gas emissions while still providing affordable food to consumers (Foresight, 2011c, p. 20).

The final Foresight report did not utilize Kearney's conclusions about localized food systems, Stockley's evidence about seasonal food consumption, or Synthesis Reports' perspectives on local food. Rather Foresight's report linked local food to issues of international trade, national food sovereignty, national food self-sufficiency, and potentially *negative* impacts on greenhouse gas reductions (Foresight, 2011d, pp. 96–98,140).

Local food was discussed in the most detail in a section entitled *Enabling GHG reduction in the food system* (Foresight, 2011d, p. 140). The way this section of the *Foresight* report addressed local food was paradoxical. The report argued for the use of a life cycle assessment on greenhouse gas emissions. It then states that *all* social, economic, and environmental impacts should be analyzed. It argued for a comprehensive and simple approach, stating that " 'eat local food' could be a good rule of thumb to reduce emissions associated with transport and very often will be so" (Foresight, 2011d, p. 140). The conclusion restates the preference to rely on greenhouse gas emissions as a primary indicator of environmental outcomes.

The sole reference for these statements is a clearly marked opinion article, shown in Figure 3.5, published by the IIED (MacGregor & Vorley, 2006). This IIED opinion article was not referenced in the relevant Synthesis Reports, Working Papers, or peer-reviewed publications (Foresight, 2011b, c; Kearney, 2010; Stockley, 2011; Zeeuw, Veenhuizen, & Dubbeling, 2011). The inclusion of an opinion article runs counter to the Foresight process' mission to provide "thorough evidence-based, peer reviewed strategic insights" (Foresight, 2011a).

Evidence about local food was used selectively in the *Future of Food and Farming* report, a narrative tailored to the report's international audience. The report was translated into five languages and included a supplement, *Implications for China*, which detailed the negative consequences of their farm subsidies

Figure 3.5 Masthead of IIED's "Fair Miles" opinion article.
(Reproduced with permission of IIED, MacGregor & Vorley, 2006, p. 1.)

(Foresight, 2011h). Trade barriers imposed during the world food price crisis, by Russia, India, and several developing countries, were considered one of the reasons there was a food shortage (The High Level Panel of Experts on Food Security and Nutrition, 2011; UN Food and Agriculture Organization, 2008). From the government's perspective, if Foresight's report appeared to communicate support for locally produced foods, it could have undermined Britain's free trade policy narrative.

For the Foresight process, local food was an inconvenient issue and evidence was manipulated to suit government policy objectives. Further, the *Future of Food and Farming's* focus on rural development was framed in a developing country context, neglecting EU rural development programs.

***The push and pull of political localism: Recentralization in rural
development policy, 2010–2013***

The Coalition government utilized a political "localism" narrative to define its rural development policy. "Localism" resulted in both centralization and localization. It was imposed from the top down, without local participation or engagement in the decision-making about what localism meant (Featherstone et al., 2012; Plunkett Foundation, 2011).

Within this discourse regionalism had no legitimacy (Hewitt & Thompson, 2012, p. 265; Stephen Gilbert [Liberal Democrat, St Austell and Newquay], 2010), as exemplified in this Q and A document explaining the RDA abolishment in 2011:

> Does the return to Defra of RDPE delivery not go against the drive towards localism and the Big Society?
>
> No. It is an opportunity to develop greater national consistency in delivering the support that is available. This will be supported by an

98 *Local food in national English policy*

on-going sub-national network of delivery support. As part of the transitional planning, Defra is exploring how stakeholders at the local level can continue to influence delivery of the Program.

(DEFRA, 2011b, p. 5)

The pullback of RDPE administration from the RDAs was an unexpected outcome of the Coalition's budget-cutting and localism agendas (Featherstone et al., 2012). The decentralized structure of the RDA had made it more difficult for centralized advocacy groups (NFU, Country Land and Businessowner's Association, and Royal Society for the Protection of Birds) to monitor government activities (Hyder Consulting (UK) Limited, 2008, p. 115).

Reflecting on the government's change in narratives, the Plunkett Foundation reported to DEFRA that community food enterprises can experience difficulty accessing programs with frequent changes:

There is an issue of policy language where there is normally a lag between policy formers deciding to use a phrase and its adoption by communities themselves. Governments (and opposition parties) will frequently change language to aid their communication (civil society for third sector, Big Society for mutualism, localism for area-based). Communities take time to understand and adopt such language and there is an interim period where such language can cause confusion or even cynicism. Policy formers need to find ways of communicating in a language which both works in policy circles and respects the current language used at grassroots.

(Plunkett Foundation, 2011, p. 59)

Frequent changes limited the ability of poorly resourced producers and community groups to apply for funding: each change required new learning on how to link local priorities to new program guidelines. Further, terms useful to mobilize community members from the bottom up lost their impact when utilized by the government.

While the Labour government proposed a significant increase in rural funding, the Coalition government identified "significant savings from RDPE to contribute to reducing the budget deficit" (Council of the European Union, 2007; David Miliband [Secretary of State for Environment], 2007; DEFRA, 2011b, p. 1). Localism was associated with the Coalition's fiscal austerity measures.

In 2010, the Coalition government reorganized the RDPE into the Rural Economy Grant (REG), with five new "themes" (DEFRA, 2011a, b). With the shift to the REG came new program priorities, grant names and categories (Table 3.5), eligibility requirements, and administrative practices (DEFRA, 2012b; RDPE Network, 2012).

Of the five themes, the Rural Tourism and Agri-food themes could provide support to non-farm entities. The Rural Tourism theme promoted "local food"

Local food in national English policy 99

Table 3.5 Proposed expenditures of Rural Economy Grant Schemes relevant for local food

Rural Economy Grant Schemes	Start year	Proposed expenditures, 2011–2013
Farmer-only Funding		
Fruit and Vegetable Scheme in the Single Farm Payment	2010	Not stated
Farmer and non-farmer funding		
Rural Economy Grant	2011	£ 60,000,000
Rural Tourism	not stated	£ 10,000,000; from total
Agri-food	not stated	not stated; from total
Special Dairy Grant	2011 only	not stated; from total
Rural Growth Networks (5 communities only)	2011	£ 15,000,000

(DEFRA, 2012d; RDPE Network, 2012; Rural Payments Agency, 2011.)

and the Agri-food theme supported "the marketing and promotion of localized products" (DEFRA, 2012b, pp. 17, 24). Other documentation on the Agrifood scheme showed it was aimed at food exports and innovations in food technology. Its purposes were the support of "locality foods" (DEFRA, 2012d, p. 6). A portion of REG funds was targeted to five communities through a Rural Growth Network.[11] By 2011, the Coalition indicated that most RDPE funds had been allocated (Robin Mortimer [DEFRA Director of Wildlife and Countryside], 2011).

The shift from the ERDP to RDPE and RDPE to REG exemplifies how policymakers' desire to implement something "new" can override programmatic stability. The same localism narrative used to justify the pullback on delivery of the RDPE to central government was used to "push down" LEADER administration to the Local Action Groups. With closure of the RDAs, LEADER administration was placed on the LAGs, which were primarily voluntary associations coordinated by a single paid staff member. There was a one-year gap in spending during the shift between the RDPE and REG, resulting in the loss of LAG coordinators. The English evaluator for the LEADER Approach considered high volunteer involvement (e.g. 70 people per LAG) a way to "reduce the financial administrative burden" (ekosgen, 2011, p. 80) and to add benefit to the LEADER Approach (ekosgen, 2011, pp. 80–81). The evaluator did not consider that large numbers of volunteers, who may be unfamiliar with government accountability procedures, was a possible sign of program inefficiency.

With increased administrative responsibilities came less local funding discretion. The Coalition government emphasized the need for LEADER to directly create jobs or growth and indicated that a minority share of LEADER funds should be used for community projects (DEFRA, 2014b). "Localism" resulted in greater central government influence in the LEADER Approach.

100 *Local food in national English policy*

Despite the increased burdens on the LAGs, the LEADER Approach became a more significant mechanism to disperse rural development funds than the REG (Robin Mortimer [DEFRA Director of Wildlife and Countryside], 2011). Although no reliable documents were available to indicate whether spending targets for the LEADER Approach coincided with the 5 percent of CAP expenditures, Leader Approach expenditures exceeded the REG (compare Tables 3.3 and 3.5).

In May 2011, DEFRA indicated that £400 million of £530 million remained available through the LEADER Approach for 2011–2013 (DEFRA, 2011b). This £530 million total budget is nearly three times what government documents indicated was originally available through the LEADER Approach, and occurred when the Coalition government had cut rural development spending (DEFRA, 2011b). Five months later, in November 2011, £320 million remained available for 2011–2013 yet total expenditures were projected *higher* at nearly £600 million for 2007–2013 (DEFRA, 2011a). None of the government documents provided information on how funding levels were calculated. Nor do the calculations made by the English LEADER evaluator, ekosgen, utilize the same methods as the government or arrive at identical expenditure figures (ekosgen, 2010). Integrated into the RDPE, the LEADER Approach became a significant means of disbursing rural development funds.

Conclusion: The available policy windows did not align with advocacy group interests

Several types of policy opportunity were present across the three eras. Very few resulted in policy actions on local food. Windows of opportunity for local food were often in rural policy. However, sustainable food and agriculture interest groups were the most vocal proponents of local food. Advocacy groups often targeted government policy narratives, not actual policies. Opportunity and advocacy group interests were mismatched, with advocacy groups not responding to the windows available for local food. These reasons are varied and explained by type of policy vehicle: consultations, legislation, government reports, and EU policies and implementation.

Consultations

Researchers and policymakers have increasingly focused attention on how to increase the participation of civil society in the policy process (Jeremy Richardson, 2000). Typically, these efforts have focused on providing opportunities for advocacy groups, non-profit organizations, and other organized associations, to provide input to inform government policy formation. The government's desire to consult did not equate with a desire to follow through on stakeholder recommendations.

Consultations in the pre-crisis era provided forums to articulate the needs of the local food sector, identify common challenges, and proposed public policy responses as with the *Low Income Project Team,* the *Independent Inquiry into Inequalities in Health,* and *National Strategy for Neighborhood Renewal.* The broad consultations of the Curry Commission resulted in hybridization of local food narratives linked to producer income, consumer demand, and unmet demands of the status quo food system. The central government remained in control of policy decisions and provided no new or additional accountability that the government would follow through on consensus recommendations. Policies supporting local food activities did not result from consultations.

Legislation

The British Parliament had a good understanding of local food issues, as shown with 174 MPs who supported the *Food Poverty Eradication Bill* and in debate on the SFFS (*Eradication of Food Poverty,* 2001; House of Commons, 2002). Legislation formed statutory QUANGOs, such as the RDAs, Food from Britain, the Countryside Agency, the Sustainable Development Commission, and the BIG Lottery, each of which supported local food activities through ad hoc activities.

However, QUANGOs' semi-autonomous operations, which insulate them from direct political manipulation, are their weakness. They are not directly accountable to elected officials. These QUANGOs made ad hoc decisions to support local food through processes that were neither transparent nor participatory. Thus, most were not stable or reliable sources of support. All those that supported local food have been abolished or had their responsibilities shifted to other agencies, except the BIG Lottery.

If a QUANGO was formed specifically for local food, this assessment would have differed, especially if its leaders adopted a participatory, cross-sector decision-making process that held QUANGO leaders accountable to stakeholders.

Government reports

For local food, the significance of inclusion in government reports was primarily symbolic. Inclusion could elevate an issue recognizing grassroots stakeholders in the field, signaling openness to hearing their concerns, and raising public awareness of an issue (e.g. *Farming & Food: A sustainable future* and *Food Matters*).

With visibility came counter-mobilization. Government reports and scientific evidence used in government reports became sites of counter-mobilization (*Food Matters, Food 2030,* and *Future of Food and Farming*). The reports' high public visibility interjected doubt about the environmental claims associated with local food. Negative environmental critiques of local food colored its social and economic goals.

Peer-reviewed and scientific evidence did not safeguard claims made about local food. Government agencies engaged in claims-making by sponsoring

102 Local food in national English policy

research of organizations engaged in counter-mobilization (Legge et al., 2006, 2008; Sarch, 2006). Narrative hybridization in policy vehicles with low political accountability (e.g. reports, government-sponsored scientific panels, agency working groups, etc.) may well have set back local food as a palatable issue for policymakers. Stakeholder-led groups lacked capacity to effectively respond to government, media, researcher, and other advocacy group critiques.

EU policies and implementation

Britain's participation in the EU and the CAP brought new policy ideas and priorities (Falconer & Ward, 2000; Lowe & Ward, 1998; Ward & Lowe, 2004). Non-agricultural rural development was not a UK priority, nor was Britain's agricultural lobby initially supportive of agri-environmental payments. Without the coercive influence of the EU, these issues would have developed differently in Britain.

The EU process provided an important conducive *alternative venue* for British environmental organizations for priorities that would have been resisted by the British government. Yet, the alternative venue at the EU level was not utilized as a vehicle for local food though rural development policy.

The EU process created an alternative venue for domestic policy formulation. New regulations and program guidelines were developed by DEFRA to comply with CAP and European Community Initiatives (LEADER). Features of the EU policy process conducive to advocacy group engagement were:

- a predictable cycle of policy formation, implementation, and redesign facilitated policy campaign formation (versus unpredictable timing of crisis events);
- the political need for British political leaders to garner public and stake-holder support for EU initiatives;
- the potential for British political leaders to gain recognition—possibly enhancing Britain's international status;
- a need for detailed and technical information for DEFRA to form programs;
- implementation requirements as a condition of EU membership;
- additional funding that needed to be spent as part of EU membership; and
- relatively strong EU accountability measures for program non-compliance (e.g. fines with England's rural payment deficiencies).

The policy windows presented by the EU policy process resulted in policy actions for agri-environmental conservation and non-agricultural rural development. Opportunities were located *domestically* within DEFRA as it adapted European frameworks for use in England. Few advocacy groups provided detailed guidance to DEFRA on how to implement rural development programs in relation to local food (e.g. FOE UK (2001)). The

Local food in national English policy 103

degree to which EU-initiated policies supported local food activities in England was a matter of *degree of engagement and less political opportunity*.

A rural policy window existed, on a predictable cycle, at two levels: the EU Commission, and at DEFRA. Given those rural policy windows, how did advocates of local food respond to those opportunities and why did government support for local food decline over time?

A mismatch of actions with opportunities for local food

Separate policy streams, followed by separate policy communities, nearly converged in the pre-crisis era concerning issues of food poverty and access to food shops in urban areas and rural towns. Concerns about spatial disparities in health gained traction in health policy (LIPT and *Independent Inquiries into Inequalities in Health*), social policy (Social Exclusion Unit), urban policy (*National Strategy for Neighbourhood Renewal*), and rural policy (Rural White Paper of 2000). The *Independent Inquiry into Inequalities in Health* linked some issues of food poverty to the CAP. The 2000 Rural White Paper linked food poverty and access to food shops to rural development policy (Department of the Environment, 2000).

While cross-issue linkages were made by policymakers, these linkages were not supported by sustainable food and agriculture interest groups with narrower, specialist interests. Convergence across policy communities occurred when collaboration was imposed (e.g. Green Groups meeting). External influences resulted in consensus formation during the Curry Commission's consultations, and the collaborative discussion paper on local food policy options sponsored by three funders (Sustain & Food Links UK, 2003). Collective action was not sustained on food poverty or the SSFF's implementation. Instead advocacy on local food increasingly focused on the food miles narrative, especially when interest in climate peaked during 2006 through 2009 (see Chapter 4).

Policy advocacy on local food during both crisis-defined eras was fragmented. There was not a consensus among advocacy groups promoting local food on its narrative, policy targets, strategy, and tactics. As advocacy groups returned to their own interests, opportunities for collective action faded.

The world food price crisis was a policy window that encouraged competition between advocacy groups, as they sought to capture limited media, public, and policymaker attention. The resulting framing contest undermined the goodwill that existed from earlier collaborations and eventually resulted in counter-mobilization. The following chapter explores the rationality of advocacy group segmentation and desire for policymakers to respond to consensus and avoid conflict, through a case study of the food miles narrative in the UK.

Notes

1 This timeline is compiled from information in: EC (1991), *Regional Development Agencies Act* (1998), ekosgen (2010), *Public Bodies Act of 2011*, and EC DGA (2014).

104 *Local food in national English policy*

2 Of the secondary sources available on the Low Income Project Team, Nelson's account is the most comprehensive. Other accounts, Wrigley (2002) and Dowler (2007), were published later and focus more on policy outcomes than on the policy narrative development.

3 The estimated expenditure for the LEADER Approach varies by source document: no single source quotes the same estimated expenditure level. For example, the 5 percent of the £3.9 billion of the RDPE identified by the government is equal to £195 million (David Miliband [Secretary of State for Environment], 2007). No other source can confirm this funding level. The English evaluator, ekosgen, indicated that £170 million was available, 4.35 percent of the RDPE (ekosgen, 2010) and the Carnegie Trust UK indicated that £105 million was available, about 2.7 percent of the RDPE (Carnegie UK Trust Rural Programme, 2010). Further, the English mid-term evaluators of the RDPE, which had access to DEFRA expenditure data, identified yet another expenditure level (Hyder Consulting (UK) Limited, 2010, p. 56). Calculation methods are unspecified in each source.

4 The decision-making authority of British and EU institutions has changed several times and likely will continue to change (Massot, 2014). The EU Commission has combined legislative and executive decision-making powers. It is a professionalized civil service led by Commissioners appointed by the EU Council. The EU Council comprises the heads of state for each EU member state. The dashed lines to and from the EU Parliament reflect the Parliament's lack of formal decision-making authority and role as an advisor to the EU Commission and the EU Council.

5 Agricultural diversification included farm product/crop diversification, diversification through marketing techniques, partial involvement in a non-agricultural rural business, or *exiting agriculture* (MAFF, 2001, p. 22).

6 The CPRE changed its name from the Council for the Protection of Rural England to the Campaign for the Protection of Rural England in 2003 (Hunt, 2006).

7 The SSFF does cite a document for this quote. The content is similar to several contemporaneous FOE-UK reports (Bullock, 2000; FOE UK, 2001; La Trobe, 2002).

8 Its public subsidy ended in 2010, forcing it to restructure into a wholly private consultancy, the European Food and Farming Partnerships, and a non-profit organization, the Food and Farming Foundation (Ashbridge, 2010).

9 Primary Care Trusts were the regional agencies responsible for the delivery of National Health Services.

10 I did not characterize the PSFPI as a local food policy because of this early shift away from local food purchasing *before* the Initiative formed in 2003. Early evidence of its impact on local food purchases was mixed. Case studies in a 2008 evaluation indicated a change in purchases toward local, yet expenditures on domestic food purchases appear similar prior to the PFSPI with decreases for some product types (DEFRA, 2010a).

11 Government documents do not indicate whether the proposed £15,000,000 for the Networks was additional funding or a portion of REG funds (DEFRA, 2012c,d; RDPE Network, 2012).

4 English case study

The co-option of local food policy by environmental interest groups

Movements may largely be born of environmental opportunities, but their fate is heavily shaped by their own actions.

(McAdam, McCarthy, & Zald, 1996, p. 15)

Uncovering overlooked policy narratives of local food

The study profiles the evolution of the term "food miles" from 1994 to 2011. It draws upon a combination of interviews, participant observation, advocacy group documents, media reports, and government policy documents. The focus is on how the global environmental orientation of the food miles narrative overcame the social, economic, and local environmental narrative of local food.

The environmental-centric food miles narrative was the main point of contention on local food in in the government's *Food Matters* (2008), *Food 2030* (2010), and *Future of Food and Farming* (2011). It was promoted by sustainable food and agriculture interest groups, such as the Soil Association (SA) and Sustain. Other narratives of local food were promoted by stakeholder-led groups, such as the National Farmers Market & Retail Association (FARMA), the Federation of City Farms & Community Gardens (FCFCG), and the Country Land and Businessowner's Association (CLA). Stakeholder participation and professional staff accountability to stakeholders were determinants of narrative selection by organization leaders.

The study explains how organization structure and stakeholder participation affected narrative selection, policy strategy (e.g. to engage with government or engage in extra-institutional advocacy), advocacy tactics (e.g. lobbying and media campaigns), and relationships between organizations (e.g. collaboration, competition, and rivalry). To do so, it was necessary to:

- recover past events;
- identify potential alternatives;
- explain the connection between internal organization structure and narrative formation; and
- show how inter-organizational relationships influenced the policy environment and local food movement structure.

106   *English case study*

Recovery of past events

Recovery of past events was possible through advocacy group documents, many of which are maintained on organization websites. In addition to narrative, reports documented relationships between individuals and organizations and provide a record of collaborative activities. Often significant advocacy group documents were jointly authored or reviewed by individuals outside the authoring organization. Similar information about narrative and organizational relationships was available through government reports, government-funded research projects, video, and media accounts.

While publically available documents offer a partial portrayal of events, the strategy of historical analysis "does not rest on the 'representativeness' of the document . . . but rather on the consistency of the account with knowledge derived from many other sources" (Clemens & Hughes, 2002, p. 208).

Identifying potential alternatives

In any policy analysis, difficulty lies in understanding individual motivations in past decision-making processes. *Why were some actions pursued and not others?*

One way to address this is to identify alternatives that were available to the decision-maker at the time the decision was made (Kingdon, 1984, pp. 16–18, 142–143). This information can be gathered from interviews, video or audio recordings from the period, and documents (meeting notes, reports with recommendations). For events close to the research activity (2010–2013, in this case), interviews were a viable strategy. For events beyond 3–6 years, other documentation was more reliable.

In many cases, English advocacy groups issued reports detailing numerous, sometimes hundreds, of recommendations. These provide a record of potential alternatives. For historical events, when documentation is the primary source of evidence, it is often not possible to recover motivations for when an alternative option was bypassed. In interviews, the chosen path may be regarded as the obvious or natural choice. To make past choice visible, it was necessary to show inaction on the alternatives (to *not* form alliances, *not* collaborate, *not* engage with policymakers). This analytical approach is especially appropriate given the rural policy windows identified in Chapter 3 and mismatch with sustainable food and agriculture interest group priorities.

Connecting internal organization structure to narrative formation

Many organizational characteristics (decision-making processes, membership composition) and organizational behaviors (tactics, narratives, alliance formation) represent choices made by organization leaders. The stability in these choices over time forms routine patterns of behavior called *structures* (Kriesi, 1996). Three organizational features resulted in significant differences between English advocacy groups:

English case study   107

- the degree to which stakeholders were involved in policy decision-making;
- the accountability of policy staff to stakeholders; and
- the composition of stakeholders, homogenous or heterogeneous in perspective.

Each of these features affected the information available for organization leaders to form policy narratives. Organizations with higher stakeholder participation and accountability articulated more pragmatic narratives than interest groups, which favored more ideological narratives.

Inter-organizational relationships, the policy environment, and movement structure

Following a line of reasoning established by McAdam (2003) on movement structure, it is useful to call out similarities and differences by organizational type. It is necessary to view organizations within the context of stakeholder relationships and other advocacy groups (Diani, 1995, 2003, 2011). Relationships between organizations have a significant bearing on the ability to form consensus, establish a collective action frame, and mobilization.

Many English food movement participants considered interest group formation, segmentation between stakeholder groups, intense framing contests, and poor inter-organization coordination as "normal." Grouping stakeholders into fairly homogenous sectors (farmers, organic farmers, rural, sustainable food, health) increased solidarity and reduced intra-organization conflict. Narrowly-defined issues were believed effective for accessing media reporting and increasing organization visibility with the public, policymakers, and funders. The analysis revealed that these normal, and seemingly fixed, practices reflected rational decisions made by advocacy group leaders. These factors combined to increase collective action costs, and resulted in intensive rivalries during cycles of contention.

Only a few organizations needed to engage in intense inter-organization competition for the overall policy environment to become competitive. This meant that a few interest groups limited policy opportunities for organizations seeking policy collaboration. It drove at least one national organization to avoid participation in the policy process. The result was a few highly visible interest groups dominating a less visible or "hidden" set of stakeholder groups (Kingdon, 1984, p. 199). Intense inter-organization competition was observed at the national level on local food policy.

Differences in policy collaboration and competition resulted in an "extreme" case

The US–UK comparison was initially considered as a comparison between "likes." For example, interviewees were asked for examples of policy collaboration for local food (see Appendix 2) for comparison to the American

108 *English case study*

Farm and Food Policy Project. Responses were consistently negative. Additionally, the Making Local Food Work (MLFW) project, a seven-organization collaboration on local food, divided policy advocacy between CPRE and Sustain. They informed each other of their advocacy but did not collaborate in joint policy advocacy (MLFW Staff, 2011). As a consequence, the American case study would be about the outcomes of policy collaboration on local food policy and the English case study would be about organizations *not collaborating* on local food policy. This resulted in a pair of *divergent* or *extreme cases* (Snow & Trom, 2002) with regard to national policy advocacy.

The emergence of an extreme case led to theoretical refinement on the conditions under which collaboration occurred or was inhibited (Charmaz, 2006, p. 102; Lichterman, 2002; Snow & Trom, 2002). The boundary crossing activities of cross-sector, multi-level, and participatory processes common to local food projects in both countries was a consistent practice in national American local food advocacy but not national British local food advocacy. The lack of many of these activities at the national level clarified boundary crossing work to overcome social divisions as a unique practice of forming local food *systems*.

There are several national British advocacy groups that were collaborative, participatory, and worked across sectors—examples include FARMA, FCFCG, and the CLA. Other examples of cross-sector collaboration included:

- the cross-sector, stakeholder-led learning network, Tasting the Future (ADAS et al., 2010; *Tasting the Future – Innovation Group Meeting*, 2011; *Tasting the Future – Second Assembly*, 2011);
- the coordinated delivery of support for local food projects through the Making Local Food Work partnership (*Making Local Food Our Future: MLFW 2012 Conference*, 2012; *MLFW 2011 Conference*, 2011; MLFW, 2012; MLFW Staff, 2011);
- the Community Food & Health network in Scotland, which includes farmers, community-based groups, and public health officials (Community food and health (Scotland), 2014); and
- the public, business, and community-based group collaborations inspired by the Sustainable Food Cities project (SA, Food Matters, & Sustain).

However, it was the competition for narrative control between better-resourced interest groups that dominated public and policymaker perceptions of local food.

To get feedback on early findings, case information was presented at eight events with a range of audiences: academic staff, students, local food practitioners, national advocacy group leaders, national policymakers, and national funders.[1] Feedback was used to refine the findings. One critical response from Sustain was that regular, participatory decision-making processes would be an unnecessary commitment of resources compared with their use

English case study 109

of staff to design and carryout policy campaigns (Sustain, 2012c). While the implications of the research are debatable in regard to what English advocacy groups *should do*, the findings themselves were not disputed at these events and were supported by several observers, including prominent advocacy organizations and food advocacy scholars.

Food miles narrative origins and intersection with local food narratives

In the case of food miles in England, the term proceeds from a period of stability (1994–2003), to partial government and industry acceptance (2005–2007), to intensive counter-mobilization and reframing (2006–2009), and finally political discrediting (2008–2011). The first two sections establish a timeline. The second section explores the intra- and inter-organizational characteristics that lead to local food being framed as a global environmental issue.

Stability in the food miles narrative, 1994–2003

In 1994, the SAFE Alliance published *The Food Miles Report: The dangers of long-distance food transport* (SAFE Alliance, 1994).[2] Several organizations provided "detailed comments, and criticisms" for the 1994 *Food Miles Report,* including FOE-UK, Greenpeace International, Oxfam, Christian Aid (an international development charity), and the New Economics Foundation (NEF) (Sustain, 1994, republished 2011, p. 2). The report is broad, detailing local and global issues related to the international food trade.

The Food Miles Report is not anti-trade. It indicates that sustainability at a national level would require food policies to be oriented to self-sufficiency, but also acknowledged that food products will be traded, and should be traded fairly.

The narrative leads with social justice issues (Sustain, 2011b, pp. 11–12; 1994, republished 2011, pp. 11–12). The report is not exclusively focused on climate change or environmental impacts. Of particular concern are impacts of British food consumption beyond its borders, such as small farmers' vulnerability from being dependent on exports markets (Sustain, 1994, republished 2011, p. 11). This is followed with local and global environmental impacts, energy use in agricultural production, and energy use in food transport (Sustain, 1994, republished 2011, pp. 23–29). The food miles narrative clearly intended to open a wider critique of social equity in the food system.

The Food Miles Report does not explicitly define the term "food miles." Rather it is used as a concept to draw attention to negative social, economic, and environmental consequences of long-distance food chains, for example:

> Prices in shops do not reflect the full cradle-to-grave environmental and social costs.

110 *English case study*

But the concept of food miles isn't just about distances. This report explores some of the wider social and ecological implications of international food trade, and suggests how to reduce excessive, unnecessary food miles.

(Sustain, 1994, republished 2011, p. 7)

Food miles serve as a lens to reveal negative consequences for "the environment," "implications for the [global] South," "small producers," "animal welfare," and "public health" (Sustain, 1994, republished 2011, pp. 7–8). A list of the "Forces behind Food Miles" is presented, including: "subsidized transport; subsidized agriculture; retail concentration; food manufactures; aid, trade, and development; the General Agreement on Tariffs and Trade (GATT); consumer choice and information; and Food From Britain" (Sustain, 1994, republished 2011, p. 5). Each of these phrases formed sections of the original *Food Miles Report*.

The report's introduction identifies the local impact of food transportation for producers and consumers in both developed and less developed countries. The first paragraph introduces how long-distance food shipping results in "comparatively little of the food we consume com[ing] from local producers; and much will have been transported over great distances" (Sustain, 1994, republished 2011, p. 7). The fourth paragraph indicates how the presence of an international food export market can affect a less developed country:

Producers: Long-distance trade in foodstuffs leads to specialisation in agriculture and the allocation of resources to production for export rather than to local needs and self sufficiency. For example, in Bangladesh shrimps rank as the country's third largest export earner. Yet the country is unable to feed its own population – a clear conflict over the use of land for local food needs, as opposed to export production.

(Sustain, 1994, republished 2011, p. 7)

Local food production, distribution, marketing, and consumption are most prominent in the report's recommendations (Sustain, 1994, republished 2011, pp. 9, 54). Retailers were encouraged to stock local produce when in season (and produced with low-impact methods) and label its country of origin or food miles. Producers were encouraged to consider diversification and value-adding for local markets. Local government authorities were encouraged to support the revitalization and development of local food shops, community growing spaces, and farmers' markets, and ensure that supermarkets are accessible to people without automobiles.

Individuals were empowered as consumers at the local and national levels. They were encouraged to purchase Fairtrade imports and favor indigenous products through a "hierarchy of purchasing priorities: locally, nationally and regionally"[3] (Sustain, 1994, republished 2011, pp. 9, 54). Individuals were also encouraged to act locally, as citizens, by forming a "local produce marketing scheme" or to "grow their own food" (Sustain, 1994, republished 2011, pp. 9, 54). They were also encouraged to "write to their MP and Member of the European Parliament (MEP), to MAFF, and to supermarkets and food manufacturers, demanding a clear labeling system showing the distance food has travelled and its country/countries of origin" (Sustain, 1994, republished 2011, pp. 9, 54).

The national government was encouraged to adopt a higher fuel tax rate, support labeling of product origin and transport method, support domestic food consumption through promotion from Food from Britain, forgive or reduce the debt of less developed countries, and require minimum worker safety standards and environmental protections in the GATT[4] treaty. SAFE indicated that: "assistance should be provided for direct marketing schemes, such as circulating information on how to set them up and cheap loans or grants" (Sustain, 1994, republished 2011, p. 55). A specific funding source or agency was not identified to implement the recommendation, nor did their recommendations include linkages to EU-funded rural development programs or LEADER. However, the recommendation for citizens to write to their MEPs indicates that SAFE was aware of an EU role in food and agricultural policy.

There are minute differences in the food miles narrative in later reports. A 1996 report published by Sustain, *Growing food in cities*, defined food miles as: "a term used to cover the social, environmental and economic effects of transporting food by road, air or other means" (Garnett, 1996, p. 89). A 1999 report, *Food Miles – Still on the road to ruin?*, focused more on economic drivers. That report identified that the increase in food miles was a result of food retailer concentration in the UK, increased road transportation funding throughout Europe, and global trade liberalization (Sustain, 1999b). Yet, the 1999 report retained linkages to economic, social, and environmental concerns. One of the new policy recommendations in *Still on the road to ruin?* was that the government reduce the 31 percent of external environmental and social costs not included in the price of fuel (Sustain, 1999b, p. 16). Another new recommendation was for the government and meat industry to support the use of mobile abattoirs in the UK (Sustain, 1999b, p. 16). As in the 1994 *Food Miles Report*, the EU CAP was not a specific policy target.

A 2001 Sustain report, *Eating Oil: Food in a changing climate*, targeted the issues of energy efficiency and pollution from food transportation and production (Sustain & Elm Farm Research Centre, 2001). Its emphasis is predominantly focused on the negative consequences from food transportation. The first major policy recommendation is to promote sustainability through Fairtrade products, reduce food imports, and support local food sourcing (Sustain & Elm Farm Research Centre, 2001, p. 4). Local food sourcing was encouraged in five of six report recommendations (Sustain & Elm Farm Research Centre, 2001, p. 4). *Eating Oil* specifically recommended that the EU rural development programs "be directed to support the development of sustainable local and regional food distribution" (Sustain & Elm Farm Research Centre, 2001, p. 72).

112 *English case study*

Eating Oil was widely endorsed and garnered some policymaker recognition. Forty-eight organizations endorsed the report, including: IIED, SA, FOE-UK, NEF, the Farm Retail Association, the Family Farmers' Association, and WWF UK. The report was referred to in a 2002 debate on the SSFF (Alan Simpson [Labour, Nottingham South], 2002). It received an "Award for Campaigning or Investigative Food Journalism" from the Guild of Food Writers in 2002 (Guild of Food Writers, 2011). While *Eating Oil* focused on energy use in the food system, the social and economic components of the food miles narrative remained present.

The consistency of the food miles narrative within Sustain after *Eating Oil*, and between organizations, can be observed in a 2003 video on food miles (Schleisman, 2003). The video shows that interviewees from CPRE, Sustain, Oxfam, and Marks and Spencer (a British food retailer) had a common understanding of the food miles narrative and its linkage to social, economic, and environmental outcomes in England and less developed countries.

The food miles narrative used by Sustain in 2003 was still focused on social, economic, and environmental issues:

> What you've got to look at is the underlying trend of who is gaining the profit. Who has got the power in the food chain. And they are the people who have the profit in the food chain. You might say a worker is getting a dollar a day rather than nothing a day by actually sending us their green beans. But what happens when that water supply runs out, when the pesticide use is too high, for this perfect produce for the Western Consumer. And also what happens when Tesco's decides 'oo – it's cheaper to go somewhere else'? And that producer, or that small worker-farmer has actually invested in producing these luxurious beans for us, they've suddenly got no market or a depleted soil or a depleted water supply.
>
> (Vicki Hird, Sustain in Schleisman, 2003)

Political inequality and social justice concerns framed Sustain's food miles narrative. It highlighted power inequities in the food system, those who gained profit, and that consumers in developed countries were insulated from the risks of food production and economic vulnerability in regard to foreign food producers. Similar concerns were voiced by Alex Renton of Oxfam Asia, who indicated that the environment and the fair wages of agricultural workers were overlooked in international development projects (in Schleisman, 2003).

Also in 2003, Sustain and Food Links UK co-authored a collaborative discussion paper, *Feeding the Future: Policy options for local food* (Sustain & Food Links UK, 2003). Compared with earlier food miles reports, there was broad input from agricultural and rural development groups, including CPRE, the British Independent Fruit Growers' Association, and the National Association of Farmers Markets. It had input from sustainability interest groups SA, IIED, and NEF.

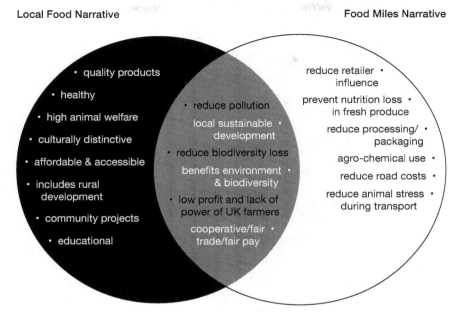

Figure 4.1 Overlapping elements of Sustain's local food policy narrative and food miles policy narrative.
(Based on section headings in Sustain and Food Links UK (2003) and Sustain (1999c).)

Comparing the 2003 *Policy options for local food* discussion paper to the 1999 *Still on the road to ruin?* report illustrates points of convergence and divergence on food miles and local food narratives (Sustain, 1999b; Sustain & Food Links UK, 2003). Figure 4.1 draws on the main section headings for each report. The "local food narrative" is based on the 2003 discussion paper and the "food miles narrative" is based on the 1999 food miles report.

Narrative elements of local food and food miles overlapped on issues of sustainable development and some marginalized social groups. The food miles narrative focused primarily on environmental issues. Some social and economic issues were excluded from the food miles narrative, such as food affordability, access, and health; rural development; community-led projects; education about food issues; and the development of quality products. Thus, *the food miles narrative did not include all the elements of the local food narrative, nor did the food miles narratives include all aspects of local food*. The local food and food miles narratives also diverged by *tone*. The food miles narrative focused on negative outcomes while the local food narrative focused on positive outcomes.

Policy options for local food focused on issues of local food and agricultural production. The first policy option listed for national government strategy was to:

114   *English case study*

> Adopt new agricultural and rural development strategies in the UK government and devolved administrations[5] that include the widespread development of sustainable, local and regional food economies as a top priority.
>
> (Sustain & Food Links UK, 2003, p. 18)

In total, 287 policy options are listed for local food. Nineteen policy options were related to EU rural development policies. For example, one "problem" was that EU rural development policy left it to each EU "member state as to how funds are distributed." The solution paired with the problem was: "National agricultural programmes should include support to develop strong local economies e.g. measures such as retail diversity, local/regional processing facilities, public food purchasing for local, organic, fair-trade produce" (Sustain & Food Links UK, 2003, p. 36). Further, the domestic implementation of EU rural development policies, including LEADER, was identified as a potential policy target for local food policy.

Throughout the report only five policy options directly mentioned food miles. A policy option to "Continue campaigning to reduce food miles" was ranked as the third of six options to address climate change problems arising from the air-freighting of fresh agricultural products (Sustain & Food Links UK, 2003, p. 48). Throughout the discussion paper, the food miles campaign was only listed once as a policy option. With 287 policy options for local food, there were literally hundreds of alternative policy options.

The food miles campaign continued despite negative reactions from other advocacy groups and allies. In 1999, Sustain indicated that some organizations had the perception that "SAFE was attacking all international trade and potentially challenging the livelihoods of developing-country farmers" after publishing the 1994 *Food Miles Report* (Sustain, 1999b, p. 10). This was "never the intention," explained Sustain, rather the "principle [*sic*] target is the unnecessary transportation of food, and that can just as easily occur with food produced and consumed in this country as it can in international trade" (Sustain, 1999b, p. 10). Sustain was aware the food miles campaign could increase contention with other advocacy groups.

Partial industry and government acceptance, 2005–2007

The food miles concept gained traction with the Department for Environment, Food and Rural Affairs (DEFRA) and the food industry. It enjoyed a short-lived period of partial acceptance by DEFRA, some food retailers, and some food distributors from 2005 through to 2007 (Andrews & Dunn, 2005; DEFRA, 2007c, d; Smith et al., 2005). Some retailers, such as Tesco and Marks and Spencer, introduced labels indicating transport method and country or origin (Journeyman Pictures, 2007; Schleisman, 2003). Some peer-reviewed evidence supportive of claims of environmental impacts was published (Pretty et al., 2005).

Figure 4.2 Logo of the *Farmers Weekly* food miles campaign.
(Reproduced with permission, *Farmers Weekly*, 2006.)

Visibility of the food miles concept increased significantly in May, 2006, when *Farmers Weekly* launched a food miles campaign. A motivation for the campaign was DEFRA's 2005 report on *The Validity of Food Miles as an Indicator of Sustainable Development* (*Farmers Weekly*, 2006). The *Farmers Weekly* campaign asserted that local food was "miles better" (Figure 4.2).

With increased attention came increased resistance, initially with international development groups and another government agency, the Department for International Development (DfID).

Contention, counter-mobilization, and discrediting

Contention and reframing in the media, 2006–2009

Contention increased when IIED published an opinion article on *Fair miles? The concept of "food miles" through a sustainable development lens* in October, 2006 (MacGregor & Vorley, 2006). It was funded by DfID and two foreign government development agencies. IIED's article was co-authored by Bill Vorley, who had been a working party member on the *Policy options for local food* paper. Individuals and organizations who had previously collaborated on local food split along their geographic focus on British or international issues.

Responding to the *Farmers Weekly* campaign, DfID hosted a roundtable meeting of NGOs on the *Airfreight of fresh horticultural produce from least developed countries* to address increasing contention about the food miles narrative (Sustain, 2006a). Attendees included Sustain, IIED, SA, FOE-UK, the Fairtrade Foundation, and the National Consumer Council. DEFRA did not attend.

116 *English case study*

Notes of the meeting were developed by Sustain and were posted on both Sustain and IIED's website, indicating that record of the meeting was acceptable to both organizations. DfID's motivation for hosting the seminar was that:

> Using simply 'food miles' as an indicator of sustainability may mean that we ignore the development benefits of the trade in fresh produce to hundreds of thousands of farmers in the poorest countries.
>
> (Sustain, 2006a, p. 2)

DfID indicated that it sought a "complementary way, to achieve shared goals" between environmental and international development organizations (Sustain, 2006a, p. 1).

While DfID hoped to "achieve shared goals" through the meeting, it was not a neutral convener. It had funded the *Fair miles* article by IIED. During the meeting, DfID indicated it continued to sponsor research by IIED (e.g. Legge et al., 2006), which IIED described as "research and opinion pieces" (Sarch, 2006, p. 5; Sustain, 2006a, p. 9). Rather than find a common ground, DfID wished to bring the environmental community in alignment with its perspective on food miles. The seminar was ineffective at reducing contention.

Advocacy group positions on food miles were well established prior to the seminar, months before the world food price crisis in 2007 (IIED, 2006; Sustain, 2006a). A short synopsis of the meeting notes on IIED's website stated that a farming NGO thought "imports of fresh fruit and vegetables by air was at odds with their promotion of sustainable and local production" (IIED, 2006, para. 4). SA was the only farming NGO listed in the notes. Also, SA was planning to debate restrictions on organic certification for air-freighted products at its January, 2007 annual general meeting (BBC News, 2007; Mukerjee, 2007; Sustain, 2006a, p. 9).

The IIED synopsis indicated that both an environmental and a development NGO "expressed strong concern that the urgent need to reduce carbon emissions is absolute, and felt that the impact of carbon emissions was in danger of being offset by developmental benefits" (IIED, 2006, para. 3). IIED was entrenched in its perspective. It continued and expanded its public communications against food miles after the seminar with funding from DfID and other countries' development agencies (Buxton, 2011; Chi et al., 2009; IIED, 2007; Legge et al., 2008; Plassmann & Edwards-Jones, 2009).

While organizations were entrenched in their perspectives, some seminar participants hoped that the media would take a more nuanced approach reporting the pros and con of the food miles concept:

- It's possible that the media will adopt a blanket approach to all food miles. However, previous experience on this issue is that the media can adopt a nuanced approach.
- The 'food miles' terminology has changed since its introduction. The focus has moved from showing who benefits and who has the power,

English case study   117

to focus more on climate change. However, these issues are still intimately inter-linked.

- Food miles terminology is still useful to educate the consumer about supply chains.

(Sustain, 2006a, p. 7)

IIED's synopsis of the seminar communicated greater frustration with the media, who rarely discussed the complexity of the issue (IIED, 2006, para. 2). The role of the media was uncertain. It seems that proponents of the food miles narrative thought favorably of media coverage, while its detractors were skeptical about media fairness.

Mainstream media reports from 2005 to 2009 (Table 4.1) illustrate their reaction to the food miles narrative. An environmental focus of the food miles narrative was established prior to the November 2006 DfID seminar, a point made in Professor Edward-Jones' March, 2006 Op-Ed (Edwards-Jones, 2006). The assumption made about the media's ability to report a complex issue with nuance was overly optimistic. For example, the BBC developed in-depth "Q & As" on global food issues in October, 2008 *after* it had reported on food miles and the world food price crisis. Food miles proponents underestimated the media's proclivity to transform, rather than just transmit, a narrative (Klandermans & Goslinga, 1996, p. 320; Zald, 1996, p. 270). Reporting on the food miles narrative focused on air-freighted products and greenhouse gas emissions, pitting British sustainability advocates and farmers against African farm workers (for an example see BBC World News, 2007).

The environmental "turn" in the food miles narrative became its fundamental vulnerability and enabled successful counter-mobilization. Two former allies of Sustain, NEF and IIED, sought to discredit the food miles narrative on the basis of its narrow, environmental-centric view of sustainability. For NEF:

It is now apparent that the notion of 'sustainable food' has important advantages over local food for framing the next phase of the debate. We define sustainable food as food associated with high levels of well-being, social justice, stewardship and system resilience. A focus on sustainable food is particularly attractive because it provides a basis for a holistic approach to the challenge of re-making the food system. Issues around well-being, social justice, stewardship and system resilience . . . are located in the UK or abroad.

(Sumberg, 2009, p. 2)

Despite history of contention over the term "sustainability," NEF considered it a better collective action frame than the increasingly contentious food miles concept.

IIED sought to reframe the food miles narrative by criticizing its narrowness and argued for a new, broader framing:

118   *English case study*

Table 4.1 Timeline of selected national media report titles on food miles and the world food price crisis

Year	Headline title	Source & date
2005	Local food 'greener that organic'	(BBC News, 2 March 2005b)
	Food movement 'harms environment'	(BBC News, 15 July 2005a)
2006	Op-Ed: Food miles don't go the distance	(Edwards-Jones in BBC News, 16 March 2006)
	Tesco reveals plans to cut 'food miles'	(*This is Money*, 15 September 2006)
	British trade minister defends NZ	(One News, NZTV, 31 October 2006)
2007	Organic imports under fire	(BBC News, 26 January 2007)
	Trying to stay true to its roots	(Mukerjee, BBC News, 31 January 2007)
	African trade fears carbon footprint backlash	(Averill, BBC News, 21 February 2007)
	The eco-diet . . . and it's not just about food miles	(Randerson, *The Guardian*, 4 June 2007)
	The ethical food debate. . . food miles or supporting farmers in developing countries?	(BBC World News, 22 August 2007)
2008	How the myth of food miles hurts the planet	(McKie, *The Observer*, 23 March 2008)
	World Bank tackles food emergency	(BBC News, 14 April 2008a)
	Long era of cheap food is over	(Loyn, BBC News, 29 May 2008)
	The cost of food: Fact and figures	(BBC News, 29 May 2008d)
	Challenges for the food summit	(Harrabin, BBC News, 3 June 2008)
	New E Africa food crisis warning	(BBC News, 23 July 2008b)
	Op-Ed: Feeling the heat of food security	(Baker, BBC News, 11 August 2008)
	Foods 'should label up eco-costs'	(Carpenter, BBC News, 8 September 2008)
	Government urged to introduce 'omnibus standards' for food	(Randerson, *The Guardian*, 9 September 2008)
	Q&A: World food prices	(BBC News, 15 October 2008c)
	Cost of food: Global roundup	(BBC News, 16 October 2008e)
2009	Food prices vary but crisis remains	(Walker, BBC News, 15 May 2009)

Many researchers and policymakers are beginning to conclude that the food miles approach, even when it accounts for the way food is transported, doesn't provide a robust enough basis for judging whether the contents of your food basket are environmentally friendly. In short, it's a lot more complex than that. There are many other aspects of the agricultural process and food supply chain that also contribute to the greenhouse gas emissions generated by the foods you eat.

(Chi et al., 2009, p. 9)

Both NEF and IIED observed that the narrative of food miles had diverged from its original inclusion of social justice and development of poor countries.

The food miles narrative was reframed in the media. The complexity of the food trade was acknowledged in the original food miles narrative. The 1994 *Food Miles Report* had stated in its second paragraph that "the forces behind food miles are complex," and in its third paragraph that there is "no single solution" (Sustain, 1994, republished 2011, pp. 8–9). However, Sustain and SA had lost control of the food miles narrative.

Discrediting, 2008–2011

During 2008–2011, *Food Matters* and the *Future of Food & Farming* discredited the food miles narrative. *Food 2030* indicated that local food could help educate consumers about food and its origins but the food miles concept was "not a helpful measure of food's environmental foot print" (HM Government, 2010, p. 26). Apart from food miles, the government was interested in other narratives about local food, especially some of the social and economic issues in *Policy options for local food* (identified in Figure 4.1). While reframing occurred in the national media, the initial reframing of food miles happened earlier, prior to the world food price crisis. The highly visible climate change-oriented narrative of food miles and local food originated from Sustain and SA's advocacy decisions (Averill, 2007; Kenneth Hayes [Soil Association], 2007; Sustain & Elm Farm Research Centre, 2001; Sustain & Food Links UK, 2003; Sustain Policy Staff (a), 2011a).

The environmental shift: Co-option of the local food narrative

Hundreds of policy options for local food were available to advocacy group leaders. The connection of the CAP programs to local food projects had been made by governmental officials and stakeholders (Acheson, 1998; Curry, 2009). The EU CAP provided a regular policy cycle that was more predictable in its timing than the media's episodic interest in food and farming issues. Yet, why did a food miles campaign become the dominant form of local food advocacy in Britain?

A principal factor was the segmentation of advocacy groups by sector (e.g. urban, rural, environmental, agricultural). Also, several of the most prominent proponents of local food were segmented internally, between professional staff and members. How advocacy groups were governed affected their narrative choice, framing processes, tactics, and mobilization strategy. Differences in these factors helped organizations define a policy niche. Some highly competitive organizations maintained their niches by "policing" the activities of other groups. A combination of these factors enabled environmental interest groups to co-opt the policy narrative of local food for their climate change campaigns.

120   *English case study*

Social movement segmentation increased the cost of collective action

English food advocacy groups have sorted their supporters into homogenous, single-sector groups, which reduces the cost of mobilizing supporters (Klandermans & Goslinga, 1996). Sorting can reduce conflict and competition over which organizations represent whom. This sorting or segmentation occurred in three ways: between national organizations and the grassroots (vertically), between advocacy sectors (horizontally), and between rural and urban geographies (spatially).

National interest groups tended to disseminate narratives *to* the grassroots, rather than *from* the grassroots *to* national organizations. This direction of communication resulted in *vertical segmentation* between local- and regional-level organizations and national-level organizations. This occurrence was not uncommon. For example, Linking Environment And Farming (LEAF) developed a national marketing label for its members' products, which it developed in consultation with retailers, but not consumers (LEAF Staff, 2011). Consumers were *talked to* but not *listened to*.

Advocacy groups were segmented by their membership groups. The NFU, Britain's largest farm advocacy group, focused on farmers. The Soil Association focused on organic-certified producers. The Country Land and Business Owners Association focused on rural landowners, of which farming may be a part of their income, and rural businesses. Sustain's organizational alliance was primarily environmental-, health-, and consumer-oriented organizations. The Campaign for the Protection of Rural England, an individual membership organization, focused on the recreational use of the countryside and limits on its economic development. The New Economics Foundation and Food Ethics Council, as think tanks, did not aim to directly engage stakeholders. Each of these organizations represented different perspectives on food and farm issues. There were few potential overlaps between potential member groups. When there were overlaps, there were conflicts, as between the NFU and CLA, and NFU and FARMA (shown later). Sustain believed that each organization had its own policy "turf," while other organizations (CLA, FARMA) felt bounded by the turf defined by dominant groups. This resulted in *horizontal segmentation* between national advocacy groups on policy.

English advocacy groups were segmented by their rural and urban orientation of their interests. This spatial or *geographic segmentation* can be illustrated through two sector mapping exercises. The RDPE Network surveyed 95 participants on their relationships with other organizations, shown in Figure 4.3 (globe, 2009, p. 75). Using a similar survey question on organization partnerships, the Food Ethics Council surveyed organizations involved in food and farming identified by the Environmental Funders Network, the Big Lottery Fund for Local Food, and Sustain's alliance members (FEC, 2011, p. 18). The partnerships identified by 226 respondents in the FEC Food Issues Census (Figure 4.4) do not overlap with the partnerships identified by the RDPE Network, except for the NFU (FEC, 2011, p. 60; globe, 2009).

The lack of overlap between rural and food organizations and the stability of rural segmentation indicate that rural interests and food interests are represented by two distinct *policy communities* (Jeremy Richardson, 2000). This three-way segmentation of stakeholders—horizontally by issue sector, vertically by national–local activity, and geographically by rural and urban orientation—increased the cost of policy collaboration. Consequently, it is unsurprising that the rural development programs and LEADER were not priorities of food groups, even though rural policy was the main public funding source for agriculture and food.

The lack of a common agenda or a joined-up food policy has been a decade-old stumbling block for English food policy:

> [A]t the local and community levels in the UK, policy alternatives are being advanced in an ad hoc fashion by local food initiatives. More structural-level interventions at the regional and local governance levels are also needed to address the social dimension of a sustainable food supply.
> (Barling, Lang, & Caraher, 2002, p. 556)

Barling, Lang, and Caraher continued, indicating that "what is missing . . . is a more strategic approach to such policy interventions" to "offer a more 'whole supply chain' approach to local food provision" (Barling et al., 2002, p. 560). Prior to Barling et al., Nelson reported that local food initiatives wanted "access to a national forum" and that pressure groups wanted a common forum (Nelson, 1997, pp. 96–97). By 2013, such a common forum had not formed.

The "sorting" that is useful for single-issue, pressure group campaigns undermined the potential for a "joined-up" collective action frame and the potential for broad, sustained collective mobilization of the local food movement. The order established by segmentation would appear to have its own merits, otherwise it would not have been maintained for decades. However, rigid advocacy group segmentation was a barrier to the formation of cross-sector, urban–rural linkages (common in local food projects) in national policy discourse.

Interest group governance and framing processes

Sustain and SA were able to frame local food to suit each organization's environmental objectives. The policy decisions of Sustain and SA are made by professional staff, not by members in participatory decision-making. Being separate from their stakeholders, especially those with an economic interest (e.g. farmers, rural communities, small food businesses), the policy staff became *elites*. Sustain and SA "do not normally depend on the direct participation of their constituents for attaining these goals" because they have sufficient resources for institutional access, authority, and expertise, and thus their actions are "typically carried out by an elite" (Kriesi, 1996, p. 153).

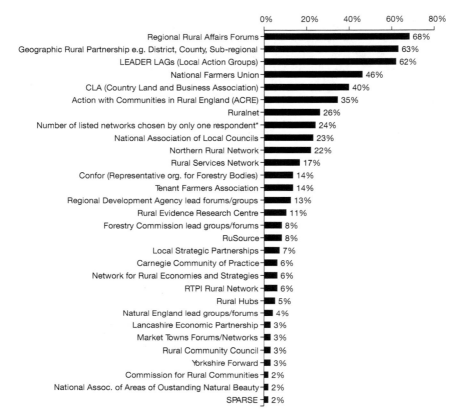

Figure 4.3 Organizations with which RDPE Network participants have an existing partnership.
(from data in globe, 2009, p. 75.)

Kriesi uses the term "elite" to characterize the influence of organization leaders over stakeholders with limited direct accountability of the leaders to stakeholders. This concept of "elite" was present, but perhaps not pervasive, within the local food movement. Cooperatives UK, a partner in the Making Local Food Work project, considered an "elite" as those with greater access to resources, status, networks, or charisma (Cooperatives UK, 2011b, p. 9).

The choice of environmental narrative was influenced by a belief among organization leaders that an evidence-based argument was best made with data from the natural sciences. In an impromptu interview of SA policy staff at its 2011 conference, the question was asked: What narratives aside from food miles were available for making the case for local food but not chosen? The staff member replied:

English case study 123

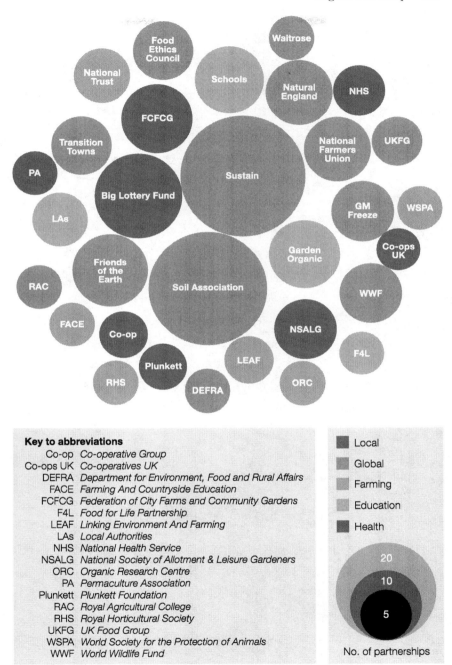

Figure 4.4 Partner organizations of Food Issues Census respondents.
(Reproduced with permission, FEC, 2011, p. 60.)

124 *English case study*

> Well, you could have made an argument based on its relationship to people
> and farmers, the economics of it, or reconnection—but that would have
> been a political argument and not science-based.
>
> (from interview notes, SA Policy Staff (a), 2011)

The SA aimed to use science to counter government narratives, as it had
done with other issues (SA, 2010a, b). Sustain considered government
manipulation of evidence as an unavoidable fact, reflecting a process of "policy-
based evidence making" instead of evidence-based policymaking (Sustain
Policy Staff (a), 2011b). Yet, both organizations still felt the need to use
evidence from the natural sciences to make their policy case. As a result, the
food miles debate proceeded on issues that were definable by natural scientists,
especially through the use of Life Cycle Assessment to measure greenhouse
gas emissions (Edwards-Jones et al., 2008).

The decision to frame local food as an environmental issue linked to food
miles and climate change was made by professional interest group staff. Sustain's
policy campaigns formed from point-to-point discussions between Sustain's
policy director and interested alliance members. An inclusive, deliberative
decision-making process was not a goal of the alliance:

> How do we get them to agree if they are all specialists?. . .
>
> We check out some of the details with some of the key allies in each
> sector. . . .
>
> We amend bits of the campaign if necessary, having spoken with them.
> . . .
>
> Having gotten the sign-on from key organizations in the sector, we then
> promote it vigorously. . . .
>
> But what we're asking them to do is sign up to the campaign as we are
> presenting it to them. We're *not* asking them if we should do it and we're
> *not* asking them how to run it.
>
> We're saying are you with us? If yes, that's great.
>
> (from a pre-recorded presentation by
Sustain Policy Staff (a), 2011a)

As a consequence, Sustain's alliance principally functioned in a one-way
relationship. Most alliance members were unable to influence the campaign's
development, including its target, message, intended outcomes, and even
whether the campaign should be developed. With Sustain identifying political
opportunities and selecting organizations to develop a campaign, Sustain
oriented the alliance's activities to the goals of Sustain.

A small minority of agricultural groups were in Sustain's alliance: 10 percent
of the membership in 2010 (Sustain, 2010). The greatest concentration of
groups was environmental in nature. This style of informal decision-making

did not provide a process that would allow for the representation of the distinct interests of a numerical minority, nor were the interests of a *majority* protected with Sustain's ad hoc decision-making processes.

The policy recommendations Sustain provided to DEFRA for the RDPE exemplify a situation when environmental priorities overshadowed agricultural priorities. Pesticides, wildlife habitats, and public health were prioritized over local food and the LEADER program (Sustain, 2006b). Further, the recommendations were by Sustain's staff and not the alliance:

> 1.3 This consultation response was compiled by officers of Sustain. It does not represent a full members' consultation response. Twelve organisations in our membership have been invited to respond in their own right and we have tried not to duplicate the issues they raise, especially on animal welfare and biomass crops.
>
> (Sustain, 2006b)

Yet, in the first point of the document (1.1), Sustain portrayed itself as an alliance: "We represent around 100 national organizations working at international, national, regional and local level" (Sustain, 2006b). For the 12 organizations, they forwent opportunities provided by an alliance to coordinate messages and cultivate broader support for their issues. For Sustain, it lost detailed information on agricultural and rural policy issues.

As a result, Sustain was an alliance "in name only" and functioned as a unitary organization (Institute for Conservation Leadership, 2005). While Sustain was ready to critique government policy, it had not developed specific, detailed, actionable recommendations that the government could implement.

Similar to Sustain, the SA's policy staff made policy decisions:

> *Interviewer:* I'm curious about the internal stakeholders you mentioned. Are these farmers, or academics, or Soil Association staff?
>
> *SA (b):* For policy (pause) it's mostly staff. We do invite others in to have discussions with on particular topics.
>
> (from audio recording, SA Policy Staff (b), 2012)

While the Soil Association is a membership-based organization, members are not engaged in its policy decision-making.[6] The policy staff report to the Director and the Director to the organizational Council. The Council's combined agricultural and rural membership is in a minority. Of the Council's 18 members, seven were engaged in agriculture (at least four as a primary vocation), four were involved in food marketing, three were journalists, two had academic backgrounds, one was a retailer, and one was a rural policy specialist (SA, ca. 2013). While agriculturalists were more numerical than other groups, they were a minority on the Council. Also, the SA's farmer and food producing members were not empowered with decision-making authority.

126 *English case study*

The lack of member empowerment was especially poignant at the SA's Annual Conference in 2011, one of the participant observation events (*SA Annual Conference 2011: Food and the Big Society*, 2011). With about 800 attendees, the main events were held in a large town hall. Panelists sat on a stage overlooking the audience. For a plenary on *Should we influence food choices?*, the SA had assembled a panel of two journalists, a food industry consultant, a large-volume organic producer, the director of Cooperatives UK, and one food cooperative manager. The panel chair was Rose Prince, a journalist who had criticized the SA's nutrition claims, elitist reputation, and farmer benefits of organic certification (Prince, 2009a, b, c).

During the plenary, Prince became increasingly critical of the complexity of the SA's message, its inability to reframe its elitist perception, and its interest in nutrition and health issues. Halfway through the hour and a half plenary, one person in the main conference hall stood up and interrupted Prince: "The audience is getting a bit uncertain here 'cause this is a conversation they are not part of" (SA, 2011). This comment was met with resounding applause.

Prince explained she was just following instructions given to her from the SA: to engage the assembled panel in a debate and then address audience questions later. The standing man responded by asking the Chair to "recognize that 49 minutes has passed without letting us ask questions" (SA, 2011). The panel leader replied that she was keeping track of time, but that if everyone wanted to open up the discussion, she would do what everyone wanted. She replied sarcastically to the "brave" standing man "that it's a democratic organization" (SA, 2011).

While the minute and a half exchange was aberrant, the SA had selected panelists the audience considered poorly suited for the topic. Prince focused the panel debate on issues she had raised in her reporting (SA, 2011). In my field notes, I observed that the panel leader "co-opted the panel for her own use and legitimized it by following her instructions" (from field notes, *SA Annual Conference 2011: Food and the Big Society*, 2011). Further, she derided the concerns voiced by the standing man through sarcasm. At no point did SA staff intervene. Nor had they effectively managed the plenary's time for audience participation. Documentation about the conference did not describe the panel selection process. A peer review process is used to review submitted proposals for conference sessions in several American food movement conferences (for example CFSC, 2011).

The reliance on informal decision-making processes in Sustain and the SA restrict participatory decision-making and accountability from stakeholders. A contrasting viewpoint is that stakeholders may not want to spend the time learning about complex issues and participating in meetings. However, stakeholders bear the risks of interest group actions. Stakeholder-led groups adopted other governance processes, different policy targets, and different narratives than interest groups like Sustain and the SA.

English case study   127

Tactics and narrative choice differed by organizations' governance processes

While Sustain and the SA were the most prominent organizations, other advocacy groups were active on local food issues at a national level. FARMA, FCFCG, and the CLA adopted organizational processes that relied upon stakeholder participation (the CLA is discussed later). Their choice in policy narratives for local food focused on social and economic issues and their tactics favored direct communication to the government.

For the FCFCG, the adoption of a federation structure was a deliberate response to the prevalence of an interest group model that utilized staff-led decision-making and single-issue campaigning.

Interviewer: You use the word federation. You use the word autonomous. Why use those words to describe the organization?

FCFCG: Because the definition of a federation is—you should know this, you come from the United States—it's made up of a group of independent organizations that mandate the federation to operate on its behalf. So we have no jurisdiction over our member groups. . .

It's very [pause] carefully considered. It's not by a mistake that we are a federation. It's actually what the members wanted. And it's a very unusual form of constitution even in England.

Interviewer: That's why I'm asking you about it. The other organizations I've interviewed, they don't adopt a structure like that—

FCFCG: No, they don't. That's why we're fairly unique.

Interviewer: Can you talk more about that? Like why—

FCFCG: Ok. I won't talk about individual organizations by name. . . doing everything they can to promote that single purpose. But at the end of the day, they are answerable to their own board of trustees which set up differently from ours. Yeah? So, our board of trustees, they say, well, we want to consult our members on what to do next with x, y, and z. So the way the Fed develops is very different than the way a single-issue campaigning group would develop.

Interviewer: I'm assuming that was a conscious decision.

FCFCG: Yeah, yeah, I mean I wasn't around when it was established, but the fact that it was set up as a *federation* was a decision made that echoes one of the fundamental principles of City Farms and Gardens is that they are managed by and for people from the local community as opposed to institutional local authorities or other organizations.

Interviewer: Ok.

128   *English case study*

> FCFCG: So it's a reflection of the desire for and recognition for the benefits of community management.
>
> (from audio recording, FCFCG Policy Staff, 2012)

The use of a federation structure, the inclusion of local-level stakeholders on the Board, and the stakeholder dialogue on policy matters reflect a participatory and deliberative decision-making process. As a result, the FCFCG has a higher level of stakeholder engagement and accountability than Sustain and the SA. The FCFCG decided not to engage on policy related to local food, in part because it was too contentious and the narrative of local food became too distant from the concerns of urban farms, gardens, and community food projects.

Like the FCFCG, FARMA is also led by a board of stakeholders, primarily farmers and farm market managers. FARMA is organized as a cooperative, with its staff hired on contract through a management company (FARMA, ca. 2013; Jackson, 2013). For FARMA, the outcomes of local food were, in order of priority: economic, social, and environmental (FARMA Policy Staff, 2012). Its policy narratives were closely linked with member interests.

> *Interviewer.* . . . What type of policy needs does your membership want you to talk about to the national government?
>
> *FARMA*: Support for the small family farms. A recognition that small family farms are an important part of the rural communities and the food supply in the UK. We would like . . . definition about what a farmers market is, what a farm shop is. . .
>
> (from audio recording, FARMA Policy Staff, 2012)

These perspectives were consistent with earlier policy statements during the world food price crisis. From FARMA's *21 reasons to support local foods*, "support your local economy" and "support local farmers" are the first and second reasons; only three relate to environmental issues, including food miles as the third-ranked reason (FARMA, 2009). FARMA preferred direct communication with government officials. However, its priorities, such as a definition of a farmers' market, were not taken up by DEFRA (FARMA Policy Staff, 2012).

By contrast the role of an interest group, like Sustain, is less about representing and communicating stakeholder positions and more about pressuring policymakers into action.

> *Interviewer.* What's your theory of change for food systems?
>
> *Sustain*: It's a bit brutal and simplistic. It's [pause] making policymakers so hideously uncomfortable causing as much political pain as possible for them to carry on doing what they're doing. And giving some kind of [pause] carrot if they change to do what we want [so], frankly, it just becomes easier for them to do what we want. . .

Interviewer: Does that ever make it difficult to have relations, with you know, sitting Members of Parliament or with folks at DEFRA?

Sustain: To be honest [pause], MPs. . . . Some of them are nice. Some of them are horrible. They use us. We use them.

We don't really have much of a deep, meaningful relationship with any of them. [laughs] . . . I can't think of any Member of Parliament that we've had a relationship with for 20 years or anything like that. It's much more focused on the short term. We want you to do *this*. You're willing to do *that*. We both get something out of that. . . .

Interviewer: Um, [pause] why do you think that things are that way?

Sustain: I just think [pause] that the nature of the political and movement system is fairly brutal. . . . I just think that this notion that we all need to do is be nice to each other and get together in partnerships and then it will all be lovely is just unspeakably naïve.

(from audio recording, Sustain Policy Staff (a), 2011b)

Even though Sustain manages the largest alliance of food and farming groups in England, which includes FARMA and the FCFCG as members, it has a negative view of working in partnership with other organizations to change policy. Rather, policy change is about sticks and carrots, about trying to exert control by boxing MPs into positions where the only positive outcome is accepting Sustain's positions.

Pressure tactics are coercive (e.g. embarrassing politicians into action), opportunistic, transactional, and aimed at achieving short-term objectives. They are not used exclusively by interest groups. For example, the CLA used pressure tactics, targeting individual policymakers. However, it was considered as a tactic of last resort: developing a reputation for targeting government officials would diminish their ability to work with other government officials (CLA Policy Staff, 2011).

For Sustain, pressure tactics were core advocacy tactics. Following an interview question about balancing short-term and long-term objectives, a Sustain staff member responded:

To be honest, I'm the world's worst at taking the long-term or strategic view. We're shamelessly opportunistic. . . . If something comes up, and it seems like a good idea, and somebody's passionate about it, and we can get some money to do it, and there is a decent range of alliance members that are keen to join in, let's do it. . . . If it doesn't work, we'll try something else. 'Cause, if I knew how to get a campaigning win reliably, every time, trust me, (laughingly) I'd do it. But I don't. And I haven't come up with anyone who does.

(from audio recording, Sustain Policy Staff (a), 2011b)

130   *English case study*

Over time, short-term opportunism can erode political influence and access—an observation made in the DEFRA staff interview.

> Like anyone really, if you're working on a really contentious, difficult issue, you have to build trust with all the people you are working with and know that it is a safe working environment that you can say things, have ideas, explore issues and know that you aren't going to be quoted in the press. Otherwise you won't make any progress.
>
> (from audio recording, DEFRA Food Policy Staff, 2011)

At a participant observation event, a DEFRA staff person sought a new "go to" organization on sustainable food policy (*Tasting the Future – Second Assembly*, 2011). This new relationship would replace an informal role that Sustain occupied during the Blair and Brown Labour Governments. Others have noted that by focusing on the short-term goals and articulating policy narratives that gain media access, advocacy group leaders can undermine their opportunities for policymaker access (Gamson & Meyer, 1996).

By early 2011, Sustain had grown increasingly frustrated with their diminished political influence after the Coalition government formed in 2010. The government was revising public sector food procurement guidelines. In 2007, Sustain had successfully advocated for the inclusion of sustainability criteria for food purchases in procurement guidelines (DEFRA, 2007b). To protect those gains and to include further sustainability criteria, for sustainable seafood, Sustain launched a *Good Food for Our Money Campaign*. It included direct communication to government (e.g. meetings, consultation responses), advocacy through its alliance and supporters, and a media campaign (Sustain, 2011c, 2012b). In 2011, Sustain communicated its frustration with direct communication publically by posting photographs of 50 temporary government passes on Sustain's website, symbolizing the government's lack of response despite their communication to the government (Sustain, 2011d).

In January, 2011 (Sustain, 2011c), Sustain increased its use of pressure tactics. Individual MPs were sent small-value checks representing the marginal, increased cost of the Parliament eateries procuring sustainable seafood (Sustain, 2011a). Copies of deposited checks were posted to Sustain's website in an effort to name and shame MPs for being "cheap."[7]

The Prime Minister was also targeted through his cat. The *Daily Mail*, a national newspaper known for its wide readership reported "Why Larry the No10 cat has shunned his rat-catching duties: His posh diet means he dines on 'greener' fish than the Prime Minister" (*Daily Mail* Reporter, 2011).

The *Good Food for Our Money Campaign* was considered a success. The government included sustainable seafood in its procurement guidelines (Jim Paice [Food Minister], 2011). Also, it won a national award from the Chartered Institute of Environmental Health (Sustain, 2011e). Pressure tactics are a valued part of the English policy advocacy and have been used by environmental

English case study   131

interest groups since at least the 1980s (Rose, 1993; Sustain, 2012a; Wilkinson et al., 2010).

However, pressure tactics are not appropriate for every situation. Policymakers favored the direct communication of a consensus on local food priorities for national policy.

> *Interviewer:* How often is a common agenda cross-sector? . . . Do you see many of those coming in and presenting policy options?
>
> *DEFRA:* No. No. Absolutely not, and it's something we really want to see more of.
> (from audio recording, DEFRA Food Policy Staff, 2011)

Similarly, a panel hosted by the All-Party Parliamentary Group on Agroecology on *How to Feed a Town* discussed the merits of a bottom-up plan for local food:

> *Baroness Miller:* Wish we wouldn't have a top down [food strategy]. Wish we would write one from the bottom-up. A top down one won't ever work. It gets sidelined by the lobbyists. The focus is always on the bottom line. Our bottom line is society's well-being. We learn more . . . but get drifted into other directions.
>
> *Mary Clear:* All the ingredients are there. Someone just needs to do it, together [on the bottom-up strategy]. I wonder why it doesn't [happen and] get on with it and do it.
>
> *Clare Deveruex:* I love the idea of a real bottom-up / top-down approach.
> (from typed notes, *How to Feed a Town or City*, 2011)

After the meeting ended, Baroness Miller indicated that government-authored policies were never government-wide and relied on input from a few Cabinet agencies. Also, they were not followed when the government changes. She indicated that Sustain once attempted a broad strategy for local food (likely the 2003 *Policy options for local food* discussion paper). When prompted about whether she thought that proposal was adequate, she replied a bottom-up plan would take in all groups, like those on the panel, and said: "We need all the groups" (Sue Miller [Liberal Democrat, Chilthorne Domer], 2011). Understanding that perspectives on local food were diverse and that the local activity was decentralized, policymakers preferred consensus mobilization as strategy for local food.

Narrative choice

The default pressure tactics of interest groups did not result in consensus policy recommendations for local food. Rather, local food was another "single issue"

132 *English case study*

in a world of single issues—an expression from a Sustain interview (Sustain Policy Staff (a), 2011b).

Sustainable food and agriculture interest groups used local food to inform the public about climate change. During 2007–2009, the UK negotiated on the EU Lisbon Treaty and prepared for the 2009 United Nations Climate Change Summit in Copenhagen. For Sustain, local food was a shorthand way to talk about sustainable food and climate change: local food was not an end in its own right. For example:

> Frankly, local is fine as a shorthand for us, *even though* it is not the most accurate way of seeing whether a food is sustainable or not. Although 'food miles' and 'local food' are popular phrases, they are not particularly accurate.

> But we don't waste any time telling the media that local food isn't quite right. If people get it as a shorthand, frankly, that's good enough for us.

> Now, when I say good enough for us, I don't mean we don't care about the language and imagery we use. I think it is really, really import to get the language right . . .
> (from a pre-recorded presentation by Sustain Policy Staff (a), 2011a)

While Sustain sought to use local food to channel public interest to climate change, the SA considered local food inherent to sustainable agriculture. The SA food miles campaign was rooted in authenticity, that agriculture's main inputs should be the soil, water, and other resources found on the farm—an issue it considered important in an era of declining oil supplies (Macalister, 2008; Mukerjee, 2007).

Neither organization's food miles campaign targeted developing local food economies or promoted bottom-up local food projects. While British environmental interest groups were successful at influencing Prime Minister Brown on climate change (Kirkup & Waterfield, 2009; Sustain, 2009; the public whip, 2008), the use of the food miles narrative came at a cost to local food stakeholders.

The environmental argument for local food was not of interest to a senior civil servant responsible for DEFRA's food policy. Following an interview question about how the case for local food had been presented, the DEFRA staff member stated:

> DEFRA: . . . In terms of the environment, it may not actually be any more sustainable. In terms of helping kids understand how to grow food—fantastic. In terms of making sure people feel connected to a place—brilliant. In terms of some of the environmental 'good things' I think it is a bit overplayed.

> *Interviewer:* So you're saying groups often come in with an environmental justification for it?

DEFRA: Yeah, which I think is not massively evidenced-based. . . . The obvious place to explore that is the debate on food miles. An obsession with the idea that food miles are innately bad, which as you know, sometimes they are sometimes they aren't. Quite a lot groups come in and say "and it helps reduce food miles" as if it's a big clincher. And it isn't really, because it's simplistic.

(from audio recording, DEFRA Food Policy Staff, 2011)

The environmental-centric food miles narrative overshadowed social and economic narratives of local food, and had to be drawn out with a follow-up question:

Interviewer: Do you think sometimes that the food miles issue doesn't have an environmental value, but has a social value?

DEFRA: Yes. I do.

. . .. the wider benefits of community engagement, helping children to focus to school, or helping to reduce vandalism, or for pride in some places looks better to get more investment, etcetera etcetera, all those things are quite tangible, clearly.

(from audio recording, DEFRA Food Policy Staff, 2011)

Despite government interest in local food concerning social issues and rural development activities, Sustain and the SA presented the government with environmental arguments for local food. The food miles narrative was not targeted to engage in a dialogue with DEFRA.

Interest groups focused on narrative control in the media, not consensus mobilization of stakeholder groups

The food miles narrative was an instrument to increase contention on food industry practices and motivate the public on climate change. As a result, its use was deliberate in "creating controversy . . . to increase opportunity by opening media access to movement spokespersons" (Gamson & Meyer, 1996, p. 288). Yet, "winning media attention requires strategies and tactics exactly the opposite to those needed to win political standing within established political institutions" (Gamson & Meyer, 1996, p. 288). The differences in policy target—media and government—are known to have different outcomes on policy formation.

Media campaigning focused sustainable food interest group leaders on "winning" a framing contest even though interest groups are rarely able to successfully reframe the debate (Former NEF Staff, 2011). Through framing contests, organizations demonstrate their ability to defend or promote their issues, inflict harm, or provide support to the government (Zald, 1996, p. 269). Engaging in the contest can be an outcome in its own right. One interviewee

134   *English case study*

likened framing contests to "street fights" where the outcomes are focused on bringing the opponent into the fight, having the opponent expend resources on an issue not of their choosing, and bloodying them a bit in the process (Former NEF Staff, 2011). Policy can be just another venue to be "in the fight;" policy outcomes need not be the primary objective.

If specific policy outcomes were an intended outcome, then "failure" can make movement participants "unwilling to invest further time, energy, political capital, or other resources in the endeavor" (Kingdon, 1984, p. 169). Failing to achieve narrative control or changing government policy can lead to a "fortifying myth" whereby losses are interpreted in ways that sustain belief in the movement (Voss, 1996).

When an advocacy group fails to influence an institutionalized authority, that failure is "proof" of the institution's control and validation of the advocacy group's challenge to an institutionalized authority. The reframing of failure as validation "allows activists to frame defeats so that they are understandable and so that belief in the efficacy of the movement can be sustained until new political opportunities emerge" (Voss, 1996, p. 253). Achieving visibility in the media is a way to maintain organization visibility to the public and funders at a time when political opportunities (and public sector resources) may be few.

A fortifying myth is still a myth. By communicating failures through a fortifying myth, activists can hide the limited effectiveness of their tactical choices. This can be shown in examples from Sustain, the SA, and CPRE.

For Sustain to say that the food miles narrative was "abused" because "too often it describes only greenhouse gasses" (Sustain, 1994, republished 2011, p. 3) removes responsibility from Sustain linking local food to a food miles campaign intended to address climate change and "reduce CO_2 emissions" (Sustain & Food Links UK, 2003, p. 48). Sustain did not protect its narratives from media mischaracterization and public misunderstanding: it used local food as an imperfect shorthand to reach consumers on climate change and sustainability (Sustain Policy Staff (a), 2011a). Furthermore, Sustain staff indicated that the EU rural development programs were "too complicated," allowing continued allocation of resources to campaigning instead of policy analysis (Sustain Policy Staff (b), 2012).

The SA focused on environmental science as evidence for local food because social and economic evidence would have been "political." This validated SA's environmental perspective and discounted efforts to build up socio-economic evidence for local food (Edwards-Jones et al., 2008). Reliance on scientific evidence, without achieving scientific consensus, resulted in the selective use of evidence by government agencies and scientific bodies to bolster governmental positions.

CPRE engaged in a local food campaign through the MLFW project, which included citizen-led local food web maps and advocacy on the National Planning Policy Framework. CPRE's comments on the draft framework about local food were in the 63rd paragraph of its 213 responses, and local food had two very brief mentions in CPRE's recommendations on pages 38 and 47 of its 60-page document (CPRE, 2011a, pp. 14, 38, 47). The placement of local food indicates it was not a top priority for CPRE. Also, the overall document length and its "laundry list" nature ignored the reality that policymakers have limited time and resources to make decisions. CPRE's response to the National Planning Policy Framework was identified as one of six national policy outcomes for MLFW (MLFW, 2012, p. 29).

When the organization's choice of tactics does not achieve its stated policy goals, a fortifying myth allows an organization to communicate its belief in the righteousness of its actions to authorities and bystanders (the public, local food stakeholders, advocacy groups) (Zald, 1996, p. 269). Without independent and direct knowledge of the policy process, it can be difficult for outside observers to separate myth from reality. Consequently, unsuccessful campaigns designed to increase controversy and gain media access (unlinked to feasible policies), or poorly delivered consultation responses can be successfully explained away in a myth. In England, this myth was primarily that the government was unresponsive to the public, and lacked legitimacy.

Drawing on a perceived sense of political inequity, English food activists utilize a frame of *unjust authority* to mobilize public support for their positions. Direct engagement with "illegitimate" authorities risks the loss of identity as an organization struggling against the unjust influence of elites and corporations on public policy (as discussed in Laclau, 1996, p. 49). It is easier to communicate to the public while *being an outsider* to the political process, than it is *being an insider* (as discussed in Gamson & Meyer, 1996, p. 288).

The unjust authority frame is oriented *upward*, focused on institutions with centralized authority in government and business (Figure 4.5). The concept of *unjust authority* is not applied introspectively to consider how NGOs may reproduce pre-existing social inequalities.

A similar pattern of behavior in England's environmental movement was observed by Chris Rose, former policy director of Greenpeace UK in the 1990s. Rose observed that Greenpeace UK had focused on a "media reality" and away from the "grassroots reality" of its stakeholders (Rose, 1993). With the turn to media-based campaigning, he saw a deficit of "delivered change," an overreliance on media mobilization, and the underdevelopment of other communication methods (Rose, 1993, p. 292). As a result, Greenpeace UK perpetuated an organizational structure that was unresponsive to new needs; it bypassed grassroots engagement and relied upon familiar, but increasingly ineffective, communications methods (Rose, 1993, pp. 294–295).

Since Rose made his observations, the then Executive Director of Greenpeace UK joined the leadership of the SA. Rose's observations resonate with the experiences of the English food movement two decades later. Its interest groups focus on the media. They continue to use pressure tactics despite increasing frustration with the outcomes from pressure tactics. Additionally, opportunities for engaging the grassroots (e.g. LEADER) were bypassed.

136 *English case study*

Figure 4.5 Wordle from the Food Issues Census depicting factors that help and hinder food issues. Greater intensity shown by text size. Graphic: responses to the questions "Thinking about the sector as a whole, who or what is currently doing most to help efforts to address food and farming issues?" (green [gray]) and "Thinking about the sector as a whole, who or what is currently doing most to hinder efforts to address food and farming issues?" (red [black]). Those shaded brown were said by some to help and by others to hinder [only DEFRA, EU, and NFU]. Note: excludes common words such as "and," "the," and "food."

(Reproduced with permission, FEC, 2011, p. 56.)

Maintaining segmentation: ideology and "policing"

Collaboration within the context of a local food project aids project outcomes. It can increase access to resources necessary for success—land, producers, a distribution network, markets, and buyers. Policy collaboration offers the benefits of greater returns than a single organization could achieve, however it imposes risks, costs, and constraints on advocacy groups. Future policy outcomes are fundamentally uncertain. Most challenges occur at the start of a collaborative project, such as how to maintain an organization's individual identity while forming the new identity of a collaborative policy project.

English case study 137

Maintaining an advocacy group's individual identity through narrative cohesion and group homogeneity requires that organization to maintain divisions between groups. Ideological narratives, while easy to communicate, result in dogma. Several individuals, outside of formal interview settings, indicated that collaboration with the SA was difficult because it promoted an "organic-only" perspective on food policy. From the perspective of Sustain: "The thing you shouldn't seize is other peoples' turf, or other people's territory" (Sustain Policy Staff (a), 2011a). Authority for these groups originated from ideological adherence and the ability to occupy and defend a policy niche, not the direct representation of stakeholders (Knoke, 1990).

To maintain existing divisions (protect their "turf"), interest groups will often "police" potential competitors to maintain influence over their issue—*even if the organization is not active in that policy area*. This relationship is one-way: interest groups *dominate* smaller, stakeholder-led organizations—a form of authoritative power (Knoke, 1990, pp. 5–6). Passive forms of policing include surveillance over other organization's behaviors and withholding political support.

The CLA's local food activities were policed by the NFU. When interviewing the CLA about their interest in local food in policy, the CLA identified local food as a "common ground" issue. The CLA did not view local food as a political issue. However, the relationships between organizations *made* local food political:

> On an issue like local food, there is some common ground. But what has tended to happen is—you know, we have a pretty good relationship with the NFU. But there are certain issues where we would expect them not to interfere with us and they would *definitely* expect us not to interfere with their issues. At times, there is an overlap between the two. When that happens, relations tend to sour.
>
> (from audio recording, CLA Policy Staff, 2011)

A few minutes later, a follow-up question addressed the politics of local food:

> *Interviewer:* What do you think is political about local food?
>
> *CLA:* [long pause] Um. [pause] Good question. [pause] What is political about local food?
>
> I think it tends to be because of all the different personalities involved. . . . if you got somebody with a massive ego who says "You're doing it my way or I'm gonna take my ball away and you can't play with it anymore," I think you back down or it doesn't work. I can provide a number of instances where we have had to back down because somebody has said "Ok, you want to do it my way or you don't bother."
>
> That's why, in fact, we developed our own [local food] policy in the first place. Because we could see there was a market in it. We understood it

138 *English case study*

was politically sensitive. But we had to create our own ... footprint or
mark ... in a political market place—which we've managed to do.

(from audio recording, CLA Policy Staff, 2011)

As a result of the NFU's policing, the CLA formed its own local food campaign
encouraging food purchasers to "Just Ask" where their food comes from (CLA,
2007; Watts, 2007).

Policing originates not from the content of an issue but from the motivation
of an organization to protect its dominance over an issue area. Within this
mindset, innovation to form a new campaign can be viewed as "interference,"
not an opportunity for cooperation or working toward mutual goals.

FARMA also experienced policing by the NFU, though its influence was
more subtle. As a smaller organization, FARMA perceived that its lack of
political influence originated from a relative lack of *resources*:

We are not like the NFU who have a major lobby in the government all
the time. ... We have a much smaller voice. And I would say, we have
not made the impact on policy we would like to have.

(from audio recording, FARMA Policy Staff, 2012)

While the NFU and FARMA did not work together on local food issues,
the NFU recognized that FARMA provided a service to the farming
community that the NFU did not:

Interviewer: Do you know if you work with FARMA?

NFU Food Chain Staff: Uh, I don't know actually, ah, no, we don't work
with them. I tend to direct people that have specific issues on local food
and farmers markets, and that kind of thing to them. Um, but we don't
have particularly close links with them.

(from audio recording, NFU Food Chain Staff, 2012)

The NFU knew it did not provide services on local food and farmers' markets
to its members. It recognized that FARMA provided that service and that
some of its members may value FARMA's expertise. Yet, the NFU did not
support FARMA's advocacy for a definition for local food and protection of
terms like farm shop and farmers market: it was a one-way, unreciprocated
relationship. The NFU's policing of FARMA was passive. It occurred through
withholding political support for FARMA's agenda, which presumably is
relevant to NFU members interested in direct marketing.

FARMA is also subjected to another form of passive policing. While
FARMA has been a member of Sustain's alliance, and its predecessors, for
about two decades, FARMA explains that it lacks political allies:

Interviewer: Have you worked with any groups on advocacy at the national
level or have you always done you policy work separately?

FARMA: We have tended to try and do own our policy and advocacy work because, of, um, [pause] I think we have an understanding with a number of different organizations, and I mean [pause] but I don't think, any other organizations, um, particularly act with our voice, if you like. No.

(from audio recording, FARMA Policy Staff, 2012)

FARMA's inability to cultivate allies through the Sustain alliance illustrates how organizational structure can be used to police an alliance member by limiting the transmission of its priorities and narratives through the alliance's network. Sustain favored environmental narratives of local food over FARMA's social and economic narratives of local food.

Dominant organizations also police the actions of individuals. The All-Party Parliamentary Group on Agro-ecology (APPGA) set up a policy briefing on National Funding Strategies for Local Food: The US and UK Experience. The briefing featured this research and a presentation from a former US Department of Agriculture appointee visiting the UK, Gus Schumacher (National Funding Strategies for Local Food: The US and UK Experience, 2012).

Having decided on a draft agenda, the APPGA coordinator reached out to one interest group to get feedback on the event concept. That group contacted me asking why they were not asked to set up the event. This interest group was the first contacted to provide feedback on the event and first invited to be part of the event's roundtable discussion. Their default response to a new policy event, which they had not developed, was defensive. When coordinating Congressional briefings in the US, both independently and with partner organizations, this type of defensive behavior had not been encountered.

Policing serves organizational interests to maintain dominance over an issue. New policy initiatives were rebuffed (e.g. with the NFU and CLA, and the NFU and FARMA). Preexisting narratives were selectively reframed (e.g. with Sustain and FARMA). An individual was put on the defensive by working directly with policymakers rather than through an intermediary. In the case of the NFU's policing, this occurred even though they were not actively providing services to its members on local food and farmers' markets. Maintaining political influence was more important than meeting the needs of local food stakeholders.

Policing had a corrosive effect on inter-organization cooperation by "souring" relations. Domination by a few interest groups over stakeholder-led organizations limited the influence of individuals who are directly engaged in local food projects. Policing between organizations can result in suppression *from within* civil society and is similar to the "discipline" practiced by central government over the grassroots and on narrative formation (Curry, 2006; Foucault, 1977; Plunkett Foundation, 2011).

140 *English case study*

Conclusion: A culture of non-participatory decision-making enabled the co-option of local food

Local food was one solution to the problems of long-distance food transport in the food miles narrative. The entities that make up local food projects—farms, farmers markets, community food projects, urban farms, rural food businesses, community gardens—utilized narratives of local food that closely followed their social and economic interests.

Because interest groups, such as Sustain, the SA and CPRE, lacked direct accountability to stakeholders, it cannot be said they represented local food stakeholders. Interest groups harnessed public support for local food to climate-change campaigns without direct accountability to stakeholders. The environmental interest groups co-opted the narrative of local food for their own purposes.

Interest groups did not achieve solidarity through consensus, but through maintaining ideological purity, movement participant loyalty, and segmentation. Segmentation undermined the cross-sector relationships formed in local food projects and resulted in a corrosive political environment characterized by intense competition, rivalry, and exclusion. National interest groups promoting local food did not embody the transformative, participatory politics of local food projects. The interest group model is far from the *food democracy* envisioned by Lang et al. (2009) and practiced by many local food groups (Cooperatives UK, 2011c; Kirwan et al., 2013; Plunkett Foundation, 2003, 2011).

The passing of two crisis-defined eras may result in a decline of contention and sharp inter-organization rivalries. With the passing of policy windows for "bigger" issues like the structure of British farm policy and climate change policy in the EU, "smaller" issues may have an opportunity to rise on the policy agenda (following from Kingdon, 1984, p. 184). A down cycle may provide an opportunity for English food movement leaders and funders to investigate advocacy models which result in consensus formation, in line with policymaker interests. This could include:

- *Expanding the use of advocacy models with stakeholder participation and accountability*, like those used by FARMA and FCFCG. This would help ensure that policy narratives and targets aim to benefit local food stakeholders.
- *Funders devoting attention and resources to collaborative advocacy strategies that reduce exclusion due to multiple forms of social division* (advocacy group segmentation, urban/rural, stakeholders vs. professionals, and ethnicity). An initial step toward cross-sector engagement was taken by the Esmée Fairbairn Foundation's support of the Sustainable Food Cities project.
- *Recognizing past English policy outcomes arriving from collaborative strategies*, and the skills needed to support those outcomes (e.g. facilitation, cooperation, conflict resolution, patience, restraint). Advocacy group

leaders will want examples of policy collaboration drawn from England and fields related to food, agriculture, the environment and rural development.

- *Greater awareness of policymaker interests*, facilitated through more frequent, direct communication with policy leaders, domestically and at the EU level, a step FARMA had taken by 2012 (EC DGA, 2012).

It is unlikely that a more holistic approach to English food policy will take hold on its own, business as usual. Segmentation has been stable for a period of two decades. Such a strong pattern of "going it alone" makes it difficult to establish the trust needed for collaboration. Rather, the right frameworks need to be established for a more inclusive, participatory, and democratic approach to food policy. With a few organizations able to define a whole policy environment, no single organization will be able to do this. Funders, by virtue of their ability to support many organizations at once, may be in a far better position to spur practices that form and sustain advocacy on a joined-up food policy.

Notes

1 These events included presentations at Cardiff University (October, 2011); the Centre for Rural Economy at Newcastle University (March, 2012); the W.K. Kellogg Foundation Food and Community Gathering (May, 2012); an informal meeting with the Making Local Food Work evaluator and three WWF UK staff (March, 2012); a workshop of six WWF UK staff from two separate policy programmes (November, 2012); a workshop hosted by the Cabinet Office (November, 2012); a presentation for the All-Party Parliamentary Group for Agroecology (November, 2012); and a presentation at the 3rd City Food Policy Symposium at City University, London (December, 2012).
2 Sustain, which was the organization formed from the merger of the SAFE Alliance and the NFA in 1999, republished the original 1994 report in 2011. Direct quotes and page sequence of those quotes are from the 2011 reprint.
3 In this instance, "regional" meant the European region.
4 The General Agreement on Tariffs and Trade, now superseded by the formation of the World Trade Organization.
5 National assemblies in Scotland, Wales, and Northern Ireland.
6 The Soil Association has a separate organic certification body of the same name, which does include producer feedback in its decision-making.
7 The website showing which Members of the House of Commons and House of Lords who accepted and returned the checks is no longer online.

5 American case study

Overcoming barriers to policy change due to civil society coordination failure

Competing narratives: Political "win" and policy "failure"

Two days before the US House of Representatives would debate and vote on the 2001 Farm Bill, Representative Kind introduced an amendment that would rewrite the Agriculture Committee's draft bill. During the Committee's debate on the Farm Bill, Kind had tried to include conservation funding measures from his Working Lands Conservation Act (WLSA) (Ron Kind [D-WI], 2001; *Working Lands Stewardship Act of 2001*, 2001). The WLSA strategy was to unite several policy communities poorly served by farm subsidy programs: fruit and vegetable growers, environmental groups, organic producers, and sustainable agriculture groups. With most provisions of the WLSA rejected by the Agriculture Committee, Kind felt many of his 145 WLSA co-sponsors would support his amendment to the Farm Bill, Amendment 10 (*Working Lands Stewardship Act of 2001*, 2001).

Many of the provisions of Amendment 10 were the same or similar to the WLSA. Included was a reduction in farm subsidies to pay for increased conservation funding (Becker & Womach, 2002). Other provisions included funding for farmland preservation, socially disadvantaged producers, wetlands protection, a new Grassland Reserve Program, urban and community forestry, organic agriculture, and assistance for state marketing campaigns. Through the introduction of Amendment 10, Representative Kind pulled several advocacy group endorsements away from the House Agriculture Committee's Bill, upsetting the Committee Chairman and most colleagues on the Agriculture Committee (*Amendment No. 10*, 2001; John Dingell [D-MI], 2001; Ganske [R-IA], 2001; Sherwood Boehlert [R-NY], 2001).

One difference was that Amendment 10 did not fund a farmers market grant program and a national campaign to promote locally grown produce. This difference reflects dissension between advocacy groups over Representative Kind's tactics of surprising the House leadership and Agriculture Committee Chairman with a last-minute amendment. The Bush Administration also opposed the House Agriculture Committee's Bill, giving momentum to Kind's Amendment 10 without endorsing it (E. Becker, 2001a; *[Debate on Amendment 10]*, 2001).

American case study 143

Over the following 48 hours, House leaders scrambled to pull support from Kind's Amendment and shore up Republican support for the Committee's Bill after the President's veto threat (Becker, 2001b; Ray LaHood [R-IL], 2001). By offering to fund the new Grassland Reserve Program (GRP) in the Committee Bill and threatening to delay Food Stamp program funding, House leaders were able to shore up support for the Committee's Farm Bill. Representative Kind's amendment failed by a narrow vote, of 226 to 200, with 218 needed for a majority (*[Debate on Amendment 10]*, 2001). The final version of the House Farm Bill sent to the Senate funded the GRP at the expense of another conservation program (Table 5.1). Representative Kind's WLSA and Amendment 10 failed to have the intended effect of transferring

Table 5.1 Comparison of funding levels of selected conservation programs between the House Farm Bill floor vote and the Farm Bill as engrossed and placed on the Senate calendar

Program	House Agriculture Committee Farm Bill as voted October 5, 2001	Final House Farm Bill as sent the Senate on October 9, 2011	Net change in funding after House Floor Vote
Grassland Reserve Program	Authorized, but not funded	$254 million for use anytime during 2002–2011	+$254 million, 2002–2011
Wildlife Habitat Incentive Program	$25 million per year until 2011	$25 million, 2002 $30 million, 2003 $30 million, 2004 $35 million, 2005 $35 million, 2006 $40 million, 2007 $45 million, 2008 $45 million, 2009 $50 million, 2010 $50 million, 2011	+$30 million, 2002–2006 +$105 million, 2007–2011
Environmental Quality Incentives Program	$200 million, 2001 $1.2 billion per year until 2011	$200 million, 2001 $1.025 billion, 2002 $1.025 billion, 2003 $1.2 billion, 2004 $1.2 billion, 2005 $1.2 billion, 2006 $1.4 billion, 2007 $1.4 billion, 2008 $1.4 billion, 2009 $1.5 billion, 2010 $1.5 billion, 2011	−$350 million, 2001–2006 +$1.2 billion, 2007–2011

NB: Spending in later years (fiscal years 2007–2011) is a projection and would not affect actual expenditure.

(Farm Security Act of 2001, 2001a, b.)

144   *American case study*

farm subsidy funds to conservation programs. Counter-mobilization, led by the House Agriculture Committee Chairman, overcame the "outsider" strategy implemented by Representative Kind principally by funding the GRP.

Despite Amendment 10's failure, the threat it posed was framed a success by some environmental groups and reporters (Becker, 2001b; Brasher, 2001; The Fading Appeal of Farm Subsidies, 2001; Lancaster, 2001; Morgan, 2001; Reiss, 2001; Shorgen, 2001; Skiba, 2001). Environmental advocacy groups had mounted a legislative campaign that posed a significant threat to the House Agriculture Committee. They were emboldened to try Kind's outsider strategy again, framing the outcome of Amendment 10 as a near win. Kind's strategy took on a mythic quality fortifying supporters (Voss, 1996). When Kind repeated his strategy in the next 5–6-year renewal cycle for the Farm Bill in 2008, he was portrayed as a "crusader" (Center for Rural Affairs, 2007).

Analyses about what strategies to use in the next Farm Bill began in the aftermath of the House's passage of the Farm Bill in 2001. The House and Senate Agriculture Committees, sensing their vulnerability, sought to shore up support among producer groups. This led to Congress passing a Specialty Crop Competitiveness Act in 2004 to address the concerns of specialty crop growers (primarily fruit and vegetable farmers).

Despite Representative Kind's actions being framed as a "win" by many environmental groups and reporters, it had exposed fissures among organizations interested in reforming farm policy. The House Agriculture Committee successfully exploited these divisions to pass a Farm Bill with minimal revision. Fragmentation between environmental and conservation policy communities on the House Farm Bill vote was considered a primary threat to reforming the Farm Bill by a Program Officer at the W.K. Kellogg Foundation (WKKF).

WKKF had funded environmental, conservation, and sustainable agriculture groups who were active on the 2001 Farm Bill (WKKF, 2002). It did not make sense to the Program Officer that some of these groups would undermine the efforts of other groups. The Program Officer sought firsthand knowledge of the Kind Amendment's failure to try to understand how to prevent future reform efforts from being "bought out" by the Agriculture Committees (NEMWI Policy Staff, 2001, p. 1).

A WKKF grantee located in Washington, DC, the Northeast Midwest Institute (NEMWI), was funded to conduct an evaluation of the Kind Amendment's failure, including interviews from advocacy groups, Congress, and state departments of agriculture (Harris, 2003). In contrast to the media narrative of a near "win," the NEMWI evaluation indicated that repeating the strategy used by Representative Kind would be ineffective: the House Agriculture Committee was already consolidating support among producer groups to neutralize future attempts to divide farm groups (Harris, 2003).

Competing analyses within the funder community on the House Farm Bill outcome shaped their funding strategies for the next Farm Bill. The Hewlett Foundation funded an alliance between environmental and fiscally conservative advocacy groups to repeat the "outsider" strategy with Representative Kind.

American case study 145

This resulted in the formation of the Alliance for Sensible Agricultural Policies (ASAP) and a media-intensive campaign to press for agricultural subsidy reforms. The WKKF adopted a different strategy, focusing on greater engagement of sustainable agriculture producer groups and community food security activists. This led to the formation of the Farm and Food Policy Project (FFFP), which favored the "insider's strategy" of organizing community leaders and farmers and mobilizing them for direct communication to their Members of Congress.

This chapter focuses on how policy collaboration became a solution to a collective action failure (the House Farm Bill). Policy collaboration in the FFFP resulted in the formation of a holistic local food system narrative. That narrative was adopted into several programs passed in law by Congress and funded by USDA.

Framing collective action failure as a policy problem

For the WKKF Program Officer, the House Farm Bill debate in 2001 was a powerful learning experience about coalition-building (from audio recording, WKKF Program Officer, 2011). The officer relied on analysis from NEMWI, NEMWI's Agricultural Policy Program evaluator (Harris), and Gus Schumacher, a former USDA appointee (Harris, 2003; NEMWI Policy Staff, 2002). Three stress factors were identified for the loose alliance of conservation groups:

> Time – The Farm Bill came up so quickly that no one had time to get up to speed. Advocates needed more time to educate members and consolidate support.
>
> No united front – Ultimately, the coalition of NGO groups was unable to present a united front, as environmental and sustainable agriculture advocates lined up on different sides of the debate . . . on conservation provisions proposed in the Kind-Boehlert Amendment in the House.
>
> Threats – Members of the House Agriculture Committee played hard ball, for example by threatening members from urban districts with the reduction of nutrition title funding.
>
> (Harris, 2003, p. 19)

The lack of a "united front" formed the basis of the WKKF Program Officer's interpretation of the Kind Amendment's outcome as an advocacy group coordination failure.

WKKF had not supported grantee lobbying activities, but invested in the "behind the scenes" work of coalition-building, public education, and educational outreach to Members of Congress. It had funded The Nature Conservancy (TNC) to "create a network of local citizen constituents for environmentally compatible agricultural practices" (WKKF, 1998–2003). TNC

146   *American case study*

co-developed a Grassland Reserve Program (GRP) with the National Cattleman's Beef Association (2001). Advocacy groups that backed the GRP were believed to have shifted their support to the House Farm Bill, enabling its passage (Hance, 2001; WKKF Program Officer, 2011). Other WKKF grantees were not part of this formal coalition but included the World Wildlife Fund, Environmental Defense Fund, and the National Association of State Universities and Land-Grant Colleges, the Soil and Water Conservation Society, and the Sustainable Agriculture Coalition (WKKF, 2002). WKKF wanted its grantees to be more effective and better prepared for the next Farm Bill.

WKKF continued to utilize NEMWI's policy expertise to design the policy component of its Food and Society initiative. The initial steps of analysis and concept development spanned 17 months and ended in early 2003 (Table 5.2). NEMWI and WKKF refined the policy cluster concept and issued pre-proposals for grant-seekers. Its policy initiative reflected the assessment that the risk of a collective action failure was a problem and that the solution was increased collaboration.

The resulting Food and Society initiative was "inspired by a vision of a future food system that provides for all Americans safe and nutritious foods grown in a manner that protects the environment, promotes health, and brings economic development to both rural and urban communities" (NEMWI, 2003b, p. 5). The community and food system were important frames for a project that would:

- ensure collaboration and joint accountability between partnering organizations;
- involve organizations with strong leadership and institutional capabilities, a history of significant impact in the policy arena, and with a record of successful collaboration;
- focus on system-wide change resulting in community impact;
- show a commitment to policy changes that impact people from diverse socio-economic and ethnic backgrounds;
- secure funding to complement WKKF support;
- demonstrate commitment to evaluations.

(NEMWI, 2003c, pp. 2–3)

These goals were to be implemented through activities that "support[ed] the creation and expansion of community-based food systems that are locally owned and controlled, environmentally sound, and health-promoting" (NEMWI, 2003c).

NEMWI indicated to WKKF that a collaborative policy project would have a central goal of "Broadening Institutional Agendas" (NEMWI, 2003b, p. 16). Collaboration was a means to a "systems" framework of policy change, addressing multiple policy goals simultaneously through collective action, in lieu of pursuing organizational pet issues.

Table 5.2 Timeline of WKKF's policy grant-making and the Farm and Food Policy Project

Stage	Activities	Duration & timing
Analysis & concept development	• Analysis of strategies used in the 2002 Farm Bill • Identification of problem (coordination failure) & solution (collaboration) • Development of an information-gathering and planning process	17 months Nov. 2001–Mar. 2003
Information gathering, consultation, & planning	• Informal outreach to policy organizations • Congressional feedback informs politically feasible priorities • Independent analysis of policy organizations and grassroots groups' issue areas, policy activity, communications activity, and capacity • Development of plan for WKKF Request for Proposals	10 months Apr. 2003–Feb. 2004
Proposal development, submission, revision, & award	• Pre-proposal request: March 2004 • Pre-proposals submitted: April 2004 • Potential grantees selected: September 2004 • Submission of full proposals: December 2004 • Successful collaborative revises and resubmits project proposal: April 2005 • Grant award: September 2005	18 months Mar. 2004–Sep. 2005
Governance structures & management processes implemented	• Finalization of decision-making & communications protocol • Development of internal file-sharing website and contact lists • Selection of Advisory Committee members • Development of issue-area Work Groups • First Coordinating Council meeting: December 2005 • Decision-making protocol reviewed	3 months Aug. 2005–Oct. 2005
Development of policy priorities & narrative	• Work Groups launched and "listening sessions" held Sept. 2005–May 2006 • "Learning Papers" on local food and healthy food • Need for increased representation of minority farmer issues: formation of Diversity Initiative in May 2006 • "Synthesis report," written June–Dec. 2006, leads to *Seeking Balance*, Jan. 2007 • Project launched; 350+ groups sign on; 450+ by May 2007	15 months Nov. 2005–Jan. 2007 *Diversity Initiative launched*
Legislative outreach & evaluation	• Introduction of "marker bills" with FFPP proposals • House Farm Bill passes: June 2007 • Senate Farm Bill passes: December 2007 • Farm Bill Conference Committee: early summer 2008 • Becomes law, overriding Presidential veto: July 2008 • Project eval. & communication of outcomes: Oct. 2008	17 months Feb. 2007–Oct. 2008
Total time elapsed		78 months (6.5 years)

Based on CBI (2007), and supplemented with information from: Harris (2003); NEMWI (2003a, b, 2004); NEMWI Policy Staff (2001, 2002).

148   *American case study*

The "insider" strategy: Working the legislative process

Consensus formation through the Farm and Food Policy Project

The selected collaboration began in September, 2005 after a proposal development process spanning a year and a half (Table 5.2). The collaboration included four core advocacy groups, 28 funded partners (five of which were advocacy coalitions), and a two-organization facilitation team, composed of NEMWI and the Consensus Building Institute (CBI). The collaboration between the four main groups, and their partners (listed below), represented the joining together of organizations across sectors, levels of activity, and varying degrees of inclusion in USDA policies. Their partnerships illustrate the breadth of social groups and organizational perspectives within the FFPP.

- *American Farmland Trust* (AFT), a national farmland preservation interest group with regional offices and which maintained good relations with mainstream farm lobby groups. Funded partners included the National Council of Churches and the Land Trust Alliance (AFT & ED, 2004a, b).
- *Community Food Security Coalition* (CFSC), a national advocacy coalition led by stakeholders and composed of community-based food project leaders, farmers market managers, rural and urban farmers, and people of color. Funded partners included: American Community Gardening Association, Congressional Hunger Center (an influential anti-hunger advocacy group), National Campaign for Sustainable Agriculture, National Council of Churches, National Family Farm Coalition, Rural Coalition, Wayne State University (Detroit, MI), World Hunger Year, and a reserve for future partners (CFSC, 2004).
- *Environmental Defense Fund* (EDF), a national environmental interest group with regional offices, which had a focus on reforming farm programs to reduce environmental harm. It had two sub-grantees, the Soil and Water Conservation Society and the William C. Velazquez Institute, a Hispanic-American organization (Environmental Defense, 2005a, b).
- *Sustainable Agriculture Coalition* (SAC), and later the national Sustainable Agriculture Coalition (NSAC), an advocacy coalition led by members and composed of rural development, sustainable agriculture, organic, and minority farmer organizations. Most members provide direct support to stakeholders. Funded partners included Center for Rural Affairs (SAC's fiscal agent), Land Stewardship Project, Michael Fields Agricultural Institute, the Minnesota Project, National Catholic Rural Life Conference, Organic Farming Research Foundation, California Coalition for Food and Farming, and the Northeast, Southern, and Western Sustainable Agriculture Working Groups (SAC, 2004, 2005a).

American case study 149

The lengthy proposal process resulted in significant collaborative learning about each organization's theory of policy change, strategy, tactics, messaging, priorities, and decision-making processes. This facilitated frame alignment and policy target selection. Thus, reform of agricultural commodity programs was not a primary target: the issue was too controversial for an "insider" strategy reliant upon Agriculture Committee access. Many issues remained unresolved, including the degree to which WKKF wanted the partnership to include minority farm groups.

Enough trust and mutual understanding formed to establish new coordination processes for the three-year and nearly $6 million project. Expectations for the collaborative process were established in a jointly authored Communications Protocol, which described processes for conflict resolution, addressing surprises, and making joint decisions (CBI & NEMWI, 2005). The FFPP alliance formed a Coordinating Council to forge consensus on policy priorities (FFPP, 2005b). A hierarchical structure was proposed with the Coordinating Council informing research needs and the direction of four policy Work Groups (Figure 5.1). During the legislative outreach phase, the FFPP's structure shifted to a policy network, reflecting the need for increased flexibility and quicker decision-making leading up to the Farm Bill debate (Figure 5.2) (CBI, 2008b).

Coordinating Council members and Working Group co-chairs were nominated based upon their ability to "wear multiple hats," commitment to support the FFPP's objectives without favoring organizational agendas, and political support from the constituency they represented (FFPP, 2005b). Throughout, there was a commitment that leadership was not vested solely in Washington, DC staff, and included the perspectives of national leaders who worked on community-based projects. Each Work Group was co-chaired by at least one individual based outside the capitol. Other criteria to promote the diversity in the alliance's leadership were "topical interest, expertise, constituency, geography, race, ethnicity, and/or gender" (FFPP, 2005b, p. 2). Thus, four Coordinating Council members were based in Washington, DC, four were non-white, four were female, three worked directly with farmers or urban gardeners, and one was a part-time farmer (FFPP, 2006b).

For nine months (September 2005–May 2006), the FFPP conducted stakeholder consultation processes to gather input on policy prioritization and proposal development. This proceeded through the Work Groups, beginning with an expansive solicitation for stakeholders to participate in the Work Groups. Most Work Groups listed 90–130 members, with 10–40 participating per call. In addition, workshops called "listening sessions" were held at in-person events, mostly as conference sessions, to solicit input from individuals and groups beyond the formal project.

Through the FFPP process and the Coordinating Council's development, it became clear that additional resources were needed to involve minority farm groups (FFPP, 2005a, 2006a, c; Rural Coalition/Coalición Rural, 2006). WKKF then funded a separate, but linked, Diversity Initiative, coordinated by the Rural Coalition (Rural Coalition/Coalición Rural, 2006).

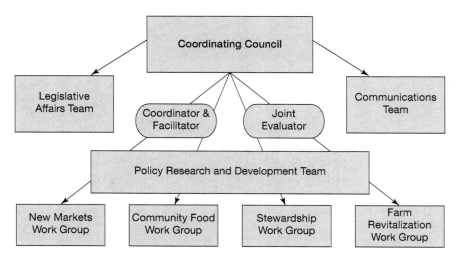

Figure 5.1 Proposed structure of the Farm and Food Policy Project.
(AFT et al., 2005, p. 6.)

Local and regional food systems as a collective action frame

FFPP leaders and stakeholders in the New Agricultural Markets Work Group, Healthy Food and Communities Work Group (originally "Community Food"), and Family Farm Revitalization Work Group considered the "localization" of agriculture and food distribution central frames for narrative formation and mobilization.

The Healthy Food and Communities Work Group (HFCWG) was a locus for social justice issues (CFSC, 2006b). This included efforts to end hunger, promote food-related employment in urban and rural areas, and empower disadvantaged communities and youth through urban agriculture projects. Their focus was on community-level improvements, not just providing individual assistance to address poverty as done in most USDA Food and Nutrition Service programs. Their aims included place-based community development strategies, local ownership, social inclusion, and city and regional coordination (HFCWG, 2006a).

Its stakeholders were local and regional organizations working with a diverse array of people: rural, urban, African-Americans, Hispanics (both old and new communities), Native Americans, small farm operators, registered dieticians, a rural sociologist, a food systems researcher, and a Catholic Brother (CFSC, 2005, 2006a). Two anti-hunger organizations and an international development organization were part of the Work Group. The local emphasis was a recognition that dedicated activists in multitudes of communities, in the US and internationally, were working towards greater empowerment through food-related projects.

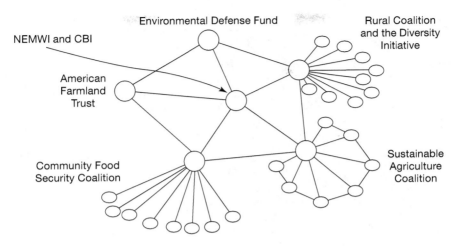

Figure 5.2 "Evolved Structure" of the FFPP.
(organization names added in italics, CBI, 2008b, p. 10.)

Specific, politically feasible policy recommendations on social justice issues were formed. One of these was an "Initiative to Build Local Ownership for a Healthy Food Supply." Within this was a proposal for "Local and regional food supply systems: Investing in the Short Term for Long Term Community-Based Food Security." It proposed to:

> Set up regional food system development authorities, drawing upon port authorities, resource conservation districts and other economic development zones as models, to facilitate planning and development of shortened food supply chains that includes the promotion of urban, local and regional food production (in conjunction with New Agriculture Markets).
>
> Create a farm-to-consumer infrastructure fund, to support thousands of new farmers markets, food bank purchase from local farms, CSA marketing cooperatives, wholesale markets for local products, and new initiatives to support the entry of new farmers or to transition commodity crop farmers to specialty crops and sustainable farming practices. (in conjunction with New Agriculture Markets).
>
> (HFCWG, 2006b, p. 6)

The HFCWG proposal integrated with a similar proposal in the New Agricultural Markets Work Group (NAMWG) (NAMWG, 2006b).

The NAMWG stakeholder composition, while overlapping with HFCWG, was more agricultural and rural (NEMWI, 2005, 2006b). NAMWG was a locus for economic development policy in the FFPP. Its work centered on

152 *American case study*

marketing strategies that would increase farm viability and community investments that would enhance or retain a community's economic viability (NAMWG, 2006a). Its regular participants included organizations that provided services to farmers and communities, two Hispanics, an African-American who was a former USDA employee, and a few farmers.

Issues related to farmers markets and local and regional food distribution were most prominent in this Work Group. The NAMWG proposed an infrastructure development recommendation, which complemented the one from the HFCWG to facilitate regional infrastructure development through a two-step grant and loan program. This program would facilitate organizational capacity development and infrastructure financing necessary for shorter-distance supply chains. Examples of projects could include: meat processing facilities; regional fruit and vegetable value-adding facilities; grading, processing, and packing facilities; warehouses; distribution centers; on-site processing facilities for public institutions; wholesale markets; and year-round retail markets for local foods (NAMWG, 2006b, p. 4).

The infrastructure proposals were new and lacked direct legal precedent. They were un-joined and undeveloped by May 2006 when the Work Group process finished. By January 2007, the FFPP *Seeking Balance* report supported local and regional food infrastructure, but policy proposal development languished for months. Without a national "local food" organization, these proposals were no one's direct responsibility.

Media outreach: Low controversy and low profile

With the FFPP focused on stakeholder consultation and joint policy prioritization, it was difficult to communicate "what" the FFPP was until a year and half into the funded project. By then, several issues were resolved. FFPP would not advocate on reforming farm commodity programs. It would pursue a strategy of incremental policy change, modifying existing policies, increasing funding for key programs, and proposing a limited number of new initiatives. It would directly communicate policy priorities to Members of Congress, enlisting the support of Members on the House and Senate Agriculture Committees. It was an alliance of interest groups, coalitions, and grassroots groups, which focused on coordinating activities through existing networks rather than building its own centralized staffing.

The FFPP's public launch came in January 2007. It issued a jointly authored report, *Seeking Balance in US farm and food policy*, with over 350 endorsing organizations, at a media event at the National Press Club in Washington, DC (FFPP, 2007c; NEMWI, 2007b). The tone of the launch and *Seeking Balance* framed the Farm Bill's policy problem as one of improving equity across underserved regions, policy priorities, and producer groups.

Seeking Balance had five major themes and 32 policy proposals (FFPP, 2007a, c). It was a critical document of farm and food policy, focusing on the metaphor of a broken food system without assigning direct blame, following recommendations from research conducted by WKKF media consultants (Bales, 2006; FrameWorks Institute, 2008a, b). While critical, its tone was not negative. It offered pragmatic, politically feasible solutions. Local food and regional systems formed the "glue" across different issues raised in the policy narratives and addressed in the policy recommendations (Table 5.3).

The launch event was the single coordinated media outreach activity of FFPP. The panel of five speakers portrayed FFPP as a broad, socially diverse, and cross-sector alliance with a consensus-based policy platform focused on incremental policy changes (FFPP, 2007b). The focus of reporter questions was on whether the FFPP was linked with another collaborative policy project, the Americans for Sensible Agricultural Policy (ASAP).[1] Two FFPP participants were also a part of ASAP and were present at the press briefing, AFT and EDF. ASAP was actively attacking the farm commodity programs and had garnered endorsements from 350 newspaper editorial boards (Environmental Working Group, 2008; Fluharty, 2008; Morgan, 2010). Reporters focused their questions on the two ASAP members at the briefing, AFT and EDF (FFPP, 2007b).

By choosing not to target the farm commodity programs, the FFPP lacked the controversy that appealed to reporters covering the Farm Bill. Of 29 reporters attending, 13 wrote a news article. This represented one half of the FFPP's total press coverage during the 2008 Farm Bill (NEMWI, 2007a, b). The FFPP had low public and media visibility: its communication resources were targeted for Congressional outreach (Headwaters Group Philanthropic Services, 2008, p. 12). While the FFPP benefited from the atmosphere of reform fostered by the ASAP, the FFPP did not want to engage in controversial communications that could limit access to policymakers.

Congressional outreach on local and regional food systems

After a March, 2006 meeting of the five core leads of the FFPP, one of the EDF representatives approached me and indicated that if I did not develop the infrastructure policy proposals, they would likely remain undeveloped. Since September 2005 my role with the FFPP had been supporting FFPP coordination, not policy development.

The infrastructure policy proposal was for a block-grant model of funding, where the federal government establishes a policy priority and then disburses funds to the states for implementation. The Work Group's concepts and the EDF representative's suggestions led to the Regional Food and Family Farm Development Act (Hunt, 2006). The opportunity to connect this idea with a legislative proposal did not develop until March, 2007.

Representative Bobby Rush [D-IL] contacted NEMWI, wanting the Farm Bill to help finance a new supermarket in his urban district. Representative Earl Blumenauer [D-OR] wanted to introduce a bill that would support local agriculture and community-based food projects. Congressional interest led to revisions of the Regional Food and Family Farm Development Act to the

Table 5.3 Excerpts of relevant policy goals and recommendations on local food systems in *Seeking Balance* (as numbered in source)

Section title	Goal "Core Farm Bill Priorities"	Recommendation "Key Farm Bill Innovations"	Policy target
1. Renewing American Agriculture	Fostering Market-Based Solutions 1. Create a balanced marketing support structure to address local, regional, national, and global markets.	Expand New Markets 1. Provide increased support for value-added agricultural enterprises and for supply chain innovations that link family farm businesses with new markets and distribution networks. 2. Make a major investment in grants to spur farmers markets and other direct farmer-to-consumer marketing innovations. 3. Reduce regulatory barriers and provide support for processing and distribution infrastructure to complement emerging retail and institutional markets for local and regional farm products, including sustainably raised meats, eggs, and milk.	Value-added Producer Grant Program Farmers Market Promotion Program Regulations for Interstate Shipment of State-inspected Meat Infrastructure Policy (TBD)
2. Healthy People: Reducing Hunger and Improving Nutrition	Reducing Hunger, Improving Nutrition 3. Increase access to healthier foods for all Americans, including through government food assistance programs.	Increase Food Access and Improve Health 1. Encourage greater consumption of fruits and vegetables by enabling federal nutrition program beneficiaries to purchase food at local farmers markets and other retail food outlets. 2. Expand innovative, community-based food programs to increase the scale and scope of institutional and emergency food-purchasing programs, including through changes in procurement policy and support for infrastructure development. 3. Create new and expanded food systems programs to help communities develop retail food markets, urban agriculture projects, and marketing networks to address the needs of underserved neighborhoods. 4. Provide funding to schoolchild nutrition programs to provide fruits and vegetables in schools, implement wellness policies, and expand nutrition education.	EBT Access at Farmers Markets Support of the Senior Farmers Market Nutrition Program Community Food Projects Allow Geographic Preference in School Meal Procurement Infrastructure Policy (TBD) Urban Agriculture Farm to School Support for the Fresh Fruit and Vegetable Snack Program

3. Vital Communities: Building Rural Businesses and Promoting Entrepreneurship	Building Rural Businesses, Improving Rural Communities	Capitalize on Rural Strengths and Promote Community Development	
	2. Promote local and farmer ownership and investment opportunities in farm-based renewable energy production.	1. Promote rural entrepreneurship and micro-enterprise business development. 2. Advance rural community and economic development through local leadership, wealth creation, entrepreneurship, and youth involvement.	Rural Micro-entrepreneur Access Program (No specific policy proposal)
4. Sustainable Lands: Cultivating Stewardship	Conserving Natural Resources and Protecting the Environment	2. Promote Local Leadership in Conservation	Cooperative Conservation Partnerships
	4. Build the technical assistance infrastructure needed to assist farmers and ranchers with becoming better stewards of the nation's lands.	1. Encourage locally led collaborations to solve environmental problems and meet community needs by establishing a Cooperative Conservation Partnerships Initiative.	
5. Diversity and Equity: Advancing Opportunities For All	Promoting Diversity and Equity	1. Eliminate Disparities and Ensure Fair Access	
	4. Expand opportunities for socially disadvantaged farmers and ranchers and communities of color to shape the future of the food system.	6. Expand innovative, community-based approaches to solving food access problems in urban and other underserved communities.	Community Food Projects Urban Agriculture

TBD = To be determined
(FFPP, 2007c, pp. 5, 7–9, 12, 14, 17.)

156 *American case study*

Domestic Market Access Act (DMAA) (Hunt, 2007b, c). The block grant funding was replaced with a four-step program providing a ladder of support: 1) funding for feasibility studies, 2) start-up grants, 3) direct and guaranteed loans, and 4) evaluation funding (Hunt, 2007b). Funding was to be available to any public, private, or non-profit entity involved in local and regional food system development.

The policy goal was to support the "missing link" between small-scale producers, processors, and distributors to "meet demand" (Hunt, 2007d). By using the term "access," the NAMWG interest in expanding producer market access was linked with the HFCWG interest in expanding consumer access to fresh, healthy, and locally produced foods. The dual purpose "access" narrative was reflected in the purpose of the proposed DMAA:

> support farm and ranch income by significantly enhancing a producer's share of the final retail product price through improved access to competitive processing and distribution systems which deliver affordable, locally and regionally produced foods to consumers, improve food access in underserved communities, and help save farm and ranch land and protect natural resources.
>
> (Hunt, 2007b, p. 1)

Outcomes and processes were incorporated into a definition of "Locally and regionally produced foods," defined as "food products distributed within the geographic area within which they are produced" and which:

> a)   maintain a transparent record of product origin, production practices, and other identifiers from which value is conveyed from the producer to the end consumer;
> b)   enhance a producer's income by maximizing the share of the retail food price retained by the farmer or rancher;
> c)   provide consumers with affordable, food products produced, processed, and distributed in their locality or region; and
> d)   ensure environmental integrity and enhance social welfare throughout the supply chain.
>
> (Hunt, 2007b, pp. 1–2)

Local and regional food was defined by: *proximity* (not distance), non-pricing information conveyed along with the product, reduced transaction costs, affordability, and a supply chain that did not minimize environmental and social concerns.

The policy problems addressed by the DMAA were twofold: 1) the declining portion of the farmer's share of the retail price of food with a growing portion of the food supply chain dedicated to distribution and marketing costs; and 2) the distancing of social relationships between producer and consumer. Focusing on the supply chain and the farmer's share of the retail price of food allowed

American case study   157

the concepts within DMAA to merge (i.e. hybridize) with existing policy (*Agricultural Marketing Act*, 1946; Ogren, 1965).

Alternative justifications were available, but turned down because they did not reflect stakeholder interests. One alternative narrative was using an environmental "food miles" narrative citing evidence from the UK's Department for Environment, Food, and Rural Affairs report *Validity of Food Miles as an Indicator of Sustainable Development* report. Food miles led the justification in a FFPP report draft, *Making the case for local and regional food systems*. It was subsequently revised to reflect stakeholder concerns, including farm income, community wealth retention, and access to fresh, locally produced foods (Anderson, 2006, 2007a, b, c).

A month after drafting, Representative Blumenauer and Senator Sherrod Brown [D-OH] included a revised version of DMAA in Farm Bill proposals (*Food Outreach and Opportunity Development for a Healthy America Act of 2007*, 2007; *Local Food and Farm Support Act*, 2007). Brown sought greater revision, notably renaming it the Healthy Food Enterprise Development (HFED) program. Brown's purpose section flipped the emphasis in the "access" narrative, beginning with health-related outcomes and ending with agricultural outcomes:

> The purpose of this section is to promote the health and well-being of all people in the United States, particularly school-aged children, low-income populations, and individuals residing in underserved communities, by increasing the availability and affordability of healthy foods, such as fresh fruit and vegetables, which, when produced, processed, and packaged locally or regionally, can significantly enhance the income of agricultural producers by increasing the share of the producers of the [*sic*] final retail price of the foods.
>
> (*Food Outreach and Opportunity Development for a Healthy America Act of 2007*, 2007, pp. 26–27)

The "access" narrative provided flexibility for targeting the interests of individual legislators, allowing the bills to gain co-cosponsors from urban, rural, suburban, and agricultural regions. This was significant in the House because Blumenauer was not on the Agriculture Committee. Blumenauer cultivated three co-sponsors on the House Agriculture Committee, all newly elected Democrats (Earl Blumenauer [D-OR] et al., 2007), as well as Representative Rush [D-IL], a former Black Panther and member of the Congressional Black Caucus.

The House Agriculture Committee was resistant to include HFED in the Chairman's Farm Bill. At issue was that USDA did not have a program that could finance projects in urban areas; it only had rural development financing programs established. At the time, USDA rural development programs were under scrutiny. The *Washington Post*'s year-long series, *Harvesting Cash*, featured investigations into the use of rural development programs in eligible, small cities under 50,000 people (Gaul & Cohen, 2007). In that climate, Congress was reluctant to introduce new financing programs or expand existing authorities.

158 *American case study*

The House Agriculture Committee preferred a strategy that would increase the use of an existing rural development program by the local food sector. Two days before the House Agriculture Committee debated its Farm Bill, the Committee's Rural Development Director agreed to set aside 5 percent of funds in the Rural Business and Industries Loan and Loan Guarantee Program for local and regional food projects (referred to as the *B&I* program hereafter). Representative Gillibrand [D-NY] introduced this compromise proposal as an amendment during the Committee's mark-up of the Farm Bill (*Amendment to the Rural Development Title Offered by Mrs. Gillibrand of New York*, 2007).

She requested that a distance-based measure be included as a definition so she could communicate to her constituents what she meant by locally and regionally produced food. It was decided that 400 miles was the upper limit of "locally and regionally produced agricultural products," accommodating the wide spaces of the Midwestern and Western US. Two other definition components were: 1) the product be "produced and distributed in the locality or region where the finished product is marketed"; and 2) "the distributor has conveyed to the end-use consumers information regarding the origin of the product or production practices, or other valuable information" (*Amendment to the Rural Development Title Offered by Mrs. Gillibrand of New York*, 2007).

While the lending provisions were included in the Committee's Farm Bill, the grant portions for feasibility studies, start-up support, and evaluation were not. Prior to the House floor vote on the Farm Bill, Representative Rush was able to get the grant-based portion included in the Chairman's Bill, as an authorized, but unfunded program. Rush had voted against the Agriculture Committee's Bill in 2001, and as a Member of the Congressional Black Caucus, could bring additional support to the Chairman's Bill during the floor vote. As a result, HFED became the Healthy *Urban* Food Enterprise Development (HUFED) Center (*Food and Energy Security Act of 2007*, 2007b). Following the House's lead, the Senate split HFED along the same lines, but provided funding to the HUFED Center. The final 2008 Farm Bill included both the HUFED Center and the locally and regionally produced food priority in the B&I program (*Food, Conservation, and Energy Act of 2008*, 2008e; *Food, Conservation, and Energy Act of 2008*, 2008f).

The HUFED Center was enacted in the same law section as the Community Food Projects program and drew on nutrition program funding. At $3 million over three years, its focus was on feasibility studies, small start-up grants, and project evaluation. The HUFED Center and the B&I priority shared nearly identical definitions of *underserved communities*, a definition that allowed both programs to support urban and rural projects (Filia, 2009). The HUFED Center purpose was "to increase access to healthy affordable foods, including locally produced agricultural products, to underserved communities" defined as:

a community (including an urban or rural community and an Indian tribal community) that has, as determined by the Secretary—

American case study 159

(A) limited access to affordable, healthy foods, including fresh fruits and vegetables;
(B) a high incidence of a diet-related disease (including obesity) as compared to the national average;
(C) a high rate of hunger or food insecurity; or
(D) severe or persistent poverty.

(*Food, Conservation, and Energy Act* of 2008, 2008e)

Even though the House Agriculture Committee split the HFED program into two parts, both the HUFED Center and the B&I program priority retained a holistic framing of the food system, spanning urban, rural, and tribal geographies; disciplinary perspectives of poverty; and addressed multiple issues simultaneously. Increasing consumer and producer access, transformative from the status quo, remained the central goals.

The definition of "locally or regionally produced agricultural products" was located in the B&I priority and changed in the final Farm Bill. The local and regional definition was relatively brief:

The term 'locally or regionally produced agricultural food product' means any agricultural food product that is raised, produced, and distributed in—
(I) the locality or region in which the final product is marketed, so that the total distance that the product is transported is less than 400 miles from the origin of the product; or
(II) the State in which the product is produced.

(*Food, Conservation, and Energy Act* of 2008, 2008f)

This brief definition should not be interpreted out of its statutory context because it only applies to defining eligibility for a priority within the B&I program.

Components of the DMAA local and regional food definition were interspersed throughout the overall B&I priority. For example, product traceability became a requirement of the loan or loan guarantee in the final law (*Food, Conservation, and Energy Act of 2008*, 2008f). Consumers were to be informed of the product's local or regional origins through agreements between the distributors and the final seller (e.g. retailer, cafeteria). Further, the overall priority was only available to entities that "support community development and farm and ranch income" through processing, distributing, aggregating, storing, and marketing locally or regionally produced agricultural food products (*Food, Conservation, and Energy Act of 2008*, 2008f).

USDA food desert and local food studies

A related initiative included in the Farm Bill was a USDA food desert study, co-developed in Chicago and Detroit (Gallagher, 2006, 2007). A Detroit report helped secure the support of food desert Michigan Senator and Member of the Senate Agriculture Committee, Debbie Stabenow [D-MI]. Although controversial, the food desert study was included in the House Farm Bill as an authorized, but unfunded study, with identical language in the Senate Farm Bill. The 2008 Farm Bill allowed a $500,000 appropriation for it (*Food, Conservation, and Energy Act of 2008*, 2008j). Issues of limited affordable, healthy food access were politically salient: Rush included his leadership on food deserts in his summer 2008 newsletter mailed to his constituents (Figure 5.3).

Following the study's authorization, a coalition of urban and rural Members of Congress advocated for its funding.[2] Once funding was secured, USDA began the study. The USDA focused on mapping areas with limited grocery store availability and low rates of car ownership (USDA, 2009a). The resulting maps became the Food Environment Atlas (USDA, 2010a). The report and Atlas were politically significant, influencing the selection of childhood obesity as Michelle Obama's signature policy (Kohan, 2010).

Congress communicated its interest in a local food system study through the Farm Bill's Manager's Amendment (Managers on the part of the House and the Senate for H.R. 2419, 2008b). The intended scope was the "potential community, economic, health and nutrition, environmental, food safety, and food security impacts of advancing local food systems and commerce" as well as descriptions of strategies used to overcome challenges (Managers on the part of the House and the Senate for H.R. 2419, 2008b). The USDA then conducted two local food system studies. One focused on national data evaluating local and regionally produced food trends (Martinez et al., 2010). The other used a case study approach focused on how local and regional food systems operate (King et al., 2010). These were the most detailed USDA analyses of the local and regional food sector since 2001 (Kantor, 2001).

Figure 5.3 Food desert newsletter from Representative Bobby Rush.

Contrasting "insider" and "outsider" advocacy strategies with policy outcomes

The presence of mobilized outsiders drives acceptance of insider proposals

The dispersion of political authority in the American federal system, and especially in the Congress, provides a political structure that aligns with the dispersion of a social movement. Many community-based organizations working across the country can cultivate allies in their elected representatives, leading to legislative changes, without the investment needed for a strong, centralized organization. The dispersion of political authority means that when one policymaker says "no" there are several others in the legislative or executive branch that can be reached. These preconditions enable the formation of national advocacy coalitions in the American local food movement.

A diversity of organization types utilizing a wide array of political strategies and communications allows social movements to benefit from a *radical flank effect* (McCarthy, Smith, & Zald, 1996). In many movements there are organizations that favor extreme tactics and moderate tactics. Extreme positions were proposed by interest groups in the ASAP alliance, such as Environmental Working Group (EWG) and EDF. They sought fundamental, structural reforms to the Farm Bill, and utilized highly controversial mass media campaigns to apply pressure on Congress to accept their proposals. Their political communications favored the use of mass-media over the direct involvement of stakeholders and citizens in policy decision-making, proposal development, and direct communication to policymakers.

While organizations like EWG and EDF pressed for policy change, their tactics were too extreme to engage directly with the House and Senate Agriculture Committees. Their presence helped to legitimate and strengthen more moderate groups (McCarthy et al., 1996, p. 12). The presence of outsiders pressing for change resulted in a political environment where Congress was receptive to the transformative proposals originating from tactically moderate organizations, such as NSAC, CFSC, and others in the FFPP. The pressure from the extreme groups—the radical flank—pushed Congress to seek out new policy ideas from advocacy groups who were willing to work with them. Local food was one of those new ideas.

Organizations that tried to play both the extreme "outsider" and moderate "insider" strategies simultaneously, like EDF, eventually were shut out of the Agriculture Committees' process. Another interest group that played both roles, American Farmland Trust (AFT), had a lower media profile. It cultivated several mainstream farm groups as allies and proposed a new commodity program that reduced expenditures, a feature that made its inclusion in the Farm Bill politically necessary. The success of the AFT proposal and FFPP may not have occurred without the outsider pressure: their influence alone was unlikely to push the Agriculture Committees to accept their proposals. These relationships

162   *American case study*

are shown in Table 5.4, with the radical flank effect shown as a by-product of the presence of the outsider alliance, ASAP, and a benefit to the insider alliance, FFPP.

Significant insider policy outcomes, few outsider policy outcomes

Locally and regionally produced food policies introduced in the 2008 Farm Bill were initiated within the Farm and Food Policy Project. The convergence of advocacy groups resulted in the formation of a holistic food systems policy. Policies utilizing this *food systems narrative* were accepted by Congressional champions on the House and Senate Agriculture Committees, and passed into law. This resulted in the USDA implementing the HUFED Center, the local

Table 5.4 A comparison of the "outsider" and "insider" strategies used in the 2008 Farm Bill

Outcomes	Outsider strategy Americans for Sensible Agriculture Policy project	Insider strategy Farm and Food Policy Project
"Success"	1) Increased attention 2) Pressure for reform 3) Legislative outcomes	1) Defense of existing policies 2) New legislation 3) Increased funding
"Change"	Fundamental; immediate; dramatic	Incremental; long-term; pragmatic
Media attention	Higher	Lower
Visibility to public & funders	Higher	Lower
Political feasibility of policy proposals	Less feasible Potential mix of options	More feasible Potential mix of options
Tactics	Adversarial	Consensus/Compromise
Authority	Moral	Political/Constituency
Needs Ag. Committee for "success"?	No	Yes
Direct legislative outcomes	Unlikely—Committee gatekeepers resent attacks	Likely, but specifics uncertain Benefits from pressure
Indirect legislative outcomes	Pressure creates a "reform environment" leading to some level of reform	+ Priorities positioned as "reasonable" − Risk of being grouped with the "outsiders"
"Failure"	Enactment of the "status quo" (anything less than a fundamental transformation)	1) Loss of existing policies or funding 2) No new legislation or funding 3) Co-option or tokenism

American case study   163

and regional food priority in the B&I program, and the local food and food desert studies. These and other earlier, incremental policy changes became the starting points for local food policy proposals in the 2014 Farm Bill (*Local Farms, Food, and Jobs Act of 2011*, 2011a, b; NSAC, 2012).

Overall, the FFPP was able to include the majority of its policy proposals in the 2008 Farm Bill. Policy opportunities related to *Seeking Balance* had expanded from 32 to 38 proposals. The FFPP's external evaluation indicated that of its 38 policy priorities, 23 were fully included in the Farm Bill (61 percent), seven were partially successful (18 percent), and eight not included (21 percent) (Headwaters Group Philanthropic Services, 2008, p. 9). Without the FFPP process, the proposals in the HFCWG, including local food policies, and the Diversity Initiative would not have occurred (Headwaters Group Philanthropic Services, 2008, p. 10). For WKKF's $5.5 million, three-year investment in policy coordination, capacity development, and communications, there was a net gain of $5 billion in mandatory program spending compared with the 2002 Farm Bill (Headwaters Group Philanthropic Services, 2008; NEMWI, 2008a).

Another outcome of collaboration was cultivation of allies in the specialty crops industry and public health community, such as the United Fresh Produce association and the American Public Health Association (CBI, 2008a; Earl Blumenauer [D-OR] et al., 2007; Headwaters Group Philanthropic Services, 2008, p. 18). The collaborative resulted in a *culture* of partnership formation: project participants gained capacity to overcome differences between organizations and learn the skills needed for collaboration (CBI, 2008a; Eukel & Beaufort, 2005).

The FFPP collaboration avoided the collective action failures of the 2002 Farm Bill (CBI, 2008a; Headwaters Group Philanthropic Services, 2008). However, its process was not free from conflicts or defections. The proposal process was lengthy, spanning two years. Participants lacked a holistic and unified understanding of what the alliance was until after it had made significant decisions. Some decisions could take months, as coalition participants needed time to review proposed FFPP actions with their boards and members prior to making decisions. Significant changes to the collaborative structure and communication processes were needed at key project milestones, resulting in short-term confusion. The personalities and leadership styles of participants conflicted: some were accustomed to top-down, quick decision-making processes and others accustomed to deliberative decision-making processes. The weakest point of the FFPP alliance was its ability to "collectively develop and implement advocacy strategy," due in part to the presence of core groups utilizing both insider and outsider strategies (CBI, 2008b, p. 4).

Concerns over whether the FFPP promoted incremental changes or fast, structural changes (e.g. a Kind Bill strategy) were not resolved until two years into the FFPP (Headwaters Group Philanthropic Services, 2008). Even with the mutual identification of priorities, some organizations remained attached to their own principal political tactics.

164　*American case study*

When the FFPP entered its legislative outreach phase, EDF became increasingly inactive in the FFPP and focused its effort in the ASAP alliance. It introduced its own legislation (*Healthy Farms, Foods, and Fuels Act of 2007*, 2007a, c). The ASAP alliance followed the Kind Amendment strategy, offering an alternative Farm Bill on the House and Senate floors (CBI, 2008a; *Healthy Farms, Foods, and Fuels Act of 2007*, 2007a, c). Because of the ASAP's controversial messaging, the agenda that EDF was able to achieve through the Agriculture Committees was far narrower than it and other ASAP participants had proposed in the Healthy Farms, Foods, and Fuels Acts of 2007.

Several outcomes of the 2008 Farm Bill were:

- the presence of "outsiders," meaning that interest groups pushing for reform in the media were necessary to create an overall atmosphere for reform;
- the presence of "insiders," meaning that advocacy groups and coalitions that directly connected stakeholders to policymakers were necessary to deliver *credible and feasible* policy recommendations;
- the FFPP's ability to influence Congress was dependent upon the pressure for reform generated from the messaging activities of the ASAP;
- the public was better informed of the ASAP's media campaigns, encouraging opposition to the Farm Bill, and a sense of "wrongness" about farm sector policies;
- the public was poorly informed of the FFPP's direct legislative campaign, and the outcomes of working directly with Congress; and
- public perceptions of the Farm Bill were more attuned to its passage being a negative occurrence, when its passage represented the largest shift in spending toward programs for environmental protection, conservation practices, socially disadvantaged producers, fruits and vegetables, and local food systems.

As a result of high-profile media campaigns critical of the agricultural policy community, popular beliefs of how to achieve policy change may well be at odds with how policy change actually occurs. The Agriculture Committees gradually included the interests of "outside" groups and granted them access as "insiders."

Conclusion: Empowerment as an alternative to rivalry

A combination of sustained practices in the 2008 Farm Bill overcame divisions observed in the 2002 Farm Bill. Deliberative decision-making established a mutual, food systems policy agenda; policy entrepreneurship actualized cross-sector policy proposals on local and regional food systems; collaborative learning and building the capacity to participate together reduced inter-organization rivalry.

American case study   165

Deliberative decision-making

Sustaining a deliberative process required inducements to collaborate and structures to sustain collaboration, including accountability mechanisms and procedures. In the FFPP, WKKF held grantees jointly accountable for project outcomes. The potential threat to rescind funding or potential for future funding—the coercive influence of *the power of the purse*—encouraged participation (Headwaters Group Philanthropic Services, 2008).

The grant proposal required participation of groups headquartered both inside and outside Washington, DC. Most organizations located outside participated in policy advocacy through coalitions which themselves practiced participatory, deliberative decision-making. Further, their decentralized structure allowed them to engage non-member stakeholders through regional listening sessions. The new decision-making processes established in the FFPP (Coordinating Council, Work Groups) benefited from a preexisting culture of participation established by advocacy coalitions. Work Group leaders were then able to both cultivate the priorities of their participants as well as represent their own organization's perspectives without dominating the Work Group process.

Policy entrepreneurship

The Diversity Initiative and the FFPP required coordinators to bridge gaps between organizations, resulting in new narratives and joint policy proposals. Instead of the FFPP's *Seeking Balance* report being written collaboratively by a Synthesis Team, as proposed, the coordinator, who was the most informed of each organization's priorities and concerns, became responsible for the report's narrative. The unfinished local food policy proposals needed someone to join the two Work Groups' proposals and link them with preexisting legal authorities. The WKKF Program Officer prompted organizations who had failed to work together in the past, to work together in the future. In each of these instances, an individual took responsibility for the whole. The ability to build bridges across different policy communities and to develop new policy approaches demonstrates the political significance of policy entrepreneurs in reframing policy problems and joining the priorities of multiple political constituencies (Kingdon, 1984; Roberts & King, 1991).

Policy entrepreneurship, a funder's support for a cross-sector collaborative policy process, and deliberative policy processes (which easily expanded to include new stakeholders and interest groups) helped overcome some dissent observed in the 2002 Farm Bill debate. The FFPP was not able to resolve *all* dissent between policy communities: dissension gained significant visibility from contentious media campaigns and radical tactics. Instead, it created new opportunities for diverse stakeholder-led coalitions which resulted in new, politically significant Congressional coalitions.

By doing so, it "made space" for a wide range of stakeholders and smaller groups from urban and rural communities representing people with low

166   *American case study*

incomes and socially disadvantaged producers. This was not an outcome those groups could achieve on their own had they acted separately or even within their own coalitions. It required an independent analysis of the policy environment as a whole, not reliant on media accounts and interest group analyses, and an individual funder with enough influence to resolve pandemic issues. It required policy institutions conducive to coalition-building (e.g. Congress), a significant investment in collaborative learning across perspectives, skilled individuals working as facilitators and policy entrepreneurs, and financial resources to support collaboration.

Collaborative learning and capacity building

Deliberative policy development, through the WKKF proposal process, the Work Groups, the Coordinating Council, and the coordination of legislative outreach resulted in four years of collaborative learning, enabling stakeholders from different perspectives to understand each others' issues and priorities. The multi-stakeholder, collaborative process of the FFPP's Work Groups made visible, and thus made legitimate, common interest issues. The deliberative process exposed the underdevelopment related to minority farmers and local and regional food systems. The increased visibility of these leadership gaps led to the Diversity Initiative's formation and NEMWI's proposals for local and regional food issues.

Collaboration resulted in new relationships, increasing the capacity of individuals to work beyond familiar organizational agendas. The internal evaluator of the FFPP process observed that:

> FFPP helped some individuals forge new or much stronger relationships with others. Some mentioned the mentoring that they received from others, learning a great deal about strategy and advocacy, as well as policy. Some mentioned they were surprised at how some of their long-time colleagues evolved and matured, and found new and powerful ways of working together.
>
> (CBI, 2008a, p. 9)

Collaboration increased individual capacities, raising awareness and acceptance of others' priorities.

An example is the Diversity Initiative, whose issues were originally excluded from the FFPP grant. FFPP participants successfully applied pressure to WKKF to fund a dedicated policy initiative on minority farmer issues. It began a year later than the FFPP, but gained significant policy access for socially disadvantaged producers. Its outcomes included several conservation program priorities and a landmark settlement for civil rights discrimination (CBI, 2008a; Cowan & Feder, 2012; Feder & Cowan, 2010; Headwaters Group Philanthropic Services, 2008).

American case study   167

Collaboration increased capacity for democratic participation

By learning how to collaborate—from raising one's own issues within a group through to negotiation and conflict resolution—individuals are better able to participate in society as citizens. The increase in individual capacity is an important outcome of grassroots mobilization, and benefits society as a whole: "The widespread possession of such skills, makes it possible to mobilize a large reservoir of support on short notice, allowing movement organizations to be both small and *professional*. But it also diffuses movement activities into the broader society" (Tarrow, 1998, p. 132). Participants in the FFPP bridged national, local, and regional levels, and engaged in policy through other forums. A venue where some FFPP participants were active was through local, regional, and state Food Policy Councils where cross-sector representatives address an area's food, agriculture, and food-related health issues (Mooney, Tanaka, & Ciciurkaite, 2014).

In contrast, media-led mobilization techniques concentrate public (and funder) attention on communication in place of the development of individual capacities and skills needed for negotiation (Kriesi, 1996; Tarrow, 1998). While a useful mobilization technique, dependency and overuse of a single strategy or tactic often reduces political outcomes over time, putting a social movement's issues at risk of marginalization (Laclau, 1996; Rose, 1993). The impact of media mobilization and outsider strategies increases when tactically moderate groups are willing to negotiate and engage with policymakers via the radical flank effect (McAdam et al., 1996). Despite their significance in policy change, the role of tactically moderate groups can be overlooked by reporters, funders, and the public.

Advocacy groups are in competition for limited policymaker attention. Outsider strategies are better conveyed through media because their controversial messages or tactics grab attention (Gamson & Meyer, 1996, p. 288). Within this case study period, the perception of outsider strategies as the norm for citizen activism was pervasive, as seen with accounts of Representative Kind as a "crusader." Also, reporters showed comparatively little interest in the less controversial FFPP compared with their interest in the ASAP. Insider strategies occupied a position of low visibility in national media reports on the Farm Bill.

For decades, the House and Senate Agriculture Committee accepted the priorities of outsiders *who were willing to work with the Committees*, over time. Outsiders who became insiders include the anti-hunger lobby in the 1960s and 1970s and conservation interests in the 1985 Farm Bill (Berry, 1982; Johnson, 1991–1992; Malone, 1986). The higher visibility of outsider strategies means that these can become established as the norm (especially for individuals without prior, direct policy experience) even when insider strategies are effective in the long term. If relatively few people have direct experience with policymakers, then the norm of outsider strategies and media mobilization can overshadow the direct engagement of citizens and stakeholders in the policy process.

168 *American case study*

Evidence in this case study shows that direct citizen and stakeholder engagement with policymakers can be a highly effective political strategy, especially when there is outside pressure. However, the public was more informed of the outsider strategy. This presents a challenge for the American food movement. Individuals wanting to engage on food policy may be more familiar with radical tactics and controversial policy proposals and less familiar with direct advocacy and communications strategies. With continued growth, the food movement will need to inform and educate new participants, organizations, and funders of the policy outcomes achieved from the direct engagement of citizens and stakeholders with policymakers.

Notes

1   ASAP was primarily funded by the William and Flora Hewlett Foundation, and included: AFT, Bread for the World, the CATO institute (a libertarian think tank), the Chicago Council on Foreign Relations, Citizens Against Government Waste, EDF, Environmental Working Group, National Wildlife Federation, Oxfam, and Taxpayers for Common Sense (Headwaters Group Philanthropic Services, 2008). All of these organizations are interest groups. Most are headquartered in Washington, DC. None are stakeholder-led, except for AFT, which included some farmers on its Board, and its President, Ralph Grossi, operated a ranch in California.
2   This included support from 28 Representatives (Bobby Rush [D-IL], Collin Peterson [D-MN], and Bennie Thompson [D-MS], 2008) and bipartisan support in the Senate (Robert Menendez [D-NJ] and Susan Collins [R-ME], 2008), an effort I supported while at NEMWI.

6 Making space for collaboration in the food system

Three practices for overcoming exclusion

This chapter directly contrasts content from the case studies of the American food movement (Chapters 2 and 5) and British food movement in England (Chapters 3 and 4). The basis for the comparison is that local food activity was similar in both countries, and that, at the national level, policymakers wanted consensus recommendations from local food stakeholders. However, the prevailing norms of internal and external communications among advocacy groups were different, to the point of extremes. Internal organizational governance processes were the critical point of difference between the UK and US.

How organizations made decisions affected their external relationships with their stakeholders, other organizations, and policymakers. These outcomes were affected by

- prevailing norms of how to conduct policy advocacy called *advocacy repertoires* (e.g. whether to protest or persuade government);
- the degree to which organizations and individuals acted to minimize their relative position of influence to organizations and individuals of lesser influence; and
- the degree of stakeholder participation in advocacy group decision-making and advocacy group accountability to stakeholders.

While the prevailing norms of advocacy work have a cultural element, organization leaders actively make choices when selecting organization structures, developing policy decision-making processes, and implementing policy campaigns.

Observing the beliefs and actions of individuals helps characterize how movement leaders draw on preexisting "cultural stock of how to protest and organize" (Zald, 1996, p. 267). Their interview comments are placed in context through participant observation and a comparison of organizational structures. After establishing the prevailing advocacy repertoires in each country's food movement, several strategies for overcoming exclusion are profiled: making space, policy entrepreneurship, and capacity building.

There was no British material to compare to the American material on making space and policy entrepreneurship. (This resulted in divergent cases

170 Collaboration in the food system

identified and discussed in the Preface.) At the observed food conferences there were no efforts to bring in people with low incomes, minorities, and, in some instances, farmers (Food Matters/Brighton and Hove Food Partnership, 2012; Hexham Community Partnership, 2012; *Making Local Food Our Future: MLFW 2012 Conference*, 2012; *MLFW 2011 Conference*, 2011; *SA Annual Conference 2011: Food and the Big Society*, 2011; Sue Miller [Liberal Democrat, Chilthorne Domer], 2011). Nor was it apparent that organizations sponsored leadership fellowships, anti-racism trainings, or hosted forums on race and inclusion as was done in the American food movement. "Making space" for typically excluded groups was not an established movement-wide practice on farm, food, and rural policy issues in England.[1]

In England, policy entrepreneurship on local food was not identified through interviews, nor was there evidence of any national-level, jointly implemented local food policy collaborations. Advocacy groups and their staff generally operated autonomously without consulting each other (CLA Policy Staff, 2011; DEFRA Food Policy Staff, 2011; Environmental Funders Network, 2011; FARMA Policy Staff, 2012; FCFCG Policy Staff, 2012; NFU Food Chain Staff, 2012; Sustain Policy Staff (a), 2011b). Information sharing across sectors was limited. For example, one organization that pioneered a consumer sustainability label did not consult with consumers on the label, only retailers (LEAF Staff, 2011). A rural advocacy group active on conservation issues in the EU CAP was not active on EU rural development policy (CPRE Policy Staff (b), 2011). When organizations did collaborate on local food policy, it was limited to activities like a jointly authored report (without follow-up, joint advocacy) (Sustain & Food Links UK, 2003), jointly appearing as speakers (but speaking to separate priorities) (Wildlife and Countryside Link, 2001b), the separate implementation of the Making Local Food Work collaborative policy priorities (MLFW Staff, 2011), and ad hoc decision-making within a coalition as described in Chapter 4.

On other issues, there was cross-sector engagement as occurred with the meat supply chain (Les Roberts et al., 1999; WWF UK Staff, 2011). The only cross-sector policy entrepreneurship related to local food was observed *internally* with a large NGO that owned both farmland and cafeterias (Former National Trust Policy Staff, 2011). Inter-organization, cross-sector policy entrepreneurship was not evidenced on local food issues at the national level in England.

Rather, it appeared that organizations and their staff preferred working in their niches because it was "safer" (less confrontation, less risk, less sharing of information with potential competitors). Also, there seemed to be a management culture whereby managers wanted to ensure staff time and resources were directly benefitting the organization (*Tasting the Future – Innovation Group Meeting*, 2011; *Tasting the Future – Second Assembly*, 2011). Both making space and policy entrepreneurship require a policy environment that supports boundary-crossing activities as a valuable use of staff time and resources. This chapter relies upon American examples to identify, describe, and discuss how

Collaboration in the food system 171

individuals, organizations, and a social movement worked to overcome pre-existing forms of social division and exclusion.

Advocacy repertoire: Political communication as a cultural script

Movement leaders often reconfigure culturally based forms of protest to create new political opportunities in response to social, economic, and political contexts (Swidler, 1986; Tilly, 1993). Often, social movement scholars liken the advocacy repertoire to a script, utilizing well-known forms of cultural expression in a public display of grievances (Tarrow, 1998). The repetition of particular strategies and tactics results in a "default" repertoire (Swidler, 1986; Tilly, 1993).

Policy change is only one of many possible intended outcomes of an advocacy repertoire. Other goals can include promoting public awareness, recruiting new supporters, or reconfirming pre-established beliefs. As a result, an advocacy repertoire can be primarily symbolic and oriented to transmitting beliefs about how policy change should occur rather than communicating successful policy change strategies (Clemens, 1996, p. 211). Connecting advocacy to familiar forms of cultural expression and ritual can aid mobilization. However, an overreliance on a single a default repertoire limits opportunities for learning and "constrain[s] the choices available for collective action" (Tilly, 1993, p. 264).

Dealing with political failure also has a script. Through a "fortifying myth," leaders can reframe a policy failure in a way that validates the beliefs of social movement supporters (Voss, 1996, p. 253). In the myth, responsibility for political change is externalized from the social movement and often placed upon government. This downplays the influence of movement leaders' deci-sions on policy outcomes. Shifting responsibility for political change from movement leaders to a government can limit a thorough examination of how movement leaders' choices of tactics and strategies impact policy outcomes (Snow et al., 1986; Voss, 1996). Thus, blaming the government for inaction may validate a movement's belief that the government does not represent the public will, and simultaneously obscure the political ineffectiveness of a default advocacy repertoire.

An important finding and central theme of this chapter is that movement leaders identify, select, and adapt preexisting elements of culture to harness public support for their issues. Thus, repertoires that reproduce or produce exclusion can be overcome or maintained, if movement leaders and their supporters (e.g. participants, funders, policymakers) choose to do so.

Contrasting American and British advocacy repertoires

A normal pattern of protest of professionalized interest groups is to identify a political opportunity and:

172 *Collaboration in the food system*

- identify the availability of preexisting problems, solutions, and narratives for framing the opportunity[2];
- publish a report, which may include "counter-science" aimed at challenging predominant understandings of the issue; and
- carry out policy campaigns through the news media.

These are familiar patterns of protest for "new social movements." Their development is often illustrated by the rise of professional environmentalism in the 1960s (for an example see Rucht, 1996). The advent of local food projects presented new possibilities for mobilization, such as cross-sector and urban–rural alliance formation, yet these approaches to mobilization ran against default advocacy repertoires.

Within English culture, social protest is often organized against institutions that concentrate political power: government and corporations. Protest on food issues is often oriented toward supermarket retailers or the government, as with adopting sustainable food procurement policies (Tasting the Future - Second Assembly, 2011; Working Group. POWER: How does local food policy development connect with other levels of activity?, 2012).

Interest groups in the US follow a similar pattern of single-issue campaigns and media-oriented mobilization. This is typically observed with environmental interest groups (Taylor, 1995). Similar to the UK, sector divisions and strong organizational autonomy can contribute to a fragmentation of political perspectives within a single policy community, as shown during the 2002 Farm Bill (Chapter 5).

While both the US and UK have environmental interest groups active on food policy, the difference is the degree to which these organizations influence food policy discourse. In the UK, the most influential food policy interest groups are linked to the environmental movement (e.g. SA and Sustain). By contrast, the American food movement has developed from a range of small farm, sustainable agriculture, community food security, social justice, civil rights, and rural development organizations. The UK has organizations covering similar issue areas, but these tend to be overshadowed by the communications-savvy environmental interest groups.

American food movement groups tend to coordinate on their policy advocacy through collaborative policy coalitions. These organizations offer a degree of consensus, professional leadership, and authentic stakeholder perspectives—factors that make them attractive organizations to work with for policymakers. The principal organizations promoting local food followed a repertoire of grassroots, community organizing. Typically they assembled stakeholders with an interest in the issue, and:

- engaged them in collaborative learning and discussion (including funders and institutions);
- facilitated a shared understanding of the issue, published as a consensus document;

Collaboration in the food system   173

- solicited membership guidance, often through a formal voting process;
- supported stakeholders in direct political communication; and
- sought allies in order to increase influence with policymakers.

An example of this approach was shown in Chapter 5. In this model of advocacy, collective action is oriented around empowering excluded or aggrieved groups to participate in the political process. These patterns can be observed with the American rural populist and agrarian movements (Brasier, 2002; Sheingate, 2001) and civil rights movements (McAdam, 1996). Gaining access to governmental institutions has helped to legitimatize the American local food movement (Coglianese, 2001).

Protest or persuasion to reach transformation?

American organizations that emerged as promoters of local food had self-organized into several advocacy coalitions. In this organization structure, members typically share in decision-making and policy advocacy. The formation of the Community Food Security Coalition (CFSC), Farmers Market Coalition (FMC), National Family Farm Coalition (NFFC), National Sustainable Agriculture Coalition (NSAC), and Rural Coalition illustrate *additive power*, where the influence of small, individual organizations is augmented through collaboration. The level of collaboration required within the coalition setting supported the development of the skills needed for collaboration (e.g. facilitation, negotiation, compromise) and fostered a culture conducive to *external* policy collaboration.

In addition to forming and maintaining relationships with national advocacy groups, these advocacy coalitions and their members hosted networking events that facilitated engagement with unaffiliated organizations and individuals from different sectors. Some examples include conferences hosted by the Midwest, Northeast, and Southeast Sustainable Agriculture Working Groups, CFSC, and the National Farm to School Network (NFSN). A single organization's perspective was not prominent at these events, in contrast to the 2011 SA conference observed in the UK (*SA Annual Conference 2011: Food and the Big Society*, 2011). Typically conferences were organized through a committee of multiple organizations, with events co-hosted by two or more organizations. Also, a peer-review process for conference session selection is a common practice (e.g. CFSC, 2011), which further opened opportunities for diverse perspectives to enter into an event and movements discourse. Both the USDA's Risk Management Agency's Partnership and Outreach program and the W. K. Kellogg Foundation (WKKF) have helped support and fund cross-sector networking events with explicit goals to increase participation of marginalized groups (WKKF, 2012d).

For example, the WKKF's 11th Food and Community Conference in 2012 focused on providing opportunities for collaborative learning, forming cross-sector relationships, and building "a more effective movement capable of

174 *Collaboration in the food system*

creating, driving and attaining transformational change locally and nationally" (Gail C. Christopher [WKKF Vice President for Program Strategy] & Lind Jo Doctor [WKKF Program Officer], 2012, p. 1). These goals extended to the design of the conference's main tracks: understanding a new-to-you issue, movement building, food value chains, food and agricultural policy, leadership development, and communications (WKKF, 2012a). Locally produced foods were featured prominently as part of WKKF's grant-making strategy and within the conference sessions. Also, local food was included in the first two of five of WKKF's value statements: equity and community determination (WKKF, 2012c, p. 5). For WKKF, local food and local community empowerment were intertwined with social justice and sustainability.

WKKF also promoted racial and social equity by inviting a diverse audience, including people of color, farm and food workers, and activists and leaders based outside the US. It used the conference's main plenary sessions to highlight this diversity and gave the stage for people from marginalized groups to speak and share their stories. One of these plenary sessions, *Building a powerful food movement: Deep knowledge, broad base, strong networks and innovative approaches to food policy change*, shared the results of a year-long learning process that identified key actions needed for policy change at each stage of the food supply chain.

One of the plenary's panelists, Richard McCarthy, explained how he came to value a collaborative approach to policymaking. McCarthy, who is white and of European descent, described how the racially charged politics of New Orleans drove him to seek out a more collaborative approach in his policy practice.

> I began this work as a rabble-rouser, hovering around the barricades of us versus them – environmental justice, neighborhood organizing and far too long around the issues of David Duke.[3]. . . It was during those Duke years that I became really weary by the soul-numbing dynamic of searching out enemies and confronting them, responding to them.
>
> And it was about 20 years ago, as a fledging guerilla gardener that I found food. I remember the first time I met . . . Ben Burkett,[4] who said "the magic about food is that unsuspecting allies find themselves sitting down at the same table. And, because food is sitting there, we are sitting there." So I traded up from hovering around barricades to hovering around the informal economy.
>
> (from audio recording, McCarthy, 2012)

McCarthy then described his first farmers market opening in the racially charged environment of 20 years earlier.

Prior to the market's opening, the health department came and indicated that they would shut it down. He consulted a food safety specialist to develop the market's own food safety guidelines. He then enlisted the political support of a local city councillor and two state senators, a conservative white man and

Collaboration in the food system 175

a liberal black woman. He made the case to the conservative about "unleashing free enterprise" and the liberal about increasing access for fresh food in the city (McCarthy, 2012). Through these two allies, the health department backed down. It was willing to accept the market's standards to prevent unwelcome legislative changes. Of the two Senators, McCarthy said, "I needed them both." He indicated later that even though the risks facing the food movement are higher today than 20 years before, he still believes it is relevant to be "reaching out to non-traditional allies and reforming them with language that is disarming. I think that alone is transformative" (McCarthy, 2012).

McCarthy explained his shift in tactics in personal terms. He had found the "us versus them" dynamic of the environmental movement "soul numbing." Through food and the tangible work of forming a farmers market, he found personal reward when finding common ground across differences. McCarthy continues to practice this collaborative approach. He and his colleagues promoted the use of Food Stamps and their electronic benefits at New Orleans Crescent City farmers' market and countrywide (Megill, 2005). These techniques have diversified the demographic composition of attendees at the Crescent City farmers' market (marketumbrella.org, 2012). In addition, McCarthy was the founding President for the Farmers Market Coalition (marketumbrella.org, n.d.), which is led by a board of farmers market managers from across the US.

McCarthy's short speech reveals many characteristics of the American food movement. These include adapting messages to the political situation, seeking out unusual allies, avoiding a default adversarial stance, and working to broaden inclusion among supporters of local food. The conciliatory approach practiced by McCarthy can be contrasted by that of Sustain in England, which engaged in adversarial policy dialogues with government policymakers.

At the 2012 MLFW Conference, Caroline Spellman, the Minister of State for Agriculture, Food, and Rural Affairs was the keynote speaker. Her comments on *Shaping the future of food: The role of community in food policy* were followed by an expert panel. In introducing Spellman, Peter Couchman, President of the Plunkett Foundation, which coordinated the MLFW project, observed "We've never had interest at that level before" (from audio recording, Couchman, 2012). A Minister of State had not previously attended and spoken at a public event for local food. To Couchman, Spellman's attendance was a significant symbol of legitimacy for the local food movement and a potential political opportunity.

Her speech covered a range of domestic and international food policy topics. She addressed policy for the local food sector most directly when she discussed improving agricultural skill development, primarily for horticultural production, and the government's sustainable food procurement efforts. After speaking for about 15 minutes and taking several questions from the audience, she stepped from the stage, presumably leaving the event. Two of her staff remained at the stage's edge, visible to the audience and panelists, to observe panelist responses to the Minister's speech.

176   *Collaboration in the food system*

Katherine Dalmeny, Policy Director of Sustain (which was one of the two policy delivery partners for MLFW) was the first panelist to respond to Spellman's comments. Unlike McCarthy's political approach, which was conciliatory and collaborative, Dalmeny responded to the Minister of State's speech with sarcasm and personally directed criticisms.

> I really think it's interesting that when she [Spellman] talks about Malawi she said things which were really, really nice and saying sensible things. But when she talks about Britain it's like we're totally divorced from who we are.
>
> [audience laughter and applause]
>
> . . .
>
> So why is that? There is something about the Malawi situation that is really clear about what is happening. . .
>
> Where in late stage capitalism it is—when the food system hits—it's all terribly complicated and lots of power struggles to be had. So it is a different setting. And unfortunately we've got a government that is representing big business quite a lot of the time. So we've got a different struggle here.
> (from audio recording, Kath Dalmeny [Sustain Policy Director], 2012)

Dalmeny then offered praise to the government for introducing a social services bill, which furthered financing for social enterprises. However, when Dalmeny came to the issue of sustainable food procurement by the public sector, an issue she has represented for nearly a decade at Sustain, she used sarcasm and personally directed criticisms to describe the government's actions.

Dalmeny described the government's support of sustainable food procurement as laughable, because only "one third of food bought by the public sector is now covered by mandatory standards." Responding to Minister Spellman's statements about the government's support of sustainable food procurement, Dalmeny stated sarcastically:

> Thank you very much, Caroline.
>
> It took us all lobbying like hell to get it. But it is in there. And it does mean that sustainable fish will be served.
>
> [dramatic pause]
>
> And that's about it, actually.
>
> [audience laughter]
>
> So it is—it is an encouragement to use more food that meets British standards. . . We're very happy about standards. [inaudible aside] . . . of the two-thirds [not covered by standards]—about a third which is schools

and the other third which is hospitals. . . . So there are no nutrition standards or sustainability standards for food in hospital—at all—in England. There are some in Ireland, Scotland, and Wales—they're always ahead of us.

There are no national standards now for Academies.[5] So one million [students] are being taken out of nutrition standards by our government. And I'm really, really angry about that, as you can probably tell.

Standards help. And especially around all these things that lead to the best package around food systems and sustainable food systems. So we've got to keep fighting back.

You asked about changing the scene? I think that most of the things we do are an uphill battle. The point of policies is to make everything plain sailing. Those who will take issues with policies that make it plain sailing to do the good stuff are hands down wrong.
(from audio recording, Kath Dalmeny [Sustain Policy Director], 2012)

Dalmeny's communication techniques established rapport with the audience while publically criticizing a Minister of State. She used her frustration and anger with the government to justify her positions, emphasizing the need for "fighting back." She adopted an "us versus them" position, indicating that the government supports big businesses and takes actions that "are hands down wrong" while advocates like herself work to promote the "good stuff." She sought to embarrass the English government into action by praising the efforts of Wales and Scotland and used sarcasm to undercut praise for the changes adopted by the government.

Throughout her response to Spellman, Dalmeny demonstrated an adversarial view of political change. What Dalmeny viewed as an opportunity to attack the government, Couchman saw as an opportunity for further engagement. The response of Sustain was to use tactics that would undermine government credibility, including the Minister's personal credibility, and arouse public support.

The differing tactics of Dalmeny and McCarthy illustrate the contrast in political repertoires in the UK and US. The choice of who to put on a stage shows differences in how peers view McCarthy's and Dalmeny's work. Both are considered important figures in food policy change. McCarthy sought to create political opportunities through cultivating allies—a food scientist, a local councillor, and two state Senators—and work across racial and political differences. Dalmeny distanced her organization from the government and used rhetoric to align the audience with her position. Dalmeny's critique illustrates how contention and conflict are resources used for shaping public opinion *against* institutions and their leaders. By contrast, McCarthy used alliances, formed from one part of government—the legislative branches of both the city and state governments—to create political opportunity with the health department—an executive agency.

178   *Collaboration in the food system*

For an English pressure group, the power of protest—of deliberately antagonizing the highest domestic policymaker on food and agricultural policy—is a logical political strategy. For an American food movement activist and leader, the persuasive power of forming unlikely alliances is viewed as a logical way to achieve food systems change. The English movement is oriented to adversarial tactics; the American movement is oriented towards collaboration and consensus-building. These tactical choices have a significant influence on how marginalized groups are included in each country's movement.

The "seriousness of movement building"

Discussions of social inequality were less visible in the English food movement than in the American movement. Despite critiques of central government's unjust authority, similar practices of centralized authority in civil society were present, but not obvious to organization leaders. For example, in a UK survey of rural NGOs, respondents identified significant mistrust between organizations on their lobbying and influencing activities. This mistrust was characterized as the presence of "hidden agendas, propaganda and domination by individuals and elites" (globe, 2009, p. 116). These issues are similar to Chapter 4, where a few organizations tended to dominate advocacy on local food.

The focus of most English advocacy group leaders has been "upward looking." Their organizations are oriented toward reducing power inequalities within centralized institutions of government, supermarket retailers, and agro-food corporations rather than addressing inequalities internal to their own organizations and their broader movement. By contrast, the American food movement is "downward looking," oriented towards empowering less privileged and marginalized social groups, and "horizontal looking," seeking allies with groups that have similar grievances.

The culture of empowerment and "seriousness" of movement building in the US were lasting impressions for a British environmental interest group worker, who participated in CFSC's 2011 conference in Oakland, California. At the time, she co-led a national food project for a well-known British environmental interest group. As an "outsider" coming to the US, her perspective is useful to balance against my impressions of an "outsider" coming to England.

At the time, the Occupy Oakland movement was encamped two blocks from the conference hotel. While the conference had no direct linkage with Occupy Oakland, its presence and attention to issues of economic and social inequality was felt, extending to the conference's themes of food access and sustainability. In an interview conducted after returning to England, the presence of Occupy Oakland was an important touchstone for her, as was the history of the civil rights movement in Oakland.

In the interview, she made distinctions between the professionalism of English advocacy groups and the inclusion in the US of people from

Collaboration in the food system 179

historically marginalized social groups at the CFSC conference. She identified their "seriousness" to movement building and their self-belief in being able to influence policy as traits she had not observed in British food policy advocacy. While she was emboldened by the sense of confidence and empowerment of the American movement, she identified a heaviness that came with considering one's own status as empowered or disempowered. She contrasted that "heavy" feeling with the creativity and playfulness of "innovation" in the professional culture of a well-established environmental interest group.

Interviewer: What were your impressions of the food security event in Oakland?

Interviewee:. . . So I have lots, I am just trying to order them. Um. So the overwhelming one is—we—how seriously organizing is in the States. I don't really, I've never come across that kind of—um, I'm looking for the word—confidence, I think.

Like, over here [in Britain] I'm not that connected to the community development world. But, I know here we call it more community development. Where—at least in my mind—it has connotation of, doesn't have a political edge so much, doesn't have this kind of intent to almost knock out the hegemony. You know, it doesn't have that kind of muscle.

Whereas in the States, at the conference, I really felt it. I felt—yeah— that kind of edge, that confidence, really trying to have a collective voice of a movement. Yeah, that's the thing. It felt like a movement whereas over here it feels like disparate "that's a nice thing to do, yes we should help our communities" but not, kind of, a credible, serious way of building an alternative system, I guess. It's more to ameliorate the impacts of the current system rather than to create a different one, is my sense over here. And I loved it. I really loved it. I love that, that kind of. . . it's more hopefulness, I think, rather than confidence, that sense of agency, um, sense of self-belief, and really, you know, we have to do this and we are in it together.

And I love that phrase "community organizer." I've heard it, of course I've heard—because you know, I know Barack Obama used to be a community organizer. And I'm sitting in that session, and they say "put your hands up if you work in policy." And I was like, I don't really. And they say, "put your hand up if you're an organizer," and I'm like "Oh, I'm an organizer!"

I really hadn't thought of myself like that. But I guess that helped me see what I actually do. I organize people to have cumulative impact. Um, yeah. It gave me hope on a level of this is a serious intent, there is a serious intent behind it and I could place myself behind it, which is always nice.

So that was one thing. The second thing is how little I heard words around innovation. I did hear it a bit, like I saw it in the program, but

180 *Collaboration in the food system*

the tone of the workshops I was in that wasn't the frame a lot of people were using to organize their work. It was more like activism (pause) or, yeah, grassroots—all these words. It's not, um, a criticism, but I think it could benefit from that kind of thinking because I could see them struggling with the same things we struggle with—how do you connect people, joint-learning—there was a lot attention paid on how do we connect for policy "asks" from all of our different endeavors, but not how do we connect to accelerate innovation or seeing what they do as innovation.

Um, I just think, I don't know enough of this myself, I know there are a lot of practices, disciplines, like design thinking for example. And it's kind of weird because I was staying with a friend who works with IDEO, the innovations consultancy. And they just launched ideo.org. So they are working with big, philanthropic institutions, like Gates Foundation, and so on. And one of the projects they are working on is how to reinvent Detroit. And like, local food was part of those conversations, and you had the guys from Detroit at the Conference as well. So it felt like they were two separate worlds, and I didn't feel them that intentionally connected.

Interviewer: Well, what does innovation mean to you?

Interviewee: Just a different way of doing things. I think, very basically, superficially, innovators attempt to disrupt the status quo, or find an alternative to the status quo. It's not about incremental change. It's about just disrupting flows of power, capital, habitual patterns, to patterns that lead to greater—call it what you want—health, balance, equality, so to me a lot of what these guys are doing is social innovation.

It's the flipside of the same coin. That they really identify with being grassroots, marginalized, disenfranchised, which is excellent because they link sustainable with other societal issues. Though, I think that was another important observation that it wasn't really a sustainability conference. It was really a gathering of people talking about their livelihoods, a sense of justice, um, kinda a sense of reclaiming their lives, you know, that kind of which I find really inspiring. I think potentially the flipside of that there is a kind of a heaviness to that, right? A kind of seeing yourself as "the other" as having to—and being disempowered or having been disempowered. Where I think innovation has more lightness, creativity, playfulness.

(from audio recording, British environmental interest group staff, 2011)

Several themes are apparent. First, she identified a belief in the American food movement that individuals working together can have real impacts. She described a hopeful outlook, with "confidence" and "intent to almost knock out the hegemony." She described community organizing as work valuable enough for a president to do, while pointing out that community development work is considered lower-status work in England. To her, community development is easily dismissed in Britain—a belief that suggests community-based work is marginalized within the professional environmental community. She described how one of the plenary speakers sought to make visible *both* the people engaged in policy and the people engaged in community organizing. She observed that American activists at the local level engaged on national policy issues.

Second, she indicated a difference between what is considered credible work in agro-food reform in the US and England. Building an alternative food movement through community organizing has a much higher status in the US. By contrast much of her work, which was focused on England, was devoted to ameliorating the existing food chain. She found that within the context of the CFSC conference, empowerment and social justice had a higher prioritization, whereas the British organizations were focused more on innovating within the confine of the existing supply chain.

Third, in her comparison of innovation to grassroots activism, there is an implicit comparison made between professional, more mainstream work, and activism. Innovation occurs through an entity, like a consultancy, or a recognizable philanthropic foundation. Also, innovation is focused on small disruptions that lead to large-scale change in "power, capital, and habitual patterns." The work practiced by IDEO in Detroit and by Detroit's community activists occurred in "two separate worlds." One of these approaches is supported by outside resources from the Gates Foundation and is described as occurring from the top down. This is contrasted with the bottom-up efforts of community activists. At the individual level, she indicated that activists brought their own personal and emotional experiences to their work: they were people "reclaiming their lives." Innovation was professional and intellectual and activism was personal and emotional.

Fourth, addressing inequality, while a rewarding activity, was more difficult than innovation because it required understanding one's own social status and power in relation to others. She linked the work of people "reclaiming their lives" and "seeking justice" to the emotional inspiration from addressing injustice: "Oh, I'm an organizer!" She described the introspection of considering oneself as "the other" as having a quality of "heaviness" when one considers oneself or others being or having been disempowered. In contrast, innovation work "has more lightness, creativity, playfulness." Societal change achieved through grassroots activism required a person to confront and address one's own position and behavior in order to empower oneself and empower others.

The "normality" of structural processes makes exclusion "invisible"

Critiques of unequal status and authority were present within the British local food movement. This was most notable within the context of managing cooperative enterprises. England's MLFW project sought to address the potential for a community food project's decision-making processes to exclude

182 *Collaboration in the food system*

volunteers, project participants, and stakeholders. To address this issue, Cooperatives UK, a MLFW partner, published two resources: a governance handbook, *Simply governance*, and a series of five guidebooks, *From conflict to cooperation* (Cooperatives UK, 2011a, c). One of these guides, on *Organizational growth and development*, indicated that informal decision-making processes can exclude democratic decision-making in what it calls a "Tyranny of Structurelessness" (Cooperatives UK, 2011b, p. 9). It directs readers to an essay by Jo Freeman, an American feminist, called "The Tyranny of Structurelessness" (Freeman, 1972 (revised)).

The reference to Freeman's essay in the Cooperatives UK guide is within a section about "managing change" as an organization shifts from an informal to formal structure (Cooperatives UK, 2011b, p. 8). Freeman's essay is used to describe how unstructured processes result in elites—those with greater access to resources, status, networks, or charisma—occupying informal leadership roles (Cooperatives UK, 2011b, p. 9). In her essay, she asserts that without a structure, there is no accountability to the group as a whole.

> This has two potentially negative consequences of which we should be aware. The first is that the informal structure of decision-making will be much like a sorority – one in which people listen to others because they like them and not because they say significant things. As long as the movement does not do significant things this does not much matter. But if its development is not to be arrested at this preliminary stage, it will have to alter this trend.
>
> The second is that informal structures have no obligation to be responsible to the group at large. Their power was not given to them; it cannot be taken away. Their influence is not based on what they do for the group; therefore they cannot be directly influenced by the group. This does not necessarily make informal structures irresponsible. Those who are concerned with maintaining their influence will usually try to be responsible. The group simply cannot compel such responsibility; it is dependent on the interests of the elite.
>
> (break between paragraphs added, Freeman, 1972 (revised), para. 21)

Freeman's observations of informal decision-making processes can be applied to English interest groups who lacked formal accountability to their members and stakeholders.

Sustain and the SA used an ad hoc policy decision-making process. In the SA, members were not consulted on policy decisions and Sustain's alliance had minimal member participation. In both organizations, professional staff was not formally accountable to members. As in Freeman's essay, group members were not involved in making policy decisions, nor could they compel policy staff in either organization to *not* make a policy decision (shown in Chapter 4). Further, stakeholders in both organizations bore the risks of

Collaboration in the food system   183

negative policy outcomes, such as diminished political opportunity, as was the case with the food miles narrative. The lack of stakeholder accountability means that both the SA and Sustain functioned as "elites," by Freeman's definition of the term.

Informal processes may work when most leaders are known to each other and are of relatively equal status. However, movement expansion will result in new leaders, new issues, and new solutions. Informal structures are challenged to accommodate movement growth. Also, the development of new organizations and issues can be threatening to leaders of well-established organizations. This was evidenced with the policing behavior in Chapter 4. Maintaining informal structures in the face of movement expansion can be considered a form of control to maintain the influence of incumbent organizations. Sustain and the SA limit direct member and stakeholder engagement in their policy decision-making and were the two most influential organizations in the English food movement (Figure 4.4).

The American food movement has had challenges with increasing inclusion due to preexisting inequalities in American society. Addressing racial inequality had been a source of contention within the Community Food Security Coalition, and led it to introduce an organization-wide effort to "dismantle [structural] racism" (CFSC, 2006b; WhyHunger, 2012). CFSC's efforts were considered inadequate by some of its members (Afri-can Foodbasket, n.d.; Growing Food and Justice for All Initiative, n.d.; Morales, 2011; Shuput, 2008). However, CFSC had facilitated several forums that increased their visibility. The resulting Growing Food & Justice for All Initiative emerged from discussions hosted on CFSC forums, including an open-access email list called COMFOOD, its Outreach and Diversity Committee, and annual conferences (CFSC, 2006b; Shuput, 2008; Slocum, 2006). Creating space and opportunities for discussion are strategies used for increasing inclusion in the American food movement. These strategies extend not just to racial inequality, but also the inclusion of local-income residents in project design and implementation (Cohen, 2002) and farmers and local stakeholders in positions of national policy decision-making (FFPP, 2005b; NFFC, 2012).

American culture and English culture both have touchstones for recognizing social inequality (race in the US, class in the UK). Consequently, a critical point of difference between the English and American movements is that American activists adopted practices to address social exclusion within their organizations and within the broader movement.

Comparing the practices of advocacy groups promoting local food in Britain and the US

Overall, groups based in England demonstrated lower levels of stakeholder participation in decision-making than American advocacy groups. These general patterns represent the default advocacy repertoires at the society level. However, advocacy groups innovate and can create their own advocacy

Table 6.1 Typology of stakeholder participation

Typology	Characteristics
0. No engagement	The concerns of stakeholders are not sought, are ignored, and/or their involvement is restricted (passively or actively).
1. Manipulative participation	Participation is simply a pretense, with "stakeholders" on official boards but they are not elected and have no power. This level is sometimes described as "tokenism".
2. Passive participation	Stakeholders participate by being told what has been decided or has already happened; this involves unilateral announcements by decision-makers without listening to people's responses. The information being shared belongs only to those in positions of authority.
3. Participation by consultation	Stakeholders participate by being consulted or by answering questions. Those with greater authority define problems and information-gathering processes, and so control analysis. Such a consultative process does not concede any share in decision-making, and professional staff has no obligation to take on board stakeholder's views.
4. Participation for material incentives	Stakeholders participate in order to gain access to a resource. The project's outcomes are partially dependent on stakeholder involvement (e.g. as a funding requirement, project implementation) but goals are defined by those in authority. It is very common to see this called participation, yet stakeholders have no stake in the project after its end.
5. Functional participation	Participation is seen as a means to achieve project goals defined by external agents (e.g. reduced costs) or organization leaders. Stakeholders may participate by forming groups to meet predetermined objectives. Such involvement may be interactive and involve shared decision-making, but tends to arise only after major decisions have already been made external agents. Stakeholder desires are framed—at worst co-opted—to fit external goals.
6. Interactive participation	Stakeholders participate in joint analysis, prioritization, and implementation. Participation is seen as a right, not just the means to achieve project goals. The process is inherently pluralistic, using methods that involve multiple perspectives, cross sector boundaries, and focus on systemic learning processes. As stakeholders take control of decisions and determine how resources are used, they have a stake in maintaining structures or practices.
7. Self-mobilization	People participate by taking initiative independently of external institutions to change systems. They develop contacts with external institutions for resources and technical advice they need, but retain control over how resources are used. Self-mobilization can spread if governments, funders, and NGOs provide an enabling framework of support. Such self-initiated mobilization may or may not challenge existing distributions of wealth and power.

(Table adapted from Pretty (1995), text utilized by permission from Elsevier.)

Collaboration in the food system 185

repertoires. For instance, in Britain, FARMA and FCFCG adopted participatory decision-making processes, intentionally rejecting the prevailing practice of policy leadership from professional staff within single-issue interest groups. In another British example, the Tasting the Future Network hosted a cross-sector learning network on food issues from the community level through to the international level. Participatory decision-making processes were more common in American food, farming, and rural advocacy groups.

Levels of stakeholder engagement are recognized approaches to discuss stakeholder participation in American and British NGO practice and research. Pretty (1995, 2008), a British sustainable agriculture professor, considers the motivations for stakeholder engagement on a seven-step scale, ranging from manipulation (1) to self-mobilization (7). Decades earlier, Lowe, a British researcher, utilized a "ladder of citizen participation" developed in the US to describe citizen participation in local environmental groups in Britain (Arnstein, 1969; Lowe, 1977). Hart's work on youth engagement utilized the ladder of participation within the context of British community planning practices (Hart, 1992). In the US, a similar "ladder of participation" was used in an international public market manager training hosted by the Project for Public Spaces in Washington DC in 2005 (American Planning Association, n.d.).

Pretty's "typology of participation" provided a concise framework for comparing levels of stakeholder engagement in American and English advocacy groups promoting local food at the national level (Pretty, 1995, 2008). Although Pretty had developed his table for sustainable development projects, it was adapted for stakeholder-led projects through findings from this research (Table 6.1). A lower level of participation was added below manipulation—no engagement (0)—to accommodate interest groups that intended to include stakeholders in their decision-making processes. Intentional exclusion of stakeholders can be a form of manipulation. However, some organizations, such as think tanks, do not aim to include stakeholders.

Advocacy organizations and policy networks involved in local food at the national level are compared by their levels of stakeholder engagement in Table 6.2. American organizations were identified from direct interactions through professional policy experiences; most were active in the FFPP. British groups were identified from an initial scan of farm, food, and rural policy organizations documented in Hunt (2011b), an initial publication of this research.

In general, organization types with a higher level of engagement included advocacy coalitions, federations, and cooperatives. Organization types with generally lower engagement included interest groups, especially those utilizing pressure tactics, and think tanks. Engagement levels in trade associations differed more by individual organization practices than by structure.

Importantly, the governance of NGOs was not universally democratic. In other words, NGOs are not universally "good" at stakeholder and citizen engagement. This was an important finding because many scholars and government leaders share a belief that the greater participation of NGOs contribute to a democratic civil society (for example Richardson (2000)).

Table 6.2 Comparison of the level of stakeholder engagement by organization/network for national-level local food policies in the US and England. Note: organizations are listed by level of engagement (highest first) then alphabetized

Organization and location		Type	Multi-sector	Policy decision-maker(s)	Stakeholder role in policy decisions	Implementation	Level of engagement
Community Food Security Coalition (CFSC)	US	Advocacy coalition	Yes	Members Board	Membership consultation through "listening sessions" Stakeholder-led Board makes policy decisions Members sign on to campaigns	Staff and members Forms alliances with other coalitions Direct lobbying	7
Farmers Market Coalition (FMC)	US	Advocacy coalition	No	Board	Stakeholder-led board makes policy decisions Members sign on to campaigns	Staff Board Advocacy campaigns Direct lobbying	7
Federation of City Farms & Community Gardens (FCFFG)	UK	Federation	No	Board	Stakeholder-led board makes policy decisions Members sign on to campaigns	Local policy outreach by members Campaigns designed to elicit local citizen engagement	7
National Family Farm Coalition (NFFC)	US	Advocacy coalition	No	Board	Stakeholder-led board makes policy decisions Members sign on to campaigns	Staff Members Direct lobbying	7
National Farmers Retail & Market Association (FARMA)	UK	Trade association; Cooperative	Yes[1]	Board	Stakeholder-led board makes policy decisions Members sign on to campaigns	Staff Members Direct lobbying	7
National Sustainable Agriculture Coalition (NSAC)	US	Advocacy coalition	Yes	Members	Stakeholder-led policy work groups Members vote on policy platform	Staff and members Forms alliances with other coalitions Direct lobbying	7

Organization	Country	Type	Independent policy	Structure	Policy process	Tactics/activities	Score
Country Land and Business Association (CLA)	UK	Trade association with regional offices	Yes	Members	Stakeholder-led policy work groups Members decide on policy	Staff Targeted media campaigns Direct lobbying	7
National Farm to School Network (NFSN)	US	Coordinating network Learning network	Yes	Advisory board Policy staff Regional staff	Formal member consultations Member review of policy platform	National and regional staff Members Direct lobbying	7
Farm and Food Policy Project (FFPP, coordinated by NEMWI)★	US	Alliance Collaborative project	Yes	Stakeholder-led work groups Stakeholder-led Coordinating Council Project partners	Stakeholders and project partners use a deliberative process to identify priorities in work groups	Direct lobbying by project partners' policy staff and local, regional, and national stakeholder organizations Limited media outreach Online advocacy	6
Rural Coalition	US	Advocacy coalition	No[2]	Board Project partners	Membership consultation through "listening sessions" Stakeholder-led board makes policy decisions Members sign on to campaigns	Staff Board Partners Direct lobbying	6
Northeast Midwest Institute (NEMWI)	US	"Think and do tank" Regional offices	Yes	NE–MW House-Senate Coalition Policy staff	NE–MW Coalition identifies priorities Coordinates with state government offices	Staff NE–MW Coalition Policy research, analysis, and outreach Forms alliances with other national/regional/local organizations	6
National Good Food Network (NGFN, coordinated by Wallace Center)★	US	Collaborative learning network	Yes	No policy	Stakeholder-led Advisory Council Wallace Center consults members and provides input to NSAC	Informs partners of relevant NSAC priorities Wallace Center is an NSAC member	6

Table 6.2 continued

Organization and location		Type	Multi-sector	Policy decision-maker(s)	Stakeholder role in policy decisions	Implementation	Level of engagement
Tasting the Future (coordinated by World Wildlife Fund UK)★	UK	Collaborative learning network	Yes	WWF-facilitated Informal stakeholder advisory group	Informal advisory group Participants volunteer to develop content for networking meetings	Staff Participants Stakeholder engagement activities at events	6
American Farmland Trust (AFT)	US	Centralized advocacy group with regional offices Public membership subscriptions	Yes	Board Policy staff Regional staff	Stakeholder-led board Stakeholder consultation through "listening sessions" coordinated by regional staff	Staff Direct lobbying Media outreach Policy communication to members (subscribers) through its magazine	5
National Farmers Union (NFU UK)	UK	Trade association with regional offices	No	Policy staff	Consulted (often through surveys) Informed of policy decisions	Staff Direct lobbying Media outreach	4
Environmental Defense Fund (EDF)	US	Centralized interest group with regional offices Pressure group Public membership subscriptions	No	Policy staff informs Director Director makes final decisions	Passive Informed of campaign objectives	Staff Media campaigns Policy campaigns Direct lobbying Forms temporary alliances with other pressure groups	2
Campaign for the Protection of Rural England (CPRE)	UK	Centralized interest group with regional offices	No	Staff	Passive Central office directs regional offices	Staff Media campaigns Policy campaigns Policy communication to	2

			Public membership subscriptions			members (subscribers) through its magazine	
Sustain: the alliance for better food and farming	UK	Centralized interest group with "alliance" members Pressure group	Yes	Informal input from selected alliance members Director makes final decisions	Small group consulted in campaign design Membership asked to sign on to campaigns	Staff Media campaigns Policy campaigns	2
Soil Association (SA)	UK	Centralized interest group Pressure group	No[3]	Staff Informal external network	Stakeholder uninvolved in policy decisions Stakeholders give image of an agricultural organization	Staff Media campaigns Policy campaigns	1
Food Ethics Council (FEC)	UK	Think tank	Yes	Board Staff	Stakeholders not included in organization	Policy communication to members (subscribers) through its magazine Projects	0
Making Local Food Work (MLFW, coordinated by Plunkett Foundation)★	UK	Collaborative project	Yes	Policy decisions delegated to Sustain and CPRE	Informal Needs identified through project work	One facilitating org./ manager Six other national partners	0
New Economics Foundation (NEF)	UK	Think tank	Yes	Staff	No members	Staff Media campaigns	0
Plunkett Foundation	UK	Rural NGO	Yes	No policy	No members	Policy implemented through project partners	0

★Denotes multi-organization project or network.

[1] Includes producers and market managers.

[2] The Rural Coalition only represents farmers; however, its membership is racially diverse, spanning the interests of African-Americans, old and new Hispanic producers, and American Indians.

[3] Council of Trustees includes representatives from within different segments of the organic sector including journalists, food processors, food retailers, food marketing, campaigners, and growers.

190 *Collaboration in the food system*

Organizations can and often do change: the characteristics shown are a snapshot in time. Opportunities for internal organizational changes can come with regular cycles of board member elections or nominations. Also, external influences, such as support from funders or funder requirements can influence organization characteristics.

Local food projects in the US and England have created situations where social inequalities can be addressed. Additionally, local food projects have been a way to enable or animate civic engagement from the local, community level to the national level. The following section identifies three practices useful for organizational and movement-wide change drawing primarily from American examples.

Sustaining change: Empowerment, policy entrepreneurship, and capacity building

Making space: Empowering the excluded

The 15th Annual CFSC Conference in 2011 provided an opportunity for the coalition's founders to reflect its work upon the founding Executive Director Andy Fisher's retirement. CFSC formed with a specific aim to influence the 1996 Farm Bill. Through the development of the Community Food Projects program, its signature policy initiative, the nascent coalition sought to transform federal farm and food policy by shifting power to lower-income communities and small and medium sized farmers. Creating space for a diversity of perspectives and people of different social statuses was an intentional goal of CFSC's founders (Gottlieb & Fisher, 1996a, b).

To meet this goal, the primarily white, educated promoters of the community food security concept had to confront their own social status and privilege through introspection and action. Their responsiveness to social difference is evidenced in the election of CFSC's first board in 1996, recounted by Hank Herrera, at CFSC's 2011 conference:

> We were there with about a hundred and fifty other folks and the audience looked very different than the audience looks today. There were only a few other Latino people, African-American people, Native people, or Asian people who were drawn to a meeting of an infant coalition with the single but the most riveting, challenging definition of community food security I have ever heard: access to fresh, healthy, affordable, culturally-appropriate food for all people at all times outside of emergency sources.
>
> Those were fighting words then and they still are today.
>
> Working in low-income communities of color, those words inspired me and others to dream of networks of locally-owned farming, distribution, and retail to achieve multiple goals. First, to increase access to healthy food in those low-income communities of color. Second, create businesses

to retain wealth and create jobs changing poverty to self-sufficiency. Third, create a foundation of hope to generate a transformational change in neighborhoods excluded from virtually all other resources this nation has to offer from education to economic opportunity.

So at that first meeting the few people of color began to talk to each other. Who among this initial gathering represents *us*? How would our needs, desires, hopes, and dreams shape the work of this coalition? Who on the proposed slate of first Board of Directors would tell our stories, influence the shape and direction of the coalition for us? We spoke up. We asked hard questions, questions which challenged the slate and we got results. Much to my surprise, at least, Andy and his crew of key people and founders of the coalition including Mark, Bob, Kathy, and Kate Fitzgerald, who I saw for the first time in a long time, opened the slate of nominations from the floor, and lo and behold three of us were elected to the board. So I honor Andy Fisher because he opened that space for us.

(from audio recording, Hank Herrera [HOPE Collaborative], 2011)

The "opening of space" for people of color was shared with another group: small, family-operated farms. On the same panel as Herrara, Kathy Ozer, Executive Director of the NFFC, described the context of the 1996 Farm Bill:

Our farmer leaders, from the beginning, embraced the urgency of linking farmers and consumers as many were already trying to do that: Patchwork Family Farms in Missouri,[6] the Federation of Southern Cooperatives,[7] and others who are here today. At that moment, in looking towards '95 and '96, for family farmers, when we look back at that, it was a time when the Republican-led House Ag. Committee was able to fully dismantle and deregulate the Farm Bill and replace it with programs which were euphemistically known then as "Freedom to Farm." In the midst of that, in the midst of that legislation came the establishment of the Community Food Projects.

. . .

Its success was due to the people in this room who worked for it but it also due to the commitment of the staff at the Department of Agriculture who truly cared that it served the communities it was intended to reach.

(from audio recording, Kathy Ozer [NFFC Executive Director], 2011)

The formation of the CFSC, enactment of the Community Food Project (CFP) grant program, and its subsequent reauthorizations, demonstrate a long-term commitment to reorienting existing patterns of exclusion with American society and its food economy. From the outset, movement building and national policy reform were viewed as essential tools to overcome preexisting social inequalities *through food projects*.

192   *Collaboration in the food system*

Inequality has many patterns, aside from race, income, and urban and rural geographies. It can occur between the local and community-based and the national and professional location of individuals. In an example from the May, 2012 WKKF Food and Community conference, Armando Nieto, Executive Director of the California Food & Justice Coalition, explained how he had contacted Ricardo Salvador, a WKKF Program Officer, asking why he had not been included in a WKKF meeting on food policy a year earlier (both Nieto and Salvador are Hispanic):

> the California Food & Justice Coalition, a relatively newcomer, maybe, to this movement with food systems and food justice. . . .
>
> . . . I had heard that the W.K. Kellogg Foundation was hosting a convening on food policy, and um, at this hotel, in May of last year.
>
> So I called Ricardo Salvador and said, "How you can you hold a food policy convening and not have the California Food & Justice Coalition?" Um, "How can you have it and not invite me? Why don't you *Google* me?" And I hung up the phone.
>
> [audience laughter]
>
> So I turned to the staff and I said: "One of two things will happen. They'll say, "What an asshole." Or they'll say "What an asshole. Let's invite him."
>
> [audience laughter]
>
> And they did. They invited me and asked to facilitate a conversation.
> (from audio recording, Y. Armando Nieto [California Food and Justice Coalition Executive Director], 2012)

Nieto continued, explaining how that meeting played out from his perspective.

> It was kinda guerilla conferencing, to be truthful. We were supposed to do something else. We convened back inside where Linda Jo and Ricardo were about to take us through the next steps of what seemed an incredibly boring conference agenda.
>
> And the grumbling in the crowd suggested that we wanted to do something else. To this day, I'm amazed with the grace of Ricardo who stepped aside and said, "What do you want to do?" And we said, "Well, leave us alone and we'll figure it out." He said, "Ok."
>
> Many hours later, like about 12 hours, and a lot of alcohol, what was developed was this policy lifeline.
>
> . . .
>
> Well, the process of doing this, shows that for those conversations that we've got to have with each other that are so difficult—*what do you mean*

Collaboration in the food system 193

I'm racist? or *well, what do you mean about institutional racism?* and all of the above and everything—they're just hard conversations and, to their credit, everyone participated in those hard conversations. It wasn't just the alcohol, it was a *moment.*

(from audio recording, Y. Armando Nieto [California Food and Justice Coalition Executive Director], 2012)

Nieto, like Herrera, ended by specifically thanking those who created space, naming three white participants, and asking those involved to stand up and be recognized by the audience.

Nieto's retelling of his phone call to Salvador shows he crossed a barrier of professionalism: not being on a national foundation's invitation list. Salvador responded, including Nieto *and* putting him in charge of facilitating a conversation on food policy. When the meeting's attendees grew frustrated with the meeting schedule, they voiced their concerns to Salvador, who, in Nieto's words, "stepped aside." Through inviting Nieto, giving him a leadership role, and stepping aside, Salvador was an active agent of self-mobilization by creating space to allow someone who was excluded to participate in defining his and others' priorities.

The end result of this engagement was the *Food Policy Lifeline for Children and Communities,* presented together by Nieto, McCarthy, and other panelists. It linked together nearly 40 policies and programs that address land and water use, production, processing and distribution, marketing and healthy food retail, consumption and child nutrition (WKKF, 2012b). Its intent was to build federal policy awareness among the more than 500 conference attendees. By creating space, activists who had felt excluded became empowered and sought to empower others through increased awareness of federal farm, food, nutrition, and rural policies.

The opening of space required individuals who were "in charge" or in a position of greater social status to respond to concerns presented to them. The practice of "making space" did not undermine the influence of individuals in the incumbent position of influence. Rather, their influence shifted from a position of unequal status to influence based upon esteem and respect. This is illustrated by the public comments of Herrera thanking Fisher for making space in CFSC, Nieto thanking Salvador for inviting him into WKKF's network, and McCarthy crediting Burkett as a mentor.

Importantly, a national foundation gave the stage to individuals like Herrera, Nieto, and McCarthy. Their stories of the "heavy work" of addressing social inequality were also stories of personal empowerment and transformation. Consequently, an advocacy repertoire common to the American food movement is the development of personal capacity to act, and taking actions, to overcome social divisions. This does not result in universal inclusion. It results in a practice of creating space to increase the participation of those who would otherwise be excluded.

An advocacy repertoire of "making space" contrasts with Allen's circumspection that food system re-localization would be pursued without

194 *Collaboration in the food system*

"directly addressing issues of participation and equity" (Allen, 2004, p. 180). This assertion has generally been argued from a theoretical or narrative approach with limited direct observation (Allen, 2004, 2010). More recently, DeLind (2011) has questioned the local food movement's commitment to social equity through a limited case study approach and personal essay. Both Allen and Delind are concerned about social justice on issues of local food. However, their observations present a limited perspective of the food movement especially when primary sources are abundant. For example, in the US there are now hundreds of federal grant recipients (e.g. Community Food Projects, Farmers Market Promotion Program, WIC and Senior FMNPs), thousands of farm-to-school projects, and 20 years of WKKF's grants addressing aspects of social equity at local, regional, national, and international levels (NFSN, 2012; WKKF, 2012d).

In the years since Allen wrote *Together at the Table*, the inclusion and participation of people of color in national-level movement leadership has diversified. This is shown through the continuing expansion of local food policies to address affordability since introduction of the Farmer-to-Consumer Direct Marketing Act in 1975 through to the passage of the 2010 Healthy, Hunger-Free Kids Act, as shown in Chapter 1. Further, the USDA Food Insecurity Nutrition Incentive program, passed in the Agriculture Act of 2014, puts a contribution of the local food movement—monetary incentives for purchases of fresh fruits and vegetables at direct markets—on the cusp of institutionalization with the Supplemental Nutrition Assistance Program (SNAP).

Similarly, early assessments of local food in Britain were narrow, focused on narrative, and relied on limited primary data. For example, Winter based his narrative of defensive localism on two survey responses and a single newspaper article (Winter, 2003). Also, the connection between food miles, climate change, and local food was primarily driven through perceptions of shoppers, media, and government less than observations of local food projects themselves. Recent research has found that community food security framings of local food have been excluded from national prominence (Kirwan & Maye, 2013) and that local food projects within the Local Food Program often aimed to increase social inclusion (Kirwan et al., 2013). In both the US and UK, leaders in the local food movement have worked to overcome boundaries between policy communities.

Policy entrepreneurship

Policy entrepreneurship "is the process of introducing innovation—the generation, translation, and implementation of new ideas—into the public sector" (Roberts & King, 1991, p. 147). Policy entrepreneurs do not always work alone. The terms "collective entrepreneurship" and "institutional entrepreneurship" are occasionally used to describe policy entrepreneurship from small groups of individuals and governmental institutions. The application of the term "entrepreneurship" is meant to focus attention on how individuals

Collaboration in the food system 195

and small groups identify and exploit political opportunities—gaps—which have not been pursued by dominant organizations or fall outside of conventional thinking (Schumpeter, 1939, 1961).

Policy entrepreneurs are critical agents for making space and promoting innovative policies in the American food movement. Policy entrepreneurs typically participate in multiple policy networks, both governmental and non-governmental, which enables them to form the trust necessary to build bridges across policy communities (Mintrom & Vergari, 1998). An example of an individual policy entrepreneur is Gus Schumacher, who as a Commissioner of Agriculture, USDA staff, and NGO staff has linked together agricultural, nutrition, and public health communities around the concept of healthy food incentives at farmer-to-consumer markets. An example of collective entrepreneurship is how the NEMWI, coordinator of the FFPP, linked together separate narratives of local food into three coherent policies in the 2008 Farm Bill. A defining characteristic of a policy entrepreneur is their ability to make connections across organizations and their policy narratives (Kingdon, 1984; Meijerink & Huitema, 2010; Roberts & King, 1991).

While policy entrepreneurs lack formal position power, their political influence originates from their ability to generate and translate ideas, define or reframe problems, and skill in working collectively with those who have position power (Roberts & King, 1991). Maintaining trust of multiple entities, with different and sometimes competing perspectives, is necessary. As a result, a policy entrepreneur's work may not be visible to the public or outsiders. Yet, their presence can be instrumental to policy change. Policy outcomes are "enhanced considerably by the presence of a skillful entrepreneur, and dampened considerably if no entrepreneur takes on the cause, pushes it, and makes critical couplings when policy windows open" (Kingdon, 1984, p. 205). Their activity can disrupt the status quo and it could be perceived as a threat. However, their work of joining together existing policy narratives can frame an innovation as a natural extension or trajectory of existing, familiar work.

Because policy entrepreneurs often work from outside of government and formal positions of influence, they generally are not formally accountable. It is important to note that policy entrepreneurship is not inherently democratic or beneficial (Henrekson & Sanandaji, 2011). However, a policy entrepreneur's influence and continued access is dependent upon maintaining trust and a reputation for political effectiveness

A freedom to explore unexploited gaps, and meet organizations and individuals with different perspectives is needed for a policy entrepreneur to be effective. A civil society policy environment with strong checks can severely constrain the ability of an individual or organization to form connections between organizations (Schnellenbach, 2007).

In England, individuals within organizations exhibited entrepreneurial behavior, such as within the MLFW project, and across organizations, as with the Tasting the Future learning network. However, policy entrepreneurship

196   Collaboration in the food system

was not observed on national-level local food policy. High sectorial segmentation and policing behaviors severely constrained the cross-sector networking needed to join separate policy streams. Additionally, individuals with good inter-organizational relationships, such as consultants, lacked the authority to convene organizations because they lacked organizational authority. Few opportunities existed for policy entrepreneurship to develop.

Much of the American food movement's political successes came from policy entrepreneurs hybridizing policy narratives and forming unusual but influential political alliances. A consistent example is the blending of local community food needs and supporting the markets for small and family farms. This can be observed with the Farmer-to-Consumer Direct Marketing Act of 1976, the advent of the FMNPs, the community food security movement and the CFP, and the evolution of the FMPP. To assemble and maintain the diverse coalitions behind these policies, policy entrepreneurs formed political narratives that united different groups, resulting in a *food systems* narrative.

In addition to the skills of policy entrepreneurs, organizations across sectors needed to be willing to work together. Contextual factors are determinants for an environment that is "more or less likely to favor the emergence of policy outsiders or insiders as policy entrepreneurs" (Mintrom & Norman, 2009, pp. 661–662). Funders have a role in the level of collaborative work undertaken in a field and the skills that individuals develop. For example, the UK's BIG Lottery's Local Food Program initiated a cross-sector forum supporting community food enterprises, an experience which was an "training ground" for developing the capacity of individuals to work across sectors and other boundaries (Kirwan et al., 2014). Similarly, many young professionals who participated in the FFPP in program support roles joined senior positions in several advocacy organizations, including the Center for Rural Affairs, the National Farm to School Network, the National Sustainable Agriculture Coalition, and at the USDA.

The role of funders in capacity building for policy collaboration

Funders have a unique role in a social movement: they select how their resources target and support movement activities. Also, they can have a unique perspective due to their broad knowledge of movement activities in their area through learning of grant-seeker needs and ideas. Further, their influence, through the "power of the purse," can align both grant recipient and grant-seeker project goals to their goals (CBI, 2008b).

In the US, the WKKF provided resources to build the capacity and increase the inclusion of individuals from marginalized social groups (WKKF, 2012d). Through the FFPP, it deliberately sought to include grassroots stakeholders from outside of the capitol in the policy decision-making process. This combination of goals and grant criteria resulted in an increase in local-level group policy capacity and representation of marginalized social groups at the national level.

Collaboration in the food system 197

The grant-making of the WKKF evolved over two decades. It began with support for small farms, sustainable agriculture projects, and rural community development in the 1990s. Throughout the 2000s its Food and Society Fellows program helped community-based practitioners enhance their communications and policy skills and actively recruited people from diverse socio-economic backgrounds (Institute for Agriculture and Trade Policy, 2013). In 2004, it explicitly encouraged organizations representing people of color to submit applications on farm and food policy (CBI, 2008a; Sherman & Peterson, 2009). In the late 2000s, WKKF targeted lower-income communities with severe, diet-related health disparities through *Foot and Fitness* (2006–2009), *Food and Communities* (2009–2012), and support for a national farm-to-school program (WKKF, 2012d). Over time, WKKF expanded its support of marginalized groups, from small farmers and rural communities to low-income communities nationally.

The US government promoted inclusion, capacity building, and self-determination in marginalized communities through USDA grant-making. It did so through the CFP by prioritizing the joining of at least two sectors of the food system, requiring applicants to explain how individuals with low-incomes were included in the project design and implementation, and selecting projects that would promote community self-reliance (*Federal Agriculture Improvement and Reform Act*, 1996; USDA, 2014a). Likewise, resources in the WIC FMNP, SFMNP, and the EBT set-aside in the FMPP prioritized resources that would increase access to local food for individuals with low incomes (*Food, Conservation, and Energy Act of 2008*, 2008b; Markowitz, 2010; Young et al., 2011). Further, advocacy by the Diversity Initiative resulted in USDA increasing the share of resources available to socially disadvantaged producers (CBI, 2008a; Headwaters Group Philanthropic Services, 2008). Combined, these resources increased the participation of individuals with low incomes and marginalized producers in the food system, and provided resources for NGOs to carry out community based projects.

Similarly, the EU provided resources to its member states to increase the local capacity and self-mobilization of rural communities, including local agriculture projects (EC, 1991). Funds provided through LEADER required the self-organization of LAGs, constituted of governmental representatives, non-governmental representatives from social and economic sectors, and at least 50 percent of representation from farmers, rural women, and young people (EC, 2005). LAG participation was cross-sector and unaligned to any single rural industry. They were empowered with grant-making authority to support a diversity of rural projects, which in turn increased the capacity and self-confidence of the individuals through the collaborative decision-making process.

Private British funders have pursued social justice with less attention to the internal processes of current and prospective grantees. There are few dedicated food and sustainable agriculture funders. The majority of those funders are family-run charitable trusts, many of which did not accept unsolicited proposals

198 *Collaboration in the food system*

and provided little public information about selection criteria. A general comparison of American and English private and government funding requirements, paired with local food project activities, is shown in Table 6.3. Funders had to make intentional decisions to include requirements for stakeholder participation, adopt peer-review processes for grant selection, and increase funding access for marginalized groups.

One British funder, the Esmée Fairbairn Foundation (EFF), had a dedicated food funding strand, begun in 2008, and provided guidance to grant-seekers on its priorities and its selection criteria. EFF was motivated to engage in food funding because of its social justice goals and awareness of issues such as health disparities in low-income communities (EFF Food Strand Staff, 2011). While EFF engaged on food issues out of its social justice mission, stakeholder and community resident participation were not criteria or priorities of the Foundation (Esmée Fairbairn Foundation, 2011, n.d.). Rather, the EFF took a move reactive, experimental approach within the first three years of the Food Strand's operation:

> So you described how one of the other foundations in the States came down the route of consultants to see what really needs doing. We came at another approach "let's just do some stuff" and see what comes out of it, what emerges. Esmée's very experimental that way.
>
> (EFF Food Strand Staff, 2011)

The experimental approach was reflected by not specifying who should be involved in its food projects and how they should be involved (Esmée Fairbairn Foundation, 2011).

How money is used has a greater impact on stakeholder engagement than on the total money available. The funding available for food policy activities was relatively similar in the US and in England, even though England has about one-fifth the population of the US. Yet, the way that organizations responded to local stakeholders and their degree of collaboration were very different.

WKKF provided about $6 million from 2005 to 2008 for the FFPP and Diversity Initiative, the main national policy efforts on sustainable agriculture and local food systems at the time (Headwaters Group Philanthropic Services, 2008, p. 4). In a similar timeframe, over $7 million was provided to the ASAP by the William and Flora Hewlett Foundation, for expanding farm conservation funding and reducing funding for farm commodity programs (Headwaters Group Philanthropic Services, 2008, p. 28). These three projects represented the main national policy efforts supported by private philanthropy during 2005–2008, totaling about $13 million across 4 years.

The annual spending of these policy projects is many times *less* than the total annual expenditures by the (smaller) English food movement. In 2011 about £18 million was spent on lobbying, and about £5 million on projects for local food (FEC, 2011, pp. 40, 52). The 2011 expenditure on NGO food

Table 6.3 Funding characteristics of local projects in the US and England

Characteristics	US	England
Local food projects		
Collaboration	Citizens, farmers, businesses, NGOs, govt., schools[G,P,R]	Citizens, farmers[G,R], businesses, NGOs, govt., schools
Inclusion	Urban & rural partnerships[R] Low-income people [G,P,R]	Some urban–rural partnerships Sometimes includes low-income[G,P]
Learning		
Networking events	Cross-sector Peer-to-peer learning[G] No debates Diverse participants recruited[G,P]	Typically single sector Peer-to-peer learning (uncommon) Debates by "experts" Not observed
Capacity building	For under-represented groups[G,P]	Cooperative partnership (e.g. MLFW)[P]
National advocacy organizations		
Structure	Advocacy coalitions	Pressure groups Think tanks Trade associations
Membership	Multi-sector[R] Urban and rural People with low incomes[R] Includes stakeholders with economic interests[R]	Typically single-sector (e.g. farmers; urban; environ.)
Decision-making	Voting by members Member-led policy committees Co-led by staff & members	Typically staff & informants Frequently ad hoc Typically led by staff
Advocacy tactics	Direct lobbying by staff & members[P] Alliance formation[P,R]	Primarily pressure through media[P] Some direct lobbying[P]
Advocacy group interaction		
Inter-group relationships	Typically cooperative[P,R] Coalitions[P] Joint campaigns[P] Joint lobbying[P] Joint messaging[P] Joint media outreach[P]	Competitive Uncoordinated Single-issue campaigns[P] Single-group lobbying[P] Single-issue messages Single-group media outreach
Outcomes		
National policy for local food	Incremental gains Increasing with time Multi-objective[G,P]	No clear "wins" for local food but wins on other targets Single-objective Inconsistent/declining with time
Political supporters	Expanding "Unusual alliances"	Limited Organizations stay within niches
Messaging	Food systems framework	Single issue Need to be more "joined up"
Resources	Expanding	Inconsistent

P Philanthropic funding; G Government funding; R Requirement for eligibility with some funders

lobbying in England exceeded the value of four years of significant farm and food policy advocacy in the US. While these are not apples-to-apples comparisons, the magnitude of difference suggests that factors other than the total funding available for policy advocacy shape advocacy practices.

Funder preferences, rather than total funding available, appear to be a determining factor for formation of collaborative policy projects, levels of stakeholder engagement in national policy processes, and the inclusion of marginalized groups (including small farm operators) in policy decision-making.

"Doing nothing" to address exclusion allows existing inequalities to persist and become established as an advocacy repertoire. National interest groups in the US and UK both had a tendency to "go it alone," relying on professional staff for policy guidance rather than the direct engagement of stakeholders in agenda-setting. In an unstructured policy environment, such as England's food movement, the resulting individual practices, organizational structures, and inter-organization behaviors have favored organizations that are the most effective in securing resources and media access over organizations including stakeholders. A highly competitive environment can undercut a movement's and a funder's broader social justice mission. By adopting a broader perspective —that of supporting a movement "ecosystem" versus supporting individual organizations and campaigns—funders of policy advocacy can become more aware of how their actions and inactions impact social justice.

Government-funded programs provided an opportunity for public input on funding priorities and grantee selection criteria. Private foundations can be more flexible and entrepreneurial, entering into undefined and emerging fields. However, private foundations are not democratic or participatory despite their legal status founded upon the provision of the public good. As a result, they have both authority and ability to use a coercive influence—the "power of the purse"—to further social justice goals. Through funding criteria and grant-making funders signal their values to prospective grantees. Just as democratic institutions require frameworks to establish norms for participation and inclusion, so too can funders structure behaviors that promote inclusion and support work that crosses social and sectorial boundaries.

A gap in both British and American philanthropy is the availability of medium- to long-term funding to support national-level, cross-sector policy collaboration targeted to stakeholder-led organizations. In the American experience, a short-term investment in inclusion, diversification, and policy entrepreneurship shifted billions of dollars in public expenditures (Headwaters Group Philanthropic Services, 2008; NEMWI, 2008c; Sherman & Peterson, 2009). An evaluation of that project, the FFPP, indicated the main question for funders is "It's not *if*, but *how much*, collaboration to undertake" (CBI, 2008b, p. 22).

Continued investment in cross-sector, stakeholder-led projects like MLFW and Big Lottery's Local Food Program, combined with support for policy collaboration targeted at EU-level rural development programs, may yield

Collaboration in the food system 201

additional public sector resources for the British local food sector. Similarly, continued investment by American funders on cross-sector policy collaborations is needed, especially in the wake of the rapid expansion of new, politically inexperienced, food organizations.

Conclusion

Internal organizational governance processes regulate the effectiveness of British and American organizations on food policy. Choices made by advocacy groups impacted the choices policymakers made about how respond to local food.

Advocacy groups conducted their policy activities differently. Some pursued policy changes directly with policymakers. Some conducted media campaigns to increase public awareness of their issues, recruit new supporters, and reconfirm preexisting beliefs. While there was a common perception that national-level advocacy groups were pursuing strategies for policy change, policy change was not always their immediate target. A failure to change policy was reframed in a new belief that the government is responsible for change or the lack of change. Placing responsibility for policy change only on the government, rather than seeing it as co-production between advocacy groups and the government, shifted scrutiny away from the effectiveness of advocacy group leaders' decisions. A belief that governmental institutions were *unjust* justified high-profile controversial media campaigns that attacked the government becoming the predominant form of political communication in an advocacy repertoire.

Preexisting advocacy repertoires influenced how advocacy group leaders conducted their policy advocacy. Some leaders innovated, and adopted organization structures and advocacy techniques different than the prevailing repertoire. Innovations included organizational processes, collaborative decision-making, and stakeholder-led governance. Other innovations, practiced between organizations and at a movement level included making space, policy entrepreneurship, and capacity building.

The approach for national-level food policy change is fundamentally different within the UK and US. In the UK, the largest influencers for food policy are large environmental interest groups. Change in policy was seen as an "us versus them" adversarial approach. In dialogue with policymakers, sarcasm and personally directed criticisms were utilized. The targets for policy change were government institutions, supermarket retailers, and agro-food corporations. Interactions with these large institutions were conducted through a narrow set of interest groups and led by professional staff. The two most visible advocates of local food focused on reducing the influence of the large institutions without encouraging the empowerment and direct participation of movement participants and without considering equality in food policy advocacy.

In the US the primary approach is small groups developing consensus to affect food policy. Cross-sector networks and policy coalitions provided opportunities for establishing a mutual understanding of farm and food policy

202 *Collaboration in the food system*

issues across the movement. Cross-sector, multi-level networking structures enabled policy entrepreneurs to join together separate policy streams.

Policy coalitions provided a participatory process to coordinate policy decision-making across otherwise decentralized, localized groups. Conciliatory and collaborative approaches helped overcome social divisions and reach consensus. Individual and social group empowerment was a principal mobilization strategy. A collective action frame of empowerment provided openings to make space for excluded groups and sustained mobilization across policy cycles, in part because *it was fulfilling to become empowered.*

Funders sought to increase social equity. Government funders developed eligibility criteria that targeted underrepresented groups: rural stakeholders, smaller-volume farmers and food producers, community residents, and minority farmers (US only). Private funders sought both policy outcomes and innovative approaches to address food-related social issues. When an American funder changed its grant-making strategy to encourage collaboration, groups collaborated. Other funder-led strategies including making space for typically excluded groups in policy projects, conferences, and movement leadership and building capacity for established and new groups to work together. By influencing intra- and inter-organizational processes, governmental and private funders were able to further democratize participation in the local food movement.

Notes

1 At least one such cross-sector collaborative policy effort was observed in the UK: Community Food and Health Scotland was a cross-sector policy forum that was a platform for collaborative advocacy issues of health, community food security, and local food procurement. Class issues and food affordability were readily apparent (Schumacher & Hunt, 2012).

2 This process is sometimes called the "Garbage Can" model of policy change—a description Ward et al. applied to the framing of the foot-and-mouth disease crisis in the UK (Ward et al., 2004).

3 David Duke is described as a white supremacist and environmental activist who "enraged black activists" in Roberts and Tofolon-Weiss (2001, p. 57). Duke's activism became an important symbol for mobilizing against racism and racial inequality, and promoting a more inclusive concept of environmental justice in New Orleans.

4 Ben Burkett, an African-American, is a small farm operator supplying New Orleans farmers markets, helped organize the Indian Springs Cooperative in Mississippi, and is on the Board of the NFFC (NFFC, 2012).

5 Like an American charter school, it is a government-funded school operated by a private entity that has more flexibility for its operations than public-funded, public-operated schools.

6 Patchwork Family Farms is a collaborative of about 15 independent hog producers (Fischer, 2002).

7 A primarily African-American farm organization associated with the American civil rights movement.

7 Toward a theory of food systems practice

Food production is fundamentally defined by multiple perspectives. For the practice of local food projects, this often means that producers, citizens (voters, shoppers, volunteers, residents, and neighbors), community-based organizations, and local government officials interact in forming projects, such as farmers markets and farm-to-school procurement. This local-level connectedness expands in two ways. First, through the formation of other local efforts. Second, through the formation of information-sharing networks and advocacy groups. Maintaining connections across perspectives requires negotiation or consensus across perspectives.

This chapter focuses on six interlinked approaches used in American and British local food movements to overcome preexisting social divisions: 1) multi-sector approaches, 2) multi-level approaches, 3) participators processes, 4) interdisciplinary analysis, 5) multi-objective goals, and 6) an inclusive orientation. The *theory of food systems practice* links these approaches together. The food systems approach represents a "play book" of American and British food movements.

The degree of inclusion and breadth of cross-sector activity varies by country, organization, project, and community. Their activities are not universally inclusive. Yet, when observed in aggregate, at the national level, there is an overall orientation towards overcoming several types of social division. The second section of the chapter discusses the shift toward movement building.

Researchers continue to make claims about the social exclusion of American and British local food movements. While there is exclusion, progress towards broader inclusion is embedded within the multi-sector, multi-level approaches of American and British local food movements. Exclusion was not a universal phenomenon observed in the field. Among practitioners, the field has moved beyond abstract concerns of inequality.

Efforts toward addressing social inequality and promoting inclusion have been practiced for decades in both countries. In England, this includes the Low Income Project Team in the 1990s (Nelson, 1997), Food Poverty Network of the early late 1990s and 2000s (*Food Poverty (Eradication) Bill*, 2001; Sustain, 1999a, 2001, 2003), and two local food grant projects in the 2010s (Kirwan et al., 2013; SERIO, 2012). In the US this includes the formation of the

204 *Toward a theory of food systems practice*

Farmers Market Nutrition Programs in the 1980s and 1990s (Commonwealth of Massachusetts, 2011; *Farmer to Family Nutrition Enhancement Act*, 1988, 2000a), and the formation of the community food security movement (Winne et al., 1997).

In both the US and UK, Hinrichs and Charles (2012) observed that local food projects are sites where community members gain capacity and engage in collaborative problem solving. It is through participatory process involving a mix of stakeholders that a more comprehensive food systems narrative emerged.

Distinctions between interest group narrative and practice and the food system narrative and practice are shown in Table 7.1, with significant differences shaded in gray. This includes a narrative defined by multiple perspectives and sectors, direct empowerment of marginalized groups, the use of multiple disciplines in analyzing a problem, and orienting benefits toward stakeholders. Its use as a distinctive policy narrative is evident in the American food movement and policymaking, and evident in practice in the UK, as shown in discussions of community food projects, projects funded by LEADER and other rural development programs, and the interviews of stakeholder-led groups.

Stakeholder-led national advocacy groups were more likely to practice engagement with policymakers. An organization may be an "outsider" pressing for change, or an "insider" engaging with governmental policymakers. It may not be both at once. Government policymakers require a degree of trust when working closely with advocacy groups. For example, if an internal draft of legislation is shared with an advocacy group for feedback, the policymaker expects that group will not share the draft with the national media if it wants to keep working with policymakers. Likewise, organizations constantly communicating through the national media *against* normal policy process will not be given the opportunity to review internal legislation drafts for feedback. When there are both outsiders pressing for change and insiders offering alternatives to the status quo, the chance of policy change increases.

Two examples of this *radical flank effect* are the local food provisions in the 2008 US Farm Bill and the increasing share of the EU CAP dedicated to LEADER, a rural development program. Both benefited from environmental pressure groups' desire to shift farm payments away from agricultural subsidies. In each case local food groups and rural development groups, respectively, lacked sufficient influence to achieve those outcomes without the benefit of outside pressure. Over time, former outsiders can become influential insiders, as has happened with the American anti-hunger groups and British wildlife groups (Berry, 1982; Lowe & Wilkinson, 2009).

Civic participation in food systems governance: A theory of food systems practice

The early endeavors of modern agriculture considered it necessary to "decontextualize the farm enterprise from the community and household

Toward a theory of food systems practice 205

settings in which it was embedded" to increase productive output (Lyson, 2004, p. 14). Over time, this form of agriculture has become not only economically and politically entrenched, but also *culturally* entrenched and, thus, resistant to change. Reforming the social relationships within agricultural production and food consumption requires overcoming preexisting divisions within the segmented *economic* roles of production, processing, distribution, marketing, retailing of farm products, and the role of the individual as consumer and citizen. Reconnecting these relationships within a business sector involves a process of re-embedding social relationships within economic relationships (Granovetter, 1985), and thus a new perspective on food system development.

American and British researchers have applied different terms to describe the interconnectedness envisioned with local food projects. This text uses "local food" without a following term. "System" is commonly used in the US while "network" or "links" is commonly used in the UK and Europe (Hinrichs & Charles, 2012). The political critique implied by the local food links narrative has many overlapping features with the local food systems narrative. One is the assertion of local influence and locally determined relationships in the food supply chain, including citizen involvement, empowerment, and capacity building (Hinrichs & Charles, 2012, p. 165). Unlike the systems narrative, which argues for a more comprehensive view of the food system, the narrative of links and networks is used more flexibly (Hinrichs & Charles, 2012, pp. 157–158). A difference with policy implications is that a system implies a higher level of interdependence than linkages alone.

Politically, a systems perspective means that the concerns of one group are not necessarily more or less important than the concerns of another. The concerns of all groups (as many as is feasible to bring together) are to be considered together because they are interdependent. This means, for example, that the concerns of farmworkers are not necessarily hierarchically above or below the needs of affordable food. Rather, their needs are viewed as important as the need for affordable food. The needs of both groups coexist as equal, intertwined, and inseparable concerns.

Promoting inclusion, building awareness of excluded groups, making space for excluded groups to be invited in, and a willingness to work across social divisions are practices utilized in the field to overcome exclusion. Six common and often interlinked approaches are used in the field to respond to preexisting social exclusion and the de-linkages from modern agriculture, including:

- *multi-sector approaches*, to overcome sectorial divisions from the specialization of roles in the food system;
- *multi-level approaches*, when agricultural and food markets have drifted toward the international;
- *participatory processes* in the food system that prioritize citizen and stakeholder engagement;
- *interdisciplinary analysis* in contrast to an agricultural policy driven by agricultural economics;

Table 7.1 A comparison of marketism, interest group, and food system narratives and practices

	Marketism narratives and practice	Interest groups narratives and practice	Food system narrative and practice
Level of political activity	States (in the US), National, International, Corporate leadership	Impact-driven—level most likely to gain public interest	Multi-level—local government through to international institutions
Breadth	Specialized, often single sector (farmers, distributors, retailers, environment) or to a single commodity	Specialized, often a single issue; Formation of coalitions of "like-minded" groups often relegated to within a policy community	Multi-perspective, including views across both the food supply chain and social groups; Multi-sector at the project-level and across policy communities; at the farm level, aimed at on-farm diversification
Analytical perspective	Natural sciences, used to improve produce and mitigate environmental and food safety harm; Economic	Natural sciences, often used to counter government or industry views; Social justice or marginalization; Analysis of public expenditures	Multi-discipline—crosses social and natural sciences; not defined by a single, dominant discipline
Role of citizens	Limited agency; Consumers; Volunteers for charity; Activists a potential threat	High agency; Consumer boycotts and purchase of "ethical" goods; Financial donations; Petitions; Protest activities	High agency; Consumers making informed and ethical choices; Project participants; Citizens concerned about community politically active
Social inclusion	Public assistance for the poor to participate in the market; Legal minimum worker safety and rights	Protection or rights for the marginalized	Direct empowerment; Incorporates marginalized social groups into projects and movement-building activities
Objectives	Oriented toward maximizing production volume or sales; Concern about minimizing risk	Preventing harm—focuses on marginalized groups and entities, including animals and nature	Multiple simultaneous objectives, often focused on community-level or society-wide goal(s)
Objective of policy interventions	Protect proprietary rights; Limit regulatory burden; Expand trade; Promote technology adoption	Attract, retain, and mobilize supporters; Change in government priorities or business practices	Benefits and reduces harm for stakeholders; includes citizens

Toward a theory of food systems practice 207

- *multi-objective goals* instead of narrow goals of production, trade or other single-issue goals; and an
- *inclusive orientation* to address economic and political exclusion and marginalization.

Responses to each of these issues form the *theory of food systems practice*.

Multi-sector approaches

Involvement of individuals and representatives from across the food system often requires a collaborative approach. Pragmatically, this often begins with a "coalition of the willing" who are already "primed" for engagement. It is combined with a strategy of inclusion, to invite new participants and make space for their full participation.

At the project level this can include working across such distinctions as gatherer, forager, farmer, rancher, fisher, *campesino*, farm worker, owner, manager, contract farmer, independent farmer, urban farmer, organic producer, farm neighbor, processor, distributor, butcher, produce stocker, deli manager, grocery store owner, procurement officer, chef, baker, cafeteria worker, restaurant worker, barista, dishwasher, shopper, consumer, eater, food bank user, the hungry, homeless, institutionalized persons, voters, and citizens. At the organizational level, this often means working with associations that represent different sectors of the food system, such as farmers, retailers, distributors, producers, consumers, and the environment. Working across sectorial differences requires individuals that are willing to engage others, who demonstrate patience, and avoid trying to dominate the concerns of others.

In the US, this has meant forming urban–rural coalitions and alliances. Working with Members of Congress on the Agriculture Committees has resulted in the food movement's access to the Committee's Farm Bill process, access contingent on the Committee's recognition that passing a Farm Bill requires off-committee, urban, and suburban votes.

The UK has faced similar issues. When the EU CAP was shifting from farm subsidies to agri-environmental payments, the agricultural policy community was resistant to those changes. Additional public support (and pressure) was needed to continue to justify farm program support. The Curry Commission utilized the "farm crisis" as a policy window to bring additional support to the farm sector in the form of agri-environmental payments, a move supported by environmental, wildlife, conservation, and some agricultural advocacy groups.

Working across sectors requires skills like those identified with policy entrepreneurs, who identify and follow through on opportunities to join together separate policy streams. Policy streams do not automatically "join up." For example, in Britain, public health, food, and rural development communities nearly converged on the issue of access to food shops and food affordability in the mid to late 1990s. They did not converge because of a lack

208 *Toward a theory of food systems practice*

of a "more strategic approach" from both national advocacy groups and national policymakers (Barling et al., 2002, p. 560).

Similarly, with the Curry Commission, advocates of sustainability and rural development argued that local food economies underpinned a more sustainable British farm sector. Since the Curry Commission, EU-initiated rural development programs have spent hundreds of millions of pounds in England. They appear to be the largest source of public sector funds available to the local food sector. Yet, British environmental groups disengaged on agricultural and rural policy, reflecting a three-decade pattern of short-term engagement on issues beyond their core interests (Wilkinson et al., 2010, pp. 339–340). Likewise, national rural advocacy groups have generally maintained a focus on equitable access to services in rural areas. As a result, urban and rural divisions persist in Britain's food advocacy.

Overcoming divisions requires a desire to overcome preexisting divisions, intentional collaborations that aim to meet short-term objectives while promoting shared long-term goals, and a culture of cross-sector engagement that catalyzes policy entrepreneurship.

Multi-level approaches

Governmental institutions at all levels—local, regional, national, and international—touch on agriculture, food, and health. Authority and management of farm programs and regulations are often concentrated at the national level even within international institutions such as the EU or World Trade Organization. The planning agencies of local governments impact farm land use, sites available for public markets, the location of a food retail store, and a homeowner's ability to have front yard gardens and backyard chickens. Governmental institutions between the local and national levels, such as counties and states in the US and the devolved authorities in the UK, may set health and safety standards for food retailers (including farms). They also manage procurement contracts for catering at public institutions. As a practice, policy knowledge and expertise is needed of all levels for producers and consumers to interact with the food system.

Another aspect is that the people who are most knowledgeable about what makes a local food project work (or fail) are involved in local food projects. For policy advocacy to be successful, it must 1) convey the concerns and needs of local food stakeholders to policymakers, and 2) translate their needs into policy proposals.

The feasibility of policy proposals often hinges upon the degree to which they fit *within the preexisting governmental frameworks*. This is difficult. It requires knowledge of stakeholder concerns; analysis of existing laws and regulations; the timing of proposal development to regular policy cycles; attention to regulatory, statutory, and budgetary processes; and supportive political messaging. Even if an advocacy group's goal is to propose an entirely new policy framework with new underlying assumptions and goals, policymakers will wish to know how it

Toward a theory of food systems practice 209

compares to existing frameworks. To understand that level of detail, a national policymaker often wants to be in direct contact with stakeholders from their constituency. A few key informants may be sufficient for educating a policymaker. A significant number of advocates and key alliances are needed to secure a legislative majority or revise a contentious regulation. The tactics of political communication are an inherent part of a policy proposal.

Likewise, the knowledge and experience of the individuals involved in forming the proposal is inherent to its content. Policy recommendations are better informed when stakeholders are involved: they have firsthand knowledge of how policy affects them. Proposals without sufficient detail can lack credibility among policymakers and other advocacy groups. This can undermine a national advocacy group's political credibility. Policymakers are loath to implement policy on a business sector without support from some groups within that sector.

Involving stakeholders can result in different policy strategy and goals. This can be an opportunity (McAdam et al., 1996), but also may introduce uncertainty for organizations that have strong, self-interested priorities. For example, the collaboratively authored *Feeding the Future: Policy options for local food* discussion paper offered 287 policy options; 19 on EU rural development programs and 5 related to food miles (Sustain & Food Links UK, 2003). A food miles campaign on greenhouse gas emissions was one option pursued by England's two most influential sustainable food advocacy groups. Neither group was led by farmers or rural businesses. Would a stakeholder group composed of farmers and rural businesses have selected other policy options?

Participatory processes

Who is and is not at the table in a local food project or in communication with policymakers matters. A combination of informal relationships and formal organizational characteristics influences the level of stakeholder participation (Pretty, 1995).

When informal relationships dominate a project or policy environment, it is difficult for new participants to join because the rules guiding participation and defining who is "in charge" are unclear. This can result in a situation described by Freeman as a "tyranny of structurelessness" (Cooperatives UK, 2011c; Freeman, 1972 (revised)). While a leader of greater social status may return a benefit to others in the group, the group lacks authority to nominate someone else as its leader.

Similarly, there is a tendency for interest groups and notable individuals to purport themselves as social movement leaders when they have no direct connection to social movement organizations. This was shown in the food miles campaign, led by Sustain and the Soil Association (SA) in the UK, and the Alliance for Sensible Agricultural Policies in the US. Even within well-organized entities, there may be a lack of direct connection to stakeholders.

210 *Toward a theory of food systems practice*

For some American anti-poverty groups, organizational leadership rests with professionals, notable individuals, and corporate sponsors, rather than people with low incomes (Feeding America, 2011; FRAC, 2010).

Formal organization types and formal decision-making processes that encourage stakeholder participation vary. These include advocacy coalition formation, stakeholder-led boards, stakeholder advisory groups, stakeholder-based membership, and voting on policy proposals and policy strategy. Examples include the high organizational autonomy within the federation structure in Federation of City Farms & Community Gardens (FCFCG), the cooperative decision-making process of the National Association of Farmers' Retail & Markets Association (FARMA), the stakeholder-led board of the Community Food Security Coalition (CFSC), and the general membership voting on policy decisions in National Sustainable Agriculture Coalition.

Formal processes are especially important for situations when a social group or sector is a numerical minority. This can help ensure that a more vocal majority does not systemically override the concerns of those with less representation or influence. In a coalition setting, such as Sustain, farm and rural groups were a numerical minority. Policy actions consistently favored health and environmental objectives over rural development and small farm issues. Organizational procedures and an inclusive culture contribute to making space for marginalized groups to participate, which in turn, builds the capacity of all involved.

For inter-organization interactions, such as conferences, publications, and funding opportunities, formal stakeholder-led peer review processes are used to help ensure stakeholder needs are met. The CFSC and National Farm to Cafeteria conferences utilized a stakeholder peer-review process for selecting conference session proposals. The W.K. Kellogg Foundation (WKKF) utilizes a conference advisory board, inclusive of stakeholders, and has resulted in the giving stage to stakeholders from a wide range of established organizations and marginalized social groups. Funders can encourage stakeholder participation as a criteria in project formation, organization governance, and staffing, a practice utilized in the US by the WKKF and USDA Community Food Project program. Government grant programs can be designed to require stakeholders in the grant selection process, as with the EU LEADER and several USDA programs.

From a policy perspective, direct stakeholder participation is needed for several reasons:

- legitimacy, which can be demonstrated publically via member's endorsements of the advocacy group's policy proposals;
- authenticity, which can be communicated directly to the public and policymakers through the use of stakeholders as spokespersons; and
- policy impact, where more detailed information results in better-designed policy proposals and potentially better programs or regulation.

As with a collaborative project, a participatory policy process often requires structures that are efficient, transparent, and promote accountability (and ultimately trust) between stakeholders and professional policy staff.

Interdisciplinary analysis

Agriculture and food systems practices cannot be defined by a single scientific approach or discipline: a narrow perspective or limited set of tools undermines stability in food availability. Advocates of sustainable agriculture have long been frustrated with the economic and production-oriented focus within the agricultural industry and agricultural policy (Lyson, 2004; Tomlinson, 2007).

Some sustainable food and agriculture interest groups have articulated their own narrow perspectives, ignoring the connection between social, economic, and environmental sustainability. Sustainability groups trade off their rich narrative, narrowing their own messages, to counter anti-environmental messages from government or industry. This results in an attempt to displace a preexisting narrative with an alternative, but narrow, narrative of the environment. Such displacement strategies are not widely effective (Gamson, 1975).

The food miles case study presents such an example. The narrow framing of reducing food miles as a way to reduce carbon emissions and help address climate change resulted in environmental groups arguing for a return to broader social, economic, and environmental sustainability (Sumberg, 2009).

It is difficult to resist the potential for elevating one's message by adopting a simpler framing of an issue, even among experienced professionals. In the short term, it may make sense to "fight back" with a counter attack, even though such efforts to reframe policy debate are unsuccessful (Former NEF Staff, 2011; Sustain Policy Staff (a), 2011a). Similarly, the American environmental movement continues to rely upon an environmental protection narrative, even though protection has been reframed successfully against employment and economic growth *for decades* (Dryzek, 1997; Shellenberger & Nordhaus, 2004). Thus, one of the great difficulties of an interdisciplinary perspective is communicating *interconnection* as the frame. Given the multiple perspectives on agricultural and food issues, a narrow perspective has a fundamentally limited potential to portray a food system.

Multiple perspectives on food are an asset. Its breadth allows it to influence issues beyond food and agriculture. This prevents a food systems movement from being limited to only a few mobilizing tactics. It provides multiple points of entry for mobilizing public and policymaker support. Individuals can support and join SMOs for a variety of reasons, including concern about family farm viability; the connection between food and health; protecting wildlife; protecting natural resources for preservation, conservation, or for hunting and fishing; preserving traditional food culture; persevering agricultural open space; addressing inequities regarding food availability and quality; countering egregious farming practices; food safety; protecting farm and food workers

212 *Toward a theory of food systems practice*

from exploitation; and addressing food-related issues beyond one's country. With different concerns come multiple traditions of analyzing and communicating issues.

In the roles described are issues discussed within the disciplines of rural sociology and agricultural economics; nutrition and public health; wildlife management; environmental management; sociology, anthropology, and cultural studies; community development and planning; journalism; microbiology; industrial and labor relations; and international development. To focus on an issue from a single perspective often has the counter effect of de-emphasizing other perspectives—explicitly and implicitly.

A food systems orientation means that no single disciplinary perspective is more legitimate than another, and that promoting one discipline above others undermines the interconnectedness of the systems perspective. A food systems perspective is fundamentally interdisciplinary, and requires cooperation and trust to work across traditional boundaries (Donovan, Sidaway, & Stewart, 2010; Harris, Lyon, & Clarke, 2008; Oughton & Bracken, 2009).

Multi-objective goals

Collaboration is not done because it is something "good to do." Organizations work together because they anticipate a greater benefit or reduced risk compared with working alone. Organizational self-interest is front and center. Participants want to know "*What's in it for me?*" Forming mutual understanding through collective framing processes is a central task for defining multi-objective goals.

For outcomes to be multi-objective, collaboration is needed across groups, meaning that the process requires negotiation between organizations with different priorities. Many organizations are used to working autonomously or with like-minded groups. As a result, it may be difficult for organization leaders to accept the up-front costs of collaboration, the uncertainty of the collaboration's intended goals and outcomes (because they require negotiation), and the potential of future harm to individual organization agendas from *too little collaboration*. Two challenges are identifying mutual objectives and their joint pursuit, and managing expectations about how organizations pursue priorities *outside* of the collaborative project.

Multi-objective goals can be and have been included in American, British, and EU policies. For example, economic development, community capacity building, and community empowerment have been central goals of LEADER since 1991 and are reflected in its use across the UK. Further, the EU CAP and American Farm Bill have broadened in scope over time, addressing the farm economy, rural development, and resource conservation. Policymakers have accepted a multi-objective approach to agriculture-related policies to maintain public support—due to political necessity.[1] These major pieces of legislation demonstrate that the policy process itself is not a barrier to policy proposals that include multiple objectives. Rather, they demonstrate that *the*

Toward a theory of food systems practice 213

politics of legislating multiple goals simultaneously can be a normal part of finding a political majority and gaining public support.

A food systems perspective implies a shift in the culture of advocacy work and communications, promoting beliefs and tactics that encourage collaboration across perspectives. Learning, sharing, and spreading a food systems perspective is a long-term project that requires broad and inclusive participation, a diverse discursive environment, consensus formation, and consensus mobilization of a social movement.

Inclusive Orientation

Previous sections describe different types of boundary crossing: across roles in the food system, across levels of activity, between stakeholders in the field and professional staff in advocacy groups, and across disciplinary perspectives. Together these approaches are oriented toward overcoming preexisting and common types of division and demonstrate an orientation toward overcoming exclusion through a system-based approach to forming local food projects.

Debate about inclusion in local food projects often focuses on the degree to which individuals or social groups with unequal levels of status or influence interact in defining project goals, project participation, and benefit from project outcomes. Three general perspectives are articulated by researchers:

- the potential for a local food project to transmit preexisting social inequality;
- the potential for a local food project to increase inequality, perhaps through project leadership, participation, and outcomes to be defined entirely by and for those with greater influence and status; and
- the potential for local food projects to reduce social inequality through empowerment.

Often, these first two points are not distinguished and are compared against a measure of "full inclusion" (Hinrichs & Kremer, 2002, p. 68). The last point, about the potential for social transformation through increasing inclusion, has received less attention. As observed by Pretty (1995), participation and inclusion exist upon a quantifiable spectrum based on organizational structures, decision-making processes, and actions.

The American food movement has a trajectory of increasing inclusion. For example, the national Farmer-to-Consumer Direct Marketing Act of 1976 sought to address the mutual needs of producers and consumers. At the time, small-volume producers were receiving a declining share of the retail food dollar, and consumers saw goods as less affordable. Later policies specifically addressed the unequal access to affordable, fresh foods by including low-income women, infants, and children as beneficiaries of additional food assistance at farmers markets (1986); increasing availability of fresh fruits and vegetables in public schools (1994); giving assistance for low-income communities to identify their own food needs (1996); and targeting low-income seniors as beneficiaries

214 *Toward a theory of food systems practice*

of additional food assistance at farmers markets, farm stands, and CSAs (2001). Multiple federal programs were developed to reduce inequality including through: set-asides for socially disadvantaged producers and beginning farmers (2008); a farm-to-school program with priority for low-income communities (2010); and a nutrition program that incentivizes the purchase of fruit and vegetables by food assistance recipients (2014). These national policies promoted by supporters of local food demonstrate a clear trajectory of societal change oriented toward increasing social inclusion in the US.

Likewise, in the EU, the advent of LEADER in 1991 sought to overcome the disempowerment of local communities relative to the influence of central government. In England, the first LEADER project was a local food project, a food festival to promote the identity and local consumption of indigenously produced foods in a region dependent upon extractive industries (e.g. metal mining). Unlike previous rural development strategies, LEADER projects are bottom up, requiring the participation of local communities to decide how EU funds are used to promote *community* development and empowerment (Lowe & Ward, 1998; Ray, 2002).

Within a more urban context, community-led activities to address food poverty were widespread throughout the UK in the 1990s (Sustain, 1999a, 2003). These projects were recognized nationally in at least two policy forums addressing social inequity, the *Low Income, Food, Nutrition and Health: Strategies for Improvement* report and the *Independent Inquiry into Inequalities in Health Report* (Acheson, 1998; Barling et al., 2002; Nelson, 1997).

More recently, the non-governmental Making Local Food Work (MLFW) project resulted in a series of community food asset mapping exercises led by volunteers (CPRE, 2011b–g, 2012a–g). Further, within MLFW, project goals often outweighed economic outcomes. Evaluators were concerned that projects would fail to meet social goals because financial realities of project sustainability were inadequately addressed (SERIO, 2012, p. 23). Within Big Lottery's Local Food (LF) grant program, social goals were prominent. Kirwan observed that "the notion of enabling change for the betterment of those involved is at the core of what projects supported by LF are intent on doing" and that as a result "food can be understood as a vehicle for facilitating the achievement of wider aims" (Kirwan et al., 2013, p. 6).

Like the American local food movement, the British local food movement adopted practices oriented toward inclusion: self-mobilization, direct citizen and stakeholder engagement, capacity building of its participants, and making space for marginalized groups. The key difference of inclusion in the two countries' food movements is the degree to which national advocacy groups promoting local food adopted these practices.

The shift toward movement building

The practices of national policy leaders on local food in the US demonstrate that long-term gains are possible within an overall political and policy

Toward a theory of food systems practice 215

framework that many movement supporters consider loathsome. Through direct engagement and working toward small, definable, feasible policy proposals, they have achieved a succession of victories that has sustained the food movement's interest in national policy as a strategy to change the American food system. These outcomes have come through a networked social movement with decentralized leadership, few professional policy staff, and a strong focus on direct stakeholder communication to policymakers. Bridging the gap between national and local perspectives, and between different types of social division, required the American local food movement to adopt *governance* processes and organizational structures that address inequality, promote trust, and encourage political participation.

Stakeholder-led groups in the UK demonstrated a similar capacity to learn *governance*. Like the American, McCarthy, who was tired of "us versus them" politics, the FCFCG adopted a federation structure. Similarly, FARMA adopted a cooperative structure, and the Country Land and Businessowners' Association (CLA) adopted a stakeholder-led policy process. In the UK, stakeholder led groups were overshadowed by dominant interest groups, such as the SA, Sustain, and the National Farmers Union (NFU). The media access and funder support (membership fees in the case of NFU) of the three interest groups helped sustain their dominance over less visible and less resourced groups which had a direct relationship to local food stakeholders. The result was local food framed as an environmental issue (which three governments rejected) and an issue of *national* interest by many traditional agricultural advocacy groups.

The external influence of private foundations and government helped to democratize the American food movement. Foundations and Congress (through the USDA) established grant programs with goals of empowering marginalized groups and underserved communities. The EU has played a similar role in rural Britain by promoting capacity building in rural areas through the LEADER program. Perhaps, like the American food movement, the British food movement could benefit from a cadre of dedicated private funders to promote inclusion and policy collaboration in the food movement.

For the British, this could include promoting the existing diversity within the British food movement by "giving the stage" to stakeholders and overlooked groups; sharing best practices from organizations that practice participatory decision-making; providing support for building the capacity of marginalized groups; and utilizing stakeholder participation as a criterion for funding decisions.

By establishing stakeholder participation norms, funders are in effect regulating a competitive marketplace by setting a voluntary standard. Applicants choose how to meet funding criteria. Because not all applicants are funded, there is a broader impact across a social movement and policy community. This "power of the purse" is a coercive power. It needs to be taken seriously: it can be misused. If developed appropriately, a funder can effectively signal to grant-seekers that their internal practices should align with the external, social justice goals of their projects.

216 *Toward a theory of food systems practice*

Power is practiced both externally, from a social movement or organization to government and society, and internally, among individuals within a social movement or organization. For power to be practiced equitably, structures and processes need be adopted that address unequal status and influence. For the food systems practice to be truly systems-focused, it must internalize the practices, skills, and self-reflection needed to overcome several forms of social division and inequality. Without attention to the internal practice of power, funders risk supporting only vocal and visible organizations, which tend to dominate the interests of stakeholders and leave out marginalized social groups.

Conclusion

A research project about national policy change on the issue of local food became an exploration into how those policies were formed (and not formed). Explaining how and why policy change did and did not occur required the development of a partial history of British and American food movements. Policy texts from each country were used extensively, as an extant or external form of evidence, to complement the researcher-developed interviews and participant observation. Through the international comparative approach it was possible to identify a shared orientation toward inclusion in the project-level work of reforming local food systems. Similarly, it was possible to identify the differences in advocacy repertoires and prevailing organizational norms as a significant factor for local food policy outcomes.

Given the similarities of American and British local food project activities, and that both countries have national democratic institutions, the main differences originate from beliefs about policy change. Organizations that provide a service to stakeholders were more likely to pursue strategies of incremental change, allocate resources to small groups, and adopt winnable policy proposals, which would return a definable benefit to stakeholders. Organizations focusing on a belief or ideology were more successful at articulating their message but less successful in policy changes with direct benefit to local food stakeholders. There are pros and cons to both approaches. While a pure vision of sustainability may be needed to envision a future world, to bring individuals, organizations, and institutions along to that vision requires a capacity to work across differences. It requires careful attention for its leaders to select short-term objectives that contribute to a longer-term strategy for change.

The theory of food system practice identifies six ways in which practitioners practice governance, through trying to overcome common types of fragmentation (sector, level of activity, discipline, and narrowly defined objectives) and exclusion (an orientation to "make space" to facilitate inclusion and the degree of stakeholder participation). It serves as a playbook used in the field and a new starting point to assess and reassess food movement-building activities in United Kingdom, the United States of America, and elsewhere.

Toward a theory of food systems practice   217

While the inclusion aimed for in local food projects was similar across two national contexts, advocacy culture and political institutions resulted in different prevailing advocacy repertoires. By recognizing where there were similarities and differences, new, powerful assessments of each country's food movement were made. Too often, studies on local food utilize references from across borders without a clear justification for doing so. By doing so, other fundamental insights about food localization and its politics are missed. It is the task of researchers to tease out their differences and similarities. This is not one local food movement, but many local food movements.

Local food, after all, is about the context of place—of how factors such as a local environment, local community, and local economy contribute to distinctiveness. This means careful attention about when it is valid to include evidence and references from other places and cultures, as well as scrutiny of whether the academic publications are rooted in primary evidence or formed from academic discourse. Participant observation, as a practitioner-researcher, helped establish what was "normal" in a country's food movement, by observing what was put on stage in the public display. While the industrialization of agriculture is a common feature in many countries, political expression in response to it varies place by place according to different advocacy repertoires.

Competition and debate are inherent to the work of food, inherent to any field that aims to cross well-established divisions. However, perpetuating separateness through the segmentation of sector-specific advocacy groups and intense competition between organizations undermines holistic policy responses.

With high competition, an issue must gain prominence by being elevated over other competing, worthy issues, resulting in displacement of others' issues. The converse task, of forming alliances, of hybridizing narratives, of addressing one's level of empowerment compared to others, is more difficult and is aided by policy entrepreneurs. It requires the skills of governance: negotiation, facilitation, inclusion, capacity building, accountability processes, patience, restraint, and listening. These skills are learned by doing. Democracy is predicated on the participation of its citizens: they must participate in their communities and engage with their policymakers in order to be powerful and counter the interests which minimize their influence. Civic engagement is a cornerstone of food system governance.

Notes

1   Much of this has come from political pressure from conservation and wildlife interest groups (Potter, 1998; Potter & Tilzey, 2005).

Appendix 1
Organizations interviewed

Interviews were in-person unless specified otherwise. Notes taken unless specified otherwise.

England

- British environmental interest group Staff – 7 December, 2011. By skype, audio recorded.
- CLA Policy Staff – 28 March, 2011. Audio recorded.
- CPRE Policy Staff (a) – 28 March, 2011. Audio recorded.
- CPRE Policy Staff (b) – 13 May, 2011. Audio recorded.
- DEFRA Food Policy Staff – 28 February, 2011. Audio recorded.
- Environmental Funders Network – 30 June, 2011.
- Esmée Fairbairn Foundation (Food Strand) – 31 March, 2011. Audio recorded.
- FARMA Policy Staff – 2 May, 2012. By telephone, audio recorded.
- FCFCG – 8 May, 2012. Audio recorded.
- Former National Trust staff – 28 February, 2011. Audio recorded.
- Former NEF Staff – 30 March, 2011.
- Former RDA Staff (a) – 4 November, 2010. Background interview.
- Former RDA Staff (b) – 31 January, 2010. Background interview.
- Hackney City Farm – 30 March, 2011. Background interview.
- LEAF Staff – 24 March, 2011. Audio recorded.
- MLFW Staff (Plunkett Foundation) – 25 March, 2011. Audio recorded.
- NFU Food Chain Staff – 10 May, 2012. Audio recorded.
- Northumberland farmer (a) – 11 March, 2011. Background interview.
- Professor Mark Shucksmith (regarding LEADER) – 19 October, 2012. Background interview.
- Soil Association (a) – 9 February, 2011. Impromptu interview.
- Soil Association (b) – 13 December, 2011. By telephone, audio recorded.
- Sustain Policy Staff (a) – 29 March, 2011. Audio recorded; 2 February, 2012. Follow-up by telephone. Audio recorded
- WWF UK – 3 March, 2011. By telephone, audio recorded.

Appendix 1 Organizations interviewed 219

United States

- Former WKKF Program Officer – 7 November, 2011.
- Merck Family Fund – 14 December, 2011. Audio recorded.
- NSAC Policy Staff – 14 December, 2011. Audio recorded.

Appendix 2
Proposed Interview Topics list

This is a list of the main topics for a semi-structured interview in draft form.

- What is your perspective on locally produced food?
  - What is local?
  - What problems are local foods trying to address?
  - What prevents those changes?
  - What enables those changes?
  - What are the ultimate goals/outcomes?
  - What are the benefits from it?
  - Who might be harmed?
  - How are natural resources like soil, water, and air treated? (in comparison to what?)
    - Animals and crops?
    - Labor?
  - To the best of your knowledge, when did you become aware of local foods?
    - Why do you think this interest began then?
    - Any stories about how you learned of it?
  - What types of producers/consumers might be interested most in local foods?
    - When you think of them, what are their ages?
  - What is the relationship between producers and consumers?
- What is the role of the market?
- What is the role of government?
  - Are key leaders and influencers mentioned?
  - Are opposition interest mentioned?
  - Are key policies or events mentioned?
  - Are there key events that led to government positions?
- In general, is there a responsibility to ensure that producers receive a fair price?
  - Whose responsibility would that be?
- In general, whose responsibility is it to regulate or police the market?
- In general, whose responsibility is it to ensure that food is affordable?

Appendix 2 Proposed Interview Topics list   221

- Accessible to low-income families?
- What is the role of NGOs and third-sector organization?
- What is the role of the media?

Appendix 3
Participation observation events

Notes taken unless specified otherwise.

United Kingdom, primarily England

Conferences, meetings, and field trips

- All-party Parliamentary Group on Agro-ecology meeting on *How to Feed a Town* – 6 December, 2011.
- BBC *Farming Today* Interview – 25 June, 2012.
- Department for Work and Pensions with London Food Board – 23 January, 2013.
- MLFW Conference (Sheffield) – 12 May, 2011.
- MLFW Conference (London) – 20 March, 2012.
- Northern Rural Network (Conference on LEADER) – 17 April, 2012.
- Northumberland farmer (b) – 21 May, 2011. Group field visit, limited notes.
- Royal Agricultural College – 12 November, 2012. with Gus Schumacher
- Soil Association Annual Meeting (Manchester) – 9–10 February, 2011.
- Tasting the Future Events
  - 2nd Assembly – 2 February, 2011.
  - 3rd Assembly – 28 November, 2011.
  - 4th Assembly – 19 June, 2012.
  - Innovation group workshop – 29 March, 2011.
  - Stewardship group meeting (held at Hackney City Farm) – 12 September, 2011.
- Workshop with town planners and rural development officers in the Peak District hosted in Bakewell – 11 May, 2011. Attended as a note-taker for Newcastle University.
- Workshop with town planners and rural development officers in the Peak District hosted in Bakewell – 11 May, 2011. Attended as a note-taker for Newcastle University.
- US-UK Fulbright Commission scheduled events.
  - Cornwall County Council – 12 January, 2011.

Appendix 3 Participation observation events 223

- Eden project – 12 January, 2011.
- Ireland and Northern Ireland field trip – 5–7 April, 2011.
- Panel on *Coalition politics and post-CSR [Corporate Social Responsibility] Britain* with Lord Stewart Wood and James Crabtree (Financial Times), Stratford Town Hall – 10 January, 2011.
- Panel on *The London Olympics: Regeneration and Legacy* with Tessa Jowell MP, Nick Falk (Director, URBED), Liz McMahon (Managing Director of Madison-Muir / former Head of International Marketing for the London 2012 Games bid) – 11 January, 2011.
- Panel on *Devolution, regional governance, and the EU* with Stephen Gilbert MP, Caroline Pidgeon AM [London Assembly Member], Mary Honeyball MEP, House of Lords – 11 January, 2011.
- Panel on the role of Parliament with Baroness Shirley Williams, David Lammy MP, Neil Mahapatra, and Baroness Diana Warwick, House of Lords – 16 September, 2010.
- WWF UK Workshop (with the Making Local Food Work evaluator) – 19 March, 2012.
- WWF UK Consulting and Workshop – November, 2012 – March, 2013.

Presentations (with/for stakeholders)

- 3rd Annual City Food Policy Symposium (London) – 12 December, 2012. Invited as a speaker.
- All-Party Parliamentary Group on Agro-ecology – 14 November, 2012. with Gus Schumacher.
- Community Food and Health (Scotland) – 15 November, 2012. with Gus Schumacher.
- Department of Communities and Local Government: Policy Picnic Series (organized by the Cabinet Office) – 13 November, 2012. with Gus Schumacher.
- FARMA workshop (London) – 30 September, 2012. Invited as a speaker.
- London Food Board – 14 November, 2012. with Gus Schumacher.

Farmers' markets attended

- Newcastle farmers' market – infrequently.
- Norwich city market – weekly during January – May, 2002.
- Queens Park Market (London) – 30 September, 2012.
- Stockbridge market (Edinburgh) – 1 May, 2011.
- Tynemouth farmers' market – monthly.
- Warwick market – 18 February, 2012.

224 *Appendix 3 Participation observation events*

Indoor public markets attended

- Coventry – 23 March, 2011.
- Durham – 2011.
- Inverness – July 2012.
- Newcastle – monthly.

Other visited farms

- Bede's World Farm (South Tyneside) – 5 March, 2011; 30 June, 2012.
- Close House (Newcastle University Farm) – October, 2010.
- Hackney City Farm – 30 March, 2011.
- Nafferton (Newcastle University Farm) – October, 2010.
- Ouseburn city farm (North Tyneside) – 19 March, 2011.
- Rising Sun Country Farm (North Tyneside) – 2012.

Other

- Hadrian's Wall Trail walks – 25–27 April, 2011; 28 May – 5 Jun, 2011.
- Hexham food festival – 24 September, 2011.
- North Shields Fish Quay – frequently.
- Northumberland County Show (Corbridge) – 25 August, 2012.
- Organic fruit and vegetable box, Deli Around the Corner, Tynemouth – weekly.
- Tynemouth food festival – 12–13 May, 2012.

United States

Participant observation events

- CFSC Conference (Oakland, CA) – 4–8 November, 2011. Audio recorded.
- Northeast Sustainable Agriculture Working Group Conference (Albany, NY) – 10–12 November, 2011. Audio recorded.
- WKKF Conference (Asheville, NC) – 21–25 May, 2012. Audio recorded.

References

7 U.S.C. § 1991(11)(b).

7 U.S.C. § 1991(11)(d)(i)(I)(aa).

7 U.S.C. § 1991(11)(d)(i)(I)(bb).

7 U.S.C. § 1991(a)(11). *Definitions. Qualified beginning farmer or rancher.* (2012).

A bill (H.R. 2559) to amend the Federal Crop Insurance Act. In Congressional Record, S1628–1642. (2000, March 23).

Acheson, D. (1998, November 26). *Independent Inquiry into Inequalities in Health Report,* Department of Health. Accessed December 8, 2008. Retrieved from www.archive. official-documents.co.uk/document/doh/ih/ih.htm

An Act to Amend the Agricultural Adjustment Act and other purposes. Section 32. (1935, August 24). U.S. Congress.

ADAS, Food and Drink Federation, FEC et al. (2010). *Tasting the Future: Collaborative Innovation for One Planet Food. Invitation to attend the second assembly.*

ADAS and SQW Limited (2003, December). *The Mid-Term Evaluation of the England Rural Development Programme,* prepared for DEFRA. Wolverhampton and Cambridge. p. 191.

ADAS and University of Reading (2003, November). *An Economic Evaluation of the Processing and Marketing Grant Scheme,* prepared for DEFRA. p. 137.

Afri-can Foodbasket. (n.d.). Food Justice: The Food Justice Movement in North America. Retrieved January 11, 2013 from blog.africanfoodbasket.com/knowledge/ food-justice/

AFT, CFSC, ED et al. (2005, Revised April 11). *Core Proposal for the Food and Society Collaborative Policy Project.* p. 12.

AFT and ED (2004a, December 10). *AFT ED Prjct Bdgt 12–04.* [Excel spreadsheet].

AFT and ED (2004b, December 10). *AFT ED Regrants Bdgt 12–04.* [Excel spreadsheet].

Agribusiness Consolidation. Hearing before the U.S. House Committee on Agriculture. 106th Congress, 1st Session. Report 106–5 (1999, February 11).

Agricultural Adjustment Act. Section 32 (as amended). 7 U.S.C. § 612c(1–3). (2012 ed.).

Agricultural Marketing Act. 7 U.S.C. § 1621. Congressional declaration of purpose; use of existing facilities; cooperation with States. (1946, August 14).

Agricultural Risk Protection Act of 1999. Report 106–300, H.R. 2559, U.S. House, 106th Congress (1999, August 5).

Agricultural Risk Protection Act of 2000. Sec. 231. Pub. L. No. 106–224. (2000, June 20). U.S. Congress.

Agricultural Risk Protection Act of 2000–Conference Report. In Congressional Record, S4416–4443. (2000, May 25).

226 References

Agriculture of the Middle. (2012, January). Agriculture of the Middle. Retrieved January 15, 2012 from www.agofthemiddle.org/

Agriculture Risk Protection Act of 2000. Value-added Agricultural Product Market Development Grants, Sec. 231. Pub. L. No. 106–224. (2000, June 20). U.S. Congress.

Alan Simpson [Labour – Nottingham South]. (2002, December 12). *Debate on the issues raised in the Sustainable Farming and Food Strategy (published on the same day) and the newly formed Department of Food, Environment, and Rural Affairs,* In Hansard, House of Commons. pp. 409–504. Accessed August 29, 2012. Retrieved from hansard. millbanksystems.com/commons/2002/dec/12/environment-food-and-rural-affairs#S6CV0396P0_20021212_HOC_184

Allen, G. (2002, August 22). *Regional Development Agencies,* Research Paper 02/50, House of Commons Library, Economic Policy and Statistics Section. p. 48.

Allen, P. (2004). *Together at the Table: Sustainability and Sustenance in the American Agrifood System.* University Park, Pennsylvania: The Pennsylvania State University Press.

Allen, P. (2010). Realizing justice in local food systems. *Cambridge Journal of Regions, Economy and Society, 3*(2), 295–308.

Allison, B. (2001). Counting Farmers Markets. *Geographical Review, 91*(4), 655–674.

Amendment No. 10, H.R. 2464, U.S. House, 107th Congress, 1st Session. In Congressional Record, H6294–6299 (2001, October 4).

Amendment to H.R. 2419 Offered by Mr. Kagen of Wisconsin, 109th Congress Session (2007, July 18) (print from House Legislative Counsel).

An amendment to the bill S. 3307, to reauthorize child nutrition programs, and for other purposes, Healthy, Hunger-Free Kids Act of 2010, SA 4589, U.S. Senate, 111th Congress, 2nd Session. In Congressional Record, S6911–S6965 (corrected). (2010, August 5).

Amendment to the Rural Development Title Offered by Mrs. Gillibrand of New York, 109th Congress Session (2007, July 18) (introduced, electronic copy from Representative Gillibrand's office).

American Planning Association (n.d.). *Ladder of Young People's Participation.* Great cities: Great markets, 6th International Public Markets Conference, October 28–31, 2005, Washington, DC. p. 2. [paper handout].

Anderson, M., FFPP (2006, November 25). *Making the Case for Local Food Systems, Farm & Food Policy Project LEARNING PAPER,* draft. p. 32. Accessed April 16, 2012. Retrieved from www.foodsystems-integrity.com/yahoo_site_admin/assets/docs/The_Case_for_Local__Regional_Food_Marketing.28645058.pdf

Anderson, M., FFPP (2007a, May). *The Case for Local and Regional Food Marketing.* p. 8. Accessed April 16, 2012. Retrieved from www.foodsystems-integrity.com/yahoo_site_admin/assets/docs/The_Case_for_Local__Regional_Food_Marketing.28645058.pdf

Anderson, M., FFPP (2007b, May). *The Case for Local Food Systems.* p. 18.

Anderson, M. (2007c, April 2). *Summary of Revisions to "The Case for Local Food Systems" FFPP Background Paper. Molly D. Anderson – April 2, 2007,* memorandum to Alan R. Hunt, Policy Analyst, NEMWI. p. 3.

Andrews, P. and Dunn, H., DEFRA, Sustainable Agriculture Division and Food Chain Analysis Division. (2005, January 20). *The Strategy for Sustainable Farming and Food.* Retrieved from www.relu.ac.uk/events/Jan05/Presentations/Policyworkshop/Andrews.pdf

Appel, P. A. (2000). Intervention in Public Law Litigation: The Environmental Paradigm. *Washington University Law Review, 78*(1).

References 227

Arnstein, S. R. (1969). A Ladder of Citizen Participation. *Journal of the American Institute of Planners, 35*(4), 216–224.

Artur Davis [D-IL] and Bobby Rush [D-IL]. (2007a, July 19). *Letter from 31 Representatives to Chairman of the House Committee on Agriculture,* Washington, DC. p. 3.

Artur Davis [D-IL] and Bobby Rush [D-IL]. (2007b, July 19). *Letter from 31 Representatives to Ranking Member of the House Committee on Agriculture,* Washington, DC. p. 3.

Ashbridge, I. (2010, September 9). English Farming & Food Partnerships to restructure, *Farmers Weekly [Online].* Retrieved from www.fwi.co.uk/Articles/10/09/ 2010/123359/English-Farming-amp-Food-Partnerships-to-restructure.htm

Austrian Institute for Regional Studies and Spatial Planning (2003a). *Ex-post Evaluation of the Community Initiative LEADER II – Final Report Volume 1: Main Report,* prepared for EC DGA. p. 260.

Austrian Institute for Regional Studies and Spatial Planning (2003b, December). *Ex-post Evaluation of the Community Initiative LEADER II Final Report Volume 4: Geographical Reports,* prepared for EC DGA. p. 464. Retrieved from www.ec. europa.eu/agriculture/eval/reports/leader2/full4.pdf

Austrian Institute for Regional Studies and Spatial Planning (2006, December 6). *Synthesis of mid-term evaluations of LEADER+ programmes Final Report,* commissioned by the EU Commission Directorate General Agriculture. Vienna. p. 230.

Averill, V. [in Nairobi, Kenya]. (2007, February 21). African trade fears carbon footprint backlash, *BBC News.* Retrieved from www.www.news.bbc.co.uk/1/hi/ business/6383687.stm

Baker, P. (2008, August 11). Feeling the heat of food security [Viewpoint], *BBC News.* Retrieved from www.news.bbc.co.uk/1/hi/sci/tech/7553958.stm

Bales, S. N. (2006, August). *Framing the Food System.* p. 17. Retrieved from www.frameworksinstitute.org/foodsystems.html

Barling, D., Lang, T. and Caraher, M. (2002). Joined-Up Food Policy? The Trials of Governance, Public Policy and the Food System. *Social Policy & Administration, 36*(6), 556–574.

Barnes, T. J. (2008). American Pragmatism: Towards a Geographical Introduction. *Geoforum, 39,* 1542–1554.

BBC News (2005a, July 15). Food movement "harms environment", *BBC News.* Retrieved from www.news.bbc.co.uk/1/hi/uk/4684693.stm

BBC News (2005b, March 2). Local food "greener than organic", *BBC News.* Retrieved from www.news.bbc.co.uk/go/pr/fr/-/1/hi/sci/tech/4312591.stm

BBC News (2007, January 26). Organic imports under fire, *BBC News.* Retrieved from www.news.bbc.co.uk/1/hi/business/6302611.stm

BBC News (2008a, October 16). The cost of food: Facts and figures. Explore the facts and figures behind the fluctuating price of food across the globe, *BBC News.* Retrieved from www.news.bbc.co.uk/1/hi/world/7284196.stm

BBC News (2008b, October 16). Cost of food: Global roundup, *BBC News.* Retrieved from www.news.bbc.co.uk/1/hi/world/7671124.stm

BBC News (2008c, July 23). New E Africa food crisis warning, *BBC News.* Retrieved from www.news.bbc.co.uk/1/hi/world/africa/7522060.stm

BBC News (2008d, October 15). Q&A: World food prices, *BBC News.* Retrieved from www.news.bbc.co.uk/1/hi/business/7340214.stm

228   *References*

BBC News. (2008e, April 14). World Bank tackles food emergency, *BBC News*. Retrieved from www.news.bbc.co.uk/1/hi/7344892.stm

BBC World News (2007, August 22). The ethical food debate. Should ethical shoppers be more concerned about food miles or supporting farmers in developing countries? *BBC News*. Retrieved from www.news.bbc.co.uk/player/nol/newsid_6950000/newsid_6959600/6959606.stm?bw=bb&mp=wm&asb=1&news=1

Becker, E. (2001a, October 4). House Rejects an Effort to Redirect Farm Policy, *The New York Times*. Retrieved from www.nytimes.com/2001/10/05/us/house-rejects-an-effort-to-redirect-farm-policy.html

Becker, E. (2001b, October 4). White House Criticizes Republican Farm Bill, *The New York Times*, New York City. Retrieved from www.nytimes.com/2001/10/04/us/white-house-criticizes-republican-farm-bill.html

Becker, G. S., Library of Congress, CRS. (2006). *Farmers' Markets: The USDA Role*, RS21652. p. 6.

Becker, G. S., Library of Congress, CRS. (2009, February 20). *Farm and Food Support Under USDA's Section 32 Program*, 7–5700. p. 21.

Becker, G. S. and Womach, J., Library of Congress, CRS. (2002, Updated March 13). *The 2002 Farm Bill: Overview and Status*, RL31195. p. 32.

Bernie Sanders [I-VT]. *Senate Amendment 3745*. In Congressional Record, S14544. (2007, November 15).

Bernie Sanders [I-VT]. (2009). FY 2010 Appropriations/Authorization. Retrieved February 24, 2012 from www.sanders.senate.gov/services/approps.cfm

Bernie Sanders [I-VT]. (2010, June 4). Release: Sanders Announces Grant for 40 Vermont School Gardens. Retrieved February 24, 2012 from www.sanders.senate.gov/newsroom/news/?id=33f2f400–4769–4928–97bd-0fde1551f7bf.

Berry, J. M. (1982). Consumers and the Hunger Lobby. *Proceedings of the Academy of Political Science*, *34*(3), 68–78.

Betty Jo Nelson [USDA FNS Administrator]. *Review of the use of Food Stamps in farmers' markets*, Hearing before the U.S. House Committee on Agriculture. Report 101–68, p. 105 (September 18, 1991).

Bingham, L. B., Nabatchi, T. and O'Leary, R. (2005). The New Governance: Practices and Processes for Stakeholder and Citizen Participation in the Work of Government. *Public Administration Review*, *65*(5), 547–558.

Blake, M. K., Mellor, J. and Crane, L. (2010). Buying Local Food: Shopping Practices, Place, and Consumption Networks in Defining Food as "Local". *Annals of the Association of American Geographers*, *100*(2), 409–426.

Bobby Rush [D-IL], Collin Peterson [D-MN] and Bennie Thompson [D-MS] (2008). *Letter from 28 Representatives to the House Appropriations Committee Agriculture sub-committee Co-chairs*. p. 3.

Braiser, K., Findeis, J. L., Hubbard, C. et al. (2012). The evolution of agriculture and agricultural policy in the UK and US. In M. Shucksmith, D. L. Brown, S. Shortall, J. Vergunst and M. E. Warner (Eds.), *Rural Transformations and Rural Policies in the US and UK* (pp. 196–214). New York: Routledge.

Brasher, P. (2001). House rejects farm bill reforms to cut subsidy, aid conservation, *Pittsburgh Post-Gazette*, Pittsburgh, PA. p. A-8.

Brasier, K. J. (2002). Ideology and Discourse: Characterizations of the 1996 Farm Bill by Agricultural Interest Groups. *Agriculture and Human Values*, *19*, 239–253.

Briggs, S., Fisher, A., Lott, M. et al. (2010, June). *Real Food, Real Choice Connecting SNAP Recipients with Farmers Markets*: CFSC & FMC. p. 86.

British environmental interest group staff (2011, December 7). *Skype interview*. [audio recorded].

Bryden, J. and Warner, M. E. (2012). Policy Affecting Rural People, Economies and Communities. In M. Shucksmith, D. L. Brown, S. Shortall, J. Vergunst and M. E. Warner (Eds.), *Rural Transformations and Rural Policies in the US and UK* (pp. 179–195). New York: Routledge.

Bullock, S. (2000). *The economic benefits of farmers' markets*. FOE UK.

Bulls Eye Resources (2008, March 2–5). *Summary of Town Hall Meeting on Child Nutrition Reauthorization from Legislative Action Conference March 2008*, Powerpoint presentation. p. 21. Accessed February 7, 2012. Retrieved from www.schoolnutrition.org/uploadedFiles_old/ASFSA/childnutrition/govtaffairs/SNATownHallReauthorization2009final.pdf

Bush, G. W., The White House. (2008, May 21). *Farm Bill Veto Message*. Retrieved from georgewbush-whitehouse.archives.gov/news/releases/2008/05/20080521–4.html

Buxton, A., IIED (2011). *A shopping trolley for change?* Retrieved September 29, 2012, from www.iied.org/shopping-trolley-for-change

Buzby, J. C., Guthrie, J. F. and Kantor, L. S., USDA, Economic Research Service, Food Assistance and Nutrition Research Program. (2003, May). *Evaluation of the USDA Fruit and Vegetable Pilot Program: Report to Congress*. p. 31.

Cabinet Office, The Strategy Unit. (2008). *Food Matters: Towards a Strategy for the 21st Century*. London: Cabinet Office. p. 124.

Caplan, R., Harrison Institute for Public Law, George Washington University, (2006, December 5). *Preemption of Geographic Preferences in School Food Procurement*, Office Memorandum. Washington, DC. p. 4.

Carnegie UK Trust (2010). *Rural Development and the LEADER Approach in the UK and Ireland*. Dunfermline. p. 25.

Carnegie UK Trust Rural Programme (2010). *A Common Rural Development Policy?* Dunfermline. p. 48.

Carpenter, J. (2008, September 8). Foods "should label up eco-costs", *BBC News*. Retrieved from www.news.bbc.co.uk/1/hi/sci/tech/7604996.stm

Carter, N. (2008). Combating Climate Change in the UK: Challenges and Obstacles. *The Political Quarterly*, *79*(2), 194–205.

Carter, N. (2014). The Politics of Climate Change in the UK. *WIREs Climate Change*, *5*(3). doi: 10.1002/wcc.274

CBI (2007). *Farm and Food Policy Project Timeline (Draft 1/8/07)*. p. 2.

CBI (2008a). *Farm and Food Policy Project Process Evaluation*. p. 35. report for NEMWI.

CBI (2008b, October 28). *Farm and Food Policy Project Process Evaluation Briefing 10/27/08*. p. 26. presentation to WKKF, Battle Creek, Michigan.

CBI and NEMWI (2005, September 25). *Communications and Decision-Making Protocol for the FFPP*. p. 11.

Center for Rural Affairs. (2007). Ron Kind: Interview with a Crusader. *Blog for Rural America*. Retrieved March 26, 2012 from www.cfra.org/blog/2007/06/24/ron-kind-interview-crusader

CFSC (2004, December 9). *Community Food Security Coalition Community Food and Nutrition Partnership Budget presented to WK Kellogg Foundation*. [Excel spreadsheet].

CFSC (2005, November 28). *Notes for HFC Conference*. p. 3. [conference call notes].

CFSC (2006a, May 26). *Synopsis Healthy Food and Communities Work Group Call*. p. 3. [conference call notes].

230   *References*

CFSC (2006b, Winter). *Working toward a diverse and inclusive coalition. Community Food Security News.* p. 20.

CFSC (2010). *Child Nutrition Act Legislation: Bills That Contain Farm to School Provisions.* Retrieved February 13, 2012 from sites.google.com/a/foodsecurity.org/child-nutrition-legislation/

CFSC (2011). *Request for Proposals.* "Food Justice: Honoring our Roots, Growing the Movement." *15th Annual Conference Oakland, California November 5–8, 2011.* p. 4.

Charmaz, K. (2006). *Constructing Grounded Theory: A Practical Guide through Qualitative Analysis.* London: SAGE Publications.

Chi, K. R., MacGregor, J. and King, R., IIED & Oxfam (2009). *Fair miles recharting the food miles map,* Big ideas in development. p. 48. Retrieved from pubs.iied.org/15516IIED.html

Child Nutrition and WIC Reauthorization Act of 2004. Access to Local Foods and School Gardens, Sec. 122. Pub. L. No. 108–265. (2004a, June 30). U.S. Congress.

Child Nutrition and WIC Reauthorization Act of 2004. Fresh Fruit and Vegetable Program, Sec. 120. Pub. L. No. 108–265. (2004b, June 30). U.S. Congress.

Child Nutrition Forum (2008, December 17). *Child Nutrition Forum: Statement of Principles for Child Nutrition Reauthorization.* p. 4.

Child Nutrition Improvement and Integrity Act, Report together with Additional Views (To accompany H.R. 3873), Sec. 302. Supporting Nutrition Education, Improving Meal Quality, and Access to Local Foods, Report 108–445, U.S. House, 108th Congress, 2nd Session (2004, March 23) (reported).

Child Nutrition Promotion and School Lunch Protection Act of 2009, S. 934, U.S. Senate, 111th Congress, 1st Session (2009a, April 30) (introduced).

Child Nutrition Promotion and School Lunch Protection Act of 2009, H.R. 1324, U.S. House, 111th Congress, 1st Session (2009b, March 5) (introduced).

Chuck Grassley [R–IA]. (2000, May 25). *Agricultural Risk Protection Act of 2000–Conference Report,* Congressional Record. p. S4437.

CLA (2007). Prime Minister launches CLA's Just Ask campaign. Retrieved January 5, 2013 from www.cla.org.uk/News_and_Press/News_Archive/Food/Food/6378.htm/

CLA Policy Staff (2011, March 28). *Personal interview.* [audio recorded].

Clancy, K. (1994). Social Justice and Sustainable Agriculture: Moving Beyond Theory. [Commentary]. *Agriculture and Human Values, 11*(4), 77–83.

Clemens, E. S. (1996). Organizational Form as Frame: Collective Identity and Political strategy in the American labor movement, 1880–1920. In D. McAdam, J. D. McCarthy and M. N. Zald (Eds.), *Comparative Perspectives on Social Movements: Political Opportunities, Mobilizing Structures, and Cultural Framings* (pp. 205–226). Cambridge: Cambridge University Press.

Clemens, E. S. and Hughes, M. D. (2002). Recovering Past Protest: Historical Research on Social Movements. In B. Klandermans and S. Staggenborg (Eds.), *Methods of Social Movement Research* (pp. 201–232). Minneapolis: University of Minnesota Press.

Coglianese, C. (2001). Social Movements, Law, and Society: The Institutionalization of the Environmental Movement. *University of Pennsylvania Law Review, 150*(1), 85–118.

Cohen, B., IQ Solutions, Inc. (2002, July). *Community Food Security Assessment Toolkit,* E-FAN-02–013, Report prepared for USDA ERS. p. 166.

Committee on Agriculture, U.S. House. (2001). *Report on Activities During the 106th Congress,* Washington, DC: Government Printing Office. Accessed January 11,

2012. Retrieved from www.gpo.gov/fdsys/pkg/CRPT-106hrpt1042/pdf/CRPT-106hrpt1042.pdf

Committee on Agriculture, Nutrition, and Forestry, *Report of the Committee on Agriculture, Nutrition, and Forestry to accompany S. 1731*, Report 107–117, U.S. Senate, 107th Congress, 1st Session (2001).

Commonwealth of Massachusetts. (2011). *Faces of Massachusetts Agriculture: August Schumacher, Jr. former Commissioner of Agricultural Resources*. Retrieved from www.mass.gov/agr/150/Gallery/pages/schumacher_gus.htm

Community Council of Devon (2010). *Removing the Barriers: Community Groups' Guide to Making your Growing Project Accessible to All*. Exeter. p. 16.

Community food and health (Scotland) (2014). *Community food and health (Scotland)*. NHS Scotland. Retrieved August 21, 2014, from www.communityfoodandhealth.org.uk/

Companies House. Select and access Company Information. Community Owned Retailing Limited (08321409) Dissolved 12/06/2001. Retrieved December 6, 2012 from www.companieshouse.gov.uk/

Conference Report to Accompany H.R. 2997. (2009, October 21). Report 111–279, U.S. Congress. p. 125.

Congressional Budget Office (2010a August 5). *Budgetary Effects of an Amendment in the Nature of a Substitute to S. 3307, reauthorizing child nutrition programs*.

Congressional Budget Office (2010b, August 25). *Congressional Budget Office Cost Estimate H.R. 5504 Improving Nutrition for America's Children Act*. p. 21.

Cooperatives UK (2011a). *From conflict to co-operation: Handy illustrated guides for community food enterprises*. [packet containing five guidebooks].

Cooperatives UK (2011b). *Organisational growth and development*, from conflict to co-operation: a handy illustrated guide for community food enterprises: MLFW. p. 19.

Cooperatives UK (2011c, June). *Simply governance: A comprehensive guide to understanding the systems and processes concerned with the running of sustainable community enterprise*: MLFW. p. 111.

Couchman, P. (2012). *Introduction for Caroline Spelman, Secretary of State for Environment, Food, and Rural Affairs*. Presented at Making Local Food Our Future: MLFW 2012 Conference, London.

Council of the European Union. (2007, March 19). *Press Release – 2790th Council meeting Agriculture and Fisheries*, Brussels. p. 28.

Countryside Agency. (1999, June 28). *News Release: Everyone's a Winner in Tomorrow's Countryside*, handout in press kit from the Countryside Agency launch event.

Countryside Agency. (2002). *Eat the view: Promoting sustainable local products*, Wetherby, West Yorkshire. p. 32.

Countryside Agency. (2004). Eat the View. The Countryside Agency. Retrieved September 29, 2004 from www.countryside.gov.uk/LivingLandscapes/eat_the_view/What/index.asp

Cowan, T. and Feder, J., Library of Congress, CRS. (2012, August 15). *The Pigford Cases: USDA Settlement of Discrimination Suits by Black Farmers*, RS20430. p. 14.

Cox, G., Lowe, P. and Winter, M. (1986). Agriculture and Conservation in Britain: A Policy Community under Siege. *Agriculture: People and Policies* (pp. 181–215). London, UK: Allen and Unwin.

CPRE (1998 (reprinted 2002)). *Food Webs: A report on local food networks in East Suffolk which demonstrates the importance of local shops and services to rural communities*. London. p. 11.

232   *References*

CPRE (2001a, October). *Farming Futures.* p. 20.

CPRE. (2001b, October). *Modulation. CPRE submission no. 4 to the Policy Commission for Farming and Food.* p. 2.

CPRE (2001c, October). *Policy Commission on Future of Farming and Food: Farming and Food – the Future CPRE Response October 2001.* p. 14.

CPRE (2001d, June). *Rural Recovery.* p. 24.

CPRE. (2001e, October). *Rural recovery. CPRE submission no. 6 to the Policy Commission for Farming and Food.* p. 2.

CPRE. (2001f, October). *The specialty and local food sector. CPRE submission no. 5 to the Policy Commission for Farming and Food.* p. 2.

CPRE (2001g, September). *Sustainable local foods.* p. 26.

CPRE (2002). *Local Action for Local Foods.*

CPRE (2011a, October). *Draft national planning policy framework – A response by the Campaign to Protect Rural England (CPRE) to the Department for Communities and Local Government consultation.* p. 60.

CPRE (2011b, April). *From field to fork: Birstall mapping the local food web.* p. 12.

CPRE (2011c, April). *From field to fork: Hastings mapping the local food web.* p. 20.

CPRE (2011d, April). *From field to fork: Kenilworth mapping the local food web.* p. 12.

CPRE (2011e, April). *From field to fork: Knutsford mapping the local food web.* p. 20.

CPRE (2011f, April). *From field to fork: Sheffield mapping the local food web.* p. 24.

CPRE (2011g, April). *From field to fork: Totnes mapping the local food web.* p. 24.

CPRE (2012a, September). *From field to fork: Darlington mapping the local food web.* p. 32.

CPRE (2012b, May). *From field to fork: Faversham mapping the local food web.* p. 28.

CPRE (2012c, May). *From field to fork: Haslemere mapping the local food web.* p. 28.

CPRE (2012d, September). *From field to fork: Hexham mapping the local food web.* p. 28.

CPRE (2012e, February). *From field to fork: Ledbury mapping the local food web.* p. 28.

CPRE (2012f, May). *From field to fork: Otley mapping the local food web.* p. 28.

CPRE (2012g, May). *From field to fork: Shrewsbury mapping the local food web.* p. 28.

CPRE Policy Staff (b) (2011, May 13). *Telephone interview.* [audio recorded].

CS Mott Group for Sustainable Food Systems (2009, August). *Summary of Child Nutrition Reauthorization Priorities for Select National Organizations/Coalitions.* Michigan State University. p. 7.

Cumbria Fells and Dales RDPE Local Action Group. (2011). *Annual Review 2010/2011,* Cumbria County Council. p. 16.

Cumulus Consultants Ltd (2006, May 16). *Analysis of scenarios of co-financing and voluntary modulation,* CC-P-432, prepared for DEFRA. p. 67.

Curry, D., SFFS Implementation Group. (2006, July). *The Sustainable Farming and Food Strategy, three years on: Reflections on progress by the SFFS Implementation Group.* p. 13.

Curry, D. (2009). *A sustainable future for farming and food in the UK: Eight years on from the Policy Commission.* Presented at 26th Edith Mary Gayton Memorial Lecture, University of Reading, Farm Management Unit.

Curry, D., Browning, H., Davis, P. et al., Policy Commission on the Future of Farming and Food. (2002). *Farming & food: A sustainable future.* p. 152. Retrieved from webarchive.nationalarchives.gov.uk/20100807034701/archive.cabinetoffice.gov.uk/farming/pdf/PC%20Report2.pdf

Daily Mail Reporter. (2011, March 2). Why Larry the No10 cat has shunned his rat-catching duties: His posh diet means he dines on "greener" fish than the Prime

References 233

Minister, *Daily Mail Online*. Retrieved from www.dailymail.co.uk/news/article-1362077/Larry-No-10-cat-shuns-rat-catching-duties-posher-diet-David-Cameron.html

Dalmeny, K., Sustain (2001, October 31). *Food Justice: An end to food poverty. Public meeting, 14th November.* [E-mail archive of] Health-equity-netowrk@jiscmail.ac.uk. Retrieved February 20, 2013, from www.jiscmail.ac.uk/cgi-bin/webadmin?A2=health-equity-network;3a36fc37.0110

David Miliband [Secretary of State for Environment, Food, and Rural Affairs] (2007). *Voluntary Modulation, Written Ministerial Statement, and related correspondence,* Parliament. Retrieved from www.parliament.uk/documents/upload/070328-miliband-voluntary-modulation.pdf

de Tocqueville, A. (1835/40 [1997]). *Democracy in America* (H. Reeve, Trans. revised and corrected 1899 ed.). American Studies Programs, University of Virginia.

[Debate on Amendment 10]. (2001, October 4). Congressional Record: U.S. House. pp. H6294-H6325.

DEFRA (2002a, December 10). *7.2 Timing, Level and Source of Funding for Measures,* [Archived web content. Last updated August 17, 2005]. Accessed August 31, 2012. Retrieved from www.www.tna.europarchive.org/20081112122150/defra.gov.uk/erdp/docs/national/section7/funding.htm

DEFRA (2002b). *Activity under the England Rural Development Programme in 2001,* ERDP Bulletin April. Retrieved from www.www.tna.europarchive.org/20081112122150/defra.gov.uk/erdp/pdfs/bulletin/bulletin_01.pdf

DEFRA (2002c, December 10; last updated February 5, 2007). *ERDP in practice,* The National Archives. Accessed October 3, 2012. Retrieved from www.tna.europarchive.org/20081112122150/defra.gov.uk/erdp/case_studies/full_list_scheme.htm

DEFRA (2002d). *The Strategy for Sustainable Farming and Food: Facing the Future,* Department for Environment, Food and Rural Affairs. p. 51.

DEFRA, Working Group on Local Food. (2003a, March). *Local Food – A Snapshot of the Sector Appendices: Report of the Working Group on Local Food.* p. 142.

DEFRA (2003b). *Policy Paper on Local Food.* p. 10.

DEFRA (2004a, July). *Report of Rural Funding Review.* p. 86.

DEFRA (2004b, July). *Rural Strategy 2004,* London. p. 101.

DEFRA. (2005, September 5). *ARCHIVE: Co-operation and collaboration for sustainable farming and food.* Accessed December 10, 2010.

DEFRA (2006a, February 2). *Closure of ERDP Project-Based Schemes,* The National Archives. Retrieved from www.tna.europarchive.org/20081112122150/defra.gov.uk/erdp/pbs-closure.htm

DEFRA (2006b). *Selling to the Public Sector – A guide to the Public Sector Food Procurement Initiative for farmers and growers,* PB 11952, London. p. 32.

DEFRA (2006c, July). *Sustainable Farming and Food Strategy: Forward Look.* p. 53.

DEFRA (2007a). *DIY Guide to Implementing the PSFPI – advice for practitioners,* London. p. 92.

DEFRA (2007b, revised December 12). *Public Sector Food Procurement Initiative (PSFPI) frequently asked questions.* p. 19.

DEFRA (2007c, April 16). *Reducing the External Costs of the Domestic Transportation of Food by the Food Industry.* p. 73. Retrieved from www.archive.defra.gov.uk/evidence/economics/foodfarm/reports/Costfoodtransport/Defra-17May2007.pdf

234   References

DEFRA (2007d, May). *Report of the Food Industry Sustainability Strategy Champions' Group on Food Transport*. p. 24.

DEFRA (2008a). *The Rural Development Programme for England 2007–2013. Chapter 5 Information on the Axes and Measures proposed for each Axis, and their description*. p. 149.

DEFRA (2008b). *The Rural Development Programme for England 2007–2013. Chapter 7 Indicative breakdown by measure, showing private as well as public expenditure*. p. 2.

DEFRA (2009a, July 21). *ARCHIVE: Regional and local food cross-departmental working group*. Accessed May 11, 2011. Retrieved from www.archive.defra.gov.uk/foodfarm/food/industry/regional/localfoodgroup.htm

DEFRA (2009b, July 21). *ARCHIVE: Regional and local food research*. Accessed July 17, 2012. Retrieved from www.archive.defra.gov.uk/foodfarm/food/industry/regional/research.htm

DEFRA (2010a, February). *Public Sector Food Procurement Initiative – Proportion of domestically produced food used by government departments and also supplied to hospitals and prisons under contracts negotiated by NHS Supply Chain and National Offender Management Service (previously HM Prison Service) Third report: 1 April 2008 to 31 March 2009*. p. 19.

DEFRA (2010b, October 1). *UK Trade Data in Food, Feed and Drink Including Indigeneity and Degree of Processing*. www.defra-stats-foodfarm-food-trade-indigeneity-110415.xls. DEFRA.

DEFRA (2011a, November). *Future delivery of socio economic elements (Axis 1, 3 and 4) of the Rural Development Programme for England (RDPE) Frequently asked questions*, RDPE Network. p. 7. Accessed October 17, 2012. Retrieved from www.rdpenetwork.defra.gov.uk/assets/files/News%20Item%20attachments/QA%20PV%207%20%282%29.pdf

DEFRA (2011b, May 27). *Future delivery of the socio economic elements (Axis 1, 3, and 4) of the Rural Development Programme for England*, RDPE Network. p. 5. Accessed October 17, 2012. Retrieved from www.rdpenetwork.defra.gov.uk/assets/files/News%20Item%20attachments/QA%20PV5.pdf

DEFRA (2012a, September 17). *Farm shops and farmers' markets*. Retrieved from www.gov.uk/farm-shops-and-farmers-markets

DEFRA (2012b, February 29). *Rural Development Programme for England (RDPE) The Rural Economy Grant (REG) Handbook – for applicants submitting an Outline Application*. p. 40.

DEFRA (2012c, March). *Rural Economy Growth Review. Enabling Businesses to Grow and Diversify: Rural Growth Networks*. p. 3.

DEFRA (2012d, March). *Rural Economy Growth Review. Overview*. p. 8.

DEFRA (2014a, March). *Consultation on the abolition of Food from Britain*. p. 4. Accessed August 16, 2014. Retrieved from www.gov.uk/government/consultations/abolition-of-food-from-britain

DEFRA (2014b, August 13). *The LEADER Approach Q&A – Transition year issues and the new approach*. p. 46 Retrieved August 19, 2014, from www.gov.uk/government/uploads/system/uploads/attachment_data/file/343450/QA_Update_7__ver_F_13_A ug_.pdf

DEFRA Food Policy Staff (2011, February 28). *Personal interview*. [audio recorded].

DeLind, L. (2011). Are Local Food and the Local Food Movement Taking Us Where We Want to Go? Or Are We Hitching Our Wagons to the Wrong Stars? *Agriculture and Human Values*, 28(2), 273–283. doi: 10.1007/s10460–010–9263–0

References 235

della Porta, D. (2002). Comparative Politics and Social Movements. In B. Klandermans and S. Staggenborg (Eds.), *Methods of Social Movement Research* (pp. 286–313). Minneapolis: University of Minnesota Press.

Democratic Policy Committee (2010, August 5). *The Lincoln Substitute Amendment to S. 3307, Healthy, Hunger-Free Kids Act*, Legislative Bulletin. p. 7.

Department of Agriculture and Rural Development. Northern Ireland (2013). Wikipedia. Retrieved October 14, 2014, from www.en.wikipedia.org/wiki/Department_of_Agriculture_and_Rural_Development

Department of the Environment, Transport and the Regions (2000, November). *Our Countryside: The future. A fair deal for rural England.* p. 176.

Deputy Speaker. *Food Poverty (Eradication) Bill*, House of Commons. In Hansard, c631. (2002, July 19) (not moved).

Diani, M. (1995). *Green Networks: A Structural Analysis of the Italian Environmental Movement.* Edinburgh University Press.

Diani, M. (2002). Network Analysis. In B. Klandermans and S. Staggenborg (Eds.), *Methods of Social Movement Research* (pp. 173–200). Minneapolis: University of Minnesota Press.

Diani, M. (2003). Networks and Social Movements: A Research Programme. In M. Diani and D. McAdam (Eds.), *Social Movements and Networks: Relational Approaches to Collective Action* (pp. 299–319). New York: Oxford.

Diani, M. (2011). Social Movements and Collective Action. In J. Scott and P. J. Carrington (Eds.), *The SAGE Handbook of Social Newtork Analysis* (pp. 223–235). Thousand Oaks: SAGE.

Doering, O. (1999). Farming's future. *Forum for Applied Research and Public Policy, 14*(3), 42.

Dollahite, J. S., Nelson, J. A., Frongillo, E. A. et al. (2005). Building Community Capacity through Enhanced Collaboration in the Farmers Market Nutrition Program. *Agriculture and Human Values, 22*, 339–354.

Donovan, K., Sidaway, J. D. and Stewart, I. (2010). Bridging the Geo-divide: Reflections on an Interdisciplinary (ESRC/NERC) Studentship. *Transactions of the Institute of British Geographers, 36*, 9–14.

Dowler, E. (2007). *Policy initiatives to address low-income households' nutritional needs in the UK.* Presented at Third Congress of Societe Francais de Nutrition with the Nutrition Society, Faculte de Medecine Henri Warembourg, Pole Recherche, Lille, France.

Dryzek, J. S. (1997). *The Politics of the Earth: Environmental Discourses.* New York: Oxford University Press.

DuPuis, E. M. and Goodman, D. (2005). Should We Go "Home" to Eat?: Toward a Reflexive Politics of Localism. *Journal of Rural Studies, 21*(3), 359–371. doi: 10.1016/j.jrurstud.2005.05.011

Earl Blumenauer [D-OR], Nancy Boyda [D-KS], Steve Kagen [D-WI] et al. (2007, May 25). *Support Healthy Food and Independent Farms – Cosponsor H.R. 2365 [sic, 2364], the Healthy Food and Farm Support Act.* p. 1.

EC (1991, March 19). *Notice to Member States laying down guidelines for integrated global grants for which Member States are invited to submit proposals in the framework of a Community initiative for rural development,* C 73 Volume 34, Official Journal of the European Community. pp. 33–37.

EC (1999). *Council Regulation (EC) No 1257/1999 of 17 May 1999 on support for rural development from the European Agricultural Guidance and Guarantee Fund (EAGGF) and*

236 References

amending and repealing certain Regulations, L 160/80, Official Journal of the European Community. pp. 1–23.

EC (2005). *Council Regulation (EC) No 1698/2005 of 20 September 2005 on support for rural development by the European Agricultural Fund for Rural Development (EAFRD)*, L 227, Official Journal of the European Community. pp. 1–40.

EC DGA (1994). *Culture and Rural Development*, Published in LEADER Magazine nr.8 – Winter, 1994. Accessed October 21, 2012. Retrieved from www.ec.europa.eu/agriculture/rur/leader2/rural-en/biblio/culture/art05.htm

EC DGA (2012, April 20). *Conference "Local agriculture and short food supply chains"*. Accessed August 25, 2014. Retrieved from www.ec.europa.eu/agriculture/events/small-farmers-conference-2012_en.htm

EC DGA (2014, July 4). *The history of the CAP*. Accessed August 14, 2014. Retrieved from www.ec.europa.eu/agriculture/cap-history/index_en.htm

Edwards-Jones, G. (2006, March 16). Food miles don't go the distance [Viewpoint], *BBC News*. Retrieved from www.news.bbc.co.uk/1/hi/sci/tech/4807026.stm

Edwards-Jones, G., Milà i Canals, L., Hounsome, N. et al. (2008). Testing the Assertion That "Local Food Is Best": The Challenges of an Evidence-based Approach. *Trends in Food Science & Technology, 19*(5), 265–274.

EFF Food Strand Staff (2011, March 31). *Personal interview*. [audio recorded].

Eileen Stommes, Deputy Administrator, USDA, AMS. (1998). *Direct Marketing Activities in USDA/AMS*. p. 3.

Eisenberg, J. (2001, July 17). *Statement of Mr. Jeff Eisenberg Senior Policy Advisor for Agriculture for The Nature Conservancy*, Hearing before the U.S. House Committee on Agriculture. Retrieved from www.lobby.la.psu.edu/_107th/123_Farm_Bill/Congressional_Hearings/Testimony/H_Agric_Eisenberg_071901.htm

Eisenhardt, K. M. (1989). Building Theories from Case Study Research. *The Academy of Management Review, 14*(4), 532–550.

ekosgen (2010, October 29). *National Impact Assessment of LEADER: The Story of LEADER in England*. Sheffield. p. 50.

ekosgen (2011, June). *National Impact Assessment of LEADER Impact Report – Final*, Sheffield. p. 87.

Eligio "Kika" de la Garza [D-TX]. (1994, Tuesday, July 10). *Healthy Meals for Healthy Americans Act of 1994*, In Congressional Record: before time 13:50. Retrieved from www.gpo.gov/fdsys/pkg/CREC-1994–07–19/html/CREC-1994–07–19-pt1-PgH59.htm

Elliott, J., ADAS Consulting Limited (2003, December). *The Mid-Term Evaluation of the England Rural Development Programme (ERDP) Processing and Marketing Grant Scheme*, prepared for DEFRA. Wolverhampton and Cambridge. p. 52.

Elliott J., Temple, M. L., Bowden, C. et al., ADAS Consulting Limited (2005). *Regional Food Strategy Evaluation Report September 2005*. Wolverhampton. p. 140.

Elsener, M. (2009, July 1). *Farm to School House targets July 2009*. [Excel spreadsheet].

England's Regional Development Agencies. (2009, September). *The Rural Development Programme for England 2007–2013: A progress report from the Regional Development Agencies*. p. 16.

English Farming and Food Partnerships. (2009, December). *Memorandum submitted by English Farming & Food Partnerships (EFFP) (DFoB 40)*, Parliament: Commons Select Committee on Environment, Food, and Rural Affairs. Accessed December 10, 2012. Retrieved from www.publications.parliament.uk/pa/cm200809/cmselect/cmenvfru/memo/dairy/ucm4002.htm

References 237

Enteleca (2001). *Eat the View Consumers Research Literature Review: Final Report Prepared for the Countryside Agency*. Richmond upon Thames. p. 25.

Environmental Defense (2005a, April 12). *ED WKKF Budget 4–11–05*. [Excel spreadsheet].

Environmental Defense (2005b). *ED WKKF Proposal 2–28–05*. p. 3.

Environmental Funders Network (2011, June 30). *Telephone interview*. [notes].

Environmental Working Group. (2008, February 11, 2008 1:36 PM). Farm Bill: All Over the Map. *The Mulch Blog*. Environmental Working Group. Retrieved December 18, 2010 from www.mulchblog.com/2008/02/farm-bill-all-over-the-map.html

Eradication of Food Poverty, House of Commons (2001, March 3) (early day motion 408).

Esmée Fairbairn Foundation (2011, January). *Applying to the fund guidance notes*. p. 12.

Esmée Fairbairn Foundation (n.d.). *Guide to applying: Food Strand*. p. 3. Accessed October 20, 2014. Retrieved from www.esmeefairbairn.org.uk/print/guide_funds/?print_ids=14006 | 14007 | 14008 | 14009

EU Committee, House of Lords. (2008, March 6). *The Future of the Common Agricultural Policy. Volume I: Report,* London: The Stationery Office. p. 88.

Eukel, K. and Beaufort, N. D. (2005, September 29). *Memorandum. To: Farm and Food Policy Communications Work Group. Subject: Communications Survey Themes and Responses*, memo analyzing interview repsonses of 10 policy leaders in the FFPP. p. 23.

European Network for Rural Development. (2012, November 13). *The LEADER Approach*. Accessed August 14, 2014. Retrieved from enrd.www.ec.europa.eu/enrd-static/leader/leader/leader-tool-kit/the-leader-approach/why-is-leader-specific/en/bottom-up-approach_en.html

Evans, J., ADAS Consulting Ltd. (2003). *The mid-term evaluation of the English Rural Development Programme (ERDP) Rural Enterprise Scheme*, prepared for DEFRA. Wolverhampton. p. 43.

Evans, S. M. and Boyte, H. C. (1986). *Free Spaces: The Sources of Democratic Change in America* (1992 ed.). Chicago: University of Chicago Press.

The Fading Appeal of Farm Subsidies. (2001, October 6). *The New York Times,* New York, New York. Retrieved from www.nytimes.com/2001/10/06/opinion/the-fading-appeal-of-farm-subsidies.html

Falconer, K. and Ward, N. (2000). Using Modulation to green the CAP: The UK case. *Land Use Policy, 17*, 269–277.

Farm-To-Cafeteria Projects Act of 2003, H.R. 2626, U.S. House, 1st Session, 108th Session (2003a, June 26) (introduced).

Farm-To-Cafeteria Projects Act of 2003, S. 1755, U.S. Senate, 1st Session, 108th Session (2003b, October 17) (introduced).

The Farm Financial Crisis. Hearing before the U.S. House Committee on Agriculture (September 15, 1999). (C-Span: www.c-spanvideo.org/program/FarmF).

Farm Security Act of 2001, H.R. 2646, U.S. House, 107th Congress, 1st Session (2001a, October 9) (engrossed).

Farm Security Act of 2001, [Report No. 107–191, Parts I, II, and III], H.R. 2646, U.S. House, 107th Congress, 1st Session (2001b, September 10) (reported from Committee).

Farm Security and Rural Investment Act. Pub. L. No. 107–171. (2002a, May 13). U.S. Congress.

238 *References*

Farm Security and Rural Investment Act. Assistance for Community Food Projects, Sec. 4125. Pub. L. No. 107–171. (2002b, May 13). U.S. Congress.

Farm Security and Rural Investment Act. Defintion of value-added Agricultural Product, Sec. 6401(a)(2). Pub. L. No. 107–171. (2002c, May 13). U.S. Congress.

Farm Security and Rural Investment Act. Farmers Market Promotion Program, Sec. 10605. Pub. L. No. 107–171. (2002d, May 13). U.S. Congress.

Farm Security and Rural Investment Act. Fruit and Vegetable Pilot Program, Sec. 4305. Pub. L. No. 107–171. (2002e, May 13). U.S. Congress.

Farm Security and Rural Investment Act. Purchases of locally produced foods, Sec. 4303. Pub. L. No. 107–171. (2002f, May 13). U.S. Congress.

Farm Security and Rural Investment Act. Purchases of Specialty Crops, Sec. 10603(b)(1–3). Pub. L. No. 107–171. (2002g, May 13). U.S. Congress.

Farm to School Improvements Act of 2010, H.R. 4710, U.S. House, 111th Congress, 2nd Session (2010, February 26) (introduced).

FARMA. (2009, May 6). About local foods: 21 Reasons to support local foods. Retrieved May 1, 2012 from www.farma.org.uk/about-local-foods

FARMA. (2010, November 8). Certification – abridged rules. Retrieved December 2, 2012 from www.farmersmarkets.net/certification2.htm

FARMA. (ca. 2013). Who is FARMA? Who runs this site? Retrieved January 5, 2013 from www.farmersmarkets.org.uk/aboutFARMA.htm

FARMA Policy Staff (2012, May 2). *Telephone interview.* [audio recorded]

Farmer-to-Consumer Direct Marketing Act. 7 U.S.C. § 3001–3006. (1976a, October 8).

Farmer-to-Consumer Direct Marketing Act. 7 U.S.C. § 3001–3006. Pub. L. No. 94–463. (1976b, October 8).

Farmer to Family Nutrition Enhancement Act, S. 2056, U.S. Senate, 2nd Congress, 100th Session (1988, February 4) (introduced).

Farmers' Market Nutrition Act of 1991, S. 1742, U.S. Senate, 102nd Congress, 1st Session (1991, September 24) (introduced).

Farmers Market Promotion Program. 7 U.S.C. § 3005 (b)(1)(A-B) (2008a, June 18).

Farmers Market Promotion Program. 7 U.S.C. § 3005 (c)(1–7) (2008b, June 18).

Farmers Weekly (2006). Join the battle for local food. Retrieved January 1, 2013 from www.fwi.co.uk/Articles/24/05/2006/94706/Farmers-Weekly-Food-Miles-Campaign-Join-the-battle-for-local.htm

FCFCG Policy Staff (2012, May 8). *Personal interview.* [audio recorded].

FDA Food Safety Modernization Act, Sec. 102. Registration of Food Facilities, H.R. 2751, U.S. Congress, 111th Congress, 2nd Session (2010, December 21).

Featherstone, D., Ince, A., Mackinnon, D. et al. (2012). Progressive Localism and the Construction of Political Alternatives. *Transactions of the Institute of British Geographers*, *37*(2), 177–182.

FEC (2011, June). *The Food Issues Census: A survey of UK civil society.* Brighton. Retrieved from www.foodissuescensus.org/

Feder, J. and Cowan, T., Library of Congress, CRS. (2010, August 15). *Garcia v. Vilsack: A Policy and Legal Analysis of a USDA Discrimination Case,* R40988. p. 12.

Federal Agriculture Improvement and Reform Act. Food Stamp Program, Sec. 401(g). Assistance for Community Food Projects, Sec. 25(a)-(h). Pub. L. No. 104–127. (1996, April 4). U.S. Congress.

Feeding America (2009). *Child Nutrition Priorities.* Washington, DC. paper handout in the 2009 National Anti-hunger Policy Conference packet.

References   239

Feeding America. (2011). Board of Directors. Retrieved December 1, 2011 from feedingamerica.org/about-us/board-of-directors.aspx

Ferd Hoefner [NSAC Policy Director] (2011, June 10). [Personal communication, e-mail].

FFPP (2005a, September 28). *October 9 FFPP Workshops*. p. 2. held at the Ninth Annual CFSC Conference: It's Homegrown: Cultivating the Roots of Real Change, October 6–9, 2005, Atlanta, Georgia.

FFPP (2005b, September 20). *Responsibilities and selection criteria: Working group co-chairs and members of the FFPP coordinating committee*. p. 3.

FFPP (2006a, March 29). ★★★*Draft 3/29/06*★★★ *Preliminary Framework for FFPP Diversity Initiative*. p. 4.

FFPP (2006b, February 15). *Farm & Food Policy Project*, two page overview. p. 2.

FFPP (2006c, July 11). *Notes from the 7/5/06 afternoon Diversity Team Meeting*. p. 3. [held concurrently with an in-person FFPP Coordinating Council Meeting, July 6–7, 2006, Washington, DC].

FFPP (2007a, January 22). *Panelist Statements for the Press Conference on "Seeking Balance in U.S. Farm and Food Policy"*. Washington, DC. p. 4.

FFPP (2007b, January 22). *Press conference transcript*. p. 20.

FFPP (2007c, January). *Seeking balance in U.S. farm and food policy*. p. 20.

Fieldman, M. S. (1995). *Strategies for Interpreting Qualitative Data*. London: SAGE Publications.

Filia, P., USDA, Rural Development. (2009, April 18). *Business and Industry Guaranteed and Direct Loan Programs Locally or Regionally Produced Agricultural Food Products, RD AN No. 4430*. p. 3.

Fischer, L. D. (2002). Missouri Hog Farmers Patch Together a Solution. *Bridges*. Federal Reserve Bank of St. Louis. Retrieved February 5, 2013 from www.stlouisfed.org/publications/br/articles/?id=673

Fisher, A. (1999). *Hot Peppers & Parking Lot Peaches: Evaluating Farmers' Markets in Low Income Communities*. Venice, CA: Communtiy Food Security Coalition. p. 63.

Fluharty, C. (2008). Toward a US Shift from Agricultural to Rural Development Policy: Forces of Challenge and Change. *EuroChoices*, 7(1), 46–51.

FMC (2009). *Position Paper from the Farmers Market Coalition 2009*. p. 4. Retrieved April 4, 2013, from www.farmersmarketcoalition.org/wp-content/uploads//2009/10/FMC_Position_Paper_2009v2.pdf

FOE UK (2001, October). *Getting real about food and farming*. p. 32.

Food and Energy Security Act of 2007, H.R. 2419, U.S. Senate, 110 Congress, 1st Session (2007a, December 14) (As passed in the Senate).

Food and Energy Security Act of 2007, H.R. 2419, U.S. House, 110 Congress, 1st Session (2007b, December 14) (engrossed).

Food Chain Economics Unit, DEFRA. (2007). *Overview of the benefits and carbon costs of the African horticultural trade with the UK*, London. p. 12.

Food Justice. (2005, February). *Memorandum by Food Justice (WP 100)* [written evidence]. Parliament: Commons Select Committee on Health. Retrieved from www.publications.parliament.uk/pa/cm200405/cmselect/cmhealth/358/358we108.htm

Food Justice Strategy Bill, 58, House of Commons (2003, February 13).

Food Justice Strategy Bill, 125, House of Commons (2004, June 23).

Food Matters/Brighton and Hove Food Partnership (2012). *Panel: Where now? The Lessons? The next steps? 3rd Annual City Food Symposium. Local Food Policies in Practice:*

240   *References*

the state of the sub-national. Cass Business School, City University, London, UK. [from notes].

Food Outreach and Opportunity Development for a Healthy America Act of 2007, S. 1432, U.S. Senate, 110th Congress (2007, May 17).

Food Poverty (Eradication) Bill, Bill 69, House of Commons (2001, March 6) (introduced).

Food Poverty Eradication Bill, 69, House of Commons (2001, December 12) (first reading).

Food, Conservation, and Energy Act of 2008. Pub. L. No. 110–246. (2008a, June 18). U.S. Congress.

Food, Conservation, and Energy Act of 2008. Farmers Market Promotion Program, Sec. 10106. Pub. L. No. 110–246. (2008b, June 18).

Food, Conservation, and Energy Act of 2008. Fresh Fruit and Vegetable Program, Sec. 4304. Pub. L. No. 110–246. (2008c, June 18).

Food, Conservation, and Energy Act of 2008. Healthy Food Education and Program Replicability, Sec. 4303. Pub. L. No. 110–246. (2008d, June 18).

Food, Conservation, and Energy Act of 2008. Healthy Food Enterpise Development Center, Sec. 4402(1–3). Pub. L. No. 110–246. (2008e, June 18).

Food, Conservation, and Energy Act of 2008. Locally and Regionally Produced Agricultural Product, Sec. 6015. Pub. L. No. 110–246. (2008f, June 18).

Food, Conservation, and Energy Act of 2008. Mid-tier Value Chain, Sec. 6202(a)(3)(A-B). Pub. L. No. 110–246. (2008g, June 18).

Food, Conservation, and Energy Act of 2008. Purchases of Locally Produced Foods, Sec. 4302. Pub. L. No. 110–246. (2008h, June 18).

Food, Conservation, and Energy Act of 2008. Section 32 Funds for Purchases of Fruits, Vegetables, and Nuts to Support Domestic Nutrition Assistance Programs. Purchase of Fresh Fruits and Vegetables for Distribution to Schools and Service Institutions, Sec. 4404(c). Pub. L. No. 110–246. (2008i, June 18).

Food, Conservation, and Energy Act of 2008. Sense of Congress Regarding Food Deserts, Geographically Isolated Neighborhoods and Communities with Limited or No Access to Major Chain Grocery Stores, Sec. 7257. (2008j, June 18).

Food, Conservation, and Energy Act of 2008. Value-added Agricultural Product, Sec 6202(a)(5)(A)(v). Pub. L. No. 110–246. (2008k, June 18).

Foresight, Government Office for Science. (2011a). *About Foresight.* Accessed October 17, 2011. Retrieved from www.bis.gov.uk/foresight/about-us

Foresight, Government Office for Science. (2011b). *Foresight Project on Global Food and Farming Futures Synthesis Report C8: Changing consumption patterns,* URN 11/628. p. 24.

Foresight, Government Office for Science. (2011c). *Foresight Project on Global Food and Farming Futures Synthesis Report C12: Meeting the challenges of a low-emissions world,* URN 11/632. p. 30.

Foresight, Government Office for Science. (2011d). *The Future of Food and Farming: Challenges and choices for global sustainability. Final Project Report,* London. p. 211.

Foresight, Government Office for Science. (2011e). *High Level Stakeholder Group.* Accessed October 18, 2011. Retrieved from www.bis.gov.uk/foresight/our-work/projects/published-projects/global-food-and-farming-futures/high-level-stake holder-group

Foresight, Government Office for Science. (2011f). *Lead Expert Group.* Accessed October 18, 2011. Retrieved from www.bis.gov.uk/foresight/our-work/projects/published-projects/global-food-and-farming-futures/lead-expert-group

References 241

Foresight, Government Office for Science. (2011g). *Our Work*. Accessed November 30, 2012. Retrieved from www.bis.gov.uk/foresight/our-work

Foresight, Government Office for Science. (2011h). *Reports and publications*. Accessed October 25, 2012. Retrieved from www.bis.gov.uk/foresight/our-work/projects/published-projects/global-food-and-farming-futures/reports-and-publications

Former National Trust Policy Staff (2011, February 28). *Personal interview*. [audio recorded].

Former NEF Staff (2011, March 30). *Personal interview*. [notes].

Foucault, M. (1977). *Discipline and Punish: The Birth of the Prison* (A. Sheridan, Trans. 1991 ed.). London: Penguin.

FRAC (2009, March). *Food Research and Action Center 2009 Child Nutrition Reauthorization Budget Priorities*, Printed handout provided in the conference packet for the 2009 National Anti-hunger Policy Conference held March 1–3, 2009, in Washington, DC. p. 4.

FRAC (2010). Board of Directors. Retrieved December 1, 2011 from www.frac.org/about/board-of-directors/

FrameWorks Institute (2008a). *How to Talk about Food Systems*. p. 4.

FrameWorks Institute. (2008b). How to Talk Rural Issues. Frameworks Institute. Retrieved from www.frameworksinstitute.org/assets/files/PDF_Rural/How_to_Talk_Rural.pdf

Freeman, J. (1972 (revised)). The Tyranny of Structurelessness. Retrieved January 15, 2013 from www.jofreeman.com/joreen/tyranny.htm

Freeman, R. E. (1984). *Strategic Management: A Stakeholder Approach*. Cambridge, UK: Cambridge University Press.

The Future of the Common Agricultural Policy. Volume I: Report, House of Lords, European Union Committee. (2008, March 6). HL Paper 54–I, London: The Stationery Office Limited. p. 88. Retrieved from www.publications.parliament.uk/pa/ld200708/ldselect/ldeucom/54/54.pdf

Gail C. Christopher [WKKF Vice President for Program Strategy] and Lind Jo Doctor [WKKF Program Officer] (2012). *Welcome*. WKKF. [Letter in conference guide for the 2012 Food & Community Conference: Assembly Required, May 22–24, Asheville, North Carolina].

Gale, F., USDA (1997). *Direct Farm Marketing as a Rural Development Tool*, Rural Development Perspectives. pp. 19–25.

Gallagher, M. (2006). *Good Food: Examining the Impact of Food Deserts on Public Health in Chicago*. p. 40.

Gallagher, M. (2007). *Examining the Impact of Food Deserts on Public Health in Detroit*. p. 16.

Gamson, W. A. (1975). *The Strategy of Social Protest*. Homewood, Illinois: The Dorsey Press. p. 217.

Gamson, W. A. and Meyer, D. S. (1996). Framing Political Opportunity. In D. McAdam, J. D. McCarthy and M. N. Zald (Eds.), *Comparative Perspectives on Social Movements: Political Opportunities, Mobilizing Structures, and Cultural Framings* (pp. 275–290). Cambridge: Cambridge University Press.

Ganske [R-IA]. (2001, October 4). In Congressional Record. pp. H6301-H6302.

Gardiner, B., Minister for Biodiversity, Landscape and Rural Affairs, Department for Environment, Food and Rural Affairs. (2006, July 5). *Rural Enterprise Scheme*, Hansard: House of Commons. c. 1144W. Retrieved from www.publications.parliament.uk/pa/cm200506/cmhansrd/vo060705/text/60705w0016.htm

242   References

Garnett, S. C., USDA FNS. (2007, January 23). *School Districts and Federal Procurement Regulations,* SP 02–2007, Alexandria, VA. p. 14.

Garnett, T. (1996, June). *Growing food in cities: A report to highlight and promote the benefits of urban agriculture in the UK.* National Food Alliance & SAFE Alliance. p. 96.

Gaul, G. M. and Cohen, S. (2007, April 6). Rural Aid Goes to Urban Areas. USDA Development Program Helps Suburbs, Resort Cities, *The Washington Post.*

Gaventa, J. and Barrett, G. (2010). *So What Difference Does It Make? Mapping the Outcomes of Citizen Engagement.* Brighton: Institute of Development Studies, University of Sussex. p. 71.

Gerlach, L. P. and Hine, V. H. (1970). *People, Power, Change: Movements of Social Transformation.* Indianapolis, Indiana: Bobbs-Merrill.

globe (2009). *Rural Development Programme for England (RDPE) Network: Market Research and Stakeholder Engagement Project,* prepared for Commission for Rural Communities, p. 132.

Goland, C. and Bauer, S. (2004). When the Apple Falls Close to the Tree: Local Food Systems and the Preservation of Diversity. *Renewable Agriculture and Food Systems, 19,* 228–236.

Gottlieb, R. and Fisher, A. (1996a). Community Food Security and Environmental Justice: Searching for a Common Discourse. *Agriculture and Human Values, 13*(3), 23–32.

Gottlieb, R. and Fisher, A. (1996b). "First Feed the Face": Environmental Justice and Community Food Security. *Antipode, 28*(2), 193–203.

Granovetter, M. (1985). Economic action and social structure: The problem of embeddedness. *American Journal of Sociology, 91,* 481–510.

Greve, C., Flinders, M. and Thiel, S. (1999). Quangos—What's in a Name? Defining Quangos from a Comparative Perspective. *Governance, 12*(2), 129–146. doi: 0952–1895.951999095

Growing Farm to School Programs Act of 2010 S. 3144, U.S. Senate, 111th Congress, 2nd Session (2010, March 16) (introduced).

Growing Food and Justice for All Initiative. (n.d.). About Us. Growing Power, Inc. from www.growingfoodandjustice.org/About_Us.html

Gubrium, J. F. and Holstein, J. A. (2003). Active Interviewing. In J. F. Gubrium and J. A. Holstein (Eds.), *Postmodern Interviewing* (pp. 67–80). Thousand Oaks: Sage Publications.

Guild of Food Writers. (2011). Past recipients. Retrieved January 3, 2013 from www.gfw.co.uk/past-recipients.cfm#Guild_of_Food_Writers_Awards_Winners_2001

Hamilton, N. D. (2004). Essay – Food Democracy and the Future of American Values. *Drake Journal of Agricultural Law, 9,* 9–31.

Hamilton, N. D. (2005). Food Democracy II: Revolution or Restoration? *Journal of Food Law & Policy, 1*(13), 13–42.

Hamilton, N. D. (2011). Moving Toward Food Democracy: Better Food, New Farmers, and the Myth of Feeding the World. *16*(1), 117–145.

Hance, A. (2001, November 6). *Re: Meeting with Oran Hesterman, Kellogg Foundation [November 2]. Memorandum to Dick Munson, Executive Director.* NEMWI. p. 2.

Hank Herrera [HOPE Collaborative] (2011, November 6). *[Impromptu panel honoring former Executive Director Andy Fisher]. "Food Justice: Honoring our Roots, Growing the Movement," 15th Annual CFSC Meeting.* Oakland, California. [audio recorded].

References 243

Hantrais, L. (2009). *International Comparative Research: Theory, Methods, and Practice.* Basingstoke: Palgrave McMillan.

Harold L. Volkmer, Desmond Ansel Jolly, Kathleen Sullivan Kelley et al., USDA, Cooperative State, Research, Education, and Extension Service. (1998). *A Time to Act: A Report of the USDA National Commission on Small Farms,* Miscellaneous Publication 1545 (MP-1545). Retrieved from www.csrees.usda.gov/nea/ag_systems/pdfs/time_to_act_1998.pdf

Harrabin, R. (2008, June 3). Challenges for the food summit [Analysis], *BBC News.* Retrieved from www.news.bbc.co.uk/1/hi/sci/tech/7431126.stm

Harris, F., Lyon, F. and Clarke, S. (2008). Doing Interdisciplinarity: Motivation and Collaboration in Research for Sustainable Agriculture in the UK. *Area, 41*(4), 374–384.

Harris, K. (2003, May 15). *Assessment of Northeast-Midwest Institute Agriculture Policy Program January 2001 – December 2002:* NEMWI. p. 23.

Hart, R. A., UNICEF (1992). *Children's participation: From tokenism to citizenship.* p. 39.

Hassanein, N. (2003). Practicing Food Democracy: A Pragmatic Politics of Transformation. *Journal of Rural Studies, 19,* 77–86.

Hassanein, N. (2008). Locating Food Democracy: Theoretical and Practical Ingredients. *Journal of Hunger & Environmental Nutrition, 3*(2–3), 286–308.

Headwaters Group Philanthropic Services (2008, October). *Informing the 2008 Farm Bill: An Assessment of the Farm and Food Policy Project: Summary,* prepared for WKKF. p. 28.

Healthy Farms, Foods, and Fuels Act of 2007, H.R. 1551, U.S. House, 1st Congress, 110th Session (2007a, March 15) (introduced).

Healthy Farms, Foods, and Fuels Act of 2007, Farmers Market Promotion Program, Sec. 306(d)(2), H.R. 1551, U.S. House, 1st Congress, 110th Session (2007b, March 15) (introduced).

Healthy Farms, Foods, and Fuels Act of 2007, S. 919, U.S. Senate, 110th Congress, 1st Session (2007c, March 20) (introduced).

Healthy Farms, Foods, and Fuels Act of 2007, Farmers Market Promotion Program, Sec. 306(d)(2), S. 919, U.S. Senate, 110th Congress, 1st Session (2007d, March 20) (introduced).

Healthy, Hunger-Free Kids Act of 2010. Access to Local Foods: Farm to School Program, Sec. 243. Pub. L. No. 111–296. (2010a, December 13). U.S. Congress.

Healthy, Hunger-Free Kids Act of 2010, 2nd Session. Senate Report 111–178, Reprt together with additional and supplemental views to accompany S. 3307, U.S. Senate, 111th congress, 2nd Session (2010b, May 5).

Healthy Meals for Healthy Americans Act of 1994. Continued funding for certain states under farmers' market nutrition program, Sec. 204(v)(2). Pub. L. No. 103–448 (1994a, November 2). U.S. Congress.

Healthy Meals for Healthy Americans Act of 1994. Continued funding for certain states under farmers' market nutrition program, Sec. 204(v)(3). Pub. L. No. 103–448 (1994b, November 2). U.S. Congress.

Healthy Meals for Healthy Americans Act of 1994. Pilot Projects. Increased Choices of Fruits, Vegetables, Legumes, Cereals, and Grain-based Products. Sec. 108(d). Pub. L. No. 103–448. (1994c, November 2). U.S. Congress.

Helping Agricultural Producers "Re-grow" America: Providing the Tools. Hearing before the U.S. House Committee on Small Business. 106th Congress, 2nd Session. Report 106–47 (2000, March 15).

244 References

Helping Agricultural Producers Regrow Rural America. Hearing before the U.S. House Committee on Small Business. 106th Congress, 1st Session. Report 106–34 (1999, September 29).

Henrekson, M. and Sanandaji, T. (2011). The Interaction of Entrepreneurship and Institutions. *Journal of Institutional Economics*, 7(1), 47–75. doi: 10.1017/S1744137 410000342

Herb Kohl [D-WI], Tom Harkin [D-IA], Jack Reed [D-RI] et al., Mike Johanns, Secretary of Agriculture (2007, May 21). Washington, DC.: U.S. Senate. p. 3.

Hewitt, S. and Thompson, N. (2012). Regionalism and Rural Policy. In M. Shucksmith, D. L. Brown, S. Shortall, J. Vergunst and M. E. Warner (Eds.), *Rural Transformations and Rural Policies in the US and UK* (pp. 261–268). New York: Routledge.

Hexham Community Partnership. (2012). *Market Town Renewal: Hexham Case Study.* Presented at Rural Development and Social Renewal. Powerpoint presentation. retrieved from www.northernruralnetwork.co.uk/archive/rural-development-and-social-renewal

HFCWG, FFPP (2006a, February 9). *DRAFT Discussion Paper – Revised February 9, 2006, Healthy Food & Communities Work Group, Farm & Food Policy Project.* p. 5.

HFCWG, FFPP (2006b, March 20). *Healthy Food and Communities: Proposed Policy Initiatives for the 2007 Farm Bill.* p. 7.

Hinrichs, C. (2000). Embeddedness and Local Food Systems: Notes on Two Types of Direct Agricultural Market. *Journal of Rural Studies*, 16(3), 295–303. doi: 10.1016/s0743–0167(99)00063–7

Hinrichs, C. and Allen, P. (2008). Selective Patronage and Social Justice: Local Food Campaigns in Historical Context. *Journal of Agricultural and Environmental Ethics*, 21, 329–352.

Hinrichs, C. and Charles, L. (2012). Local Food Systems and Networks in the US and in the UK. In M. Shucksmith, D. L. Brown, S. Shortall, J. Vergunst and M. E. Warner (Eds.), *Rural Transformations and Rural Policies in the US and UK* (pp. 156–176). New York: Routledge.

Hinrichs, C. and Kremer, K. S. (2002). Social Inclusion in a Midwest Local Food System Project. *Journal of Poverty*, 6(1), 65–90.

HM Government (2002, December). *Response to the Report of the Policy Commission on the Future of Farming and Food by HM Government.* p. 59.

HM Government (2010). *Food 2030,* London: DEFRA. p. 84.

HM Government (2013, February 23). *Devolution settlement: Northern Ireland.* Accessed August 6, 2014. Retrieved from www.gov.uk/devolution-settlement-northern-ireland

Holstein, J. A. and Gubrium, J. F. (1995). *The Active Interview* (Vol. 37). London: SAGE Publications.

House of Commons. (2002, December 12). *Debate on the issues raised in the Sustainable Farming and Food Strategy (published on the same day) and the newly formed Department of Food, Environment, and Rural Affairs,* Hansard: House of Commons. c. 409–504. Accessed August 29, 2012. Retrieved from www.hansard.millbanksystems.com/commons/2002/dec/12/environment-food-and-rural-affairs#S6CV0396P0_20021212_HOC_184

How to Feed a Town or City, Meeting of the All-Party Parliamentary Group on Agroecology. (2011, December 6). House of Lords [from typed notes].

References 245

Howlett, M. (2002). Understanding National Administrative Styles and Their Impact Upon Administrative Reform: A Neo-Institutional Model and Analysis. *Policy and Soceity, 21*(1), 1–24.

Hugh-Jones, S. (2010). The Interview in Qualitative Research. In M. Forrester (Ed.), *Doing Qualitative Research in Psychology: A Practical Guide* (pp. 77–97). London: SAGE.

Hunger Prevention Act of 1988, S. 2056, U.S. Senate (1988, June 23) (enacted).

Hunt, A. R. (2003). *Preserving the economic viability of the agricultural landscape: A contingent valuation study of locally produced beef.* Bachelor of Science, Bates College, Lewiston, Maine.

Hunt, A. R. (2005). *Conserving the agricultural landscape through farmers' markets.* Master of Environmental Management in Environmental Economics and Policy, Duke University, Durham, NC.

Hunt, A. R. (2006, March 20). *Regional Food and Family Farm Development Act.* p. 3.

Hunt, A. R. (2007a). Consumer Interactions and Influences on Farmers' Market Vendors. *Renewable Agriculture and Food Systems, 22*(1), 54–66.

Hunt, A. R., NEMWI (2007b, April 20). *Domestic Market Access Act.* p. 7. [final draft].

Hunt, A. R., NEMWI (2007c, March 22). *Domestic Market Access Act.* p. 8.

Hunt, A. R., NEMWI (2007d). *Domestic Market Access Act – Overview and Examples.* p. 1.

Hunt, A. R. (2009, April 2). *USDA April 2, 2009 Conference Call, Farm to School Draft Notes.* p. 4. [Conference call notes].

Hunt, A. R. (2011a, April 15). *Summary of Interview Highlights March 2011.* p. 4. [interview goals and notes, Word document].

Hunt, A. R. (2011b). *Would more media campaigning secure more policy wins? Insight for the US Farm Bill from initial findings of a US-UK comparison on national policymaking for locally and regionally produced foods,* prepared for Sustainable Agriculture and Food Systems Funders. p. 42.

Hunt, A. R. (2013). *Civic engagement in food systems governance: A comparative perspective on American and English local food movements.* Ph. D., Newcastle University, Newcastle upon Tyne, UK.

Hunt, A. R. and Kalb, M. (2008, October 6). *NANA Draft: September 2008. Child Nutrition Reauthorization Recommendations.* Washington, DC. p. 6. Revisions to draft by Wallace Center at Winrock International and the National Farm to School Network.

Hunt, T., Campaign for the Protection of Rural England (2006). *Making our mark: 80 years of campaigning for the countryside.* p. 12.

Hyder Consulting (UK) Limited (2008, December 23). *Ex Post Evaluation of England Rural Development Programme,* prepared for DEFRA. p. 911.

Hyder Consulting (UK) Limited (2010, May 4). *Defra Rural Development Programme for England 2007–2013 Mid Term Evaluation Volume One,* prepared for DEFRA. p. 1151.

IIED. (2006, December 11). Airfreight Seminar. Retrieved January 3, 2013 from www.agrifoodstandards.net/es/resources/global/airfreight_seminar

IIED. (2007). Politicians and consumers could harm poorer nations with token reactions to "food miles" concerns. Retrieved September 29, 2012, from www.iied.org/politicians-consumers-could-harm-poorer-nations-token-reactions-food-miles-concerns

246   References

Ilbery, B., Watts, D., Little, J. et al. (2010). Attitudes of Food Entrepreneurs towards Two Grant Schemes under the First England Rural Development Programme, 2000–2006. *Land Use Policy, 27,* 683–689. doi: 10.1016/j.landusepol.2009.09.002

Improving Nutrition for America's Children Act, Sec. 208. Access to Local Foods: Farm to School, H.R. 5504, U.S. House, 101th Congress, 2nd Session (2010, June 10) (introduced).

Institute for Agriculture and Trade Policy, IATP Food and Community Fellows (2013, April 12). *Cultivating Equity and Leadership in the Food System.* [e-mail sent to the open-access COMFOOD listserv] from us1.campaign-archive1.com/?u=0cc2b 8c112986f1267e57a058&id=38f24a3d0c&e=

Institute for Conservation Leadership (2005, October 1). *What structure fits our work?* p. 17. Retrieved from www.icl.org/resourcefree/six-models-cooperative-efforts

It's win-win: From farm to school. (February 6, 2001) *the Extension Connection* (Winter). Iowa State University Extension. Retrieved from www.extension.iastate.edu/ Connection/2001Winter/winwin.html

Jackson, S. (2013). Letter from the Chair. *FARMA.* Retrieved March 5, 2015, from www.farma.org.uk/news/letter-from-the-chair/

Janow, D. (1996). *How Does a Policy Mean?: Interpreting Policy and Organizational Actions.* Washington, DC: Georgetown University Press.

Jim Paice [Food Minister]. (2011, June 16). *New Government Buying Standards for food and catering,* DEFRA, Government Buying Standards team. Accessed May 8, 2012. Retrieved from www.sd.defra.gov.uk/2011/06/new-government-buying-standards-for-food-and-catering/

John Ashcroft [R-MO]. S. 2745. *A bill to provide for grants to assist value-added agricultural businesses; to the Committee on Agriculture, Nutrition, and Forestry,* The Value-added Development Act for American Agriculture, U.S. Senate. In Congressional Record, S5271-S5272. (2000, June 15).

John Dingell [D-MI]. (2001, October 4). In Congressional Record: U.S. House. p. H6304.

John McCain [R-AZ], Saxby Chambliss [R-GA] and Pat Roberts [R-KS]. (2010, April 27). *Letter from three Senators concerning USDA's "Know Your Farmer, Know Your Food Initiative".* p. 2.

Johnson, D. W. (1991–1992). Saving the Wetlands from Agriculture: An Examination of Section 404 of the Clean Water Act and the Conservation Provisions of the 1985 and 1990 Farm Bills. *Journal of Land Use & Environmental Law.*

Johnson, R., Library of Congress, CRS. (2008, November 6). *The 2008 Farm Bill: Major Provisions and Legislative Action* RL34696. p. 199.

Johnson, R., Cowan, T. and Aussenberg, R. A., Library of Congress, CRS. (2012, January 20). *The Role of Local Food Systems in U.S. Farm Policy,* R42155. p. 53.

Joseph, H. (2014, February 5). *Origins of FMNP.* [Personal communication to Gus Schumacher, e-mail].

Journeyman Pictures. (2007, November 26). Kenya – Change in the Air. Retrieved from www.youtube.com/watch?v=hdap-gxEWWWI

Kantor, L. S., USDA ERS. (2001, January-April). *Community Food Security Programs Improve Food Access,* Food Review. Accessed April 5, 2013. Retrieved from www.pdic.tamu.edu/pdicdata2/FarmBill/pdfs/FRV24I1.pdf

Kath Dalmeny [Sustain Policy Director]. (2012). *Closing plenary, response to Caroline Spelman, Secretary of State for Environment, Food, and Rural Affairs.* Presented at Making Local Food Our Future: MLFW 2012 Conference, London.

References 247

Kathy Ozer [NFFC Executive Director] (2011, November 6). *[Impromptu panel honoring former Executive Director Andy Fisher]. "Food Justice: Honoring our Roots, Growing the Movement," 15th Annual CFSC Meeting.* Oakland, California. [audio recorded].

Kearney, J. (2010). Food Consumption Trends and Drivers. [Review]. *Philosophical Transactions of the Botanical Society, 365,* 15.

Keith, R., C. Library of Congress. (2010). *The Statutory Pay-As-You-Go Act of 2010: Summary and Legislative History,* R41157. p. 26.

Kenneth Hayes [Soil Association]. (2007). Interviewed in Kenya - Change in the Air. Youtube.com.

King, R. P., Hand, M. S., DiGiacomo, G. et al., USDA, Economic Research Service. (2010, June). *Comparing the Structure, Size, and Performance of Local and Mainstream Food Supply Chains.* p. 73.

Kingdon, J. W. (1984). *Agendas, Alternatives, and Public Policies* (Second, updated 2011 ed.). London: Longman.

Kirkup, J. and Waterfield, B. (2009, November 3). Lisbon Treaty: More of Britain's powers surrendered to Brussels, *The Telegraph.* Retrieved from www.telegraph. co.uk/news/worldnews/europe/eu/6496336/Lisbon-Treaty-more-of-Britains-powers-surrendered-to-Brussels.html

Kirwan, J., Ilbery, B., Maye, D. et al. (2013). Grassroots Social Innovations and Food Localisation: An Investigation of the Local Food Programme in England. *Global Environmental Change, 23*(5), 830–837.

Kirwan, J., Ilbery, B., Maye, D. et al. (2014, March). *Local Food – Final Evaluation Report.* p. 74.

Kirwan, J. and Maye, D. (2013). Food Security Framings within the UK and the Integration of Local Food Systems. *Journal of Rural Studies, 29,* 91–100.

Klandermans, B. and Goslinga, S. (1996). Media Discourse, Movement Publicity, and the Generation of Collective Action Frames: Theoretical and Empirical Exercises in Meaning Construction. In D. McAdam, J. D. McCarthy and M. N. Zald (Eds.), *Comparative Perspectives on Social Movements: Political Opportunities, Mobilizing Structures, and Cultural Framings* (pp. 312–327). Cambridge: Cambridge University Press.

Knoke, D. (1990). *Political Networks: The Structural Persepctive.* USA: Cambridge University Press.

Kobayashi, M., Tyson, L. and Abi-Nader, J. (2010). *The Activities and Impacts of Community Food Projects 2005–2009* USDA funded study. p. 28.

Kohan, E. G. (2010). Big Day At White House For Launch Of "Let's Move," First Lady's Child Obesity Campaign *Obama Foodorama.* Retrieved February 27, 2012 from www.obamafoodorama.blogspot.com/2010/02/big-day-at-white-house-for-launch-of.html

Kriesi, H. (1996). The Organizational Structure of New Social Movements in a Political Context. In D. McAdam, J. D. McCarthy and M. N. Zald (Eds.), *Comparative Perspectives on Social Movements: Political Opportunities, Mobilizing Structures, and Cultural Framings* (pp. 152–184). Cambridge: Cambridge University Press.

La Trobe, H., FOE UK (2002). *Local food, future directions: A report for Friends of the Earth.* London. p. 71.

Laclau, E. (1996). *Emancipation(s).* London: Verso.

Lancaster, J. (2001, October 2). Federal Farm Subsidies Are Hardy Perennial; Despite Years of Criticism, House Legislation Would Perpetuate and Expand Crop Support Programs, *The Washington Post,* Washington, DC. p. A6. Retrieved from www. pqasb.pqarchiver.com/washingtonpost/access/82568297.html?dids=82568297:82568

248   *References*

297&FMT=ABS&FMTS=ABS:FT&type=current&date=Oct+02%2C+2001&auth
or=John+Lancaster&pub=The+Washington+Post&desc=Federal+Farm+Subsidies+
Are+Hardy+Perennial%3B+Despite+Years+of+Criticism%2C+House+Legislation
+Would+Perpetuate+and+Expand+Crop+Support+Programs&pqatl=google

Lang, T., Barling, D. and Caraher, M. (2009). *Food Policy: Integrating Health, Environment and Society*. Oxford: Oxford University Press.

Lang, T., Dibb, S. and Reddy, S. (2011). *Looking Back, Looking Forward: Sustainability and UK Food Policy 2000–2011*, Sustainable Development Commission. p. 58.

Larsen, S. and Forster, T., CFSC (2008). *Community Food Projects. Geographic Preferences for Schools*, paper handout. p. 1.

LEAF Staff (2011, March 24). *Personal interview*. Stoneleigh Park: Linking Environment and Farming.

Legge, A., Orchard, J., Graffham, A. et al., Natural Resources Institute (2006). *The production of fresh produce in Africa for export to the United Kingdom: Mapping different value chains*, prepared for DfID. p. 98.

Legge, A., Orchard, J., Graffham, A. et al. (April, 2008) Mapping different supply chains of fresh produce exports from Africa to the UK. *Fresh Perspectives* (12). Retrieved March 8, 2013, from www.agrifoodstandards.net/en/filemanager/active?fid=118

Lehrer, N. (2008). *From competition to national security: Policy change and policy stability in the 2008 farm bill*. Ph. D. Dissertation, University of Minnesota, St. Paul.

Les Roberts, Chief Executive, ACRE, Tim Harris, European Secretary, Animal Transportation Association, Gordon Gatwood, Director, Arthur Rank Centre et al. (1999, October 8). *Letter to the Minister of Agriculture, Fisheries and Food – The Future of Small to Medium-sized Abattoirs and cutting plants* [organization sign-on letter, 68 endorsers]. Select Committee on Agriculture Minutes of Evidence: Parliament. Retrieved from www.publications.parliament.uk/pa/cm199899/cmselect/cmagric/931/931ap09.htm

Library of Congress. (2000). Bill Summary & Status 106th Congress (1999–2000) H.R. 2559 All Congressional Actions with Amendments. Retrieved January 11, 2012 from www.thomas.loc.gov/cgi-bin/bdquery/z?d106:HR02559:@@@S

Lichterman, P. (2002). Seeing Structure Happen: Theory-Driven Participant Observation. In B. Klandermans and S. Staggenborg (Eds.), *Methods of Social Movement Research* (pp. 118–145). Minneapolis: University of Minnesota Press.

LIPT, Department of Health, Nutrition Task Force, (1996). *Low Income, Food, Nutrition, and Health: Strategies for Improvement: A Report*. UK.

Little, J., Ilbery, B., Watts, D. et al. (2012). Regionalization and the Rescaling of Agro-Food Governance: Case Study Evidence from Two English Regions. *Political Geography, 31*(2), 83–93.

Local Farms, Food, and Jobs Act of 2011, S. 1773, U.S. Senate, 112th Congress (2011a, November 18) (introduced).

Local Farms, Food, and Jobs Act of 2011, H.R. 3286, U.S. House, 112th Congress (2011b, November 18) (introduced).

Local Food and Farm Support Act, H.R. 2364, U.S. House, 110th Congress, 1st Session (2007, May 17) (introduced).

Local Harvest. (2012). About Local Harvest. Retrieved March 2013, 2013 from www.localharvest.org/about.jsp

Lockwood, M. (2013). The Political Sustainability of Climate Policy: The Case of the UK Climate Change Act. *Global Environmental Change, 23*(5), 1339–1348.

References 249

Long, C., USDA, FNS. (2008, July 9). *Applying Geographic Preferences in Procurements for the Child Nutrition Programs,* SP 30–2008, Alexandria, VA. p. 2.

Long, C., USDA, FNS. (2011, February 1). *Procurement Geographic Preference Q&As,* SP 18–2011, Alexandria, VA. p. 9.

Lorelei DiSogra [United Fresh Produce Vice President] (2012, January 18). *Legislative history of the FFV Program.* [Personal communication, e-mail].

Lott, M., CFSC (2009a, November 2). *Hill Team Call 11–2–09.* p. 2. [conference call notes].

Lott, M., CFSC (2009b, November 9). *Hill Team Call 11–9–09.* p. 2. [conference call notes].

Lott, M., CFSC (2009c, November 16). *Hill Team Call 11–16–09.* p. 2. [conference call notes].

Lowe, P. (1977). Amenity and Equity: A Review of Local Environmental Pressure Groups in Britain. *Environment and Planning A, 9,* 35–58.

Lowe, P. and Ward, N. (1998). Regional Policy, CAP Reform and Rural Development in Britain: The Challenge for New Labour. *Regional Studies, 32*(5), 469–475.

Lowe, P. and Wilkinson, K. (2009). How Do Environmental Actors Make Governance Systems More Sustainable? The Role of Politics and Ideas in Policy Change. In W. N. Adger and A. Jordan (Eds.), *Governing Sustainability* (pp. 76–98). Cambridge: Cambridge University Press.

Loyn, D. (2008, May 29). Long era of cheap food is over, *BBC News.* Retrieved from www.news.bbc.co.uk/1/hi/business/7425078.stm

Lyson, T. (2004). *Civic Agriculture: Reconnecting Farm, Food, and Community.* Lebanon, New Hampshire: University Press of New England.

Macalister, T. (2008, April 21). Co-op takes on Soil Association in food miles fight, *The Guardian.* Retrieved from www.guardian.co.uk/business/2008/apr/21/supermarkets.carbonemissions

MacDonald, J. M., Ollinger, M. E., Nelson, K. E. et al., USDA. (2000, February). *Consolidation in U.S. Meatpacking,* AER 785. p. 47.

MacGregor, J. and Vorley, B., IIED (2006, October). *Fair Miles? The concept of "food miles" through a sustainable development lens.* London. p. 2. Retrieved from pubs.iied.org/11064IIED.html

Madison, J. (1788, February 1). *Federalist No. 47 The Particular Structure of the New Government and the Distribution of Power Among Its Different Parts.* From the New York Packet. Retrieved August 6, 2014, from www.thomas.loc.gov/home/histdox/fed_47.html

MAFF. (2001, February). *England Rural Development Programme 2000–2006 Executive Summary.* p. 67.

Making Local Food Our Future: MLFW 2012 Conference. (2012). London. participant observation, from notes.

Malone, L. A. (1986). A Historical Essay on the Conservation Provisions of the 1985 Farm Bill: Sodbusting, Swamp Busting, and the Conservation Reserve. *University of Kansas Law Review,* 577–597.

Managers on the part of the House and the Senate at the Conference for H.R. 2559. (2000, May 24). *Joint Explanatory Statement of the Committee for H.R. 2559, Agricultural Risk Protection Act of 2000,* Value-added agricultural product market development grants In Congressional Record. p. H3801.

Managers on the part of the House and the Senate for H.R. 2419. (2008a). *Joint Explanatory Statement of the Committee of Conference,* Expansion of Fresh Fruit and Vegetable Program. pp. 105–106.

250 *References*

Managers on the part of the House and the Senate for H.R. 2419. (2008b). *Joint Explanatory Statement of the Committee of Conference,* Study of impacts of local food systems and commerce. p. 423.

Managers on the part of the House and the Senate for H.R. 2419. (2008c). *Joint Explanatory Statement of the Committee of Conference,* Seniors Farmers' Market Nutrition Program. p. 107.

Managers on the part of the House and the Senate H.R. 2646. (2002a, May 1). *Joint Explanatory Statement of the Committee of Conference for H.R. 2646, Farm Security and Rural Investment Act of 2002,* Subtitle C—Miscellaneous. (53) Purchase of Locally Produced Foods In Congressional Record. p. H1939.

Managers on the part of the House and the Senate H.R. 2646. (2002b, May 1). *Joint Explanatory Statement of the Committee of Conference for H.R. 2646, Farm Security and Rural Investment Act of 2002,* Subtitle D—Administration. (52) Commodity Purchases In Congressional Record. pp. H1918–1919.

Managers on the part of the House and the Senate H.R. 2646. (2002c, May 1). *Joint Explanatory Statement of the Committee of Conference for H.R. 2646, Farm Security and Rural Investment Act of 2002,* Subtitle C—Miscellaneous. (55) Fruit and Vegetable Pilot Program In Congressional Record. p. H1939.

marketumbrella.org. (n.d.). Staff - Richard McCarthy. Retrieved January 11, 2013 from www.marketumbrella.org/index.php?page=staff

marketumbrella.org (2012). *MarketMatch SNAP Incentive Program.* [Paper handout in conference packet for] Assembly Required: Working better together toward a good food future for all, 11th Food and Community Conference, May 22–24 Asheville, North Carolina, USA. p. 3.

Markowitz, L. (2010). Expanding Access and Alternatives: Building Farmers' Markets in Low-Income Communities. *Food and Foodways: Explorations in the History and Culture of Human Nourishment, 18*(1–2), 66–80.

Marsden, T., Munton, R., Ward, N. et al. (1996). Agricultural Geography and the Political Economy Approach: A Review. *The New Rural Geography, 72*(4), 361–375.

Marsden, T. and Sonnino, R. (2008). Rural Development and the Regional State: Denying Multifunctional Agriculture in the UK. *Journal of Rural Studies, 24,* 422–431.

Martinez, S., Hand, M., Pra, M. D. et al., USDA, Economic Research Service. (2010, May). *Local Food Systems Concepts, Impacts, and Issues,* ERR 97. p. 80.

Mason, J. (2002). *Qualitative Researching* (2nd ed.). London: SAGE.

Massot, A., European Parliament. (2014, March). *The Common Agricultural Policy (CAP) and the Treaty.* Accessed August 18, 2014. Retrieved from www.europarl.europa.eu/aboutparliament/en/displayFtu.html?ftuId=FTU_5.2.1.html#

Mathison, S. (1988). Why Triangulate? *Educational Researcher, 17*(2), 13–17.

McAdam, D. (1996). The Framing Function of Movement Tactics: Strategic Dramaturgy in the American Civil Rights Movement. In D. McAdam, J. D. McCarthy and M. N. Zald (Eds.), *Comparative Perspectives on Social Movements: Political Opportunities, Mobilizing Structures, and Cultural Framings* (pp. 338–355). Cambridge: Cambridge University Press.

McAdam, D. (2003). Beyond Structural Analysis: Toward a More Dynamic Understanding of Social Movements. In M. Diani and D. McAdam (Eds.), *Social Movements and Networks: Relational Approaches to Collective Action* (pp. 281–298). New York: Oxford.

McAdam, D., McCarthy, J. D. and Zald, M. N. (1996). Introduction: Opportunities, Mobilizing Structures, and Framing Processes – Toward a Synthetic, Comparative

References   251

Perspective on Social Movements. In D. McAdam, J. D. McCarthy and M. N. Zald (Eds.), *Comparative Perspectives on Social Movements: Political Opportunities, Mobilizing Structures, and Cultural Framings* (pp. 1–20). Cambridge: Cambridge University Press.

McCarthy, J. D., Smith, J. and Zald, M. N. (1996). Public, Media, Electoral, Governmental Agendas. In D. McAdam, J. D. McCarthy and M. N. Zald (Eds.), *Comparative Perspectives on Social Movements: Political Opportunities, Mobilizing Structures, and Cultural Framings* (pp. 291–311). Cambridge: Cambridge University Press.

McCarthy, R. (2012, May 22–24). *[Plenary panel on] Building a powerful food movement: Deep knowledge, broad base, strong networks and innovative approaches to food policy change. Assembly Required: Working better together toward a good food future for all, 11th Food and Community Conference hosted by WKKF*. Asheville, North Carolina. [audio recorded].

McKie, R. (2008, March 23). How the myth of food miles hurts the planet, *The Observer*. Retrieved from www.guardian.co.uk/environment/2008/mar/23/food.ethicalliving

Megill, L., Congressional Hunger Center (2005). *Bridging the Technological Divide: A guide to accepting Food Stamps at farmers' markets*, Emerson National Hunger Fellowship Hunger-free Community Report. New Orleans. p. 13. Retrieved from www.hungercenter.org/wp-content/uploads/2011/07/Bridging-the-Tech-Divide-Food-Stamps-at-Farmers-Markets-Megill.pdf

Meijerink, S. and Huitema, D. (2010). Policy Entrepreneurs and Their Change Strategies: Lessons from Sixteen Case Studies of Water Transitions Across the Globe. *Ecology and Society*, 15(2), 21.

Metis GmbH, AEIDL and CEU (2010, December 15). *Ex-post evaluation of LEADER*, prepared for the EC. Vienna. p. 358.

Mintrom, M. and Norman, P. (2009). Policy Entrepreneurship and Policy Change. *The Policy Studies Journal*, 37(4), 649–667.

Mintrom, M. and Vergari, S. (1998). Policy Networks and Innovation Diffusion: The Case of State Education Reforms. *The Journal of Politics*, 60(1), 126–148.

Mitchell, R. K., Agle, B. R. and Wood, D. J. (1997). Toward a Theory of Stakeholder Identification and Salience: Defining the Principle of Who and What Really Counts. *The Academy of Management Review*, 22(4), 853–888.

MLFW (2008). Making Local Food Work. Plunkett Foundation. Retrieved November 30, 2010 from www.makinglocalfoodwork.co.uk/

MLFW (2012, October). *Making Local Food Work Final Report 2012: Connecting land and people through food*: P. Foundation. p. 61.

MLFW 2011 Conference. (2011, May 12). Sheffield. [participant observation, from notes].

MLFW Staff (2011, March 25). *Personal interview*. Plunkett Foundation, Woodstock. [audio recorded].

Mooney, P. H., Tanaka, K. and Ciciurkaite, G. (2014). Food Policy Council Movement in North America: A Convergence of Alternative Local Agrifood Interests? *Alternative Agrifood Movements: Patterns of Convergence and Divergence* (pp. 229–255).

Morales, A. (2011). Growing Food *and* Justice: Dismantling Racism through Sustainable Food Systems. In A. H. Alkon and J. Agyeman (Eds.), *Cultivating Food Justice: Race, Class, and Sustainability* (pp. 149–176): Massachusetts Institute of Technology.

Morgan, D. (2001, October 4). White House supports reformers on farm bill, *Reprinted from The Washington Post in The Post and Courier*, Charleston, South Carolina. p. A13. Retrieved from www.news.google.com/newspapers?id=MJ1IAAAAI

252 *References*

BAJ&sjid=CAsNAAAAIBAJ&dq=white%20house%20supports%20reformers%20on%20farm%20bill&pg=4597%2C741643

Morgan, D. (2010). *The Farm Bill and Beyond*, Economic Policy Paper Series. Washington, D.C.: German Marshall Fund of the United States. p. 62.

Morgan, K. and Sonnino, R. (2006). Empowering Consumers: The Creative Procurement of School Meals in Italy and the UK. *International Journal of Consumer Studies*, *31*(1), 19–25.

Morgan, K. and Sonnino, R. (2008). *The School Food Revolution: Public Food and the Challenge of Sustainable Development*. London: Earthscan.

Moyer, H. W. and Josling, T. E. (1990). *Agricultural Policy Reform: Politics and Process in the EC and USA*. London: Harvester Wheatsheaf.

Mukerjee, S. (2007, January 31). Trying to stay true to its roots, *BBC News*. Retrieved from www.news.bbc.co.uk/go/pr/fr/-/1/hi/uk/6316905.stm

NAMWG, FFPP (2006a, January 10). *Draft – New Agricultural Markets Workgroup Goals And Objectives, prepared for the SSAWG conference, January 19–22, 2006*. p. 5.

NAMWG, FFPP (2006b, March 18). *New Agricultural Markets: Proposed Policy Initiatives (Draft)*. p. 6.

NANA (2004, June 6). *Promoting Fruit and Vegetable Intake in Schools*. p. 4.

NANA (2008a, November 19). *Child Nutrition Reauthorization Recommendations*, Final. p. 5.

NANA (2008b, October 2). *NANA Draft: September 2008. Child Nutrition Reauthorization Recommendations*. p. 5. Draft for comment.

NANA (2009). *Child Nutrition Reauthorization Recommendations [and endorsers]*, Last updated, September 9, 2009. p. 8.

NAO (2004, September 16). *Helping Farm Businesses in England*. London: Stationery Office. p. 50.

NAO (2006, October 16). *The Delays in Administering the 2005 Single Payment Scheme in England*, London: The Stationery Office. p. 50.

NAO (2009, October 15). *A Second Progress Update on the Administration of the Single Payment Scheme by the Rural Payments Agency*, London: The Stationery Office. p. 39.

NAO (2011). *Report of the Comptroller and Auditor General on the Department for Environment, Food and Rural Affairs 2010–2011 accounts*, London: The Stationery Office. p. 6.

National and State Organization Sign-On Letter Urging Support for Prioritizing Low-Income Children's Access to Healthy Meals. (2009, March 26). p. 11 Retrieved February 14, 2012, from www.frac.org/newsite/wp-content/uploads/2010/05/cnr_access_signon_letter_mar26_2010.pdf

National Assembly for Wales. (2014). *Governance of Wales: Who is responsible for what?* Accessed August 6, 2014. Retrieved from www.assemblywales.org/abthome/role-of-assembly-how-it-works/governance-of-wales.htm

National Consumer Council (2001, Autumn). *Feeding into food policy: A submission to the Policy Commission on the Future of Farming and Food on the views of low-income consumers*. p. 20.

The National Farm to School Act, U.S. House (2009, November 10) [draft legislation developed by Representative McCollum's office prior to submission to House Legislative Counsel].

National Funding Strategies for Local Food: The US and UK Experience, Meeting of the All-Party Parliamentary Group on Agroecology. (2012, November 11). Retrieved

References 253

from www.agroecologygroup.org.uk/index.php/events/previous-meetings/2012–11–14/

Natural Environment and Rural Communities Act 2006. Chapter 16 (2006). Great Britain. Available at The National Archives from www.legislation.gov.uk/ukpga/2006/16/contents

Nelson, M. (1997). Developments in the UK: Work of the Low Income Project Team. *Proceedings of the Nutrition Society,* (56), 91–100.

NEMWI (2003a, March 26). *Agriculture and Food System Policy Work at the Northeast-Midwest Institute: A Proposal to the W.K. Kellogg Foundation.* p. 11.

NEMWI (2003b, September 30). *Reconfiguring the FAS Policy Cluster.* p. 23. [Powerpoint presentation to WKKF].

NEMWI (2003c, November 23). *W.K. Kellogg Foundation's Food and Society Policy Cluster Request for Pre-proposals,* prepared for WKKF. p. 3.

NEMWI (2004, December 17). *Final Narrative Report to the W. K. Kellogg Foundation on the Agriculture Policy Program and the Policy Planning Initiative at the Northeast-Midwest Institute (9/31/03–5/31/04).* p. 15.

NEMWI (2005, November 29). *New Agricultural Markets Conference Call Notes.* p. 8. [conference call notes].

NEMWI. (2006a, March 20). *FFR contacts 3–20–06.* [Spreadsheet].

NEMWI (2006b, February 22). *New Markets Call.* p. 2. [conference call notes].

NEMWI (2007a, January 30). *Attendance at the FFPP Press Conference January 22nd 2007 reporters who wrote about the event highlighted in pink.* [Excel spreadsheet].

NEMWI (2007b, January 30). *News Clips for the Farm and Food Policy Project Press Conference on January 22, 2007.* p. 35.

NEMWI (2008a, September 30). *Checklist of Farm and Food Policy Project Priorities in the Food, Conservation, and Energy Act of 2008.* p. 18.

NEMWI (2008b, January 13). *FFPP Declaration Sign On List.* Washington, DC. p. 3.

NEMWI (2008c). *FFPP Farm Bill Wins 10–16–08,* Published on www.farmand foodproject.org, no longer available online. Washington, DC. p. 1.

NEMWI Policy Staff (2001, November 6). *Re: Meeting with [Program Officer], Kellogg Foundation [November 2].* Memorandum to [excerpted], Executive Director. p. 2.

NEMWI Policy Staff (2002, December 13). *Confidential Memorandum. Re: FAS Policy Initiative.* To: [WKKF Program Officer] and [WKKF Program Officer B], CC: Gus Schumacher. Washington, DC: NEMWI. p. 3.

Newton, D. and MacDonald, J. M. (2009). Farm Structure: Glossary. Retrieved January 15, 2012 from www.ers.usda.gov/Briefing/Organic/Demand.htm

NFFC (2012). NFFC 2012 Executive Committee. Retrieved January 9, 2013 from www.nffc.net/Who%20We%20Are/Executive%20Committee/page-executive.htm#BenBurkett

NFSN (2011, April 11). *How to Apply a Geographic Preference.* p. 2.

NFSN (2012). FarmToSchool.org. Retrieved February 20, 2012 from www.farmtoschool.org

NFSN, School Food FOCUS, CFSC et al. (2009, August 8). *The Farm to School Collaborative,* Supporting the Common Goals of Healthy Kids, Healthy Farms and Healthy Communities, handout: CFSC. Accessed February 13, 2012. Retrieved from www.foodsecurity.org/policy/Legislator_Info-50mil_Mandatory_F2S.pdf

NFU Food Chain Staff (2012, May 10). *Telephone interview.* [audio recorded].

NSAC (ca. 2009). Senior Farmers' Market Nutrition Program. Retrieved April 4, 2013 from www.sustainableagriculture.net/publications/grassrootsguide/local-food-systems-rural-development/farmers-market-nutrition-program/

254   *References*

NSAC (2010). *NSAC's Agriculture Appropriations Chart Fiscal Year 2011.* p. 7.

NSAC (2011). *NSAC's Agriculture Appropriations Chart for Fiscal Year 2012 Conference Report.* p. 7.

NSAC (2012). Bill Summary Local Farms, Food, and Jobs Act S. 1773, H.R. 3286. Retrieved June 11, 2012 from www.sustainableagriculture.net/our-work/local-food-bill/bill-summary-2/

Obama for America (2008a). *Obama and Biden: Tackling Domestic Hunger.* p. 3.

Obama for America (2008b). *Real Leadership for Rural America.* p. 13.

Office of the Deputy Prime Minister. (2006, March). *Ex-Post Evaluation of the English, Scottish, and Welsh Objective 5B Programmes Final Report 2004,* London. p. 266.

Ogren, K. E. (1965). Marketing Costs and Margins: New Perspectives in a Changing Economy. *American Journal of Agricultural Economics,* 47(5), 1366–1376 doi: doi:10.2307/1236394

Oliveira, V. and Frazao, E., USDA, Economic Research Service. (2009, April). *The WIC Program: Background, Trends, and Issues, 2009 edition.* p. 90.

Oliveira, V., Racine, E., Olmsted, J. et al., USDA, ERS, Food and Rural Economics Division. (2002, September). *The WIC Program: Background, Trends, and Issues.* p. 44.

Ollinger, M. E., Nguyen, S. V., Blayney, D. et al., USDA, Economic Research Service. (2005, March). *Structural Change in the Meat, Poultry, Dairy, and Grain Processing Industries,* ERR 3. p. 32.

Olsho, L., Klerman, J. and Bartlett, S., Abt Associates (2011, September 2). *Food and Nutrition Service Evaluation of the Fresh Fruit and Vegetable Program (FFVP) Interim Evaluation Report,* prepared for USDA FNS. p. 52. Retrieved from www.fns. usda.gov/ora/MENU/Published/CNP/FILES/FFVPInterim.pdf

OMB (2002). *Budget of the United States Government Fiscal Year 2003,* Department of Agriculture Washington, DC: Government Printing Office. pp. 65–201.

OMB (2003). *Budget of the United States Government Fiscal Year 2004,* Department of Agriculture Washington, DC: Government Printing Office. pp. 55–186.

OMB (2004). *Budget of the United States Government Fiscal Year 2005,* Department of Agriculture Washington, DC: Government Printing Office. pp. 67–199.

OMB (2005). *Budget of the United States Government Fiscal Year 2006,* Department of Agriculture Washington, DC: Government Printing Office. pp. 63–202.

OMB (2006). *Budget of the United States Government Fiscal Year 2007,* Department of Agriculture Washington, DC: Government Printing Office. pp. 61–201.

OMB (2007). *Budget of the United States Government Fiscal Year 2008,* Department of Agriculture Washington, DC: Government Printing Office. pp. 55–181.

OMB (2008). *Budget of the United States Government Fiscal Year 2009,* Department of Agriculture Washington, DC: Government Printing Office. pp. 69–201.

OMB (2009). *Budget of the United States Government Fiscal Year 2010,* Department of Agriculture Washington, DC: Government Printing Office. pp. 67–199.

OMB (2010). *Budget of the United States Government Fiscal Year 2011,* Department of Agriculture Washington, DC: Government Printing Office. pp. 65–202.

OMB (2011). *Budget of the United States Government Fiscal Year 2012,* Department of Agriculture Washington, DC: Government Printing Office. pp. 59–190.

One News (2006, October 31). British trade minister defends NZ, *TVNZ.* Retrieved from www.tvnz.co.nz/view/page/411749/876493

Oughton, E. and Bracken, L. (2009). Interdisciplinary Research: Framing and Reframing. *Area, 41*(4), 385–394.

References   255

Patrick Leahy [D-VT], Arlen Specter [R-PA], Jeff Bingaman [D-NM] et al. (2006, April 5). *Letter from 20 Senators to the Agricultural Appropriations Sub-committee Chair and Ranking Member requesting funding for Section 122 of the Child Nutrition and WIC Reauthorization of 2004.* p. 3.

Payne, T., USDA, AMS. (2002, May). *U.S. Farmers Markets–2000 A Study of Emerging Trends.*

Peak District National Park Authority. (2005). Welcome to the Environmental Quality Mark. Retrieved February 16, 2005 from www.peakdistrict.org/eqm/intro.htm

Pike, A., Tomaney, J., Coombes, M. et al. (2012). Governing Uneven Development: The Politics of Local and Regional Development in England. In N. Bellini, M. Danson & H. Halkier (Eds.), *Regional Development Agencies: The Next Generation?: Networking, Knowledge* (pp. 102–121). Routledge, Oxon.

Plassmann, K. and Edwards-Jones, G. (2009). *Where does the carbon footprint fall? Developing a carbon map of food production,* Sustainable Markets Discussion Paper Number 4: IIED. p. 41. Retrieved from www.pubs.iied.org/pdfs/16023IIED.pdf

Plunkett Foundation (2003, September 30). *Encouraging collaborative and co-operative initiatives between farmers and rural businesses,* RE 0115, prepared for DEFRA. p. 22.

Plunkett Foundation (2011, August). *Can Community Food Enterprises Inform and Deliver Food Policy? Insights from Case Studies,* prepared for DEFRA Centre of Expertise on Influencing Behaviour. p. 63.

Policy Action Team 13. (2000). *National Strategy for Neighourhood Renewal [spelling error in official copy]. Improving Shopping Access for People Living in Deprived Neighborhoods. A Paper for Discussion,* Department of Health. p. 103.

Policy Commission on the Future of Farming and Food. (2001, September 25). *Press Release: Farming Future and Food – The Future. Consultation Document,* archived web content. p. 3.

Potter, C. (1998). *Against the Grain: Agri-environmental Reform in the United States and European Union.* Oxford: CAB International.

Potter, C. and Tilzey, M. (2005). Agricultural Policy Discourses in the European Post-Fordist Transition: Neoliberalism, Neomercantilism and Multifunctionality. *Progress in Human Geography, 29*(5), 581.

Pretty, J. (1995). Participatory Learning for Sustainable Agriculture. *World Development, 23*(8), 1247–1263.

Pretty, J. (2008). Participatory Learning for Sustainable Agriculture. In J. Pretty (Ed.), *Sustainable Agriculture and Food: Policies, Processes and Institutions* (pp. 109–135). London: Earthscan.

Pretty, J., Ball, A. S., Lang, T. et al. (2005). Farm Costs and Food Miles: An Assessment of the Full Cost of the UK Weekly Food Basket. *Food Policy, 30*(1), 1–19. doi: 10.1016/j.foodpol.2005.02.001

Prince, R. (2009a, July 30). Ignore the FSA, it is still better to buy organic, *The Telegraph.* Retrieved from www.telegraph.co.uk/foodanddrink/5942078/Ignore-the-FSA-It-is-still-better-to-buy-organic.html

Prince, R. (2009b, May 7). Is organic food too posh for its own good?, *The Telegraph.* Retrieved from www.telegraph.co.uk/earth/agriculture/organic/5286371/Is-organic-food-too-posh-for-its-own-good.html

Prince, R. (2009c, September 30). The virtues of the next best thing to organic food, *The Telegraph.* Retrieved from www.telegraph.co.uk/foodanddrink/6243562/The-virtues-of-the-next-best-thing-to-organic-food.html

256   *References*

Public Sector Food Procurement Initiative, DEFRA. (2006). *How to increase opportunities for small and local producers when aggregating food procurement Guidance for buyers and specifiers.* p. 32.

Pujol, D., EC, DGA. (1994 (revised 1995)). *Exploiting local agricultural resources: Part II: Exploiting local agricultural resources via quality,* revised version published at Rural Europe website. Accessed October 22, 2012. Retrieved from www.ec.europa.eu/agriculture/rur/leader2/rural-en/biblio/produ/art02.htm, www.ec.europa.eu/agriculture/rur/leader2/rural-en/biblio/produ/art03.htm, www.ec.europa.eu/agriculture/rur/leader2/rural-en/biblio/produ/art04.htm, www.ec.europa.eu/agriculture/rur/leader2/rural-en/biblio/produ/art05.htm, www.ec.europa.eu/agriculture/rur/leader2/rural-en/biblio/produ/art06.htm, www.ec.europa.eu/agriculture/rur/leader2/rural-en/biblio/produ/art07.htm, www.ec.europa.eu/agriculture/rur/leader2/rural-en/biblio/produ/art08.htm

Putnam, R. D. (2000). *Bowling Alone: The Collapse and Revival of American Community.* New York: Simon & Schuster.

Pyle, J. (1971). Farmers' Markets in the United States: Functional Anachronisms. *Geographic Review, 61*(2), 167–197.

Randerson, J. (2007, June 4). The eco-diet . . . and it's not just about food miles. Focus on distance is too narrow, say researchers. "Only 2%" of impact due to transport from farm to shop, *The Guardian.* Retrieved from www.guardian.co.uk/uk/2007/jun/04/lifeandhealth.business

Randerson, J. (2008, September 9). Government urged to introduce "omni-standards" for food. Expert calls for a comprehensive labelling system integrating all available information of the environmental, health and social impact of food, *The Guardian.* Retrieved from www.guardian.co.uk/environment/2008/sep/09/food.ethicalliving

Ray, C. (1998). Territory, Structures and Interpretation—Two Case Studies of the European Union's LEADER I programme. *Journal of Rural Studies, 14*(1), 79–87. doi: 10.1016/s0743–0167(97)00039–9

Ray, C. (2000). Endogenous Socio-economic Development in the European Union—Issues of Evaluation. *Journal of Rural Studies, 16*(4), 447–458. doi: 10.1016/s0743–0167(00)00012–7

Ray, C. (2002). A Mode of Production for Fragile Rural Economies: The Territorial Accumulation of Forms of Capital. *Journal of Rural Studies, 18*(3), 225–231. doi: 10.1016/s0743–0167(02)00003–7

Ray LaHood [R-IL]. (2001, October 4). In Congressional Record: U.S. House. p. H6304.

RDPE Network (2009, August). *RDPE Regional Implementation Plan (RIP) Themes/priorities.* p. 2.

RDPE Network (2012). Rural Economy Grant (REG). Retrieved October 17, 2012 from www.rdpenetwork.defra.gov.uk/funding-sources/rural-economy-grant

RDPE Network and Rural Services Network (2009, July 8). *Discussion on Integrated Delivery.* p. 6.

Regional Development Agencies Act 1998. (1998). Parliament, Great Britain. Available at www.legislation.gov.uk/ukpga/1998/45/contents

Reiss, C. (2001, October 3). Putnam stand on Farm Bill a surprise, *Lakeland Ledger,* Lakeland, Florida. pp. B1–B2. Retrieved from www.news.google.com/newspapers?id=8MtOAAAAIBAJ&sjid=jf0DAAAAIBAJ&dq=florida%20farm%20bill&pg=2341%2C1101787

References 257

Richardson, J. (2000). Government, Interest Groups, and Policy Change. *Political Studies, 48*, 1006–1025.

Richardson, J., Library of Congress, CRS. (2010, August 6). *Child Nutrition and WIC Reauthorization: Issues and Legislation in the 111th Congress,* R41354. p. 21.

Ritchie, S. M. and Chen, W.-T., USDA, National Agricultural Library, Alternative Farming Systems Information Service. (2011). *Farm to School: A Selected and Annotated Bibliography,* Beltsville, MD. Retrieved from www.nal.usda.gov/afsic/pubs/srb1102.shtml

Robert Menendez [D-NJ] and Susan Collins [R-ME] (2008). *Letter to the Senate Appropriations Committee Agriculture sub-committee.* p. 1.

Robert Wood Johnson Foundation (2011, May 31). *Farm to School and the Child Nutrition Act: Improving school meals through advocating federal support for farm-to-school programs,* Program Results Report. p. 7.

Roberts, J. T. and Tofolon-Weiss, M. M. (2001). *Chronicles from the Environmental Justice Frontline.* Cambridge University Press.

Roberts, N. and King, P. (1991). Policy Entrepreneurs: Their Activity Structure and Function in the Policy Process. *Journal of Public Administration Research and Theory, 2*, 147–175.

Robin Mortimer [DEFRA Director of Wildlife and Countryside]. (2011, June 29). *"Dear Stakeholder..."* [on the transition of the RDPE from the Regional Development Agencies to DEFRA]. p. 2.

Robinson, F., Shaw, K. and Davidson, G. (2005). "On the Side of the Angels": Community Involvement in the Governance of Neighbourhood Renewal. *Local Economy, 20*(1), 13–26.

Roe, E. (1994). *Narrative Policy Analysis: Theory and Practice.* Durham, North Carolina: Duke University Press.

Ron Kind [D-WI]. (2001, October 4). In Congressional Record. p. H6309.

Rose, C. (1993). Beyond The Struggle for Proof: Factors Changing the Environmental Movement. *Environmental Values 2*(4), 285.

Roulston, K. (2010). *Reflective Interviewing: A Guide to Theory and Practice.* London: SAGE Publications.

Rountree, J. H. (1977). Systems Thinking—Some Fundamental Aspects. *Agricultural Systems, 2*(4), 247–254.

Rucht, D. (1996). The Impact of National Contexts on Social Movement Structures: A Cross-movement and Cross-national Comparison. In D. McAdam, J. D. McCarthy and M. N. Zald (Eds.), *Comparative Perspectives on Social Movements: Political Opportunities, Mobilizing Structures, and Cultural Framings* (pp. 185–204). Cambridge: Cambridge University Press.

Ruckelshaus, W. D. (1996). Stopping the Pendulum [editorial]. *Environmental Toxicology and Chemistry, 15*(3), 229–232.

Rural Coalition/Coalición Rural (2006, May 5). *Food and Farm Policy Project Diversity Initiative.* p. 18. [proposal submitted to WKKF].

Rural Partnerships Limited. (2003, June 30). *Provide advice on methods to improve the promotion and facilitation of the Rural Enterprise Scheme,* DEFRA. p. 4.

Rural Payments Agency. (2011, July 7). *Allocation of New SPS entitlements for 2010.* Accessed October 17, 2012. Retrieved from www.rpa.defra.gov.uk/rpa/index.nsf/53f9502f3074384e80256cae00506fcc/49416bc7895d139980257497003d735a!OpenDocument

258   *References*

SA (2010a). *A rock and a hard place: Peak phosphorus and the threat to our food security.* Bristol. p. 23.

SA (2010b). *Telling Porkies: The big fat lie about doubling food production.* Bristol. p. 11.

SA (2011). Panel discussion: should we influence food choices? SA Annual Conference 2011: Food and the Big Society.

SA (ca. 2013). Council. Retrieved March 15, 2013 from www.soilassociation.org/aboutus/whoweare/council

SA, Food Matters and Sustain. (ca. 2014). Sustainable Food Cities. Retrieved August 21, 2014, 2014 from sustainablefoodcities.org/

SA Annual Conference 2011: Food and the Big Society. (2011, February 9–10). Manchester, England. [from notes].

SA Policy Staff (a) (2011, February 9). *Personal conversation.* SA Annual Conference 2011: Food and the Big Society, Manchester, England. [from notes].

SA Policy Staff (b) (2012, December 13). *Telephone interview.* [audio recorded].

Sabatier, P. A. (1993). Policy Change over a Decade or More. In P. A. Sabatier and H. C. Jenkins-Smith (Eds.), *Policy Change and Learning: An Advocacy Coalition Approach* (pp. 13–40). Oxford: Westview Press.

Sabatier, P. A. and Jenkins-Smith, H. C. (1993). The Dynamics of Policy-Oriented Learning. In P. A. Sabatier and H. C. Jenkins-Smith (Eds.), *Policy Change and Learning: An Advocacy Coalition Approach* (pp. 41–56). Oxford: Westview Press.

SAC (2004, December 10). *Sustainable Agriculture Partnership.* p. 35.

SAC (2005a, March 25). *Summary – SAP Subcontracts.* [Excel spreadsheet].

SAC (2005b, June 25). *Sustainable Agriculture Coalition's FY2006 Agricultural Appropriations Chart.* p. 5.

SAFE Alliance (1994). *The Food Miles Report: The dangers of long distance food transport.*

Sarch, T., DfID, Renewable Natural Resources and Agriculture Policy Team. (2006, November). *Food Miles and Developing Countries,* Powerpoint presentation. p. 7. Accessed March 8, 2013. Retrieved from www.agrifoodstandards.net/es/filemanager/active?fid=29

Schleisman, P. J. (2003, posted April 11, 2008). *Food Miles.* Youtube.com: Patrick Rose [New Zealand]. from www.youtube.com/watch?v=rca8VkjXw8k

Schlesinger, A. M., Jr. (1992). Leave the Constitution Alone. In A. Lijphart (Ed.), *Parliamentary versus Presidential Government* (2000 ed., pp. 90–96). Oxford: Oxford University Press.

Schnellenbach, J. (2007). Public Entrepreneurship and the Economics of Reform. *Journal of Institutional Economics, 3,* 183–202.

Schofer, D. P., Holmes, G., Richardson, V. et al., USDA, AMS, Transportation and Marketing Programs. (2000, February). *Innovative Marketing Opportunities for Small Farmers: Local Schools as Customers.* p. 51.

School Nutrition Association (2008a, March). *2008 Legislative Issue Paper: A Matter of Standards.* p. 1. Accessed February 7, 2012. Retrieved from www.schoolnutrition.org/uploadedFiles/School_Nutrition/106_LegislativeAction/SNAPositionStatements/IndividualPositionStatements/SNA.Final.IP.2008.pdf

School Nutrition Association. (2008b). *Town Hall Meeting Reauthorization 2009 The Wish List.* Presented at School Nutrition Association Legislative Action Conference. [Powerpoint presentation].

Schumacher, G. and Hunt, A. R. (2012, November 15). *[presentation and discussion at] Community food and health (Scotland).* Edinburgh.

References 259

Schumpeter, J. A. (1939). *Business Cycles: A Theoretical, Historical, and Statistical Analysis of the capitalist process*. New York: McGraw-Hill.

Schumpeter, J. A. (1961). *A Theory of Economic Development*. Oxford: Oxford University Press.

Scott, P., US DOD. (2006, February 7). *Changes to the DoD Fresh Program*. p. 2. Accessed February 6, 2012. Retrieved from www.fns.usda.gov/fdd/programs/dod/DoD_FreshChanges2-7-06.pdf

Scottish Parliament. *Devolved and reserved matters explained*. Retrieved from www.scottish.parliament.uk/visitandlearn/25488.aspx

Senate Amendment 2585, Sec. 457. Purchases of Locally Produced Foods, 107th Congress, 1st Session. In Congressional Record, S13204–13221. (2001, December 13) (as proposed and agreed by voice vote).

SERIO, Plymouth University (2012, August). *Making Local Food Work: Understanding the Impact – Final Report* p. 47. Accessed November 2, 2014. Retrieved from www.makinglocalfoodwork.co.uk/reports.cfm

Shakow, D. (1981). The Municipal Farmer's Market as an Urban Service. *Economic geography, 57*(1), 68–77.

Sheingate, A. D. (2001). *The Rise of the Agricultural Welfare State*. Princeton: Princeton University Press.

Shellenberger, M. and Nordhaus, T. (2004, September 24). *The Death of Environmentalism*. Retrieved from heartland.org/policy-documents/death-environmentalism-0

Sherman, J. and Peterson, G. (2009). Finding the Win in Wicked Problems: Lessons from Evaluating Public Policy Advocacy. *Foundation Review, 1*(3), 87–99.

Sherwood Boehlert [R-NY]. (2001, October 4). In Congressional Record: U.S. House. p. H6299.

Shorgen, E. (2001, October 5). House narrowly defeats farm funding change, *Los Angeles Times*. p. A30. Retrieved from www.pqasb.pqarchiver.com/latimes/access/83279609.html?dids=83279609:83279609&FMT=ABS&FMTS=ABS:FT&type=current&date=Oct+05%2C+2001&author=ELIZABETH+SHOGREN&pub=Los+Angeles+Times&desc=THE+NATION%3B+House+Narrowly+Defeats+Farm+Funding+Change&pqatl=google

Shucksmith, M. (2000). Endogenous Development, Social Capital and Social Inclusion: Perspectives from LEADER in the UK. *Sociologia Ruralis, 40*(2), 208–218.

Shucksmith, M. (2009). *Sustainable Rural Communities: Constructing sustainable places beyond cities*. Presented at XXIII European Society of Rural Sociology Congress, Vassa, Finland.

Shucksmith, M. (2012, April 17). *How can rural communities thrive in "interesting times"? Lessons from 20 years of LEADER*. Newcastle University, England: Northern Rural Network Seminar on Rural Development and Social Renewal.

Shucksmith, M. and Herrmann, V. (2002). Future Changes in British Agriculture: Projecting Divergent Farm Household Behaviour. *Journal of Agricultural Economics, 53*(1), 37–50.

Shucksmith, M. and Rønningen, K. (2011). The Uplands After Neoliberalism? The Role of the Small Farm in Rural Sustainability. *Journal of Rural Studies, 27*, 275–287.

Shuput, J. (2008, October 9). Reflections on the First Annual Gathering of the Growing Food and Justice for All Initiative. *Food Systems Network NYC*. Retrieved January 11, 2013 from www.foodsystemsnyc.org/article/reflections-first-annual-gathering-growing-food-and-justice-all-initiative

260   References

Skiba, K. M. (2001, October 3). Kind is at center of farm dispute, *Milwaukee Sentinel-Journal*. p. 3A.

Slocum, R. (2006). Anti-racist Practice and the Work of Community Food Organizations. *Antipode*, *38*(2), 327–349. doi: 10.1111/j.1467–8330.2006.00582.x

Smith, A., Watkiss, P., Tweddle, G. et al., AEA Technology (2005, July). *The Validity of Food Miles as an Indicator of Sustainable Development: Final Report produced for DEFRA*. Oxon. p. 229.

Snow, D. A., Burke Rochford, J., Worden, S. K. et al. (1986). Frame Alignment Processes, Micromobilization, and Movement Participation. *American Sociological Review*, *51*(4), 464–481.

Snow, D. A. and Trom, D. (2002). The Case Study and the Study of Social Movements. In B. Klandermans and S. Staggenborg (Eds.), *Methods of Social Movement Research* (pp. 146–172). Minneapolis: University of Minnesota Press.

Social Exclusion Unit. (2001, January). *National Strategy for Neighbourhood Renewal: Policy Action Team Audit*, Cabinet Office. p. 277.

Southeast England Development Agency. (2009, July). *Rural Development Programme for England [Newsletter]*. p. 7.

Specific powers of Corporation. 15 U.S.C. § 714c(e) (2012 ed.).

Starr, A. (2010). Local Food: A Social Movement? *Cultural Studies <=> Critical Methodologies*, *10*(6), 479–490.

Stephen Gilbert [Liberal Democrat, St Austell and Newquay] (2010, September 16). *[Panel discussion on] "Devolution, Regional Governance, and the EU" hosted by the US-UK Fulbright Commission*. House of Lords.

Stockley, L., Government Office for Science. (2011). *Foresight Project on Global Food and Farming Futures. WP2: Review of levers for changing consumers' food patterns*, URN: 11/598. p. 124.

Sue Miller [Liberal Democrat, Chilthorne Domer]. (2011, December 6). *How to Feed a Town or City*, Meeting of the All-Party Parliamentary Group on Agroecology, [from typed notes].

Sumberg, J., NEF (2009, August). *Re-framing the great food debate: The case for sustainable food*. London. p. 20. Retrieved from www.neweconomics.org/publications/entry/re-framing-the-great-food-debate

Sustain (1994, republished 2011). *The Food Miles Report: The dangers of long distance food transport*. p. 62. Retrieved from www.sustainweb.org/publications/the_food_miles_report/

Sustain (1999a, July). *Developing local networks to tackle food poverty: A summary report of five seminars organised by the Food Poverty Network in partnership with local food and health workers between January and May 1999*. p. 33.

Sustain (1999b, October). *Food miles – Still on the road to ruin? An assessment of the debate over the unnecessary transport of food, five years on from the food miles report*. p. 22. Retrieved from www.sustainweb.org/publications/food_miles_still_on_the_road_to_ruin/

Sustain (1999c, January). *Making Links: A toolkit for local food projects*. p. 135.

Sustain (2001, September). *Food poverty: Policy options for the new millennium*. p. 90.

Sustain (2003, January). *Community food projects: A directory of projects on the Food Poverty Projects Database*. p. 84. Retrieved from www.sustainweb.org/publications/community_food_projects_a_directory/

Sustain (2006a, November 20). *Airfreight of fresh horticultural produce from least developed countries. A round-table seminar, 20 November 2006 held at Friends Meeting House, London*, meeting notes. Accessed December 23, 2012. Retrieved from www.sustainweb.org/images/sustain/DfID_airfreight-meeting-notes_201106.pdf

References   261

Sustain (2006b, May 22). Response - Rural Development Programme for England. Retrieved January 4, 2013 from www.sustainweb.org/news/05_2006_response_ rural_development_programme_for_england/

Sustain (2009, November 25). Sustain welcomes Government announcement on health and climate change. Retrieved March 14, 2013 from www.sustainweb. org/news/nov09_govt_eat_less_meat/

Sustain (2010, July 29). Sustain members list. Retrieved May 2, 2013 from www.sustainweb.org/membership/sustain_members_list/

Sustain (2011a). Charity pays for better fish served to Cameron and his millionaire Cabinet. Retrieved March 18, 2013 from www.sustainweb.org/news/march 2011_gffom_83p_cheques/

Sustain (2011b). *The Food Miles Report: The dangers of long-distance transport*. p. 62. Retrieved from www.sustainweb.org/publications/the_food_miles_report/

Sustain (2011c, January 24). *Good Food for Our Money Campaign response to Defra's consultation on the Impact Assessment for "Government Buying Standards" specifications for food and food services*. p. 16. Retrieved from www.sustainweb.org/pdf/11/GFFOM_ response_GBS_consultation.pdf.

Sustain. (2011d). Good Food for Our Money Campaign: Portcullis Counter. Sustain. Retrieved June 1, 2011, 2011 from www.sustainweb.org/goodfoodforourmoney/ portcullis_counter/

Sustain (2011e). Sustain wins CIEH President's Award. *Good Food for Our Money Campaign news*. Retrieved October 26, 2012 from www.sustainweb.org/news/ sustain_wins_cieh_presidents_award/

Sustain (2012a, March 15). Awards won by Sustain and its staff. Retrieved May 6, 2013 from www.sustainweb.org/about/awards_won_by_sustain_and_its_staff/

Sustain. (2012b, June 9). Good Food for Our Money Campaign. Retrieved October 25, 2012 from www.sustainweb.org/goodfoodforourmoney/

Sustain (2012c). *Panel: Where now? The Lessons? The next steps? 3rd Annual City Food Symposium. Local Food Policies in Practice: The state of the sub-national*. Cass Business School, City University, London, UK. [from notes].

Sustain and Elm Farm Research Centre (2001, November). *Eating Oil: Food Supply in a Changing Climate*. p. 98. Retrieved from www.sustainweb.org/publications/ eating_oil/?section=

Sustain and Food Links UK (2003). *Feeding the Future: Policy options for local food – A discussion paper*. p. 72. Retrieved from www.sustainweb.org/publications/feeding_ the_future/

Sustain and MLFW (2009, Autumn). *Building a Sustainable Food Hub*. p. 9. Retrieved from www.sustainweb.org/publications/?id=176

Sustain Policy Staff (a). (2011a). *Panelist presentation in workshop: Local – Global Connections View from Across the Pond: Can Campaigning Deliver Systems Change?* Presented at "Food Justice: Honoring our Roots, Growing the Movement," 15th Annual CFSC Meeting, Oakland, CA. [recorded Powerpoint presentation].

Sustain Policy Staff (a) (2011b, February 28). *Personal interview*. [audio recorded].

Sustain Policy Staff (b). (2012, November 11). *National Funding Strategies for Local Food: The US and UK Experience*, Meeting of the All-Party Parliamentary Group on Agroecology. [from notes].

Swidler, A. (1986). Culture in Action: Symbols and Strategies. *American Sociological Review, 51*(2), 273–286.

262   References

Sylvander, B., EC, DGA. (1993 (revised 1995)). *Exploiting local agricultural resources: Part I: "Specific Quality Products," an opportunity for rural areas,* Published in LEADER Magazine No. 3 [revised version published at Rural Europe website]. Accessed October 21, 2012. Retrieved from www.ec.europa.eu/agriculture/rur/leader2/rural-en/biblio/produ/art01.htm

Tarrow, S. (1998). *Power in Movement: Social Movements and Contentious Politics.* Cambridge: Cambridge University.

Tasting the Future – Innovation Group Meeting. (2011, March 29). London. [from notes].

Tasting the Future – Second Assembly. (2011, February 3). London. [from notes].

Tauber, M. and Fisher, A., CFSC (2001). *A Guide to Community Food Projects.* p. 19.

Taylor, B. (1995). Popular Ecological Resistance and Radical Environmentalism. In B. Taylor (Ed.), *Ecological Resistance Movements: The Global Emergence of Radical and Popular Environmentalism* (pp. 334–354). Albany, New York: State University of New York.

The Blue Dogs of the Democratic Party. (November 8, 2006) Blue Dogs Howl in Victory: Coalition Will Grow to 44 Members. Press Release. Retrieved January 16, 2012, from www.bluedogs.us/blue_dogs_howl_in_victory_coalition_will_grow_to_44_members.htm

The High Level Panel of Experts on Food Security and Nutrition, UN Food and Agricultural Organization, Committee on World Food Security. (2011, July). *Price volatility and food security.* p. 83.

the public whip. (2008). Lisbon Treaty – Approves of the government's policy towards the Lisbon Treaty with regards to climate change – 27 Feb 2008 at 16:06. Retrieved December 23, 2012 from www.publicwhip.org.uk/division.php?date=2008–02–27&number=103

This is Money. (2006, September 15). Tesco reveals plan to cut "food miles". Retrieved from www.thisismoney.co.uk/money/markets/article-1602412/Tesco-reveals-plan-to-cut-food-miles.html

Tilly, C. (1993). Contentious Repertoires in Great Britain, 1758–1834. *Social Science History, 17*(2), 253–280.

To amend the Richard B. Russell National School Lunch Act to reauthorize and expand the fruit and vegetable pilot program, S. 1393, U.S. Senate, 108th Congress, 1st Session (2003, July 10) (introduced).

To promote improved nutrition for students by expanding the Fruit and Vegetable Pilot Program under the Richard B. Russell National School Lunch Act, H.R. 2832, U.S. House, 108th Congress, 1st Session (2003, July 23) (introduced).

Tom Harkin [D-IA], Saxby Chambliss [R-GA], Max Baucus [D-MT] et al. *SA 3855. An amendment to amendment SA 3500 proposed to the bill H.R. 2419, to provide for the continuation of agricultural programs through fiscal year 2012, and for other purposes.* In Congressional Record, S15692. (2007, December 14).

Tomlinson, I. J. (2007). *Transforming British Organics: The role of central government 1980–2006.* Ph. D. Dissertation, University College London.

Trarieux, J.-M., Delegation of the EC to the US. (2005, July 27). *The European Union on the move: CAP reform and the WTO negotiations.* [Powerpoint presentation prepared for NEMWI, Washington, DC].

Tropp, D. and Barnham, J., USDA, AMS, Market Services Division. (2008, March 13). *National Farmers Market Summit Proceedings Report,* National Farmers Market Summit, Baltimore, Maryland, November 7–9, 2007. p. 63.

References   263

Tropp, D. and Olowolayemo, S., USDA, AMS, Transportation and Marketing Programs. (2000). *How Local Farmers and School Food Service Buyers are Building Alliances.* p. 30.

Tuckermanty, E., Pothukuchi, K., Toombs, D. et al., USDA. (2007). *Healthy Food Healthy Communities.* p. 26.

UK - Rise in number of farm shops. (2011) *Meat Trade News Daily.* Retrieved March 29, 2013, from www.meattradenewsdaily.co.uk/news/220511/uk_rise_in_number_of_farm_shops_.aspx

UN Food and Agriculture Organization. (2008). *Soaring food prices: Facts, perspectives, impacts, and actions required.* Presented at High-level conference on world food security: The challenges of climate change and bioenergy, Rome.

United Fresh Produce. (March 20, 2010) United Fresh Applauds Prominent Role of Produce in Sen. Boxer's School Nutrition Bill. *Beginning Farmers.* Retrieved February 14, 2012, from www.beginningfarmers.org/united-fresh-applauds-prominent-role-of-produce-in-sen-boxer%E2%80%99s-school-nutrition-bill/

USDA, FNS (1994a, June 10). *National School Lunch Program and School Breakfast Program: Nutrition Objectives for School Meals; Proposed Rule,* Federal Register. Accessed February 6, 2012. Retrieved from www.gpo.gov/fdsys/pkg/FR-1994–06–10/html/94–14092.htm

USDA. *Part 248 – WIC Farmers' Market Nutrition Program (FMNP). Definitions.* 7 C.F.R. § 248.2 (1994b).

USDA, AMS, Transportation and Marketing Programs (1998). *Farmers Markets,* retrieved from the Clinton Library Archive. p. 2. Retrieved from www.clintonlibrary.gov/assets/storage/Research%20-%20Digital%20Library/ClintonAdmin HistoryProject/81–90/Box%2090/1756276-history-usda-archival-documents-chapter-1–00-agricultural-marketing-service-3.pdf

USDA, FNS (2000a, November 2). *Seniors Farmers' Market Nutrition Pilot Program: Opportunity To Submit Grant Applications,* Federal Register. pp. 65825–65828. Accessed January 9, 2012. Retrieved from www.gpo.gov/fdsys/pkg/FR-2000–11–02/xml/FR-2000–11–02.xml

USDA, FNS (2000b, March). *Small Farms/School Meals Initiative Town Hall Meetings. A Step-by-Step Guide on How to Bring Small Farms and Local Schools Together,* Alexandria, VA. p. 22.

USDA, AMS, Transportation and Marketing Programs, Wholesale and Alternative Markets (2001a, March). *Farmer Direct Marketing Bibliography,* Bibliography and Literature of Agriculture No. 135. p. 52.

USDA, RBCS (2001b, March 6). *Notice of Funds Availability (NOFA) Inviting Applications for the Value-Added Agricultural Product Market Development Grant Program (VADG) (Independent Producers),* Federal Register. pp. 13490–13495. Accessed January 12, 2012. Retrieved from www.gpo.gov/fdsys/pkg/FR-2002–06–24/pdf/02–15910.pdf

USDA, RBCS (2002, June 24). *Notice of Funds Availability (NOFA) Inviting Applications for the Value-Added Agricultural Product Market Development Grant Program (VADG) (Independent Producers),* Federal Register. pp. 42531–42538. Accessed January 12, 2012. Retrieved from www.gpo.gov/fdsys/pkg/FR-2002–06–24/pdf/02–15910.pdf

USDA, RBCS (2003, September 4). *Notice of Funds Availability (NOFA) Inviting Applications for the Value-Added Agricultural Product Market Development Grant Program (VADG) (Independent Producers),* Federal Register. pp. 52565–52572. Accessed January 12, 2012. Retrieved from www.gpo.gov/fdsys/pkg/FR-2003–09–04/pdf/03–22506.pdf

264   *References*

USDA, RBCS (2004, June 15). *Announcement of Value-Added Producer Grant Application Deadlines and Funding Levels*, Federal Register. pp. 33348–33360. Accessed January 12, 2012. Retrieved from www.gpo.gov/fdsys/pkg/FR-2004–06–15/pdf/04–13392.pdf

USDA, RBCS (2005a, December 21). *Announcement of Value-Added Producer Grant Application Deadlines*, Federal Register. pp. 75780–75790. Accessed January 12, 2012. Retrieved from www.gpo.gov/fdsys/pkg/FR-2002–06–24/pdf/02–15910.pdf

USDA, RBCS (2005b, March 7). *Announcement of Value-Added Producer Grant Application Deadlines and Funding Levels*, Federal Register. pp. 10938–10951. Accessed January 12, 2012. Retrieved from www.gpo.gov/fdsys/pkg/FR-2005–03–07/pdf/05–4310.pdf

USDA, FNS (2005c). *Eat Smart–Farm Fresh!* p. 39.

USDA, AMS (2006, March 15). *Notice of Funds Availability (NOFA) Inviting Applications for the Farmers Market Promotion Program (FMPP); Notice of Emergency Approval of New Information Collection*, Federal Register. pp. 13332–13336. Accessed January 15, 2012. Retrieved from www.gpo.gov/fdsys/pkg/FR-2006–03–15/pdf/E6–3709.pdf

USDA, RBCS (2007, April 16). *Announcement of Value-Added Producer Grant Application Deadlines*, Federal Register. pp. 18949–18959. Accessed January 12, 2012. Retrieved from www.gpo.gov/fdsys/pkg/FR-2007–04–16/pdf/E7–7110.pdf

USDA, RBCS (2008, January 29). *Announcement of Value-Added Producer Grant Application Deadlines*, Federal Register. pp. 5157–5167. Accessed January 12, 2012. Retrieved from www.gpo.gov/fdsys/pkg/FR-2008–01–29/pdf/E8–1532.pdf

USDA, Economic Research Service (2009a, June). *Access to Affordable and Nutritious Food: Measuring and Understanding Food Deserts and Their Consequences. Report to Congress.* p. 160.

USDA, RBCS (2009b, September 1). *Announcement of Value-Added Producer Grant Application Deadlines*, Federal Register. pp. 45165–45177. Accessed January 12, 2012. Retrieved from www.gpo.gov/fdsys/pkg/FR-2009–09–01/pdf/E9–21030.pdf

USDA, RBCS (2009c, October 5). *Inviting Applications for Value-Added Producer Grants*, Federal Register. pp. 51126–51126. Accessed January 12, 2012. Retrieved from www.gpo.gov/fdsys/pkg/FR-2009–10–05/pdf/E9–23939.pdf

USDA, Economic Research Service (2010a). *Food Environment Atlas.* Retrieved from ers.usda.gov/FoodAtlas/

USDA, FNS (2010b). *Supplemental Nutrition Assistance Program Feasibility of Implementing Electronic Benefit Transfer Systems in Farmers' Markets. Report to Congress,* Alexandria, VA. p. 16. Retrieved from www.fns.usda.gov/snap/ebt/pdfs/Kohl–Feasibility.pdf

USDA, RBCS (2011a, June 28). *Announcement of Value-Added Producer Grant Application Deadlines*, Federal Register. pp. 37774–37779. Accessed January 12, 2012. Retrieved from www .gpo.gov/fdsys/pkg/FR-2011–06–28/pdf/2011–16121.pdf

USDA, FNS (2011b). *Department of Defense Fresh Fruit and Vegetable Program,* Alexandria, VA. p. 1. Accessed February 6, 2012. Retrieved from www.fns.usda.gov/fdd/programs/dod/DOD_FreshFruitandVegetableProgram2011.pdf

USDA, AMS (2011c, January 19). *Farmers Market Promotion Program Regulation; Notice of Request for Approval of a New Information Collection*, Federal Register. pp. 3046–3054.

USDA, FNS (2011d, April 22). *Geographic Preference Option for the Procurement of Unprocessed Agricultural Products in Child Nutrition Programs,* Federal Register. pp. 22603–22608.

USDA, National Institute for Food and Agriculture (2011e). *Peoples Garden Grant Program.* p. 21. Accessed February 24, 2012. Retrieved from www.sustainable agriculture.net/wp-content/uploads/2011/08/11_peoples_garden.pdf

References 265

USDA, FNS (2011f). *Request for Applications (RFA) Food and Nutrition Service People's Garden School Pilot Program.* p. 30. Accessed February 24, 2012. Retrieved from www.fns.usda.gov/outreach/grants/garden_rfa.pdf

USDA, FNS (2011g, December 16, 2011). *Supplemental Nutrition Assistance Program: A Short History of SNAP,* Alexandria, VA. Retrieved from www.fns.usda.gov/snap/rules/Legislation/about.htm

USDA (2011h, April 7). *USDA Announces People's Garden School Pilot Program to Promote Garden-Based Learning Opportunities. People's Gardens Aim to Provide Nutritious, Safe and Healthier Choices for Children and Communities,* Release No. 0155.11, FNS Office of Communications. Accessed February 24, 2012. Retrieved from www.usda.gov/wps/portal/usda/usdahome?contentidonly=true&contentid=2011/04/0155.xml

USDA. *Abbreviations and definitions. Family farm.* 7 C.F.R. § 761.2 (2012a).

USDA. *Definitions. Socially disadvantaged farmer or rancher.* 7 C.F.R. § 4284.902 (2012b).

USDA. *Definitions. Socially disadvantaged, limited resource, or beginning farmer or rancher.* 7 C.F.R. § 760.107 (2012c).

USDA (2012d, April 13). *Farm to School Grant Program Request for Applications.* p. 50.

USDA, AMS (2012e, June 5). *Notice of Intent to Request New Information Collection,* Federal Register. pp. 33156–33158. Accessed March 25, 2013. Retrieved from www.gpo.gov/fdsys/pkg/FR-2012–06–05/pdf/2012–13497.pdf

USDA, FNS (2012f, June). *Senior Farmers' Market Nutrition Program.* p. 2. Accessed April 4, 2013. Retrieved from www.fns.usda.gov/wic/SFMNP-Fact-Sheet.pdf

USDA, FNS. (2012g, April). *WIC Farmers' Market Nutrition Program.* p. 2. Accessed April 4, 2012. Retrieved from www.fns.usda.gov/wic/WIC-FMNP-Fact-Sheet.pdf

USDA, FNS (2013a, April 4). *The Farm to School Census.* Retrieved from www.fns.usda.gov/cnd/f2s/f2s-census.htm

USDA, AMS (2013b, August 3). *National Count of Farmers Market Directory Listing Graph: 1994–2013.* Accessed August 5, 2014. Retrieved from www.ams.usda.gov/AMSv1.0/farmersmarkets

USDA, National Institute for Food and Agriculture (2014a). *Community Food Projects Competitive Grant Program. 2014 Request for Applications.* p. 36.

USDA, FNS (2014b). *The Farm to School Census: National Overview.* Accessed August 5, 2014. Retrieved from www.fns.usda.gov/farmtoschool/census#/

Value-added Agricultural Products Market Access Act of 1997, S. 219, U.S. Senate, 105th Congress, 1st Session (1997, January 28) (referred to the Committee on Finance).

Value-Added Development Act for American Agriculture, H.R. 3996, U.S. House, 106th Congress (2000a, March 15).

Value-Added Development Act for American Agriculture. S. 2745, U.S. Senate, 106th Congress (2000b, June 15). (referred to the Committee on Agriculture, Nutrition, and Forestry).

van Eeten, M. J. G. (2007). Narrative Policy Analysis. In F. Fischer (Ed.), *Handbook of Public Policy Analysis* (pp. 251–269). Hoboken, New Jersey: CRC Press.

Verney, D. V. (1992). Parliamentary Government and Presidential Government. In A. Lijphart (Ed.), *Parliamentary versus Presidential Government* (2000 ed., pp. 31–47). Oxford, UK: Oxford University Press.

von Meyer, H., Saraceno, E., Bontron, J. C. et al. (1999, March). *Ex-Post Evaluation of the Leader I Community Initiative 1989–1993 General Report,* Brussels: CEMAC. p. 181. Retrieved from www.ec.europa.eu/agriculture/rur/leader1/index_en.htm

Voss, K. (1996). Collapse of a Social Movement: The Interplay of Mobilizing Structures, Framing, and Political Opportunities in the Knights of Columbus. In D. McAdam,

266 *References*

J. D. McCarthy and M. N. Zald (Eds.), *Comparative Perspectives on Social Movements: Political Opportunities, Mobilizing Structures, and Cultural Framings* (pp. 227–258). Cambridge: Cambridge University Press.

Walker, A. (2009, May 15). Food prices vary but crisis remains, *BBC News*. Retrieved from www.news.bbc.co.uk/1/hi/business/8052353.stm

Wann, J. L., Cake, E. L., Elliot, W. H. et al. (1948). *Farmers' Produce Markets in the United States* (Vol. Part 1 History and Description). Washington, DC: USDA.

Ward, N., Donaldson, A. and Lowe, P. (2004). Policy Framing and Learning the Lessons from the UK's Foot and Mouth Disease Crisis. *Environment and Planning C: Government and Policy, 22*.

Ward, N. and Lowe, P. (2004). Europeanizing Rural Development? Implementing the CAP's Second Pillar in England. *International Planning Studies, 9*(2–3), 121–137.

Ward, N., Lowe, P. and Bridges, T. (2003). Rural and Regional Development: The Role of the Regional Development Agencies in England. *Regional Studies, 37*(2), 201–214.

Watts, A. (2007, January 9). Blair and Miliband back CLA food campaign, *Farmers Weekly*. Retrieved from www.fwi.co.uk/Articles/09/01/2007/100586/Blair-and-Miliband-back-CLA-food-campaign.htm

Watts, D., Ilbery, B., Maye, D. et al. (2009). Implementing Pillar II of the Common Agricultural Policy in England: Geographies of the Rural Enterprise Scheme and Processing and Marketing Grant. *Land Use Policy, 26*, 683–694.

Weaver, R. K. (1986). The Politics of Blame Avoidance. *Journal of Public Policy, 6*(4), 371–398.

WhyHunger. (2012). Race and the Food System. Retrieved January 11, 2013 from www.whyhunger.org/portfolio?topicId=24

Whyte, W. F. (1984). *Learning from the Field*. London: SAGE Publishing.

WIC Farmers' Market Nutrition Act of 1992. Pub. L. No. 102–314 (1992a). U.S. Congress.

WIC Farmers' Market Nutrition Act of 1992, S. 2761, U.S. Senate, 102nd Congress, 2nd Session (1992b, May 20) (engrossed).

WIC Supplemental Benefits Act of 1991, H.R. 3711, U.S. House, 102nd Congress, 1st Session (1991, November 5) (introduced).

Wiggins, S., Keats, S. and Compton, J., DfID, UKaid, Overseas Development Institute. (2010, March). *What caused the food price spike of 2007/08? Lessons for world cereals markets*. p. 15.

Wildlife and Countryside Link (2001a). *Brief: Market-Proofing Green Policy Demands for the Future of Farming and Food*. p. 2. [Briefing paper on the coordination of the "Green Group stakeholder meeting with the Policy Commission on the Future of Farming and Food"].

Wildlife and Countryside Link (2001b, November 6). *Green Groups Stakeholder Meeting with Policy Commission on Food and Farming*. p. 3. [pre-meeting agenda draft].

Wildlife and Countryside Link (2001c). *Local Food Economies: Linking competitiveness and sustainability*. p. 15.

Wilkinson, K., Lowe, P. and Donaldson, A. (2010). Beyond Policy Networks: Policy Framing and the Politics of Expertise in the 2001 Foot and Mouth Disease crisis. *Public Administration, 88*(2), 331–345. doi: 10.1111/j.1467–9299.2010.01831.x

Winne, M. (2008). *Closing the Food Gap: Resetting the Table in the Land of Plenty*. Boston: Beacon Press.

References   267

Winne, M., Joseph, H. and Fisher, A., CFSC (1997, February). *Community Food Security: A guide to concept, design and implementation.* p. 45.

Winter, M. (2003). Embeddedness, the New Food Economy and Defensive Localism. *Journal of Rural Studies, 19*(1), 23–32. doi: 10.1016/s0743–0167(02)00053–0

WKKF (1998–2003). [Grant to the Nature Conservancy, Inc. for $2,870,000]. Retrieved April 14, 2013 from www.wkkf.org/grants/grants-database.aspx

WKKF (2002, March). *W.K. Kellogg Foundation Food Systems and Rural Development, Food and Society Initiative Grants & Related Projects March 2002.* p. 16.

WKKF (2012a). *2012 Food & Community Conference: Assembly Required.* 11th Food and Community Conference, May 22–24, 2012, Asheville, North Carolina. [conference guide].

WKKF (2012b). *A Food Policy Lifeline for Children and Communities.* Assembly Required: Working better together toward a good food future for all, 11th Food and Community Conference, May 22–24, 2012, Asheville, North Carolina. p. 1. [paper handout in conference packet].

WKKF (2012c, May). *Message Guide.* Assembly Required: Working better together toward a good food future for all, 11th Food and Community Conference, May 22–24, 2012, Asheville, North Carolina. p. 27. [included in conference packet].

WKKF (2012d). *Seeding the good food movement: 80 years of the W.K. Kellogg Foundation and food systems change.* Assembly Required: Working better together toward a good food future for all, 11th Food and Community Conference, May 22–24, 2012, Asheville, North Carolina. p. 1. [handout in conference packet].

WKKF Program Officer (2011, November 7). *Personal interview.* [audio recorded].

Womach, J. and Becker, G. S., Library of Congress, CRS. (2001, January 8). *Farm Economic Relief and Policy Issues in the 106th Congress: A Retrospective,* RL30794. p. 21.

Woods, J., Williams, A., Hughes, J. K. et al. (2010). Energy and the food system. *Philosophical Transactions of the Botanical Society, 365,* 2991–3006. doi: 10.1098/rstb.2010.0172

Working Group. POWER: How does local food policy development connect with other levels of activity? (2012, December 12). *3rd Annual City Food Symposium. Local Food Policies in Practice: the state of the sub-national.* Cass Business School, City University, London, UK. [from notes].

Working Lands Stewardship Act of 2001, H.R. 2375, U.S. House, 107th Congress, 1st Session (2001, June 28).

Wright, W. P., Arminio, M., Reimer, P. et al., USDA, FNS. (1998). *Technical and Cost Feasibility of EBT Equipage in Farmers' Markets and Mobile Food Retailers* p. 83. Retrieved from www.fns.usda.gov/ora/MENU/Published/snap/FILES/Program Operations/EBTFarmersMarket.pdf

Wrigley, N. (2002). "Food Deserts" in British Cities: Policy Context and Research Priorities. *Urban Studies, 39*(11), 2029–2040.

WWF UK Staff, Sustainable Consumption group (2011, March 3). *Telephone interview.* [audio recorded].

Y. Armando Nieto [California Food and Justice Coalition Executive Director]. (2012, May 22–24). *[Plenary panel on] Building a powerful food movement: Deep knowledge, broad base, strong networks and innovative approaches to food policy change.* Presented at Assembly Required: Working better together toward a good food future for all, 11th Food and Community Conference, Asheville, North Carolina.

268 *References*

Yin, R. K. (1993). *Applications of Case Study Research*. London: SAGE Publications.

Yin, R. K. (2003). *Case Study Research: Design and Method* (3rd ed.). Thousand Oaks, California: SAGE Publishing.

Young, C., Karpyn, A., Uy, N. et al. (2011). Farmers' Markets in Low Income Communities: Impact of Community Environment, Food Programs and Public Policy. *Community Development, 42*(4), 208–220.

Zald, M. N. (1996). Culture, Ideology, and Strategic Framing. In D. McAdam, J. D. McCarthy and M. N. Zald (Eds.), *Comparative Perspectives on Social Movements: Political Opportunities, Mobilizing Structures, and Cultural Framings* (pp. 261–274). Cambridge: Cambridge University Press.

Zeeuw, H. D., Veenhuizen, R. V. and Dubbeling, M. (2011). Foresight Project on Global Food and Farming Futures: The Role of Urban Agriculture in Building Resilient Cities in Developing Countries. *Journal of Agricultural Science*, 11.

Index

access narrative 66–67, 156–157
advocacy coalitions 6, 13, 19, 145, 148, 161, 165, 173
advocacy groups: collaboration 18, 19–20, 56, 77, 88, 103, 107–108, 136–137, 140–141, 146, 148, 163, 166–168; competition, UK 103, 107–108, 119, 137, US 42–43, 47, 142–146, 167; co–option by environmental interest groups, UK 105–141; degree of collaboration/segmentation, UK 74, 76, 88–89, 103, US 145–146; funding effects UK 140, US 144–146, 165, US compared with UK 198–201, 218; governance, UK 121–122, 127–128, 182–183; internal organization structure, UK 106–107, 121–131; pressure tactics 128–129; relationships with policy makers 129–130; segmentation, UK 119, 120–121, 136–139, 170; stakeholder accountability, UK 105, 107, 122, 126, 128, 140; stakeholder participation 169; types of organization 6–7
advocacy repertoires, British–American comparisons 12–13, 171–190
AFNs see Alternative Food Networks
AFT see American Farmland Trust
agency learning activities, local food in schools US 43–44
Agricultural Risk Protection Acts, US 33
agricultural subsidies; see also Common Agricultural Policy; Farm Bills, US

Alliance for Sensible Agricultural Policies (ASAP) 145, 153, 161–162, 164, 198
Alternative Food Networks (AFNs) 1
American Farmland Trust (AFT) 148, 153, 161
ASAP see Alliance for Sensible Agricultural Policies

BIG Lottery Fund, UK 62, 101, 196, 200, 214
Blair, Tony 76
Bush, George W. administration, farmers markets 30, trade policy 43, farm bill opposition 142

Campaign (formerly Council) for the Protection of Rural England (CPRE) 75, 76, 77, 88–89, 108, 112, 134–135
CAP see Common Agricultural Policy
capacity building: EU LEADER project 69–70, 87; US group collaboration 41–42, 163, 166, 196–201; US making space for exclude groups 169–170, 190–194, 195
CFP see Community Food Project
CFSC see Community Food Security Coalition
Child Nutrition Acts, US 43, 50, 53–54; provision of fresh/healthy/local food in schools, US 25, 29, 43–55; WIC (Women, infants and children) Farmers Market Nutrition Program, US 24, 37–40
civic participation, food system governance 207–218

270 *Index*

CLA *see* Country Land and Business Association

climate change, influence on food policies, UK 90, 96

Clinton, Bill, administration 32, 34, 38–39

collaboration, among advocacy groups 18, 19–20, 56, 77, 88, 103, 107–108, 136–137, 140–141, 146, 148, 163, 166–168, 196–201, in local food projects US 8, 40–41, 55–56, UK 80, US and UK 19, 204, 206

collaboration, food supply chain UK 62, 72, 79–80, 83, 117, 121

collaboration versus contention, British–American comparisons 19, 174–178, UK 59–60, 114–119, 140

collective action, social movements 5, UK 75, 120–121, US 145–146, 150–152

Common Agricultural Policy (CAP), EU 15–16, 63, 64, 74, 76, 79, 102, 119, 207

Community Food Project (CFP) program, US 24, 40–43, 191, 196, 197

community food security (differs from food security), 41–43, 190–191

Community Food Security Coalition (CFSC), US 49–50, 52, 148, 173, 183, 190–191; Conference 2011 178–179, 181, 190–193

Community Food Security Learning Center, US 42

community provision, local food policy narrative 9–10, 12

competition, between advocacy groups UK 107–108, 119, 137, 140; US 42–43, 47, 142–145

conservation: US Farm Bill 2001 142–143; W. K. Kellogg Foundation funded groups 144–147

consumer empowerment, UK 110–111; US *see also* food democracy

context building, research 2, 12–18

co–option of local food policy by environmental interest groups 105–141

corporate provision, local food policy narrative 10, 12

Country Land and Business Association (CLA), UK 108, 120, 137–138, 170, 215

Countryside Agency, UK 60, 62, 101

CPRE *see* Campaign for the Protection of Rural England

crises, British food policies 59–60, 76, 90

cultural comparisons, UK/USA 2–3, 12–13

Curry Commission; *see also* Policy Commission on the Future of Farming and Food

decentralization of social movements 4, 6

decision making: deliberative 165; Farm and Food Policy Project 149; identifying potential alternatives 106; informal structures excluding democratic processes 182–184; organization comparison 186–189; Soil Association 124, 125–126; stakeholder participation 169, 181–185, 186–189, 209–210; Sustain 124–125

DEFRA *see* Department for Environment, Food and Rural Affairs

deliberative decision making 165

democracy: American and British processes 12–18; importance 220; stakeholder participation xv–xvi, 9, 68, 209–210, 217; *see also* food democracy; stakeholder participation

Department of Defense (DOD), FRESH program, US 24, 44–48

Department for Environment, Food and Rural Affairs (DEFRA), UK: ending support for local food 83, 85; EU policy implementation 102–103; food miles research 90, 92–93, 114–115; renaming of MAFF 60; role in promoting local food 81–83; Rural Development Program for England 97–98; social and economic benefits of local food 79–80

Department for International Development (DfID) 93, 94, 115–117

developing countries, effects of local food promotion 91, 93

devolution, UK 69–71

DfID *see* Department for International Development

Diversity Initiative (US) 147, 149, 151, 163, 165, 166, 197, 198

DMAA *see* Domestic Market Access Act

document study 17, 18–19

DOD *see* Department of Defense

Domestic Market Access Act (DMAA), US 156–157, 159

Eating Oil: Food in a changing climate, Sustain 111–112

EBT, *see* Electronic Benefits Transfer

economic consequences of food miles 109, 111, 112

EDF *see* Environmental Defense Fund

Electronic Benefits Transfer 30, 32–33, 40, 56, 57, 154, 197

elicited information 18

elite leadership of UK advocacy groups 121–122, 182–183

empowerment: collaborative working 164–168; consumers 110–111; of the excluded 179–181, 190–194; *see also* capacity building; movement building

enabling policies, local food in schools, US 43–44

English Rural Development Program (ERDP) 71–74, 83

Environmental Defense Fund (EDF), US 148, 153, 161, 164

environmental interest groups, UK 105–141, US 148, 153, 161–162, 164

environmental issues, link with food miles UK 91–93, 109–111

episodic policy change, English–American comparison 59

ERDP *see* English Rural Development Program

Esmeé Fairbairn Foundation 140, 198

European Union (EU): effects on UK policies 60, 62, 63; policy implementation in UK 99–100, 102–103; UK institution relationships 71; *see also* Common Agricultural Policy; LEADER program

events list, participation observation 225–227

extant information 18

Fair miles? the concept of "food miles" through a sustainable development lens, IIED 115

Farm and Food Policy Project (FFPP) 108, 145, 148–153, 161–167, 196, 198

Farm Bills, US 2, 15, 30–43, 142–144, 153–160, 167, 190–191; comparison to EU Common Agricultural Policy 15–16

farm crisis, British food policies 59–60, 76–90

Farm–to–Cafeteria Acts, US 51, 213

Farm to School Collaborative, US 52, 53

farm to school movement, US 29, 43–44, 48–49, 50–55

farm to school programs: US 50–55, 197

FARMA *see* National Association of Farmers' Retail & Markets Association 6, 105, 128–129, 138–139

Farmer–to–Consumer Direct Marketing Act (1976), US 24, 29–30, 33, 39, 194, 213

Farmers Market Nutrition Programs (FMNPs), US 24, 25, 37–40

Farmers Market Promotion Program (FMPP), US 25, 30–33

Farmers markets 5–6, US policy 29–33, 37–40, 215; English policy 67, 72, 75, 78, 80, 88, 92, 128

Farmers Weekly, food miles campaign 115

Federation of City Farms & Community Gardens (FCFCG), UK 6, 105, 127–128

Feeding the Future: Policy options for local food, Sustain & Food Links UK 112–114, 119, 131, 209

FFPP *see* Farm and Food Policy Project

FMD *see* Foot and Mouth Disease

FMNPs *see* Farmers Market Nutrition Programs

Food 2030 (HM Government, 2010) 91, 101, 105, 119

food chain, use of term in UK 62, 72, 80, 83

food democracy 6, 140

food desert UK 66, 77; *see also* food shop access; US 27, 157–160, 163, Bobby Rush 157, 160

272   *Index*

Food from Britain (QUANGO) 62, 78, 101, 110, 111
Food Issues Census 123
Food Links UK 112–114
Food Matters 90, 91–93, 101, 105, 119
food miles: contestation 91, 93; 115–119; definitions 109, 111; environmental emphasis 117; evaluation of effects 82, 92–93, 95; evolution of term 105; local food narrative comparison 113; origins of narrative 109–115; use of narrative in US 157
The Food Miles Report: The dangers of long–distance food transport, SAFE Alliance 109–110
food movements: definitions 5; structural characteristics 20
food security, protecting imports versus local food 15, 94, 96, *differs from* community food security
food shop access, UK connection to health policy 65–66; *Rural White Paper* 66–67; urban redevelopment 67–68; *see also* food desert
food systems 4, 204–216
Foot and Mouth Disease (FMD), UK outbreak 2001 59–60, 76
Foresight think–tank 93–97
fortifying myth 134–135, 144, 171
framing contests 133–134
framing processes, xiv, 20, 91, 134, 144, 149, 195–196, 211–212; food miles, UK 109–119, 121–124, 133, 139, US 157; local food UK 62, 75, 78, 150–152, 215; local food systems US 62, 146, 150–159, 199
Fresh Fruit and Vegetable Snack Program, US schools 25, 45–48
funding: BIG Lottery UK 62, 101, 196, 200, 216; capacity building for policy collaboration 196–201; influence on advocacy groups 165; social justice goals 197, 198, 200; US–England comparison 199; W. K. Kellogg Foundation 144–147
Future of Food and Farming: Challenges and choices for global sustainability, Foresight 94–97, 101, 105, 119

geographic preference in school meal procurement, US 48–50, UK 81, 130, 175–177
geographic segmentation, advocacy groups 120
global food issues, Britain's connection 90–100
Good Food for Our Money Campaign, Sustain, 130
government interference US EBT, geographic preference, UK *Food Matters,* food miles, Foresight, localism agenda
government policies, British–American comparisons 12–16; national American policy 1976–2012 22–58; national English policy 1991–2012 59–104
government provision, local food policy narrative 10, 12
government consultation, process in US 14–15; UK 100–101,
Grassland Reserve Program (GRP), US 143, 146
greenhouse gas (GHG) reduction 96, 118
grounded theory approach to research 2
GRP *see* Grassland Reserve Program

Healthy Food and Communities Work Group (HFCWG), US 150–152, 156, 163
Healthy Food Enterprise Development (HFED) program, US 157–159
historical analysis 18, 21, 22, 106
holistic local food system narrative 19, 117, 141, 145, 159, 162
horizontal segmentation of advocacy groups 120

identifying potential alternatives, decision making 106
IIED *see* International Institute for Environment and Development
inclusion: empowering the excluded, US 179–181, 190–194, 202; food systems orientation US and UK 209, 215–216; UK 65, 75, 216; US 40–43, 55–57, 127–128, 183 *see also* community food security; food democracy

Index 273

Independent Inquiry into Health Inequalities, UK 66–67
individualism, local food policy narrative 11, 12
inequalities 7–8, 178–181
informal structures excluding democratic decision making, UK example 124–125, 182–183
information sources 16–19
insider strategy 145, 148–160
instrumental narrative, local food policy 10, 12, 62
interdisciplinary analysis, food systems 211–212
interest groups: definition 6, 121; narratives and practice 208
International Institute for Environment and Development (IIED), objection to food miles narrative 94, 95–96, 119
interviews: methods 16, 17, 18; organizations interviewed 218–219; topics list 220–221

Kind, Ron 142–145

labeling of food 8, 10, 74, 110, 111, 120
LEADER (Liaison Entre Actions de Développement de l'Économie Rurale) program, EU 9, 62, 68–70, 74, 86–88, 99–100
less developed countries, effects of local food promotion 91, 93
LIPT see Low Income Project Team
local food: definitions 8–9, 156, 159; main narratives 9–12
local food movements: definitions 5; UK examples 5–6; US examples 5
Local Food program (LF) UK
local food projects, definitions 8–9
"localism" agenda, UK 91, 97–100
locality foods 8, 63, 81, 99
lottery funding, UK 62, 101, 196, 200, 216
low–income community food systems, US 40–43; UK 65–66, 203–204
low–income groups, healthy food access US 37–43; see also food desert, UK 66–67; food shop access

Low Income Project Team (LIPT), UK 65

MAFF see Ministry of Agriculture, Fisheries and Food
Making Local Food Work (MLFW) project, UK 5, 62, 108, 134
marketism narrative 10, 12, 78, 92, 206
media campaigns, UK 15, 63
media outreach, Farm and Food Policy Project 152–153
media role, food miles narrative 117, 118, 133–136
Miliband, David 82, 98
Ministry of Agriculture, Fisheries and Food (MAFF) 60, 72–73; see also Department for Environment, Food and Rural Affairs
MLFW see Making Local Food Work
movement building, 4–6, food systems 178–181, 214–216; see also repertoires of action
multi–level approaches, food systems 4, 208–209
multi–objective approaches, food systems 4, 212–213
multi–sector approaches, food systems 4, 207–218

NANA see National Alliance for Nutrition and Activity
NAO see National Audit Office
narrative analysis 17, 19, 22
narrative hybridization 23, 55, 63, 102
narratives, local food 9–12
national, equating with local in UK 9
National Alliance for Nutrition and Activity (NANA), US 47, 52
National Association of Farmers' Retail & Markets Association (FARMA) 6, 105, 128–129, 138–139
National Audit Office (NAO), UK 83, 85
National Commission on Small Farms (US) 44
National Farm to School Network (NFSN), US 6, 52, 173; see also farm–to–school movement

274 *Index*

National Farmers Union (NFU), UK 9, 120, 137–139
National Food Alliance (NFA) 74, 75; *see also* Sustain
National Sustainable Agriculture Coalition (NSAC), US 6, 52, 148, 161
Natural England 62
The Nature Conservancy (TNC), US 145–146
networks–system distinction 4
New Agricultural Markets Work Group (NAMWG) 151–152, 156
new social movements, definitions 4–5
NFA *see* National Food Alliance
NFSN *see* National Farm to School Network
NFU *see* National Farmers Union
non–governmental organizations (NGOs): British food programs 14, 60, 62; degree of democratic governance 185; *see also* Quasi–Autonomous Non–Governmental Organizations
Northeast Midwest Institute (NEMWI) 144, 145, 146, 148, 153, 166, 195
NSAC *see* National Sustainable Agriculture Coalition
nutrition and health, food shop access UK 65–68

Obama, Barack, administration 56; campaign platform 53
Obama, Michelle 52, 160
observations, events list 222–224
Occupy Oakland movement 178–181
organization structures of groups affecting narrative formation, UK 106–107, 121–131
outsiders versus insiders, political process 23, 135, 161–164, 196

participation observation 17, 18; events list 222–224; role in theory formation 216–217
participatory processes 6; food systems 183–190, 209–211; typology 184; comparison of American and British advocacy groups 185–190
People's Garden 28, 52

persuasion versus protest, advocacy repertoires 173–178
pilot projects, local food in schools, US 43–44
PMG *see* Processing and Marketing Grant
policing, of advocacy groups by advocacy groups, UK 136–139
Policy Commission on the Future of Farming and Food (Curry Commission), UK 76–79, 81, 83
policy entrepreneurship 37–39, 165–166, 169–170, 194–196, 207–208
policy narratives of local food 9–12
Policy options for local food; see also *Feeding the Future: Policy options for local food*
political processes, British–American comparisons 13–14
post–farm crisis era, England 59–60, 76–90
power, upward– and downward–looking, 135, 178
pre–crisis era, England 59, 65–76
pressure tactics, UK advocacy groups 129; US advocacy groups 161
private sector provision, local food policy narrative 10, 12
Processing and Marketing Grant (PMG), UK 62, 72–73, 78, 82, 83, 85, 89
producer market development narratives, US 29–37; UK 77–79
protest versus persuasion, advocacy repertoires 173–178
Public Sector Food Procurement Initiative (PSFPI) 81
public sector provision, local food policy narrative 10, 12

Quasi–Autonomous Non–Governmental Organizations (QUANGOs), British food programs 14, 60, 62, 101

racial issues 43–44, 157–160, 174–175, 178–181, 183, 190–194, 197
radical flank effect 161, 207; insider and outsider strategy 162, 164
radicalization of social movements 23
RDAs *see* Regional Development Agencies

Index   275

RDPE *see* Rural Development Program for England

Regional Development Agencies (RDAs), England 62, 69–71
regional food, definitions 156, 159; *see also* locality foods
Regional Food and Drink Groups, UK 62, 71
repertoires of action, British–American comparisons 12–13, 171–190
RES *see* Rural Enterprise Scheme
research methods: grounded theory approach and context building 2; information sources 16–19; international comparison 2, 13
reticulation, social movements 4
rural development, capture by farm lobby UK 89
Rural Development Program for England (RDPE) 85–86
Rural Enterprise Scheme (RES), UK 62, 72–73, 78, 82, 83, 85, 89

SA *see* Soil Association
SAFE Alliance *see* Sustainable Agriculture Food and Environment Alliance
schools: gardens 50; provision of fresh/healthy/local food, US 25, 29, 43–55; UK 81–82, 130, 176–177
Schumacher, Gus xiv, 37–39, 139, 145, 195
Seeking Balance in US farm and food policy 152–153, 154–155
segmentation, social movements 4, 119, 120–121, 136–139, 170, 195–196
self–determination and self–reliance, low–income community food systems, US 40–43, 190–191
Senior Farmers Market Nutrition Program (SFMNP), US 25, 37–40
single–issue campaigns 21, 121, 127, 131–132, 172, 185
SMOs *see* social movement organizations
SNAP *see* Supplemental Nutritional Assistance Program
social consequences of food miles 109–110, 111, 112

Social Exclusion Unit UK 66–68
social inclusion/exclusion 1–2, 7–8, 181–183, 194, 200, 203, 205–207, 213–214, 216–217; *see also* segmentation
social inequalities: local projects relationship 7–8; local projects relationship in UK 67–68; movement building 178–181
social justice: community development 40–43, 150–151, 174; food miles narrative 109, 112, 119; funding goals 197, 198, 200; sustainable food 117
social movements, definitions and types 4–5
social movement organizations (SMOs), definition 6
Soil Association (SA), UK: decision making 124, 125–126; general 6, 105–141; governance 121–122; scientific versus socio–economic evidence 134
Spellman, Caroline 175–177
SSFF *see* Strategy for Sustainable Farming and Food
stakeholder participation 7–8, 9, 209–211, 217; advocacy group decision making 169, 181–185, 186–189; British–American comparisons 14–15; food democracy 6; ladder of participation 185; typology 184
stakeholders: accountability of interest groups 105, 107, 122, 126, 128, 140; consultation 100–101; definition 7; government accountability to stakeholders US 14, UK 63, 100–101, EU 102
start–up support, local food in schools 50–55
Strategy for Sustainable Farming and Food (SSFF), UK 79–83, 84
Supplemental Nutritional Assistance Program (SNAP), US 15
Sustainable Agriculture Coalition (SAC), US 148
Sustainable Agriculture Food and Environment Alliance (SAFE Alliance): UK 74–75, 109–110; *see also* Sustain

276   *Index*

sustainable development, food miles relationship 115–117

sustainable agriculture 1; groups US 6, 33, 44, 55–57, 142–146; UK 63, 103, 106, 121–126, 130–140

sustainable food: environmental aspects of local food, UK 62, 113; public sector procurement, UK 81, 130 ; versus local food 81, 92, 117

Sustain (the alliance for better food and farming), UK: decision making 124–125; general 6, 105–141; governance 121–122; Making Local Food Work project 108; merger of the SAFE Alliance and the NFA 74, 75; RDPE recommendations 89

The Nature Conservancy (TNC), US 145–146

transformation narrative: general 9–10, 12; UK policy 62, 79, 80, 92, 95; US policy 29–30, 35, 40, 41–44, 55–56, 190–191

tyranny of structurelessness 182

United Kingdom (UK): English case study 105–141; national English policy 1991–2012 59–104; political processes 13–14; US comparisons 12–16, 169–202

United States of America (USA): Farm Bills 15, 30–43, 142–144, 153–160; national American policy 1976–2012 22–58; UK comparisons 12–16

United States Department of Agriculture (USDA): development programs 145, 148, 157; directories of local food movements 5; Farmer–to–Consumer Direct Marketing Act (1976) 24, 29–30; food desert and local food studies 159–160

unjust authority narrative 135, 201

urban agriculture 5, 75, 150, 154–155

Value–Added Producer Market Development Grant Program (VAPG), US 33–37

value of local food 9

vertical segmentation of advocacy groups 120–121

W. K. Kellogg Foundation (WKKF): US 144–147, 173–174, 192, 196–197, 198, 213; *see also* Farm and Food Policy Project

WIC (Women, infants and children) Farmers Market Nutrition Program (WIC FMNP), US 24, 37–40

Working Lands Stewardship Act (WLSA), US 142–143

world food price crisis era, UK 60, 90–100